INTELLIGENCE AND EXPERIENCE

J. MCV. HUNT

PROFESSOR OF PSYCHOLOGY
UNIVERSITY OF ILLINOIS

THE RONALD PRESS COMPANY   •   NEW YORK

Library of Congress Catalog Card Number: 61-15613

To

Esther, Judy, and Carol

Preface

For over half a century, the leading theory of man's nature has been dominated by the assumptions of fixed intelligence and predetermined development. These beliefs have played a large role in psychological theorizing and investigation; they have provided a conceptual framework for the measurement of intelligence and for accounting for the development of human abilities, which have been regarded as the unfolding of capacities almost completely predetermined by inheritance. Recently, however, a transformation has been taking place in this traditional conception of intelligence and its relationship to experience. Evidence from various sources has been forcing a recognition of central processes in intelligence and of the crucial role of life experience in the development of these central processes.

This transformation in the conception of intelligence and its roots is the subject of this book. The transformation is still incomplete, however, and although the trend of both the evidence and the conceptualizing appears to be clear, the conclusions at various points must remain tentative.

This book is, then, a kind of case history in behavioral science, presented before all of the case has become history. It examines the historical roots of the assumptions of fixed intelligence and of predetermined development and the evidence that was interpreted to support them. It describes the changes that have taken place in the relevant portions of psychological and neuropsychological theory and reviews the investigations of learning sets, problem-solving, and the effects of early experience on later problem-solving capacity. It considers the programming of electronic computers with strategies for processing information to solve problems and the approximate analogues of computer-components that are beginning to be recognized in the brains of higher mammals and men. The observations of Piaget and his collaborators on the development of intelligence and logical thinking in children are treated extensively and systematically. They help to show how the human brain is "programmed" in the course of the experiences of living. Finally, the book indicates how these various developments point the way to further investigation and to reinterpretations of key issues in the psychology of intelligence and suggests implications for education and child-rearing that diverge significantly from the practices sanctioned by the assumptions under question. In one particular, this evidence leads to a serious questioning of the immutability of the IQ; instead, the IQ is regarded as a phenotype, like height or weight, for which the genes set limits of potential development but which is finally developed through encounters with the environment.

I have tried to tell the story and to present the evidence, deriving as it does from such a range of sources, with a minimum of technical jargon. Since I believe the developments I am describing are leading to an important reorientation in both theory and practice, I wish to reach that wider audience to whom these trends should be of interest and concern. Although this book is not intended primarily as a textbook, it may be useful as a synthesis for students in advanced-undergraduate and graduate courses.

My work has been made possible by the support of two foundations. The Russell Sage Foundation has generously supplied secretarial help and summer salary for several years to give me an opportunity to examine the investigations in the behavioral sciences and to formulate their implications for child-rearing. The Commonwealth Fund of New York has generously awarded me one of their fellowships for senior scientists to permit me to give full time to this work throughout the academic year of 1959–60. For this support I am deeply grateful.

It is not the fault of these foundations that my task got out of hand, so to speak, and that what were originally intended to be but chapters on the experimental roots of intelligence and of motivation became book-length works. This book is thus to be followed, hopefully, by one on motivation and experience and, hopefully again, by the ultimate completion of the originally planned volume on the implications of the findings of the behavioral sciences for child rearing.

In connection with writing this book I have incurred a series of debts that I want to acknowledge. I should like to thank Dr. Zella Luria and my colleagues, Wesley C. Becker and Charles Eriksen of the Department of Psychology and B. J. Diggs of the Department of Philosophy at the University of Illinois, for reading the original version of this work and making helpful suggestions. E. G. Holley and P. S. Grove of the Psychology Library at the University of Illinois have given me countless accommodations that went well beyond the traditional call of duty. To Professor Jean Piaget of Switzerland I am much indebted for permission to quote extensively from his observations of the development of intelligence in children, and to his colleague, Professor Bärbel Inhelder, I am also indebted for the use of various illustrative figures and protocols. I also want to thank Piaget's publishers (Basic Books, W. W. Norton, and the International Universities Press of New York; Routledge & Kegan Paul, and William Heinemann, Ltd., of London) for permission to quote extensively from Piaget's observations. Moreover, I wish especially to express my appreciation to three of my colleagues, Wesley C. Becker, Rogers Elliott, and Harry Triandis, and to my wife, Esther, for reading various or all of these chapters in their penultimate version, for pointing out errors and clumsy expressions, and for lending their wonderfully helpful counsel. Of course, none of these persons should be held responsible for any of the shortcomings of the final product.

My secretaries of the past four years, Mrs. Marie McBride and Mrs. Roberta Garner, have played an important role in this effort. Both of them have my gratitude for their patience and skill in reading my mind via sounds from a dictaphone or pencilled scribbles on typed copy.

Finally, I owe a great debt to my daughters, Judy and Carol, and to their mother. Not only have they endured months of those faraway looks in a supposedly listening father or husband, but life with them has made human development and the role of experience in intelligence a fascinating topic for me. It is entirely fitting that the book should be dedicated to them.

J. McV. Hunt

Estes Park, Colorado
August, 1961

Contents

INTELLIGENCE
AND
EXPERIENCE

CHAPTER 1

Introduction

Intelligence has long been of central concern to those seeking to understand the behavior of living organisms and especially the behavior of man. It is in connection with intelligence and the tests which measure it that some of the most violent polemics in psychology and in all the behavioral sciences have raged. These polemics have concerned the nature of man's intellectual capacities, how they should be measured, how mutable or immutable they are, and what the implications of the decisions on these issues should be for educating and improving the race.

In spite of these polemics, one traditional set of answers was dominant from before the turn of the twentieth century through World War II. This traditional set of answers has rested on two beliefs which have had the status of basic faiths. One of these may be called the assumption of "fixed intelligence." The other may be called the assumption of "predetermined development." Taken together these assumptions or faiths justified the notion of intelligence as an innate dimension of personal capacity which increases at a fixed rate to a predetermined level. In other words, they justified the notion of a constant IQ. These assumptions were also part of the general conception that intellectual capacity and the behaviors taken to indicate it unfold automatically with anatomic maturation, and that anatomic maturation proceeds at a fixed rate so long as the metabolic requirements of the infant and child are met. Furthermore, any measurement of this rate at any one stage of development was conceived to be predictive, within the limits of error, of all future measurements because basically and predominantly this maturation rate was supposed to be fixed, once and for all, by the individual's genetic constitution.

Such basic beliefs about human nature and human development had many implications. These implications influenced both the science and the practice related to the development, education, and welfare of children. In relation to science they shaped the general nature of a major share of the investigations of child nature and child development. For instance, normative studies became the mode. This normative approach was considered to be reasonable, for, if development is predetermined, measurements of the anatomy and of behavior at successive ages could be considered to be explanations as well as measurements. The result was a spate of measuring. All kinds of characteristics were forced into scales and these scales were correlated with age and with each other. The semantics of *dimensions* and *scales* for these characteristics may actually have hampered the development of understanding. They encouraged, for instance, the business of attaching numbers to characteristics, indicating more or less of them, before the observations required to ascertain the basic nature of these characteristics had been made (see Chapter 8). The work of those who strayed from the normative path, moreover, met either disinterest or especially careful scrutiny and all too often disapproval as well. The work of those who attempted to determine the basic nature of behavior that is more or less intelligent tended to meet with disinterest. The assumptions of fixed intelligence and predetermined development led to a general attitude that investigations of the effects of various kinds of early experience on later intellectual capacities would be useless. The special scrutiny and disapproval of investigations concerned with the effects of education and training on later ability tended actively to discourage them. In consequence, the impetus for studies of the later effects of early experience came during the fourth and fifth decades of the century from the impact of psychoanalysis, and these investigations were concerned with effects on the supposedly more mutable traits of emotional response and personality rather than with effects on the supposedly immutable dimension of intelligence.

In relation to practice, the implications of the assumptions of fixed intelligence and predetermined development influenced education. One influence was salutary. The tests of intelligence showed that capacity increases with age and that individual differences in capacity exist. As Anderson (1956)[1] has pointed out, the existence of these measurable differences between children, and between children of

[1] References are to the bibliography at the end of the book and are made by author's name and the year of publication.

various ages, coupled with their association with school achievement removed the onus of moral blame from school failure. They also removed justification for some of the brutality that was all too often associated with teaching. Another side of this same influence, however, was not so salutary. It encouraged a neglectful attitude toward intellectual development, for, if such development were predetermined, then it would do no good to try to cultivate it. One result was conceptual justification for the recently much deplored relinquishment of standards for intellectual excellence. The pendulum of opinion swung hard toward the side of "not pushing children in their intellectual development," of allowing their basic natures to unfold, of letting them be themselves, but of helping them toward life-adjustment. Other lines of influence, particularly that which came down from Rousseau through Pestalozzi and Froebel and that which derived from Freud, participated in this swing of the pendulum, but the fact that intellectual capacity was supposed to unfold automatically supplied an important part of the conceptual justification.

The implications of these assumptions also influenced the advice given by supposed experts to parents about their child-rearing. The business of the newborn and the very young infant was to grow, or so it was believed. This growth was conceived to be an essentially automatic process. Moreover, since the responses of the child's repertoire were supposed to depend upon the maturation of his anatomical structures, parents were urged to feed their children on schedule but to leave them alone and let them grow. In fact, parents were warned, especially during the period of 1915 to 1935, against playing with the young infant lest he get too much stimulation. That stimulation might interfere with his growth. Even Watson (1928), who stood out as an extreme environmentalist, believed the basic response repertoire had to come via maturation before learning could get in its licks, and he warned parents against overstimulating their infants and especially against spoiling them with a lot of fussy loving.

Finally, the implications of these assumptions were seen in personnel practice. Because intelligence and many other characteristics were assumed to be fixed, it became especially important, figuratively speaking, to keep square pegs out of round holes and vice versa. Since personnel practices typically concerned the job placement of adolescents and young adults, in whom intelligence and other characteristics have become fairly stable, this emphasis had a substantial basis. Even so, the assumption that intelligence and other personal characteristics are fixed has probably led to some unwarranted overemphasis on the matter of personnel selection and some unwarranted underemphasis on the matter of personnel training and on the business of arranging the social climate of institutions to foster personal interest and change.

As the title of this book indicates, it is concerned with the role of experience in the development of intelligence. This is not to deny an important role to the genes in determining intelligence (see Fuller & Thompson, 1960). It is obviously true, for instance, that one cannot get apple trees by planting radish seeds, nor can he get chimpanzees by breeding rats. Moreover, no one has ever taught a chimpanzee to solve problems with the calculus, or even to speak. Neither has anyone ever got, nor will he get, a chimpanzee interested in abstract art or in the principles and methods of behavioral science. Neither is it argued that one can get every human being to learn to use the calculus or to get interested in the principles and methods of behavioral science. It is obvious that the genes operate both to prescribe certain basic directions in organismic development and to set irrevocable limits on the range of capacities that can be developed within an organism. Moreover, they undoubtedly prescribe these directions and set these limits much more finely than these illustrations, purposely posed broadly to make the general point obvious, would imply. Various breeds of dogs, for instance, differ in the ease with which various skills can be taught them (Fuller & Scott, 1954). They also differ in the temperamental characteristics that influence the motivations they develop under various kinds of conditions (Scott & Charles, 1954). Similar influences on the development of human beings undoubtedly reside in existing genotypes.

As the data to be reviewed here will show, however, the belief that the wherewithal to solve problems comes automatically with the maturation of somatic tissues, especially with the maturation of the neural tissues of the cerebrum, is being shown to be palpably false. Even the development of such relatively static skills as the human infant's abilities to sit alone, to stand, and to walk, for instance, depend upon his getting varied stimulation from the environment and opportunities for appropriate interaction with it. Whereas home-reared children nearly always sit alone at nine months of age, Dennis (1960) reports in a very recent paper that 58 per cent of children aged from one to two years in an orphanage in Teheran, where for lack of sufficient personnel they got little variation of stimulation and few opportunities for interaction, did not yet sit alone. Moreover, whereas nearly all home-reared children walk alone by age two, only 15 per cent of the children in this Teheran orphanage who were aged between three and four years walked alone. Similarly, even the capacity to respond adaptively to painful stimulation appears to be dependent upon opportunities for stimulation and for behavioral interaction with the environment. For example, Melzack & Scott (1957) have shown that dogs reared in relative isolation, even though they be physically healthy, are either slow to learn or fail at all to learn to avoid an electric shock when the onset of this shock is repeatedly signaled ahead of time. When their noses are burned with a lighted match or cigarette, they jerk away reflexively, but they return immediately to sniff the burning material again and again. To paraphrase the adage, apparently the child must have been burned, and *as a child,* if he is later to avoid the fire adeptly.

Thus, without denying an important role to the genes in the development of intelligence, this book focuses on the relatively new evidence concerning the role of experience in the development of intelligence. Actually, important as the genes are, relatively little that is new has been learned recently about their role in the development of intelligence (see Fuller, 1960). On the other hand, the full implications of the interaction between genotype and environment in the development of the phenotype have all too seldom been fully appreciated in connection with the measurement and the development of intelligence, which is, of course, a special case of the phenotype. Even though this distinction between genotype and phenotype and the principle of interaction between genotype and environment in the production of the phenotype are as old as the epochal genetic work of Johannsen (1903, 1909), it is still necessary to bring their implications into the conception of intellectual development. Put briefly, these implications mean, for one thing, that the genes set limits on the individual's potential for intellectual development, but they do not guarantee that this potential will be achieved and they do not, therefore, fix the level of intelligence as it is commonly measured. On the whole, however, the new evidence demanding changes of conception concerns largely the experiential side of the matter where the genotype-environment interaction occurs.

The following discussion of intelligence and experience does several things. In the first two chapters, it describes the historical, conceptual, and evidential bases for the belief in fixed intelligence and the belief in predetermined development which were dominant in the thinking of behavioral scientists, and especially of psychologists, from the turn of the century through World War II. These beliefs are still widely held. Chapter 2 concerns the belief that intelligence is an innate capacity which is essentially fixed in ultimate amount and which develops at a constant rate. Chapter 3 concerns the belief that development is predetermined by genetic inheritance, and also describes the history of the argument whereby the organism was conceptually emptied of its mind that was once so richly populated with hypothetical faculties.

Chapter 4 shows how stimulus-response methodology (as distinct from stimulus-response theory) has been rediscovering "mind," or at least has been rediscovering that something important is going on between the ears. The new "mind," however, is quite different from the old one. Where the old one consisted of footloose faculties, the new "mind" consists of "hypothetical constructs" or "intervening variables" which are tied both to the history of the organism's interaction with the environment and to its observed response characteristics. It can be said that stimulus-response methodology has been undoing stimulus-response theory. Or, at any rate, stimulus-response method has produced evidence that has demanded so much revision in stimulus-response theory that the new theory has few resemblances to the one which originally went by that name. Chapter 4 also reviews Harlow's (1949) work on "learning sets," Riesen's (1958) work on the effects of rearing chimpanzees in darkness, and the work on the effects of early experience on later adaptive capacities that has been stimulated by Hebb's (1949) theorizing. It attempts further to show how the streams of theorizing that derive from such lines of investigation are coalescing with other streams, one from those who program electronic computers to solve problems (Newell, Shaw, & Simon, 1958; von Neumann, 1958) and another from neuropsychologists (Pribram, 1960; Miller, Galanter, & Pribram, 1960), to form one large stream in which the conception of the brain and its functioning is being radically revised.

Chapters 5 and 6 review the work of Piaget and his collaborators on intellectual development in children, hopefully with enough observational and empirical detail to make intelligible Piaget's fresh, and therefore strange, concepts. Chapter 7 examines the main themes of Piaget's work, and the principles deriving from them, in the light of that existing evidence which appears to the writer to be relevant. It also attempts to point both to some of the new problems raised for investigation and to some of the implications for education and child-rearing.

Chapter 8 examines the implications of the semantics of *dimension* and *scale* for intelligence and suggests the alternative semantics of *sampling behavior for evidences of intellectual structures*. It distinguishes between *predictive* validity and *criterion* validity and points up their implications for the infant-tests of intelligence. It reinterprets the evidence that was once seen to support the assumptions of fixed intelligence and predetermined devlopment in the light of the new conception of intelligence and of its origins. It also attempts to reinterpret both the heredity-environment controversy, and especially the search for a general answer to the question concerning the proportions of variance in tested intelligence contributed by heredity and by environment, and the implications of the work on differential fertility.

Chapter 9 sums up the argument and attempts to state the conclusions.

CHAPTER 2

The Belief in
Fixed Intelligence

The view that intelligence is a capacity fixed once and for all by genetic inheritance has had wide currency. Although exceptions can easily be cited (e.g., Dashiell, 1937), most of the general textbooks written before World War II tended to present the view that the IQ is essentially constant because intelligence is fixed. Treatises on intelligence, moreover, appear to have been especially prone to accept this view. For instance, Boynton (1933) defined intelligence as "an inherited capacity of the individual which is manifested through his ability to adapt and to reconstruct the factors of his environment in accordance with his group." And similarly, Burt *et al.* (1934) wrote:

By intelligence, the psychologist understands inborn, all-round, intellectual ability. It is inherited, or at least innate, not due to teaching or training; it is intellectual, not emotional or moral, and remains uninfluenced by industry or zeal; it is general, not specific, i.e., it is not limited to any particular kind of work, but enters into all we do or say or think. Of all our mental qualities, it is the most far-reaching; fortunately, it can be measured with accuracy and ease (pp. 28–29).

In view of the fact that, throughout history, mankind has looked to improvements in education in order to better his lot, why should students of behavior, and perhaps especially students of individual differences, hold that intelligence is fixed and predetermined by the genes? The reasons appear to be of several kinds. They are appar-

10

ently, first, historical, second, conceptual, and third, empirical in the sense that a fairly substantial body of evidence was gathered which was easy to reconcile with this conception.

HISTORICAL AND CONCEPTUAL REASONS

The notion of fixed intelligence has roots in Charles Darwin's (1859) theory of natural selection. In *Origin of the Species* he presented the well-known view that the various species of animals have evolved through a process in which chance variations and mutations which were inherited tend to survive and reproduce their kind only if their inherited characteristics enabled them better to survive and to reproduce. This view rapidly took the place of Lamarck's earlier notion that the characteristics of species had arisen out of a process whereby those parts and functions enhanced with use come to be inherited. Darwin's conceptions created a furor of controversy, and in consequence they were widely disseminated. Thereby, they set in motion a major conceptual tradition.

The influence of this doctrine on the concept of intelligence, however, came indirectly by way of Darwin's brilliant cousin, Francis Galton. Galton took up the problem of mental inheritance in his study of *Hereditary Genius* (1869). The study showed that men of great reputation and distinction in Great Britain tended to come from a relatively small group of families. Without recognizing that the children of leading families may have not only a greater opportunity for experience but also greater opportunity to achieve distinction by virtue of the fact that they have what in the vernacular is called "pull," Galton concluded that genius is inherited. From this conclusion, which was apparently dictated to a large degree by the conception borrowed from his cousin of evolution as the survival of inherited characteristics, Galton turned to anthropometric measurement.

Galton's (1883) *Inquiries into Human Faculty* launched the study of individual differences. He devised many tests of simple sensory and motor functions. His sensory tests included such threshold measures as the number of vibrations required to be heard as a tone, the amount of pressure necessary to produce pain, the separation of two lines in visual angles required if the lines are to be seen as two, and the degree to which two points touching the skin must be separated in order to be felt as two. His motor tests included the number of taps an individual can make in a half-minute, measures of the reaction-time required for an individual to respond to the onset of a sound, a light, or a touch on the skin. He used, as the threshold of immediate memory, the number of letters, words, or names of objects that an individual can repeat after one hearing. Galton also founded a laboratory where people could learn their capacities by taking his tests for a price of three pence. Over 9,000 persons took the tests, and as Boring (1950) says, "If Galton had not thought these individual differences were inherited, he would not have bothered with them."

In his life's program, Galton appears to have seen a place for his "anthropometric measures" in the function of improving the human race, for, with thorough consistency, he founded the eugenics movement. The implicit line of reasoning was simple. If human characteristics are inherited, the way to improve man's lot is to breed better men. Had Galton's types of tests proved efficient in differentiating those who would achieve with distinction from those who would not, the use of the tests to determine those who should reproduce themselves would have been only a short step. It is a tribute to Galton's logical consistency that he turned to simple sensory and motor tests, for these are probably the functions most closely associated with the constitutional nature of the individual. But the statistical technique of correlation, which Galton (1886) also invented, discovered little relationship among these various tests (Sharp, 1898) and little relationship with such independent estimates of intelligence as came from teachers' ratings (Bolton, 1891) or academic grades (Wissler, 1901).

The tests which did show some relationship to each other and which proved to be relatively successful in differentiating between those who do and do not achieve successfully in school came from another source. As early as 1895, Binet and Henri set forth what have become two of the principal problems of differential psychology, namely, to determine the nature and extent of individual differences in psychological processes, and to discover the interrelationships of mental processes within the individual. They criticized the Galtonian tests as being too largely sensory, and too simple. They suggested instead the measurement of more complex functions, such as memory, imagination, comprehension, and esthetic appreciation. Within a year after the French Minister of Public Instruction appointed Binet in 1904 to a commission to study the problem of retardation among children in the public schools of Paris, Binet & Simon (1905) published the first scale for the purpose of yielding an over-all index. This scale utilized the more complex psychological functions in order "to assess the intelligence."

Although Binet & Simon (1916) argued that nearly all of the phenomena with which psychology concerns itself are phenomena of intelligence, they considered it useless to bring into the examinations any measures of sensation and simple motor responses. Binet & Simon (1916) wrote:

It seems to us that in the intelligence there is a fundamental faculty, the alteration or lack of which is of the utmost importance for practical life. This faculty is *judgment,* otherwise called good sense, practical sense, initiative, the faculty of adapting oneself to circumstances. To judge well, to comprehend well, to reason well, these are the essential activities of the intelligence . . . Indeed the rest of the intellectual faculties seem to be of little importance in comparison with judgment . . . (p. 42).

With this conception of intelligence guiding them, Binet & Simon turned to tasks of comprehension (such as: "What's the thing to do when . . .?"), defining words, and answering questions involving reasoning (such as: "Why do we have houses?"). As has been the practice ever since, these tests were graded in difficulty according to the proportion of individuals who could pass them and the age of the individuals who could pass them. As Stoddard (1943) has indicated, "difficulty and complexity have always been among the hallmarks of intelligent behavior."

Alfred Binet (1909), however, did not contend that intelligence is fixed (see Varon, 1936). The commission he had accepted called for a different faith. After nearly two decades of work on intelligence Binet (1909) deplored the fact that

. . . some recent philosophers appear to have given their moral support to the deplorable verdict that the intelligence of an individual is a fixed quantity . . . We must protest and act against this brutal pessimism . . . A child's mind is like a field for which an expert farmer has advised a change in the method of cultivating, with the result that in place of desert land, we now have a harvest. It is in this particular sense, the one which is significant, that we say that the intelligence of children may be increased. One increases that which constitutes the intelligence of a school child, namely, the capacity to learn, to improve with instruction (pp. 54–55).

Inasmuch as it was Binet's complex tests that turned out to be the ones that best predict which people will achieve well and which poorly, why is it that a major share of psychologists and the majority of those who have been concerned with the testing of intelligence have taken the faith of Galton so succinctly expressed by Burt *et al.* (see page 10).

Probably one of the reasons is a matter of historical accident. The idea of using tests was brought to America by J. McK. Cattell, who was a student of Galton rather than a student of Binet. It was Cattell who coined the term *mental test* in a paper that he wrote in 1890. By 1893, Cattell was advocating that tests be given in the schools, and shortly thereafter he began publishing the results of the mental testing of students at Columbia University. Boring (1950) has contended:

Cattell more than any other person was in this fashion responsible for getting mental testing underway in America, and it is plain that his motivation was similar to Galton's and that he was also influenced, or at least reinforced, by Galton. Presumably, the theory of evolution determined Cattell less than did the spirit of hard-headed American common sense, but all these things are wrapped up together. Later it was the existence of the tests that raised again the nature-nurture problem which Galton had posed (p. 283).

Perhaps the historical accident has another aspect: It was Goddard who first brought the Binet-Simon scale to America. He translated it into English in 1908, and he used it in his studies of the feebleminded at the Vineland Training School (Peterson, 1925). Goddard, the author of the well-known study of the Kallikak family published in 1912, was an ardent hereditarian. His experience with the feeble-minded had not encouraged much faith in their educability. He not only preached the doctrine of fixed intelligence, but he also made propaganda for the eugenic movement.[1]

Yet another factor may also be of some importance. It has often been observed that faith in nature, as opposed to nurture, appears to be more common among those psychologists who are professionally concerned with individual differences, and especially with the measurement of intelligence, than among those concerned with learning, personality, or social behavior. Although no actual count is available to our knowledge, this observation has been made often enough to warrant asking why those concerned with intelligence should be more prone to faith in nature. The professional psychometrician's function may make him especially prone to believe in fixed intelligence. The very significance of his research and practice lies in the capacity of the tests to predict performance at a later time and to predict other kinds of performance. A faith in intelligence as a basic and fixed dimension of a person is probably the faith on which one can most readily rest such a professional function. With such a faith, when the exigencies of a testing effort fail, one can proceed in the hope that better instruments will improve the state of affairs. With such a faith and its resulting hope, failures in practice engender a minimum of what Festinger (1957) has termed "cognitive disso-nance." In his own professional life history, the writer finds in himself some evidence of just such a factor. So long as he was professionally identified with the testing function, it was highly comforting to be-lieve that the characteristics tested were fixed in individuals. Evi-

[1] For the history of intelligence testing, see Peterson (1925, 1926).

dence hinting that these characteristics might not be fixed produced intense dissonance, for it threatened both his belief in fixity and the adequacy of his professional function as well. Such a factor may help to explain the sometimes excessive violence of the polemics concerning the constancy of the IQ and the effects of early training that were common in the years just previous to World War II.

EMPIRICAL SUPPORT FOR FIXED INTELLIGENCE

Various kinds of facts have readily lent themselves to an interpretation which gave support to this faith in fixed intelligence. First of all, performance on the complex, Binet-type tests improves with age. For instance, while three-year-old children can typically copy a circle, very few of them can copy a square without rounding the corners, but by age five they can typically copy a square without rounding the corners. For another instance, if a child of eight is shown a drawing of a large circle on a piece of paper, is told that this is a field with a fence around it into which he has accidentally thrown his ball, and is asked what he would do, he readily proposes entering the field to look for it. But his looking is unplanned. It is not until children are 12 years old that they typically devise a plan of walking around the field so that no point will be missed from their scrutiny. Binet & Simon (1905) noted this improvement with age immediately, and it led them, in their 1908 revision, to grade their tests according to age, and, in their 1911 revision, to introduce the concept of mental age. A test was considered to be typical of a given age if approximately three-fourths of the children of that age passed it successfully. Wilhelm Stern (1912) should probably be given the credit for suggesting the intelligence quotient (IQ). Binet & Simon (1911) had used absolute differences between mental age and chronological age as the basis for estimating the degree to which some children were retarded or advanced in their development. Stern pointed out that a difference of two years between mental age and chronological age is functionally much greater at age four than at 12 years of age. He saw intelligence as something comparable to a dimension of the body which grows at a rate which may be either below or above that of chronological age. As a consequence, Stern wrote:

I should like to recommend the relating to chronological age not of the difference, but of the mental age itself. We would then obtain the mental quotient . . . This quotient would show what fractional part of the intelligence normal to his age a feebleminded child obtains. Mental quotient equals mental age over chronological age. An eight-year-old child with a mental age of six has, then, a mental quotient of six divided by eight equals 0.75. A twelve-year-old child with a mental age of nine has the same mental quotient (1912, p. 80).

In developing the Stanford-Binet revision of the Binet-Simon tests, Terman (1916) adopted this recommendation but termed it the "intelligence quotient" or IQ. Coupling this finding that an improvement in capacity occurs at a given rate with age and the widely held belief of that day that development is predetermined by genetic inheritance (see Chapter 3) made it easy to differ with Binet's (1909) view of plasticity in intelligence. The inference was "fixed intelligence."

CONSTANCY OF THE IQ. Second, support for this inference came from the fact that the average IQ from age to age is highly constant. This constancy of the average IQ for children in the population is, of course, an artifact of the manner in which the tests were chosen. In this choosing Binet & Simon assumed that, for any given age, one-fourth of the children would fail from stupidity, but the typical (middle half) and, of course, the upper quarter would pass. In all Binet-type scales the tests for each age level are chosen on the basis of such an assumption. The fact that the mean IQ for groups is highly constant then shows merely that sufficient consistency exists to make average performance roughly reproducible from sample to sample. This fact says nothing about constancy of the IQ in individual children.

Third, the IQ's of individual children were also found to show considerable constancy from test to test through the school years to adulthood. This constancy was conceived to mean that the tests were reliable. They gave approximately the same IQ value again and again. Exceptions occurred, but these were seen as errors of measurement (see Jones, 1954). One could plot these errors; they tended to fit the bell-shaped curve approximating the mathematical ideal of the normal curve which, in other settings, had been shown to describe the typical distribution of errors of measurement. Thus, these exceptions could be readily made consonant with a faith in fixed intelligence.

It was only when tests were devised for measuring intelligence in preschool children that the idea of constancy in the IQ was challenged. This point will be discussed further below.

INTERCORRELATION OF TEST-SCORES. Fourth, scores on the various Binet-type tests of intelligence showed considerable correlation with each other. It was this fact that led Spearman (1904) to the view that intellectual activities have in common a single *general* factor or *g*. He assumed each test to be caused in part by *g*, in part by some specific, or *s*, factor, and in part by error, or an *e* factor. He suggested that tests highly "saturated" with *g* should be chosen for test batteries, and he found that the most highly saturated were tests dealing with abstract relationships such as the analogies test. In later writings, Spearman (1927) found in addition to g and s various correlational clusterings or group factors, but g continued to represent for him the concept of general intelligence. The g factor he conceived as the "mental energy" which the individual expresses through his various s factors, conceived as the specific neurone patterns involved in each activity. The multiple-factor theories of intelligence proposed by Kelley (1928) and by Thurstone (1938) reinforced the general finding that there is some consistency in performance on various tests. It was, then, easy to see the general factor as fixed.

VALIDITY OF INTELLIGENCE TESTS. Fifth, intelligence tests showed evidence of being valid in the sense that scores from them did a fair job of predicting school achievement and success in various other lines. Correlation of test performance with teachers' estimates of intelligence and with academic achievement were noted from the beginning (Binet & Simon, 1905; Terman, 1916). Furthermore, whereas children with IQ's below 85 were typically found to be retarded by one or two years in school (Terman, 1916), children picked in their early school years on the basis of high IQ's tended to progress more rapidly through school than most children, to be popular, and to achieve substantially more than the average (Terman, 1925; Terman & Oden, 1947). Similarly, Cox (1926) found that historical persons who were eminent in various lines of endeavor had also shown in their achievements as children evidences of precocity. Moreover, Hollingworth's (1942) gifted children, like Terman's, tended to be larger of stature, more skilled in various areas like music, and socially better adjusted than average. During World War I, performance on the first group tests of intelligence served fairly well to differentiate those who achieved success in the officer's role from those who did not (Yoakum & Yerkes, 1920). Finally, such occupations as accountant, engineer, scientist demand minimal IQ's well above the average (Wolfle, 1954), and those with scores below the average are regularly found in such occupations as unskilled labor (Fryer, 1922; Stewart, 1947). Such evidence readily lent itself to an interpretation that intelligence is a relatively fixed capacity.

HEREDITARY VERSUS ENVIRONMENTAL DETERMINATION. Sixth, the various types of evidence for hereditary determination of intelligence-test scores lent support to the assumption of fixed intelligence. One approach was to compare the correlations between the scores of people of varying degrees of genetic relationship. These correlations have typically run as follows: for identical twins, who presumably share the same set of genes, about +.9; for siblings, about +.5; for parents and their children, about +.5; for cousins, about +.25; for grandparent-grandchild, about +.15, and for unrelated children about .00.[2]

Another approach has been to hold the environment constant and to vary the degree of genetic relationship. One way has been to compare the degree of correlation between intelligence-test scores for identical twins (about +.9) and fraternal twins (about +.65) (Stocks & Karn, 1933; Newman, Freeman, & Holzinger, 1937). A second way was to compare the degree of correlation between scores for children and their parents with that between scores for foster children and their foster parents (about +.2). In both instances, effects of heredity are evident in the fact that the more closely related show the higher degree of correlation. On the other hand, a comparable approach has yielded evidence of an effect from nurture. Fraternal twins and siblings have the same degree of genetic relationship. Fraternal twins, however, by virtue of the fact that they grow up simultaneously, have presumably a more similar environment than have pairs of siblings separated in age. Correlations between intelligence-test scores for fraternal twins range between +.64 and +.70,[3] and these are significantly larger than that of +.5, which is typical of siblings. As Richardson (1936) showed, part of the higher correlation between the scores for fraternal twins may result from the fact that they are tested at the same age. When he correlated the scores for twins obtained at differing ages, the correlation dropped from +.7 to +.57 in 45 pairs. This correlation of +.57 was not significantly larger than the +.49 that he had obtained for pairs of siblings.

Various attempts were made by way of statistical manipulations to estimate the proportion of the variance for measures of intelligence attributable to genetic inheritance and to environment. One method, for instance, has been to start with the variance in IQ within the adult population, and divide this variance into the variance for samples in which either heredity or environment is somehow kept under control (Cattell, 1950). Since the variance in IQ's for identical twins is about a fifth that for the population at large, it has been estimated that genetic inheritance accounts for about 80 per cent of the variance in IQ. Several attempts have been made to estimate the variance at-

[2] See Elderton (1923), Hildreth (1925), Wingfield (1928), Lawrence (1931), Stocks & Karn (1933), Newman, Freeman, & Holzinger (1937), and Conrad & Jones (1940). These data for cousins, grandparent-grandchild pairings, and pairings of unrelated children come from Wingfield (1928) alone. For a more extensive review of these data, see the reviews of Anastasi (1958) and Jones (1954).

[3] See Stocks & Karn (1933), Richardson (1936), and Newman, Freeman, & Holzinger (1937).

tributable to environment from studies of foster children in which their IQ's are correlated with the IQ's of their foster parents. Leahy's (1935) estimate gave home environment credit for about 4 per cent of the variance. Burks (1928) got a somewhat more liberal estimate of 17 per cent. Several of the general textbooks of psychology published before World War II gave currency to the conclusion that heredity accounts for 80 per cent of the population variance in IQ, while environment accounts for only about 20 per cent of it. (See a critique of this approach in Chapter 9.)

So much for the empirical support for the assumption of fixed intelligence. It was impressive. It was widely accepted. Although the faith appears to be weakening, the conceptual scheme derived from this evidence as outlined here is still widely accepted. On the other hand, not all the evidence lent support to the assumption of fixed intelligence. Some of it was, in fact, highly dissonant with the assumption of fixed intelligence. Some of the evidence was faulty. Sometimes claims were made that the evidence would not support. These factors, combined with what one must suppose is an especially ardent desire to believe in the assumption of fixed intelligence, produced polemics of a rare height of violence.

EVIDENCE DISSONANT WITH FIXED INTELLIGENCE

The dissonant evidence came chiefly from three sources: (1) from the studies of identical twins reared apart, (2) from repeated testing of the same children in longitudinal studies, and (3) from studies of the effects of training.

IDENTICAL TWINS REARED APART. First, the evidence from the studies of identical twins reared apart. In the strategy of such studies, it is assumed that identical twins come from the same ovum and therefore share the same set of genes. Thus, if differences appear in any characteristic between pairs reared apart, it must be attributed to variations in environment or experience. Several of the reports dealt with single pairs of twins. Newman, Freeman, & Holzinger (1937) assembled data on 19 pairs. Seven of these pairs had been separated by the age of six months, nine more by the age of two years, and the other two by the ages of three and six years. The differences in IQ between these pairs is 10 or more points in seven of the pairs. The largest difference is 24 points, the next largest 19, then 17, then 15. When the discrepancies in educational advantage were also rated and correlated with discrepancy in IQ, the correlation was +.79. From these data, Newman *et al.* concluded that environmental opportunities can account for substantial differences in measures of intelligence with the gene pool held constant. Various critics pointed out that the average separation in IQ for the 19 pairs was only 8.2 points, that this is not greatly different from the average separation of 5.9 points for identical twins reared together, and that it is slightly less than the average separation of 9.9 points for fraternal twins reared together. Woodworth (1941) moreover, emphasized that when identical twins are subjected to environments differing only about as much as is typical for children in the community, the twins remain much more alike than random children in the community. From this he argued that interfamilial and educational differences are not of great importance in determining the variations that do exist in general population. Woodworth's argument probably holds for the variation within the children of America's middle class today. But the potential genius of the approach by way of identical twins consists in determining how much effect variations in series of encounters with the environment can have on tested intelligence. From such an investigative standpoint, it is unfortunate that twins are seldom placed in homes that differ much in any way. The fact that twins are reared separately need not mean that their encounters with the environment differ appreciably in any psychologically significant way. One of the characteristics of a culture is the uniformity it dictates for the way children are reared.

When substantial differences exist in the IQ's of identical twins whose circumstances of life have varied, these differences suggest how much effect the circumstances in life can have. Further analysis indicates those kinds of variations which significantly affect IQ, and those which do not. The fact that ratings of "educational advantages" correlate +.79 with twin-differences in IQ suggests strongly that the circumstances identified as "educational advantages" are significant. But what about other factors? Ratings of the quality of the social and physical environments showed correlations of only +.51 (p.<.05) and +.30 (not significant), respectively. Most of the other studies of identical twins reared apart[4] add little to the information from this classic study by Newman, Freeman, & Holzinger (1937). The fact that they found differences of 24 and 19 points in two of their pairs of twins should probably be accepted as evidence that variations in educational and social opportunities can have an effect upon IQ of this order of magnitude. If the variation in opportunity were exaggerated further, the difference in IQ might possibly be even larger.

Variations in circumstances that injure brain tissue can certainly produce even larger differences in IQ. Hobbs (1941) has reported one pair of identical twins, tested at 13 years of age, that differed

[4] See Muller (1925), Saudek (1934), Yates & Brash (1941), and Burks (1942).

52 points in IQ. These twins were reared together, and the origin of the difference in IQ derives from the circumstances of their birth. The mother had two eclamptic seizures. The normal twin (IQ = 109) was then already well down the birth canal and was delivered without difficulty. The retarded twin (IQ = 57) required the use of high forceps, and the head was reported by the attending physician to have appeared "squeezed" during the birth. Experiments of nature in which identical twins happen to be exposed to greatly differing sets of developmental circumstances will continue to be highly informative, but instances in which they are merely reared apart can probably add nothing.

CONSTANCY OF THE IQ. Second, the studies of the constancy of the IQ within individuals have posed a severe challenge for the assumption of fixed intelligence. These studies are of two kinds. One kind is concerned with the stability with which individuals maintain their positions within a given sample of individuals from one testing to another testing separated by various intervals of time. Another kind is concerned with the variations of IQ within specific individuals.

R. L. Thorndike (1933, 1940) first reviewed the test-retest studies concerned with the stability of the position of individuals within given groups of subjects. For teen-agers and young adults, these studies showed that on immediate retest, the typical test-retest correlation is +.89. With 10 months separating the tests, this falls to +.87, with 30 months to +.81, and with 60 months to +.70. For younger groups, this stability drops even further. Ebert & Simmons (1943) have reported test-retest correlations for testings separated by 36 months as follows: for tests at ages nine and twelve, +.85; at seven and ten, +.76; at five and eight, +.7; at four and seven, +.55; at three and six, +.56. For testings at two and five (Honzik, Macfarlane, & Allen, 1948), the correlation went to +.32. With testings at even earlier ages, the correlation drops even further. When Bayley (1940) combined the scores from the California Preschool schedules obtained at ages seven, eight, and nine months and correlated the combined score with such scores obtained three months later, the correlation was +.81. Twenty-one months later, this correlation had dropped to +.39; 30 months later, to +.22, and when these combined scores were correlated with intelligence performance at age six, the correlation dropped to approximately zero. For scores obtained from developmental scales during the first six months, several investigators have even reported small, and nonsignificant, negative correlations with later IQ.[5]

[5] See Furfey & Muhlenbein (1932), L. D. Anderson (1939), and Bayley (1940).

Such data from the longitudinal studies at California, the Berkeley Growth Study (Bayley, 1949) and the Berkeley Guidance Study (Honzik, Macfarlane, & Allen, 1948), bring this instability of status over the years into sharp focus. In Figure 2–1, from Jones's (1954) review, the correlations of intelligence-test scores at age 18 with scores obtained on the same individuals at successively earlier ages appear. The upper curve from Bayley's (1949) data is based on from 40 to 50 individuals observed repeatedly from birth to the final age of 18. The lower curve, from Honzik, Macfarlane, & Allen (1948), is based on from 140 to 153 individuals. Immediate test-retest correlations for young adults is above +.90; as time separating the testings increases, the correlation remains at the order of +.70 at age seven after children have had some exposure to the relatively standardized experiences of school, but drops rapidly thereafter to zero for tests made during the first year of life.

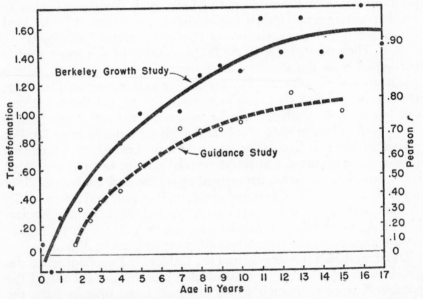

Fig. 2–1. Correlations of intelligence scores at 18 years-of-age with scores at successive earlier ages. From Jones (1954, p. 639).

One way of preventing such data from becoming dissonant with the assumption of fixed intelligence has been to consider the infant tests of development and intelligence as either unreliable or invalid. But they are not unreliable for any given time. Bayley (1940) got a reliability coefficient of +.94 from correlating scores from the odd and even items of a combination of the tests given to her sample at seven, eight, and nine months of age. Moreover, as already noted, the combined scores from these three testings correlated $+.81$ with scores obtained from testings three months later. The validity of the infant tests has also been questioned (Furfey & Muehlenbein, 1932; Goodenough, 1939; L. D. Anderson, 1939). Insofar as validity is defined as predictive value, these infant tests are apparently invalid. The scores from them indicate little about an individual's ultimate level of intelligence. J. E. Anderson (1940) has reasoned that this lack of predictive capacity for the infant tests may be a matter of their behavioral content. The behavioral elements for the infant tests have little in common with those for later tests. As age increases, the proportion of elements common from one age to another increases markedly. Thus, fixed intelligence over the course of development, while empirically untrue according to test-scores, has been defended nevertheless, on the ground that the correlation between children's test-scores and parental test-scores increase with the age at which children are tested (e.g., see Honzik in Jones, 1954). Deciding between the assumption of fixed intelligence and the alternative assumption of plasticity calls for evidence showing whether and to what degree variations in early experience of various kinds are associated with variations in intelligence at later stages when the predictive capacity of the tests has stabilized. Practical difficulties and ethical issues, however, make such studies almost unfeasible with human beings.

Studies of variation of the IQ within individuals over long periods of time corroborate the findings from the studies of stability of position. Such studies, like those correlating intelligence at 18 with earlier measures going back to infancy, awaited the completion of the longitudinal studies. These have been completed only fairly recently. The testing movement got underway in substantial fashion only after World War I. It took time to see the need for longitudinal studies and to get them underway. Then it took nearly 20 more years for the children who served as subjects to grow up. In 1942, however, Goodenough & Maurer reported individual growth-curves in intelligence in which changes of from 20 to 50 points of IQ appeared during the course of nine years. Honzik, Macfarlane, & Allen (1948), moreover, found variations of 30 or more IQ points occurring during a period of from 6 to 16 years in 10 per cent of the sample of 222 children in the Berkeley Guidance Study. In between 3 and 4 per cent of the cases, changes of a size-order of three standard deviations occurred. These are changes of the order of 60 points in IQ. Growth curves depicting such extreme changes in both directions appear in Figures 2–2 and 2–3.

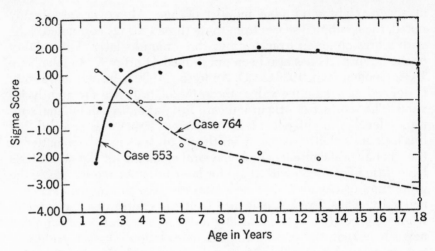

Fig. 2–2. Two contrasting mental growth curves. From Honzig, Macfarlane, & Allen (1948) and from Jones (1954, p. 641).

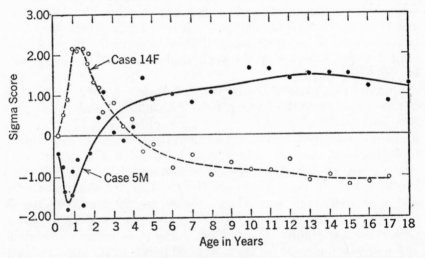

Fig. 2–3. Two contrasting mental growth curves from the original data of the Berkeley Growth Study. After Jones (1954, p. 642).

The interpretations of such findings have varied. Goodenough & Maurer (1942) saw no environmental bases for the shifts in IQ that they found, so they assumed that they must be attributable to inherited patterns of mental growth and to errors of measurement. Hints of experiential influences do appear, however, if one looks for them. Case 553 from the California Guidance Study, depicted in Fig. 2–2, had a poor health history, especially during his early years. Only one six-month period in his life had been free from illness, and family relationships were often strained. Somehow he came to find security in his intellectual interests. The "how" is not clear. With these interests go the rising IQ. Case 764 started at age two with an IQ or DQ of 133; by age four years it had dropped to average, and by age 18 years to 77, three SD units below average. She was born when her mother, who had an IQ of the order of 65 to 70, was 44. This mother is described as one "who lived to feed her (daughter) and to keep her young." In consequence obesity began in preschool years and increased to age 14 when therapy was instituted. Decreased obesity, however, was not associated with any upward change in the IQ. The obesity is probably unimportant by itself, but the maternal overindulgence may well have kept the girl from a variety of experiences and from opportunities to develop self-motivating interests that would foster intellectual growth. Such are the variations in IQ to be found in individuals. They are genuine. While their existence cannot prove that intellectual capacity is plastic during the early years, as Jones (1954) has noted, "it is equally hypothetical to regard the trends as produced solely by intrinsic growth changes." Again one faces the need for studies of the effects of experimentally controlled experiences during the early years on later intelligence.

THE EFFECTS OF SCHOOLING. Third, the studies of the effects of schooling were an attempt to get evidence concerning the effects on later intelligence of experimentally controlled experiences at various ages. In general the design of such studies is to compare the change in intelligence-test performance from a group that has had training with the change in performance from a group that did not have the training. This would appear simple, but probably no series of investigations in the history of science has produced polemics of greater intensity, partly because of the intensity with which the faiths in either fixed intelligence or human plasticity have been held, and partly because it is so difficult to control the various factors which are relevant to the outcome in investigations with human subjects.

Jones (1954) has enumerated several factors relevant to the outcome which have typically been inadequately controlled. First, the trained group and the untrained group should consist of matched pairs from a given population in which one member of each pair is randomly assigned for training and the other member for no training; however, the groups that receive training are usually "given" to the investigator by virtue of their membership in a school sample. If the training is something special, it is likely that the parents are self-selected for both higher intelligence and higher motivational interest, and higher gains in the schooled group may thereby be a matter of increasing approximation to the parental level of intelligence. Second, it is important that the trained and untrained groups come from a homogeneous population, for if a group of children of below-average ability happens to get selected for special training, retests will show an improvement based on regression toward the mean in compensation for the selective errors of measurement on the low side which occurred in putting them in the low group in the first place. Third, in the matching, comparable conditions of testing must be maintained for both groups, for if the trained group gets tested early in a nursery school experience before rapport with strange adults is established while the controls are tested within the security of the home setting, and if, after training, this procedure is repeated, the factor of rapport favors change in the trained group but favors lack of change in the untrained group. Fourth, since the predictive significance of tests increases with age, the testing program must be continued to an age at which the tests do become predictive of the final IQ. Fifth, it is important that the nature of the training experience be described well enough to be repeated and to supply a basis for determining whether any effects are a matter of simple transfers of specific skills involved in test-taking, are a matter of attitude changes and incentive, or are more generalized improvements in intellectual efficiency. Seldom has it been possible to control all of these factors properly, yet conclusions have been drawn and claims made. Result: polemics.[6]

Consider first the effects of schooling in school-age children. Goodenough (1940) summarized the investigations available before World War II with the conclusion that the measurable effects of various kinds of school practice had been "disappointingly meager when suitable controls have been employed," and that with the methods employed, effects on intelligence were even less clear. In an article called "Schooling makes a difference," however, Lorge (1945), examined the intelligence-test scores of 130 men at age 34 who had been tested 20 years earlier. He divided this sample into groups of comparable IQ at age 14, and then compared the retest scores of those who had completed more grades in school with the retest scores of those who had completed fewer grades. Result: those who had continued in school showed significantly higher test-scores than those who did not. When Vernon (1948) examined the patterns of

---

[6] For some of the polemics, see Goodenough (1939, 1940), McNemar (1940, 1945), Stoddard (1943), Stoddard & Wellman (1940), and Wellman, Skeels, & Skodak (1940).

test-performance in boys who drop out of school at age 17, he found that performance on those tests closely related to scholastic ability declined while performance on tests of mechanical aptitude continued to gain. Thorndike (1948) has shown that gains in intelligence scores are common among students in college populations even though such gains in a representative sample of those who do not go to college seldom appear after the age of 19 or 20. In Holland, deGroot (1948, 1951) has noted that during the war, when the schooling of children of all ages was badly interrupted by the bombings, the mean IQ's of the successive classes entering an industrial training school tended to drop. After the war, as the schools were rehabilitated, the mean IQ's for successive groups of applicants gradually rose again to the level that had been characteristic of applicants before the war. Although these results certainly suggest that, to quote Lorge, "schooling makes a difference," it is nevertheless true that the critics who hold a faith in fixed intelligence can point and have pointed to the fact that in all these instances, save that reported by deGroot, those who took more schooling were self-selected. Thus, even though the argument be *ad hoc*, differential rates of or differential potential for intellectual growth cannot be ruled out as factors which may be reflected both in continuing with school and in the higher later test scores. In the case of the systematic drop and rise in the IQ for the successive classes in the industrial training school reported by deGroot (1948, 1951), it has been claimed that sampling variation has not been ruled out, but the chances of such orderly change in 10 successive classes of applicants from sampling error would be exceedingly slight. On the other hand, various factors other than disruption of education are associated with war, and these rather than education could possibly have been the effective causes of the variation in IQ. Such an argument would admit that intelligence may not be fixed, but it would save it from modification by education.

Consider next the effects of nursery school and orphanages. The nursery school presumably provides an unusually stimulating environment while the understaffed orphanage provides an unusually unstimulating environment. Probably the first report of an improvement in intelligence from nursery schooling came from Wooley (1925). It was followed by a study reported by Barrett & Koch (1930) and by Ripin (1933) in which the test performance of a group of orphanage children was raised by nursery schooling. When Hildreth (1928) and Goodenough (1928), two of the leaders in the field of child psychology, reported negative findings from studies of this sort and criticized the results of these former studies as invalid,

most investigators withdrew from the field. As Jones (1954) writes:
"It is to the credit of the Iowa group of investigators that they maintained a persistent interest in the possible effects of nursery school
education and formulated an extensive and versatile program of research" (p. 681).

The work done by Beth L. Wellman, Harold Skeels, and their colleagues of the Iowa group appeared to show substantial effect of
early environmental factors on intelligence. In consequence, it was
claimed, for instance, that "some geniuses are made" and "some children are made feebleminded" by their experience (Stoddard, 1939).
Since the studies failed to control all the relevant factors described
above, the critics answered. Sometimes they "raised their voice" in
exasperation (see Simpson, 1939) or wrote in derision. Goodenough
(1939), for instance, wrote derisively:

> The many and unexpected facts that have turned up in recent and well-
> controlled experiments in human behavior have rendered many unsophisticated
> readers well-nigh as credulous as were those who fled from Orson Welles' Mar-
> tians, and even the best informed may easily be misled when a scientist of
> recognized standing "summarizes" only the positive findings of a piece of re-
> search and "concludes" from this incomplete presentation that certain principles
> are true. An outstanding example of this is to be seen in . . . the claim put
> forth that by proper training, especially such as is provided in the modern
> nursery school, the (true) intelligence of children can be raised to an astounding
> degree. Feebleminded children, it is said, can be made normal and as proof
> thereof they cite an experiment in which every member of a group of 13 "feeble-
> minded" infants was brought within the range of normal mentality through
> training by moron nursemaids in an institution for the feebleminded! . . . I
> believe that their data have been grossly misinterpreted . . . A large share of
> the results can be traced directly to . . . [the assumption] that intelligence
> tests given to infants and to children of two or three years of age have the same
> predictive value for later mental development as those given after school age,
> [and to the assumption] that the reliability of such tests . . . is so nearly per-
> fect that the effect of statistical regression due to errors of measurement may be
> safely ignored . . . (pp. 74–76).

Consider some of the specific studies. One is the "orphanage preschool project." In it, Skeels, Updegraf, Wellman, & Williams (1938)
established a model nursery school on the grounds of an orphanage
which was characterized by a nonstimulating atmosphere for children. The nursery school started with 21 children ranging in age from
18 months to 5.5 years. Each of these children of the school sample
was paired with another child, matched in chronological age, mental
age, IQ, and previous stay in the orphanage. Both groups continued
to live within the orphanage, but the schooled group got five or six
hours of experience during five days of each week in the nursery
school, while the control children remained in the orphanage en-

vironment. Over the period of three years, retests were made about every six months. The practical exigencies of foster-home placement, adoption, etc., forced modifications of this plan. As children from the schooled and control groups dropped out, others were chosen to replace them with the result that 46 children got experience in the nursery school and there were finally 44 controls. In the replacements, matching was less successful. On the initial tests, the nursery-school group averaged 4.5 points higher in IQ than the controls.

The results, as reported, showed gains in IQ for the schooled children but losses for the children who remained wholly in the orphanage environment. For those who got 200 to 399 days of nursery school, these gains averaged 3.7 points; for those getting 400 or more days, the gains averaged 4.6. In contrast, the controls for these two groups lost an average of 1.2 and 4.6 IQ-points respectively. The differential results for both these groups were reported as highly significant. When McNemar (1940) reanalyzed these data, however, he found that a case-count, in which each individual participated more than once, had inflated the number used as a basis for testing significance. Using the uninflated number of individuals in the formula to estimate the standard error left the difference between the schooled and control groups without statistical significance. Because the investigators had remarked on the shyness of the orphanage children, McNemar (1940) also attributed the remaining nonsignificant difference between the groups to the development of greater capacity for rapport with examiners in the children who had the experience of nursery school.

Wellman, Skeels, & Skodak (1940), in their answer to McNemar, reanalyzed the data for the 11 schooled children with an initial IQ above 80 who had 400 or more days of nursery school and the 11 control children with similar initial IQ and orphanage residence. The former dropped 2.2 IQ-points while the latter dropped 15.6 points. Since the mean of the net differences for these two groups of 11 children was statistically significant, they took issue with McNemar's conclusion that the difference was not statistically significant. For the 10 schooled children and 11 controls whose initial IQ's were below 80, the former averaged a gain of 8.2 points, the latter of 4.2 points. This difference, however, was not significant. Although a systematic selection of subjects produced one difference of significance, McNemar's point held: For all children in the study, the difference in net change was not significant. In answering McNemar's rapport argument, Wellman *et al.* noted that the test-retest shift is downward for the brighter children and upward for the dull, and they ask how the rapport factor can work both ways. They had a point, but it was dulled by the fact that statistical regression may have outweighed any differential effects of rapport. Moreover, since no attempt was made to obtain follow-up retests five or more years later, the permanence of even statistically significant changes would remain unknown.

In another study, Wellman (1940) compared the spring and fall test performance of 652 children for whom the appropriate data were available out of the 808 who had enrolled for at least one regular academic year in the nursery school at the Iowa Child Welfare Research Station. The tests given in the spring, after a year in nursery school, averaged 7.0 IQ-points higher than those which had been given the previous fall. For 228 children who had two years of experience in the nursery school, the gain for the second year was 4.0 more points. Fractional losses in IQ occurred over the summer, however, so the net gain for the two years averaged but 10 IQ-points. For 67 children who attended nursery school for a third year, the mean gain was 8.0 points for the first year, 4.0 points for the second year, and 2.0 points for the third year. Losses over the two summers reduced the total net increase to 11 points. Because the children tended to show a loss between the spring tests and the fall tests when they were without the nursery-school experience, the investigators attributed the gains to this experience.

Recognizing that such data can hardly be interpreted meaningfully without a control group, Wellman (1940) matched a group of 34 of her nursery-school children with 34 children from the community who did not attend the school. Between the fall and spring testings, the schooled group gained 7.0 points, while the unschooled group lost an average of 3.9 points. The difference in net gain of about 11 points was statistically significant. While these data are suggestive, those believing in fixed intelligence had no difficulty in pointing to other factors which could explain the gains. The absence of matched control-subjects for the main population left it possible to attribute the gains between fall and spring testings to such factors as the following. (1) To practice in taking intelligence tests: Jones & Jorgensen (1940), for instance, found a correlation of +.34 between IQ gains and length of nursery-school attendance at California, but when the number of tests taken was held constant by means of partial correlation, this correlation dropped to an insignificant value of approximately zero. (2) To increased security in the situation and to improved rapport with strangers who do the testing: For instance, when McHugh (1943, 1945) also found such gains in a public-school kindergarten, he attributed them to the fact that initial tests come when the children tend to be disturbed by both the strangeness of the situation and the examiner, while the retests come in the spring, when the children are secure in both. (3) To intrinsic factors in development: It is over the age range from two to five that the correlation between the IQ's of children and their parents is increasing most rapidly. Since the sample of parents of the children at Wellman's nursery school was distinctly above average (73 per cent of fathers and 53 per cent of mothers were college graduates), this sample of children might be expected to be improving in IQ unless some influence were hampering their development. In answer to this, Wellman *et al.* (1940) called attention to the fact of the loss over summer and to the fact that fall-to-spring gains occur in the children from families of lower educational status as well as in the children of families of higher educational status.

The control-group check with 34 matched pairs, the critics pointed out, capitalized on statistical regression. Since the parents of the nursery-school children came from a distinctly superior portion of the population, matching children from this group for initial IQ with children from the community must have meant picking children from the lower portion of nursery school reference population and picking community children from the upper portion of their reference population. Inasmuch as test-retest correlations over the span of six or seven months for such young children is below +.6 (Honzik *et al.*, 1948), each group of 34 could be expected to revert in retest toward the mean of its reference group on the basis of uncorrelated chance factors. At least a portion of the improvement in the nursery-school sample of 34 and a portion of the loss in the community sample of 34 could thus be expected on the basis of statistical regression alone. Who knows how large this portion is?

What may have been regression effects were also attributed to environmental influence in certain of the other Iowa studies. Unstimulating environments were seen to have a leveling effect upon intelligence; "the relatively dull move upward and the relatively bright show losses" (Crissey, 1937; also Wellman, 1938). To explain this, it was assumed that when superior children find their experience unchallenging, they tend to lose on retest. However, those low in the distribution of IQ are presumed to be sufficiently challenged to continue to grow. Such an hypothesis demands that the variability in IQ from initial test to retest should decrease, but no such decrease occurred. In consequence, critics found no reason not to attribute this so-called leveling to statistical regression.

Skeels & Dye (1939) also reported a highly suggestive study, not of schooling per se but of the effects of a shift from an orphanage to an institution for the feebleminded. This study, to which Goodenough

(1939) referred with derision (see page 28), was prompted by a "clinical surprise." Two residents of a state orphanage, one aged 13 months with a Kuhlmann IQ of 46 and another of 16 months with an IQ of 46, were committed to an institution for the feebleminded. They were committed not only because of poor performance on intelligence tests; the younger one at 13 months made no attempt to stand even with assistance and displayed no manipulative or vocal play, and the older at 16 months could not walk even with help, did not vocalize or play with materials. Both looked obviously feebleminded. At the institution, they were placed on a ward with moron girls who ranged in age from 18 to 50 years and in mental age from five to nine years. Some six months after this transfer, a psychologist visiting the wards noted with surprise that these two children had shown a remarkable development. When they were tested again with the Kuhlmann scale, the younger one had an IQ of 77, and the older one an IQ of 87: improvements of 31 and 52 points respectively. At the end of a year on the ward, the IQ of the younger was 100, and that of the older one 88. When these children were 40 and 43 months of age respectively, their IQ's were 95 and 93.

As the ward environment was examined, it was noted that

. . . the older and brighter girls on the ward became very much attached to the children and would play with them during most of their waking hours. Moreover, the attendants on the ward also took a great fancy to the babies, took them with them on their days off, took them to the store, brought them toys, picture books, and play materials. On the basis of this clinical surprise, came the fantastic plan of transferring mentally retarded children, one to two years of age, from the orphanage nursery to an institution for the feebleminded in order to make them normal (p. 5).

A group of 13 with a mean IQ of 64.3 and a range between 36 and 89, and with chronological ages ranging from seven to 30 months, were actually transferred to such wards. After being on these wards for periods ranging between six months for the seven-month-old youngster, and 52 months for the 30-month-old youngster, these children were retested. Every one of the 13 showed a gain. The minimum gain was seven points. The maximum was 58 points. All but four showed gains of over 20 points. On the other hand, 12 other youngsters with a mean IQ of 87, an IQ range from 50 to 103, and an age range from 12 to 22 months were left in the orphanage. When these children were retested after periods varying between 21 and 43 months, all but one showed a decrease in IQ. One decrease was of only eight points, but the remaining ten children showed decreases that ranged between 18 and 45 points, with five exceeding 35 points.

Here the effect of the two institutional environments in IQ appears to be great. But a critic can readily find fault. On initial tests, the two groups differed by 22 points. Since the group that remained in the orphanage had the higher mean IQ, it could be expected to show a drop in mean IQ on retest because of statistical regression alone. Conversely, the group submitted to the feebleminded institution could be expected to show an apparent improvement in IQ on grounds of statistical regression. The large size of the changes suggest general effects, but whether, after regression effects are subtracted, there remains more change in performance than could be accounted for on the basis of improved relationships with people in general, including psychometricians, cannot be determined from the data.

The evidence from these Iowa studies is highly suggestive, but no doubter who believes in fixed intelligence need relinquish his cherished belief or feel intellectually dishonest.

Perhaps the studies of R. A. Spitz (1945, 1946a, 1946b) have had more influence than any others in convincing many people, especially from the professions of psychiatry and social casework, that intelligence is not fixed but plastic and modifiable and that mothering is crucial during the first year of life. Spitz (1945) compared the development, as measured by the Hetzer-Wolf (1928) baby tests, of the babies in two institutions. One he called "Foundling Home." There the infants got very little attention or variation of stimulation of any kind after their mothers ceased to nurse them at three months of age. The other he called "Nursery." It was a nursery attached to a penal institution for delinquent girls where the mothers were permitted to care for and play with their children every day throughout the first year. "Foundling Home" cared for the progeny of socially well-adjusted mothers "whose only handicap is inability to support themselves and their children (which is no sign of maladjustment in women of Latin background)"; "Nursery" "provided for a markedly negative selection since the mothers are mostly delinquent minors as a result of social maladjustment or feeblemindedness, or because they are psychically defective, psychopathic, or criminal" (Spitz, 1945, p. 60). The mean developmental quotient (DQ) for the 61 children in "Foundling Home" dropped progressively during the course of this first year of the infants' life from a starting level of 131 for months 2–3 to a final level of 72 for months 10–12. The means for the first four months was 124, and for the last four months, 72. At "Nursery," on the other hand, the mean DQ for the 69 children was about 97 for months 2–3, rose to 112 at months 4–5, remained level to months 8–9, then dropped to 100 for months 10–12. The means for the first four months was 101.5; for the last four months, 105. Although no tests of statistical significance were reported, the difference in DQ-change between the two institutions would in all likelihood be significant. Spitz attributed the decrease in DQ at "Foundling Home" to lack of mothering. The infants in "Nursery" were mothered. Spitz reports that segregation in the penal institution frustrated the mothers' usual outlets, so they lavished their tenderness and pride on their infants each day.

The drop in DQ Spitz termed "hospitalism." He (1946b) has also reported a syndrome called "anaclitic depression." This consists of weepiness, withdrawal, loss of weight, decline in DQ, and susceptibility to infection. Spitz attributed both hospitalism and anaclitic depression to lack of mothering.

For all the tremendous attention that these studies by Spitz attracted, and for all the influence they have had in convincing people that the infant is highly plastic and that a close personal relationship between infant and mother during the first year of life is crucial for proper development, the study has major defects, as Pinneau (1955) has so ably pointed out. The conclusions do not follow from the evidence. The loss in DQ may in part be due to the manner in which the Hetzer-Wolf baby tests were originally standardized. Vagueness of reporting make it exceedingly difficult to come to critical grips with the results without suspecting that some of the facts are carelessly reported. The reports of lack of variation in stimulation, lack of toys, and even lack of light suggest that these factors may be more important than any lack of strongly emotional, personal relationship with mother in producing the drop in DQ at "Foundling Home." Again, the facts reported are suggestive, but the doubter who believes in fixed intelligence need not be relieved of his doubts.

It is relatively easy to conceive of designs for studies which would be logic tight giving human subjects from orphanage institutions experience in nursery schools and various other kinds of stimulation. Carrying them through to completion is another matter. Considerations other than the logic of evidence enter repeatedly into conduct of such investigations. It is because of this that, after an examination of the assumption of "predetermined development," the discussion in subsequent chapters will turn both to new conceptual developments and to investigations utilizing animal subjects.

CHAPTER 3

The Belief in
Predetermined Development

Faith in fixed intelligence has received a good deal of conceptual support from another belief which has been widely held in varying degrees. This is the belief in genetically predetermined development. An assumption of genetically predetermined development is implied in the concept of unlearned behavior. At various times unlearned behavior has been termed reflexes, tropisms (Loeb, 1918), and instincts (McDougall, 1908; Tinbergen, 1951). This assumption is explicit in the writing of Arnold Gesell, one of the students of G. Stanley Hall. Gesell (1940) described development or mental growth as "a progressive morphogenesis of patterns of behavior . . ." (p. 7). Elsewhere he has written, in a fashion not unlike his recapitulationist teacher: "Infancy is the period in which the individual realizes his racial inheritance. This inheritance is the end product of evolutionary processes which trace back to an extremely remote antiquity" (1954, p. 335). "The basic configurations, correlations, and successions of behavior patterns are determined by the innate processes of growth called maturation" (1945).

According to this conception of development, behavioral organizations unfold more or less automatically as a function of morphological development. Munn (1955) describes the process as follows:

Sensitivity evolves with the evolution of structures responsive to stimulating aspects of the environment. As visual, auditory, and other specialized receptors arise, the organism is better attuned to its surroundings, hence can be influenced by environmental details and can more readily adjust its behavior to changing

35

circumstances. Motor dexterity, or facility in moving around in and changing the environment, is also basically structural. It depends upon cues provided by the receptors, but demands flexible motor organs like joints, tendons, and muscles. Most organisms are equipped from the start with certain behavior patterns which depend upon inherently connected structures. Reflexes and complex inborn patterns of behavior like those sometimes called "instincts" have such a basis. These unlearned modes of adjustment depend upon inborn nervous connections which route impulses over pre-established channels from receptors to effectors; that is, to muscles and glands (p. 13).

In a sense, the notion of a constancy of the intelligence quotient may be seen as but a corollary of this principle of genetically predetermined development. Like the assumption of fixed intelligence, the idea of genetically predetermined development has historical roots. It has flourished among psychologists in America, partly again as a matter of historical accident, partly as a function of the conceptions of behavioral development that grew out of Darwin's theory of evolution, and partly because the evidence from the early experimental studies of behavioral development seemed to lend support to the idea that both the course of development and its ultimate culmination were essentially predetermined.

OTHER CONCEPTIONS OF DEVELOPMENT

Two other conceptions of development may be distinguished. The first, which is now of only historical interest, has been labeled *preformationism*. The second, which has been emerging since shortly after the turn of the century, may be called *interactionism*.

PREFORMATIONISM. Although preformationism is now a conceptual relic of only historical interest, it may be worth examining as an illustration from the history of science of the power of an idea to confuse observers and interpreters.

The notion of preformation has roots deep in antiquity. In his essay on the development of the child, Hippocrates foreshadowed the idea as follows: "Everything in the embryo is formed simultaneously. All the limbs separate themselves at the same time and so grow, none comes before or after other, but those which are naturally bigger appear before the smaller, without being formed earlier" (Needham, 1959, p. 34). The conception undoubtedly had a basis also in the kind of verbal logic to which the debators of ancient Greece were prone. Anaxagoras, for instance, who concerned himself with the origin of things, is credited with conceiving that "hair cannot come out of not-hair, nor flesh out of not-flesh" (Cornford, 1930). The idea of preformation is also full blown in Seneca's *Quaestiones Naturales,* where the following passage can be found:

"In the seed are enclosed all the parts of the body of the man that should be formed. The infant that is born in his mother's wombe hath the rootes of the beard and hair that he shall weare one day. In this little masse likewise are all the lineaments of the bodie and all that which Posterity shall discover in him" (Needham, 1959, p. 66).

Aristotle was not a preformationist. From his categories of form and substance, he credited the dynamic form-giving factor to the semen from the male, while the plastic substance out of which the embryo was formed he presumed to be the menstrual blood from the female. In one sense he anticipated the theory of recapitulation in his doctrine of the progressive acquisition of souls:

> For nobody would put down the unfertilized embryo was soulless or in every sense bereft of life (since both the semen and the embryo of an animal have every bit as much life as a plant) and was productive up to a point . . . as it develops it also acquires a sensitive soul in virtue of which an animal is an animal . . . for first of all such embryos seem to live the life of a plant, and it is clear that we must be guided by this in speaking of the sensitive and rational soul. All three kinds of souls, not only the nutritive, must be possessed potentially before they are possessed actually (Needham, 1959, p. 49).

Moreover, Aristotle observed, probably in the chicken's egg, the development of the embryo. He realized that previous speculations on the formation of the embryo could be formulated according to the antithetical conceptions of preformation and epigenesis, and he decided from these observations in favor of the idea that the embryo is formed by a series of transformations or successive differentiations.

The significant controversy between the preformationists and the epigenesists came into prominence at the end of the first quarter of the seventeenth century. Joseph DeAromati, having noted that one can see in bulbs and some seeds the rudiments of many parts of the plant, suggested that "the embryo is already roughly sketched out in the egg, and probably in all animals as well as plants." [1] Further erroneous empirical support came about half a century later from several sources.

Swammerdam (1672) found the butterfly folded up and perfectly formed within the cocoon. Prepared by the notion of preformation, he assumed that the butterfly must have been there throughout the caterpillar's life. Simultaneously, Marcello Malphigi (1672) described the chick embryo during the first hours of incubation, and presumably before incubation, through a simple microscope. His observations led him to take issue with Harvey, discoverer of the circulation of the blood, concerning Harvey's report that the heart

---

[1] What follows concerning this topic is a synopsis of the story as given in Joseph Needham's (1959) history of embryology.

does not pulsate before the appearance of the blood. Harvey's observations had been made with only hand-lenses of low power, so his preoccupation with the circulation of the blood could well have dictated his observation that the heart does not pulsate in the chick embryo before the blood appears. With a simple microscope and also with less preoccupation with the blood, Malphigi observed that the heart does beat before blood appears. Moreover, he added that as soon "as ever you can see this red pulsing particle with the beneficial observation of the microscope, you shall most distinctly see it to be the whole heart with both auricles and both ventricles . . . [Generalizing to man, he concluded:] So admirable is every organ of this machine of ours framed that every part within us is entirely made, when the whole organ seems too little to have any parts at all" (Needham, p. 167). These observations on the egg supported Swammerdam's on the butterfly, and Swammerdam saw in these observations an explanation of the religious notion of original sin: "In nature there is no generation but only propagation, the growth of parts. Thus original sin is explained, for all men were contained in the organs of Adam and Eve. When their stock of eggs is finished, the human race will cease to be" (Needham, 1959, p. 170).

The stage was set for the controversy among preformationists that later helped to destroy the belief in preformationism when van Leeuwenhoek, the inventor of the compound microscope, studied various animal fluids, including semen, under his microscope. Leeuwenhoek & Ham (1677) asserted that there were spermatic animalcules of both sexes, for a slight difference near the tails of these animalcules could be seen, that they copulated, that the females became pregnant and gave birth to little animalcules. Others claimed to have seen a microscopic horse in the semen of a horse, an animalcule with very large ears in the semen of a donkey, and minute roosters in the semen of a rooster. A reproduction of Hartsoeker's (1694) drawing of the human spermatozoon appears in Figure 3–1. Such is the power of an idea that it can over-rule all but the most dissonant perceptions. The central processes which mediate ideas may become so autonomous and persistent that they alter all but the most discrepant receptor inputs to fit their established organization. The perception of the tiny spermatozoon afforded by the early microscopes was sufficiently indistinct to permit theoretical expectation to rule the instrumentally facilitated observation without difficulty. In fact, this instrumental facilitation of perception apparently served only to increase the degree of credence attributed to the empirical support for the theory of preformation. For more than a century after the microscope was invented, preformationism remained the dominating conception of both the origin and the development of the embryo. Like the history of the phlogiston theory in chemistry, the history of preformationism in embryology exemplifies Conant's (1947) principle that "a well-established concept may prove a barrier to the acceptance of a new one."

Fig. 3–1. Hartsoeker's drawing of a human spermatozoon. From Hartsoeker (1694, sec. 88), in Needham (1959, p. 206).

The preformation controversy was not only bound up with religious issues, but was also concerned with the question of spontaneous generation. If lower animals like rotifers and protozoa could arise *de novo* out of such inanimate substances as slime, then their parts must take form through an epigenic series of successive differentiations. If epigenesis could occur in such lower animals, presumably it might also occur among higher ones. When Spallanzine and Pasteur demonstrated that animals the size of rotifers and protozoa do not originate spontaneously from broth, the preformation theory got another boost.

Preformationism was weakened by the split between the *ovists,* who saw the connection between the generations in the ova from the female, and the *animalculists,* who saw the connection in the spermatic animalcules from the male. Their controversy lasted a century. Both positions were threatened by the facts of heredity and the difficulty of considering one sex more essential than the other.

It was argument that weakened the idea of preformationism to a point where controlled observations coupled with new ideas could transform the conception. The arguments against the preformationist position were mainly three. First, if all animals have been preformed, how can monsters be explained? Second, how explain the observed facts of regeneration of such parts as the claw of a crayfish? Third, the small embryos of mammals, birds, and reptiles looked too much alike to fit the preformation theory.

It was the Russian investigator, D. F. Wolff, who in controversy with the great von Haller, finally disposed of the preformation theory at the level of embryology. On the theoretical side, Wolff (1795) borrowed from Leibniz the idea of a monad developing into an organism by means of its own inherent force and thereby gave birth to a precursor of the concept of predetermined epigenesis. On the observational side, he pointed out that if the embryo pre-exists, it should be seen fully formed as soon as it is visible at all. If it does not pre-exist, then one should see a series of appearances, each one different from the preceding one, as one shape changes into another shape. His first test case concerned the development of the blood vessels of the blastoderm. His method was to observe what he saw in batches of eggs after successively longer periods of incubation. He concluded that the blood vessels were not present at first, but that the "homogeneous surface of the blastoderm partially liquefies and transforms itself at these points into a mass of islands of solid matter, separated by empty spaces filled with a colorless liquid, but afterwards with red liquid, the blood. Finally the spaces were covered with membranes and become vessels. Consequently it was demonstrable that the vessels had not been previously formed, but had arisen by epigenesis" (Needham, 1959, pp. 220–21).

Von Haller (1767) answered that Wolff had no right to deny the presence of a structure simply because he could not see it. He argued that the blood vessels had been there continuously but did not become visible until Wolff saw the islands forming.

Wolff (1768) replied with another demonstration which showed that the chick's intestine also gets formed epigenetically from a fold in the ventral surface of the embryo which transforms itself into a closed tube. As fixatives and stains for tissues were developed during the course of the next half century, Wolff's observations were replicated in a fashion that all could see and that no one could escape.

Preformationism was done, but in its place was predeterminism. The force in predeterminism could be mystical, as in the case of the religious notion of predestination, or it could be chemical. The chemists of the early nineteenth century were gaining ground. The influence of Darwin was to attribute the predetermining force to heredity. As the genes came into being, first as logical constructs and then as entities seen with the electron microscope, the predetermining force was attributed to them, so the predetermining force has remained within the domain of chemistry.

Predeterminism has within it, of course, an element of truth. Potatoes do not come from tomato seeds, nor can one get a dog by breeding rats. It is the nature of this predeterminism and its limitations that men still debate.

INTERACTIONISM. Interactionism, the third conception of development, emerged shortly after the turn of the century with the classical genetic work of Johannsen (1903, 1909). It was Johannsen, whom many geneticists rank with Mendel as a father of scientific genetics (Srb & Owen, 1957), who distinguished the *genotype*, the constellation of genes that an organism receives from its progenitors, from the *phenotype*, the organism as it appears and may be measured at any point in development. The genotype of an organism can only be determined by observing its effect on the phenotypes of its progeny or by studying its ancestry.

From the standpoint of interactionism, the fertilized ovum is at once an organism in adaptive interaction with its environment. Thence, the phenotype of any organism at any given moment is "determined not only by the environment that prevails at any particular moment but also by the whole succession of environments he has experienced during his life time" (Sinnot, Dunn, & Dobzhansky, 1958). On the biochemical side, the newly formed organism incorporates the substances of the environment, acts upon them, and assimilates them into its transforming and growing structures. The genes appear, according to the work of Beadle (1945), to control the biochemical processes of metabolism, and each gene appears to monitor one step in the metabolic processes. But the chemical conditions surrounding a cell also have a controlling effect, for if cells from that portion of the embryo which is to become skin are transplanted to the region that is to become brain, the transplanted cells alter their development and become part of the brain instead of the skin (Jennings, 1930). Physical conditions surrounding the embryo may also alter the direction of development. (Harnley 1940), for instance, has found that in fruit flies (*Drosophila melanogaster*) of one strain phenotypic variations in wing size and structure vary directly with the temperature in which the larvae develop, while in another strain they vary inversely with temperature. Ecological investigations have shown, moreover, that marked phenotypic variations develop when plants from various environments to which they have become adapted are divided, to keep the genotypes constant, and each variety is replanted in the same sample of environments. What the genotype appears to do is to provide controlling directives for development and to set limits for the range of phenotypic variation. As Sinnot, Dunn, & Dobzhansky (1958) point out, however, it is impossible to know the entire range of possible phenotypic variation for any genotype because to know the entire range would require that the genotype would have to be exposed to not only all existing environments but also to all possible environments. This principle, which comes from geneticists, has been poorly appreciated by those students of behavior who have seen the genes as predeterminers of development and fixers of the level of intelligence.

The phenotype of human intelligence constitutes no exception to these principles. The encounters that the infant and child have with the environment in the course of development collaborate with the human genotype in determining the development of those structures and those organizations of central processes within the child's brain that mediate his intelligent behavior. Beginning at conception, the human organism, like all others, lives in the ever-moving now. It responds to the circumstances encountered with those structures, both somatic and neuropsychological, that it has already developed. In the course of maturation and in accommodating new variations in those circumstances, these structures change. Thus, at any given stage of development, the phenotypic intelligence of a child, to paraphrase the works of Dobzhansky (1956), depends on his genotype, on the diet he has ingested, and on the succession of circumstances that he has encountered. Relatively little is yet known about the important issue of how much phenotypic intelligence can be altered either by impoverishing or enriching children's encounter with their environment. But this gets ahead of the story, which will be resumed in Chapters 7 and 8. It is sufficient to observe here that a major share of the evidence to be reviewed in the chapters to follow lends support to this view called interactionism.

HISTORICAL BASES FOR BELIEF IN PREDETERMINED DEVELOPMENT

Although the conception of interactionism in development exists, the notion of development as an unfolding of behavioral patterns predetermined by inheritance is still widely believed. Or, even though this notion may be denied as a general proposition, its corollary implications are still believed. Like the notion of fixed intelligence, this notion of the predetermined development of intelligence and behavior has its modern roots in Darwin's (1859) theory of natural selection of inherited variations as the basis for evolution. Darwin's influence on American psychological thought was, of course, in part a matter of the *Zeitgeist*, but it also came through two relatively independent traditions of psychological investigation and personal influence. The first of these is the personal intellectual influence of G. Stanley Hall. The second, which involves a more complex personal and conceptual story, comes through the students of animal behavior.

G. STANLEY HALL'S INFLUENCE. Although Hall wrote much, it is likely that his influence endured more through the profound effect he had upon his students than through the effect of his writing. Boring (1929) in comparing Hall with James has written: "Both were enthusiasts, but, where James' penetrating, sympathetic whimsicalities won him a quiet supporter, Hall's torrential, fervid vividness won him an ardent disciple" (pp. 504–5). It can be noted, for what it is worth, that Hall's students include a majority of those names associated with the early development of intelligence tests in America. They are H. H. Goddard (Ph.D., Clark University, 1899), F. Kuhlmann (Ph.D., Clark, 1903), and L. M. Terman (Ph.D., Clark, 1905). Hall's students also include Arnold L. Gesell (Ph.D., Clark, 1906), who exploited the normative approach to child behavior and whose point of view was quoted in the opening paragraph of this chapter. Gesell's approach has been concerned with describing what is characteristic of children at each age. The conceptual significance of this so-called normative approach is based upon the faith that development is inherently or genetically predetermined. In the light of this faith the description of forms constitutes also explanation. It could well be that Gesell derived this faith from his teacher.

An admiration for the theory of evolution was probably the unifying thread in Hall's intellectual life. The evolutionary hypothesis appears to have motivated nearly all of his thinking. About himself, he has said: "As soon as I first heard it in my youth I think I must have been hypnotized by the word 'evolution;' which was music to my ears and seemed to fit my mouth better than any other" (Pruette, 1926, p. 208). It was Hall's ambition to become "the Darwin of the mind." Hall's training was broad; his scholarship included philosophy, psychology, physiology, and theology. Even though he was familiar with the cosmic, idealistic evolution of Hegel, Hall tied all mental life to the biological. One of his favorite aphorisms was: "No psychoses without neuroses." He assumed that mind and body had evolved together through millions of years on earth and that when physical life began in a single-celled creature, mind began in that same creature. Following the single-celled animals came the many-celled. They became active in their quest for food, for, as Hall wrote, "every thought and feeling has as its motive the feeding of the hunger of some group of cells" (Pruett, 1926, p. 210). Locomotion not only made these primitive organisms more efficient in seeking food but it also enabled them to escape enemies. The nervous system developed; vertebrate forms appeared; cold-blooded, scaly reptiles were transformed into warm-blooded animals, and in due time man evolved. For Hall, mind evolved with action: As man used his hand, his brain began to develop, "for the mind of man is hand made."

Hall thought he saw in the development of each individual the recapitulation of the evolution of the race. Moreover, he saw in recapitulation an explanatory principle. Just as he thought the human embryo recapitulates stages similar to those through which the race had passed in its morphological history, so he thought the human infant repeats the behavioral characteristics of the various stages of human social evolution. In the evolutionary theory he saw an explanation for human courtship, the care of the young, crimes, fears, subconscious habits, and the like. He saw play as "practice for the powers of the mind," and he argued that it was pleasurable to both young and old because it is instinctive.

The importance of the stages in the autogenetic development of the individual, in Hall's thinking, is illustrated by his parable of the tadpole's tail. Adult frogs lack tails, but tadpoles have them. If the tail is not tampered with, it is absorbed and gradually disappears, but if it is cut off, the back legs fail to grow. Thus, the appearance and disappearance of the tail appears to be essential to morphological development. The parable was presumed to hold also for behavioral development. The behavior of each stage was conceived to be essential to the appropriate development of the behavioral patterns to come. This is the faith in a predetermined unfolding of behavioral patterns which Hall passed on to his students and to the common sense of America, for Hall was also a popular influence who was instrumental in starting the child-study associations that influenced ideas about human development very widely.

This view did supply an important corrective. The notion of the preformation of behavioral patterns, which was tied up with that of original sin, was still widely believed in the latter years of the nineteenth century. The texts of teaching and child rearing of the day said nothing about the maturation or of individual differences of children (see, e.g., Combe, 1871). Thus, the failure of any child to fit a teacher's or parent's notion of what he should be was commonly construed as a moral lapse, a matter of laziness or what not. Hall's notions helped to provide a new perspective which appeared later to be confirmed, in a partial sense, and elaborated by Binet's tests of intelligence. On the other hand, Hall's conception of behavioral recapitulation was rigid. It failed to take into account that learning was in substantial part a matter of the circumstances to which the developing child had to adapt. Moreover, this faith in recapitulation allowed descriptive norms of behavior at various ages to serve also as explanations of that behavior.

INFLUENCE VIA THE STUDY OF ANIMAL BEHAVIOR. The influence of Darwin's theory of natural selection on conceptual developments in the study of animal behavior was less direct. This influence leads to and through some of the major transformations in modern psychological theory.

The first applications of Darwin's theory to behavior accepted such conceptual entities as mind, intelligence, and emotion. Darwin (1872) himself shifted his study of evolution from body to mind in his study of the expression of the emotions in men and animals. Thus, he himself provided the basis for what has come to be called *comparative psychology*. The task was to show that there is a gradual transition between men and the lower animals for the various entities of mind. Romanes (1882, 1883) took up this same task in attempting to show that man's mind and intelligence have evolved. The strategy was to show that animals are capable of intelligent behavior. The evidence employed by both Darwin and Romanes was anecdotal. Research for Romanes consisted primarily in collecting stories of clever behavior in various pets and marshaling them to demonstrate the continuity of intelligence between these animals and man.

It was the merit of Lloyd Morgan (1894) to see that it was reasoning by very loose analogy to impute to dogs, cats, and the like, the same kind of conscious processes that man could report. When he introduced his version of the doctrine of parsimony, psychology began "to lose its mind." [2] Morgan (1894) argued: "In no case may we interpret an action as the outcome of the exercise of the higher psychical faculty, if it can be interpreted as the outcome of the exercise of one which stands lower in the psychological scale."

It was at about this same time that Jacques Loeb (1890) first applied the concept of tropism to animal behavior. Tropisms were conceived as forced movements in plants and animal organisms by stimulation from the environment. An example is the turning of the sunflower toward the sun. In 1832, DeCondolle had termed this *heliotropism* and had attempted to show that the turning was forced by the chemical constitution of the plant in response to light stimulation. An example of what is typically regarded as tropism in an animal is a tendency in the newly hatched turtle to move toward any bright light. Inasmuch as a sea turtle lays its eggs in the sands of the beach near water, this tropism helps to insure the survival of the

[2] The reference here is to the story of a Chinese student who was studying the history of psychology sometime in the 1920's. He pointed out that psychology had originally meant the science of the soul. With the British associationists and the German students of consciousness, psychology had lost its soul. It became, instead, the science of the mind. Then, with the development of the American behaviorism, psychology lost its mind.

species. The waves reflect light. The capacity of this reflected light to attract the infant turtle helps to assure that it reaches the water where it can find circumstances appropriate for its development (Daniel & Smith, 1947).

Although such biologists as Jennings (1906) objected that even the behavior of such simple organisms as paramecia is too variable to fit Loeb's notion of the tropism, the notion was nevertheless applied, following the parsimony canon, to the behavior of higher animals. Its application, coupled with the notion of natural selection applied to responses rather than organisms, set the stage for what became trial-and-error learning.

Thorndike (1898) did the classical American experiments in comparative psychology. While still a graduate student at Harvard he did the first experiments on chicks in William James' basement. For this work, Thorndike invented the puzzle box. The chick was confined in a box from which it could escape by means of a predetermined act or series of acts. After the study with chicks, Thorndike used cats, dogs, and monkeys (1901, see 1911). In the behavior he observed in this situation, Thorndike saw no evidence of inferential reasoning. His animal subjects appeared to learn by trying one thing after another until they hit by chance upon a particular combination that permitted escape. In his original monograph (1898) Thorndike spoke of chance formations of associations in the random experience of his subjects. For such learning, it was Lloyd Morgan (1900) who coined the term trial-and-error. What any animal, even man, does in an unfamiliar situation is to try out now this action and now that, until something works. Stated more formally, the situation gives rise to response R-1, then R-2, then R-3 . . . R-n, when some specified goal, like escape from the puzzle box, is achieved. The response which occurs at a given moment is a matter of chance.

According to this conception, the responses that occur were themselves conceived to be largely functions of the structure, somatic and neural, of the animal. Learning was seen as a matter of strengthening the connection between the response that achieved the goal and the situation that evoked the response. This was stimulus-response, or S-R, theory.[3] The organism between S and R had been pruned of its mental contents with Ockham's razor of parsimony as wielded by Morgan (1894).

The question of what strengthened the bond between the correct

[3] S-R theory should be distinguished from S-R method. In emphasizing the observables of situation (or stimulus: S) and overt behavior (or response: R), the method is utterly sound. On the other hand, as will be seen in Chapter 4, the method soon led to refilling the empty organism between S and R, but with processes better tied to both stimulus, or to stimulus history, and response.

response and the stimulus early became a matter of dispute. Such psychologists as Watson (1914) attempted to explain this strengthening of the correct S-R bond on the basis of the principle of exercise. The animal was presumed to make the correct response more often than any other, and thus the correct response presumably gained in strength relative to the others. Observers of such behavior quickly noted, however, that the correct response might occur much less frequently than certain others and survive nevertheless. The principle of recency was conceived to be another factor. Inasmuch as the correct response was typically the last one of a series in a situation, the next time the animal found itself in that same situation, the correct response would occur because it was the most recent one (Guthrie, 1935). This recency hypothesis is difficult to test. From the observation that the correct response survives even though it may occur much less often than some of the wrong responses, Thorndike (1911, p. 244) formulated the *law-of-effect*. He phrased it as follows: "Of several responses made to the same situation, those which are accompanied or closely followed by satisfaction to the animal will, other things being equal, be more firmly connected with the situation . . . ; those which are accompanied or closely followed by discomfort to the animal will, other things being equal, have their connections with that situation weakened . . . the greater the satisfaction or discomfort, the greater the strengthening or weakening of the bond." When the critics applied Lloyd Morgan's parsimony to this imputation of affective states to animals, Thorndike (1911, p. 245) tried to define these states by observables, and independent of the fact of learning: "By a satisfying state of affairs is meant one in which the animal does nothing to avoid, and often doing such things as to attain and preserve it. By a discomforting state of affairs is meant one in which the animal avoids and abandons." At any rate, the occurrence of a response simply provided the opportunity for its subsequent effects to get in their reinforcing work. Such a notion corresponds in many ways to Darwin's theory of natural selection. Responses, like variations in organisms, occur by chance. They survive or persist because they are adaptive.

Such a conceptual picture of learning made but a very small place for central processes in the control of action. Along with this picture of learning came a static picture of the central nervous system. Chemistry was then the conceptual model for the biological and psychological sciences. A search for the unit of behavior, comparable to the chemical element or the morphological cell, was underway. It was found in the reflex arc, a concept originally named by M. Hall (1837) after being suggested by his observations of nerve-muscle preparations. The concept was further developed by Sherrington (1893). Moreover, the invention of the telephone appears to have played a role in the manner in which the concept of the reflex got applied in explanation of behavior. This new instrument of communication was so dramatic that it helped to reinforce a conceptual model in which the various reflexive responses could be connected and disconnected within the cerebrum from various stimulus inputs. In this stimulus-response connectionism model, the brain was conceived to be analogous to a telephone switchboard. The conception survived and spread in spite of the fact that, even before Sherrington (1906) popularized it, John Dewey (1896) argued eloquently that students of behavior should be interested in total reactions of organisms and that these total reactions could not be reduced to any system of reflex arcs. In the survival, Thorndike, as already noted, used the model to explain problem-solving, and still later Watson used it in his concepts of reflex-chaining to explain complex behavior.

As applied to development, stimulus-response connectionism had maturation going on independently of learning. Maturation and learning were conceived as essentially distinct and independent processes. The repertoire of responses came automatically with the unfolding of the neural and somatic structures which provided their basis. Marquis (1930) expressed the point of view thus: "Maturation . . . is a modification of the organismic pattern in response to stimuli present in the intracellular and intercellular conditions which at any given moment are independent of external influences." Learning, from this point of view, is superimposed upon the maturation process. It serves to tie various responses of the repertoire to various situations appropriate for adaptive purposes.

The Gestalt psychologists took issue with this stimulus-response connectionistic picture of problem-solving behavior and learning of the early behaviorists. Köhler (1925) saw his chimpanzees putting sticks together in order to use them as a tool, if the sticks were present in the animal's visual field at the time he was looking at the sought-for bananas, to reach the bananas beyond arm's length. This was *insight*. It assumed that an organizational field existed within the brain which could put things together in such an insightful manner. But, for the Gestalt psychologists, these organizational fields within the brain were conceived to be inborn. In similar fashion, Köhler (1929) attempted to demonstrate the phenomena of perception as a patterning of the field of forces set in motion within the brain by stimulation. Kurt Goldstein (1939) placed something analogous to Köhler's insight, which he called abstract-ability, into the frontal lobes of the brain. Unless Tolman and his students be considered within the

Gestalt group, this group has been relatively uninterested in learning or in the role of experience in development. Just as the early behaviorists saw the basic units of the response repertoire coming automatically with the maturation of the structures of the organism, the Gestalt group saw the cerebral organizations underlying insight and abstract-ability also coming automatically with the maturation of brain structures.

Thus, two major theoretical systems within psychology have lent conceptual support to maturation as the unfolding of gene-determined structures which in turn determine behavior. To these influences, one should add the tradition in neurology and psychiatry which has seen behavior and behavior disorders as a matter of malfunctioning of the brain (see Henry, 1941; Wertham, 1934). In certain instances, and in a certain sense, of course, behavior disorders do arise from a malfunctioning of the brain. The point is that the existence of an implicit faith in a genetically predetermined and automatic unfolding of behavior patterns following automatically on a predetermined unfolding of somatic and neural structures can blind observers to facts implying the inadequacies of the faith.

EVIDENCE SUPPORTING THE CONCEPT OF GENETICALLY PREDETERMINED DEVELOPMENT

As was true in the case of the faith in fixed intelligence, the early research on the developmental process itself yielded facts which, at the time they appeared, seemed to fit the faith well. The issue was cast in terms of the relative importance of maturation and learning. As such, the issue was part of the heredity-environment controversy, for in the maturation-learning dichotomy, maturation stood for heredity while learning stood for environment.

DEVELOPMENT IN ANATOMY AND BEHAVIOR. Of tremendous influence was the monumental work of Coghill (1929) relating the development of behavior patterns to histological or microscopical studies of neuromuscular growth. For a subject, he used the salamander, or technically the *Amblystoma*, one of the lower amphibious vertebrates. He noted parallels between morphological and behavioral development. Just as the head portion of the organism develops first morphologically, so the head is also the portion to show the first movements. It is a progression of muscular contractions starting first at the head end and proceeding tailward. At first, the infant salamander is nonmotile. Although muscular contractions can be stimulated by mechanical or electrical means, they are not initiated by the organism. At a somewhat later stage, the little fish-like sliver of a salamander would flex its head to one side or the other. As the development proceeded, this muscular contraction proceeded tailward. At a third stage, this flexure changed into a tight coil. Then, as the contraction producing flexure to one side started and rippled along the organism it was immediately followed by a flexure in the opposite direction producing what Coghill called the S-reaction constituting the fourth stage. As this S-reaction speeded up, it merged into the typical swimming movement of amphibian larvae. Other investigators had observed this cephalocaudal progression in the development of muscular contractions of many of the vertebrates, but they made less of its theoretical significance. For Coghill, the fact that function follows the development of structure implied that function also follows causally from the development of structure.

Coghill noted next that just as the forelimbs make their appearance in time before the hindlimbs appear, the forelimbs also begin to function ahead of the hindlimbs. As Coghill saw it, the forelimbs move at first only as part of the larger trunk movements, and then gradually develop an appearance of action which is independent of the trunk. This process he labeled the proximodistal principle in behavioral development.

Correlated with these stages of behavioral development, Coghill thought he found microscopic changes in anatomical structure. For instance, the shift from nonmotility to motility he reported to be associated with microscopic changes in nerve terminals. He wrote of this as follows:

> Growth of the terminals of axons and dendrites through microscopic dimensions is sufficient to have profound effect in behavior. This we have demonstrated in the first lecture in a vertebrate of such primitive form as *Amblystoma*, which, by the growth of the terminals of nerve cells over a distance of less than .01 mm, transforms itself from an animal that must lie helpless where chance places it into one that can explore its environment in response to impulses from within or stimulation from without. This is for *Amblystoma* a discovery, so to speak, of incalculable significance. It is to all intents and purposes a solution of one of the crucial problems of life (1929, pp. 84–85).

Coghill went on to assert that "the normal experience of the animal with reference to the outside world appears to have nothing to do with the determination of the form into which the behavior of the animal is cast" (p. 87). Although, as Kuo (1932b) has pointed out, this was an interpretation going well beyond Coghill's observations, it was powerful support for the notion of maturation as an unfolding process predetermined by inheritance.

To Coghill, the behavior of *Amblystoma* appeared to fit better the notions of Gestalt theory than the notions of stimulus-response theory with its trial-and-error learning. He emphasized that, at every stage, the behavior of the organism appeared to be an integrated system of action and that the development of partial patterns, like reflexes, arose "by a process of individuation within a primarily integrated total pattern." He argued further that the behavior of the organism does not arise by any system of interconnecting independent reflexes. Later this became a point of long debate among the observers of the behavior of embryos (see Carmichael, 1954), but it is hardly relevant to our story. The point is that Coghill appeared to provide an empirical basis for the notion that maturation operates as an unfolding of structures and behavioral patterns predetermined by inheritance.

The notion got further support from the work of Mary Shirley (1931, 1933) who pointed out that these developmental principles of Coghill could be applied to the human being. She wrote, for instance, that "motor control begins headward and travels toward the feet. Beginning with the eye muscle, and progressing through stages in which the head and neck muscles are mastered, arms, and upper trunk come under control . . . the baby at last achieves mastery of his entire body . . ." (pp. 204–5). When she found that all of the correlations between the orders in which responses appeared in her 20 individual children and the order of the modal series were above +.93, and that 60 per cent of them were +.97 or above, she concluded: "Motor development sweeps in an orderly course, and apparently is little influenced by the exigencies of time, place, and cultural fashion in child dress and child training." Shirley's work has been quoted widely.

There is no denying the orderly development, but her contention that this order is uninfluenced by the circumstances of development went well beyond her data. Her contention constituted an untested statement about environmental influence on the phenotype of motor development. Recent observations by Dennis (1960) have shown, moreover, that the contention is untrue. For instance, where nearly all of Shirley's children locomoted by creeping before they walked, the children who have lain unstimulated in cots in an orphanage in Teheran almost never creep. When they finally learn to walk, at between three and five years, it is scooting rather than creeping that precedes walking. The high correlations that Shirley found between the sequences of motor development in individuals and the typical sequence are probably a function of both the genetic influences common to the species and the typical sequences of experience that come with growing up in a human family.

Evidence from Subtracting and Adding Experience or Practice. The issue of whether variations in experience might alter the course of development has been considered. The strategy of the investigations was either to subtract or to add practice in a skill at various stages of development and to note the effect on the later quality of behavior in that skill.

One approach has been to subtract social experience and to note its effect upon various patterns of behavior which are characteristic of the species. Thus, various investigators have reared both male and female rats in isolation from weaning to puberty to determine whether the typical mating patterns of rats are inhibited or altered by such isolation. In general the various findings agree that when the isolated rats reach puberty, the female shows the usual pattern of receptivity, and the male shows the usual copulatory responses when placed with a receptive female. Similarly, the maternal pattern of behavior in rats, which includes care of the young at birth, nesting behavior, retrieving, and nursing, is essentially the same whether or not the rat has had other litters or opportunity to observe maternal behavior beyond the time of its own infancy. These studies have been well reviewed by Munn (1950). Such evidence has led most investigators to agree that the patterns of behavior involved in sex and the care of the young are outcomes of structural growth for which previous relevant experience is unnecessary. On the other hand, it was noted fairly early (Bingham, 1928) that chimpanzees reared in isolation do not exhibit the typical mating pattern of chimpanzees, but are in fact inhibited sexually. Such evidence suggested that structural growth is not sufficient to produce in a higher organism a pattern uniform in the species, and even more troublesome evidence has been turned up for the lowly rat (see below).

One of the early studies that subtracted experience was carried out by Carmichael (1926) on the embryos of *Amblystoma* and frogs. Just preceding the stage at which bodily movements appear, Carmichael added chloretone to the water in which the experimental embryos were developing. The chloretone was added in amounts sufficient to anesthetize the embryos, but not strong enough to interfere with cellular growth. Other embryos from the same egg-laying were placed in tap water to develop under ordinary conditions. The experimental group was kept in the chloretone solution for five days. Although they grew somewhat less rapidly than did the controls, they showed the same general patterns of body development. At the point where the embryos raised in tap water had begun to show swimming movements. Carmichael removed the embryos from the chloretone solution and put them in clean water. Within 12 minutes, these chlorotoned embryos had begun to respond to external stimulation. In less than 30 minutes after the first movement was observed, all of them showed coordinated swimming that was difficult to distinguish from the swimming of the control group which had been free swimmers for five days.

These results raised a question. Did the 30-minute period indicate that such embryos require a half an hour of practice, or did it mean that a half an hour was required to eliminate the effects of the chloretone? In another experiment Carmichael (1927) found that, when embroys which had been swimming for some time were chloretoned, it took approximately a half an hour for them to resume swimming when the water was changed. This supported the conclusion that the delay was a matter of eliminating the effects of the chloretone and that the embryos needed no practice. Carmichael's (1928) next approach was to add artificial stimulation and to observe its effects. One sample of *Amblystoma* eggs was in an aquarium placed in a noisy, vibrating work shop. The aquarium for a second group was placed in a quiet part of the building, and that for a third group on a deep pad of cotton on a cork floor of a room with both sound- and light-proofing. As soon as the embryos from the work shop and the laboratory were swimming, those in the sound-proof room were examined with a flashlight. They began immediately to swim, and apparently as efficiently as the stimulated groups. This finding was interpreted to support the assumption that in *Amblystoma* and in frogs, swimming behavior develops with efficiency in the absence of external stimulation and that adding vibratory stimulation fails to speed the development appreciably. Thus, Carmichael's studies were interpreted to furnish further evidence that behavior unfolds automatically as the structures subtending behavior mature in an order predetermined by inheritance.

Studies of the pecking response, or instinct, in chicks have a longer history. Spalding (1873) probably first called attention to the accuracy of the pecking response as something measurable. He kept one group of chicks from a hatching in a darkened basket and compared the accuracy of their pecking with that of chicks allowed practice from hatching. The chicks kept in the basket proved nearly as accurate in their pecking as those allowed full practice. Breed (1911) got a different picture when he analyzed the pecking response into its three components: (1) striking the grain, (2) seizing it, and (3) swallowing the grains. If pecking behavior is defined to include all three acts, initial accuracy falls to something like 15 per cent, but rises in the course of about 25 days to about 84 per cent. Shepard & Breed (1913) posed the issue of what would happen if chicks were prevented from pecking at visual objects for several days after hatching. Would the older chicks have a higher initial accuracy than the younger ones? Would they improve more or less rapidly than chicks allowed to peck at visual objects continuously from the time of hatching? The answer that Shepard & Breed got has since been got by various investigators and is probably best illustrated by the comprehensive studies of Cruze (1935, 1938).[4]

Cruze (1935) subtracted pecking practice by raising part of his chicks in darkness. These experimental chicks were fed by placing food pelletts in their mouths by hand. They got water from a medicine dropper. Cruze used groups numbering approximately 25. The groups were taken from the dark room and put into the test at 24, 48, 72, 96, and 120 hours after hatching. A test consisted of placing a chick on a well-lighted table and placing before it one kernel of grain at a time. For each group, the tests were separated by a period of 24 hours, and were run till the chicks were 20 days old. Cruze observed both whether the chicks struck the grain and whether the chicks swallowed the grain.

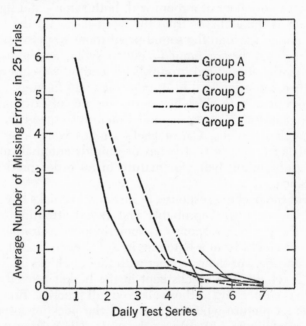

Fig. 3–2. Missing errors in pecking for chicks taking their initial tests at one, two, three, four, and five days after hatching. Adapted from Cruze (1935, p. 386).

The results for accuracy of pecking are depicted in Figure 3–2. The chicks kept in the dark improved in the accuracy of their peck-

[4] Two of these other investigators are Bird (1925, 1926, 1933) and Moseley (1925).

ing even without practice. Those kept in the dark for 24 hours averaged, on their first test, six errors per 25 trials, and on the first day of practice, those kept in the dark for 120 hours averaged only one error per 25 trials. Improvement had apparently occurred with maturation alone. On the other hand, improvement also occurred with practice. On day two, for instance, those chicks that had had a day of practice averaged only two errors per 25 trials, while those chicks which had been kept in the dark for 48 hours averaged slightly over four errors per 25 trials in their first experimental practice.

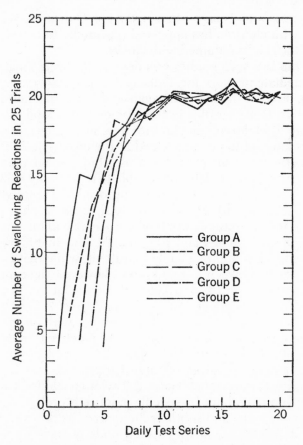

Fig. 3–3. Progressive increase in the number of swallowing reactions with pecks in chicks taking their initial tests at one, two, three, four, and five days after hatching. Adapted from Cruze (1935, p. 391).

The results for the occurrence of swallowing with pecking appear in Figure 3–3. In each group, the proportion of pecks accompanied by swallowing is low at first, but it increases rapidly with practice. The rate of improvement, moreover, is faster in the older chicks than in the younger ones. Thus, following day 10 the average number of swallowing reactions per 25 trials has leveled off at approximately 20. Such data were interpreted to mean that the pecking response, and presumably therefore most responses, unfolded automatically as the appropriate structures mature. Practice might have an effect in the perfecting of the response, but the amount of practice required to reach the given level of perfection is much less for the more mature than for the less mature.

SUBTRACTING AND ADDING EXPERIENCE FOR CHILDREN. Work of this same sort with children has appeared repeatedly to corroborate this picture of the results obtained with chicks.

One of the first such studies was done by Gates & Taylor (1925). Using immediate memory for digits as the skill, they gave periods of practice on each of 78 days in the course of four and a half months to a group of 16 four-year-olds in the Horace Mann kindergarten. Another group of children, matched for age, mental age, and memory for various kinds of items, was tested at the beginning of this schedule of practice, and again at the close, but got no practice. The practiced group gained. After being able to repeat only 4.33 digits on the average at the opening test, they improved to a point where they could repeat back 6.40 digits on the final retest. Such a gain is of about the same magnitude as that which occurs without special practice between the ages of 4 and 10 years. An immediate memory span for four-year-olds is approximately four items, while that for 10-year-olds is six items. Between test and retest, however, the control group had also improved from 4.33 to 5.06 without any intervening practice. This was also improvement, but to a lesser degree. Following the second semester of approximately four months without practice for either group, they were tested again. The practiced group had lost its superiority. It averaged 4.71 while the control group averaged 4.77. After another program of intensive practice had left the two groups approximately equal, Gates & Taylor concluded that the improvement brought about by specific practice is probably due to the acquisition of special and subtle techniques of work which are evanescent, and that the capacities which underly such a function are fundamentally a product of maturation.

In another widely quoted study, Josephine Hilgard (1932) followed this same experimental play in giving a group of 10 preschool children practice in cutting with scissors, climbing a ladder, and buttoning. The practice was given over a period of 12 weeks. At this point, the members of the practice group were definitely superior in all of these skills to the matched children in the control group. The control group had, of course, received no special practice. One week of practice in these skills for the control group, however, brought their performance to a level equal to that of the experimental group who had received the 12 weeks of practice.

Similar results were reported in two studies (Gesell & Thompson, 1929; Hilgard, 1933) which employed identical twins as subjects. In these studies both twins in each pair were given initial tests. Then one twin was given training in various skills. Following the training both were tested again, and finally the amount of training required to bring the control twin up to the level of the practiced twin was determined. It appeared fairly clear from these studies that direct practice in such skills as stair-climbing, cube-building, cutting with scissors, climbing a ladder, and buttoning is largely lost motion. In each case the control twin gained the attained level of the practiced twin at a later age with much less practice. Gesell & Thompson (1929) concluded: "There is no conclusive evidence that practice and exercise ever hasten the actual appearance of such types of reactions as stair-climbing and tower-building with blocks. The time of appearance is fundamentally determined by ripeness of the neural structures . . . although function enters into growth, training does not transcend maturation."

With the same issue at stake, Dennis & Dennis (1940) examined the consequences of the cradling practices of the Hopi Indians on the age at which the Hopi children learn to walk. Before contact with white civilization, Hopi mothers reared their children through most of the first year on a cradle board. When bound to the board, an infant can move only its head. On the other hand, it can listen and look about, and while being carried is exposed to an unusually wide variety of visual and auditory stimuli. Typically, the child is kept bound to the board for the greater part of the day until near the end of the first year, but after the age of three months most of the infants are given short daily periods of freedom. In this investigation, Dennis & Dennis compared the ages at which mothers recalled the onset of walking for children reared on the board and for other Hopi children whose mothers had given up this practice. The mean age of walking reported for these two groups did not differ significantly. From this the Dennis's concluded that walking is an autogenous response which requires little environmental stimulation for its evocation and integration.

On the basis of these results, Dennis & Dennis (1935, 1938, 1941) undertook to rear a pair of fraternal twins, Dell and Ray, from the beginning of the second month to the end of the 14th month of their lives under conditions which they characterized "as restricted practice and minimal social stimulation." Care was limited to an excellent diet and physical comfort. They then compared the age of first appearance of 50 behavioral items with norms for these items compiled for the developmental records of 40 subjects of baby biographies (Dennis & Dennis, 1937). The results show that both twins were somewhat retarded in the establishment of visually directed reaching, grasping, and sitting alone, and in standing with support. On the other hand, smiling, laughter, attempting to rise, and attempting to turn seemed to appear *de novo* and not to be derived from any antecedent reactions of the infants. In their conclusion of this study, Dennis & Dennis were somewhat less convinced about the autogenous nature of infant responses. On the one hand, they reiterated the conclusion that "practically all of the common responses of the first year of life may be developed autogenously, i.e., infants will develop these responses without encouragement of instruction, without reward or example." On the other hand, they also concluded that

. . . in the development of the autogenous responses of the first year, learning plays an important part. The dichotomy of learned and unlearned responses is difficult to employ, but if we are to employ these concepts, the evidence indicates that there is little reason to believe that infant responses are made up exclusively of unlearned elements except in the case of a very few reactions . . . Maturation in and of itself seldom produces new developmental items, but maturation of structures when accompanied by self-directed activity leads to new infant responses (1941, p. 130).

DISSONANT EVIDENCE

In view of such abundant confirmation of the conception that the basic behavior patterns unfold automatically as somatic and neural structures mature, it is hardly surprising that those crediting experience with any major effect on development have been looked upon as somewhat "softheaded." It is hardly surprising that any evidence they may have found implying such a major role for experience is examined with maximum skepticism. On the other hand, dissonant evidence has appeared. The retardation in the onset of various behavior patterns in Dell and Ray, the twins reared under minimal stimulation by Dennis & Dennis, is but one example.

Evidence pointing toward the need for a broader view of experience in the process of development has come from studies of the effect of subtracting certain experiences in the development of the lowly rat upon even such "instinctive" items of behavior as mothering and nest-building. From observations that female rats will not "mother" pups which have been washed with soap and water until certain substances characteristic of vaginal tissues have been smeared on the pups' skins, Birch (1956; also personal communication) guessed that odors from these substances were part of the instigation and control of the mothering behavior. He reasoned further that maternal licking of the young might well be a generalization of an experienced relationship between the animal and parts of itself. The female rat's licking of its own genitalia, and in particular the intense self-licking of pregnancy, would thus provide an experiential basis for eating the afterbirth and licking the pups following parturition, and perhaps also for the pup-licking of the nursing period. If such a guess were true, it would follow that any procedure interfering with the genital self-licking of the female rat during its development would serve to disrupt this typical pattern of maternal behavior.

To test this guess, Birch (1956) devised rubber collars, like the ruffs worn through the Elizabethan period, and put them on female pups at the time of weaning. These ruffs were large enough to prevent self-licking. They did not interfere appreciably with most other activities. In adulthood, the rats so reared conceived readily and had normal pregnancies. Just before parturition, the ruffs were removed. Parturition was itself normal. On the other hand, these mother rats were slow to pay any attention to their young. When they did, the maternal pattern became grossly abnormal. When the females so reared did start to lick their pups, for instance, they ate them. Only 5 per cent of the pups of these animals survived the period immediately following birth. These survived only because they got under nesting materials and were not retrieved. The pups which were retrieved were badly suckled. One animal insisted in keeping them under her neck, between her forepaws and her lower jaw where they could not possibly reach the teats.

The tendency of female rats reared with ruffs to eat the young is especially interesting. Birch has guessed that this may result from the fact that female rats ordinarily learn to inhibit chewing and swallowing with objects characterized by the odor and taste of the vaginal area through having suffered pain from biting their own genitalia. At any rate, here is an example in which the subtraction of experience results in a marked disorganization of a pattern of behavior which, in the past, has commonly been regarded as instinctive.

Reasoning in similar fashion about nesting behavior in the rat, Riess (1950) inferred that developmental experiences with materials might be essential for later nest-building. He therefore reared female rats in cages containing nothing that could be picked up or transported. As the time for their first litters approached, they failed to build nests even though appropriate materials were available. In a repetition of this experiment, Riess (1954) reared female rats in complete isolation from mother rats following early weaning and allowed them nothing in the cages that could be carried or manipulated. At the time of parturition, these animals exhibited some nesting behavior, but it was very unskillful. The resulting nests were poor in quality. Another unexpected effect also appeared. These females made no attempt to suckle their young. Instead, they treated the pups as inanimate objects to be carried about.

Cruze's (1935) study of pecking behavior in chicks also produced troublesome evidence. Besides the groups of chicks discussed above, Cruze had three others. These three groups were kept in the dark for 20 consecutive days. They saw light and had pecking-experience only during the tests themselves. One of the three groups got 12 pecks of practice during each of the 20 consecutive daily tests. Another group got 25 practice pecks during each daily test. The third group got 12 pecks per day for 10 days, then 25 pecks thereafter. These groups failed to attain a high level of accuracy in pecking. The group with only 12 pecks per day exhibited almost no improvement in the striking-seizing-swallowing sequence of behavior. In the group given 12 pecks per day for 10 days, then 25 pecks thereafter, marked improvement followed the increased amount of practice. While the Cruze study demonstrated that the cluster of factors labeled maturation is important, so is the cluster of factors labeled experience. Furthermore, the fact that the group that continued to remain in the dark except during the test period improved so much less than the others suggests that the varied stimulation that comes from living in the light may be quite as important as practicing the pecking act for the development of accuracy. Perhaps the cluster of factors labeled experience, environment, and learning have been seen too narrowly. Perhaps it is not practice of any given act that is important, but other quite different experiences.

Although Navajo infants reared on cradle boards, where they have little opportunity to exercise their legs, walk just as early as do Navajo infants reared with full opportunity to use their limbs, as Dennis & Dennis (1940) have found, the assumption that such behavior patterns as sitting, creeping, and walking and those on the Cattell infant scale will unfold automatically without sufficient opportunity for environmental stimulation has nevertheless been called into serious question by two more recent studies by Dennis. In the first of these, Dennis & Najarian (1957) compared the development of the institutional children at Creche, an infant's orphanage in Beirut, Lebanon, with children of similar ages who were brought to a Well-Baby Clinic in the same community. The social class of the institutional and comparison groups was similar. For financial reasons, the infants at Creche got very little attention during their first year of life; there was only one adult staff-member for every 10 infants. They lay swaddled in cribs that had white covering around the sides to protect the child from the drafts and which permitted the child to see only the homogenous white ceiling and those particular adults who came near only for feeding and necessary care. Light, air, food, and sanitation at Creche were better than satisfactory, but attention and stimulation were minimal. Feeding consisted, for example, of getting a bottle propped up on a pillow. The results show that from the third to the twelfth month, the mean of the scores for the Creche infants on the Cattell infant scale was 63 and that of the comparison group was 101, a difference in DQ of 38 points which is highly significant ($p<.001$). No Creche baby between 3 and 12 months of age had a DQ of above 95. Since children are kept to about age six at Creche, Dennis & Najarian (1957) also compared Creche children aged 4.5 to 6 years with children of the same age range at the Well-Baby Clinic. Because procedures of administration at the Creche home had not changed, it was assumed that these 4.5 to 6-year-old youngsters had previously shown the same retardation during the first year as those studied. On Goodenough's draw-a-man test, on the Porteus mazes, and on the Knox-cube test, these children produced median DQ's of 93 (mean = 93), 89 (mean = 95), and 100. From these data Dennis & Najarian concluded that the unfolding of the response patterns that underlie the performance on the Cattell infant scale require opportunities for learning as well as maturation. On the other hand, inasmuch as these 4.5 to 6-year-olds had returned nearly to normal on the tests which were chosen to minimize the environmental effects, they argue that the retardation was not permanent.

In a still more recent study, Dennis (1960) studied the locomotor development of children from an orphanage in Teheran where the opportunities for variations in patterns of stimulation and of experience were even less than at Creche. The data from this study challenge even more severely the still widely held view that motor development consists in the automatic unfolding of a behavioral sequence based upon the maturation of structures. Dennis writes:

Shirley's chart of the motor sequence is a textbook favorite. It shows sitting alone at seven months, creeping at 10 months, and walking alone at 15 months. The present study shows that these norms are met only under favorable environmental conditions. Among the children of Institution I (for children up to three years of age), not only was sitting alone greatly retarded but in many cases creeping did not occur. Instead, an alternate form of locomotion (scooting) was employed. These facts seem to indicate clearly that experience affects not only the ages at which motor items appear but also their very form (1960, p. 57).

Evidence has also turned up which calls into question the Gestalt theory that pattern perception (Köhler, 1929) and insight (Köhler, 1925) depend only on the maturation of the relevant cerebral structures. Von Senden (1932) has reviewed the published reports of the first visual perceptions of some 66 patients who have regained their sight through surgical intervention for congenital cataracts (see Hebb, 1949; Gibson, 1950). In the case of a cataract, the lens becomes semi-opaque. The individual may see diffused light but is blind to pattern. After bandages were removed, following the operation, these patients had their first chance to see. What did they see? The answer is that they were at first bewildered. Such questions as "Are things projected in space?" were meaningless to them. The figure-ground relation of Gestalt theory was present from the first. The patients could also apply the words *same* or *different* to objects. Two strips of cardboard, one 10 cm. and one 20 cm. long, were seen as different, but the patient could not say which was the longer. These patients soon learned to name colors, to distinguish large from small, and to distinguish far from near, but it took months to learn the innumerable names for the immense variety of visual shapes so that they could identify objects, places, events, and people. Context proved an important problem. Recognition of a cube of sugar, for instance, might be learned fairly quickly so long as the cube was seen in the investigator's hand or upon a table, but when it was suspended by a thread it was not recognized without much more visual experience. Riesen's (1947, 1958) studies of the effects upon later perception of rearing chimpanzees in darkness, to be reported in Chapter 4, tend to confirm the substance of these reports reviewed by von Senden (1932).

Similarly, various studies of the insightful behavior of chimpanzees have called into question Köhler's (1925) contention that insight occurs independently of past experience. For instance, Bingham (1929) found that chimpanzees which had been trained, or given a chance to learn, to get on top of a square box to reach a banana could then be taught to stack one box on another for the same purpose. On the other hand, a chimpanzee which had not had the opportunity to learn the first skill of using boxes could not be taught the second problem. By pyramiding such training, Bingham got certain of his chimpanzee subjects to stack four boxes, one on another. From such evidence, he concluded that the solution of box problems demands little if any behavior that is strictly new. Originality appears in the regrouping of skills already acquired. In relating this conception to Köhler's (1925) conception of insight, Bingham agreed that a solution might occur suddenly. What he argued was that instances of sudden insight come about through the combining and recombining of central processes derived from past experience in which organized patterns of behavior are combined and recombined as new situations might demand.

Other investigators have also obtained evidence suggesting that previous experience is required for sudden and insightful problem-solving, but how close the content of the experience needs to be to the problem is unclear. Jackson (1942) found that the chimpanzees in his sample did not use a tool in the process of trying to get a banana that is out of reach unless they had been observed to play with tools. Birch (1945) tested six champanzees with the hoe problem. In this problem the animal is provided with a stick which has attached to its further end another stick at right angles. The problem is one of getting food out of reach by using this tool. The food is put somewhere near the juncture of the blade and the handle of the hoe. The six chimpanzees in Birch's study were four to five years old. They had been reared in the laboratory. Only two of the six solved this problem within half an hour. One of these solutions appeared to be accidental. The other solution was made by a chimpanzee that had been observed to use sticks regularly in its spontaneous play. The animals were given an opportunity for stick play in their cages for three days, then they were tested again. At this point, five of the six subjects failed, and again the one that succeeded was that chimpanzee who had used sticks adaptively in his cage before the experiment began.

SUMMARY

The notion of fixed intelligence has received supplementary support from the assumption of genetically predetermined development, i.e., the notion that the basic behavioral repertoire unfolds automatically as a function of maturing somatic and neural structures. Historically, the notion of predetermined development took the place of the notion of preformationism, and it must now give way to a third conception of development which may be termed *interactionism*.

The conception of predetermined development has its most important roots in Darwin's theory of natural selection. Its spread in America may be attributed to the *Zeitgeist* of the last decades of the nineteenth century, to the influence of G. Stanley Hall's popularization of the recapitulation corollary, and to the train of conceptual developments in comparative psychology that followed Lloyd Morgan's application of the canon of parsimony to the attribution of mental capacities to animals, that utilized Loeb's tropisms, and that culminated in the Thorndikian trial-and-error or S-R theory of problem-solving and the notion of the empty organism coupled with the notion of the brain as a static switchboard.

The assumption of predetermined development got empirical support from Coghill's observations that behavioral development follows the same principles as somatic development and from Shirley's finding of a characteristic sequence in the appearance of developing patterns of behavior. The assumption got further apparent support from many of the studies of the effects of adding and subtracting practice on motor responses in sub-human animals and children. While a group given practice on a performance for a period of time did show some superiority in the quality of that performance over the unpracticed group, the unpracticed group typically caught up after only very little practice.

On the other hand, deprivations of experience have been found to make a difference in the rate at which infant organisms develop behaviorally. The more severe the deprivations of experience, the greater the decrease in the rate of behavioral development. Moreover, the effects of deprivations of experience may show most plainly when the experiences of which the young animal or infant has been deprived are quite different from the performances measured. This last fact suggests that the earlier investigators saw experience, learning, and practice in too narrow a fashion. The fact that the effects of some of these deprivations of experience have been so pronounced calls the assumption of predetermined development into serious question, and suggests that the concept of continuous environment-organism interaction would better fit the facts.

CHAPTER **4**

Information-Processing
and Experience

The concepts of fixed intelligence and of predetermined development have both rested on the assumption that unlearned behavior patterns and various capacities are somehow derived directly, automatically, and more or less completely from somatic cerebral structures and their functional properties. There is no question that somatic and cerebral structures with their functional properties are important, but it has become more and more clear that experience is required for the development of these behavioral patterns and capacities, and especially for the development of those central organizations for the processing of information that are required to solve problems.

Stimulus-response methodology yielded evidence that soon prompted behavioristic students of animal behavior, who had given up instincts[1] and mental entities, to begin filling the empty organism with conceptual processes intervening between stimulus and response. These intervening processes or variables fortunately were

[1] This refers to instincts conceived as adaptive patterns of behavior by Spalding (1873), Hall (see Fisher, 1925), McDougall (1908), and Hingston. Such constructs suffered from the criticism of Morgan (1894), but they did not go out of fashion till the 1920's from the criticism of Dunlap (1919), Kuo (1921, 1922, 1932d; see Chapter 8), Bernard (1924), and Watson (1924). Although the conception of instincts as inherited behavior patterns has been revived by the work of the ethologists (Lorenz, 1952; Tinbergen, 1951), the significance of the ethological conception probably belongs more in the sphere of motivation than in that of intelligence (Hess, 1959).

65

tied to both stimulus and response in the past experience of subjects. Investigations of human problem-solving suggested that active central mechanisms for the processing of information are involved. Harlow (1949) demonstrated how learning sets, which may be seen as techniques of information-processing, are acquired in monkeys. Hebb (1949) found, within the developments of neurophysiology, suggestions concerning the nature of these central processes, and these suggestions have been elaborated and modified as neurologists have considered the strategies for processing information learned from programming electronic computers. Their suggested nature has in turn prompted investigations of the effects of early experience which indicate that the perceiving of forms and objects and the capacity for insightful solution of problems, which the Gestalt theorists attributed directly to the properties of cortical fields, requires experience for their development.

So much for a bird's eye view. Consider the story in somewhat more detail.

INTERVENING PROCESSES OR VARIABLES IN
BEHAVIORISTIC THEORY

Shortly after Lloyd Morgan (1894) had extirpated the various mental entities from mind with Ockham's razor of parsimony, Thorndike & Woodworth (1901) knocked out such old-fashioned mental faculties as memory with studies showing that such practices as the daily memorization of a few lines of poetry did not improve the individual's capacity to memorize other types of material. Watson's deletion of consciousness from the glossary of useful psychological concepts completed the destruction of mental entities traditionally used to explain behavior. Inasmuch as most of these mental entities had merely described behavioral phenomena in other terms, the result was salutary. On the other hand, the consequence was an essentially empty organism between stimulus and response.

Efforts to make sense out of problem-solving and learning by various species of laboratory animals soon prompted the invention of new conceptions of what goes on when an animal solves a problem or learns. The nature of the new conceptions has varied and thus has led to a multiplicity of disputes among the adherents of the various theories (see Hilgard, 1948; Spence, 1942, 1951). Many of these issues are outside the scope of our discussion of intelligence and experience, but the issue of the existence of central mediational processes and their nature is essential. The demonstration of the existence of such processes did not come from the relatively simple Pavlovian (1927) method of associating a conditional stimulus, which ordinarily does not impel a given action, with another stimulus which does: a business which turns out to be far from simple after all. Neither did the demonstration come from Thorndikian problem-solving. Central processes were suggested rather by the work on delayed reaction and double alternation. After noting that higher animals, such as children, chimpanzees, and even racoons can utilize cues to locate food even after substantial delays between seeing the cue and going to the food, whereas animals like rats cannot, Hunter (1912) argued that the so-called higher animals must be capable of some kind of *symbolic process*. Evidence for the symbolic process was strengthened when the animal could go directly to the food following a delay even though the animal had been moved about and had engaged in various kinds of activity during the delay between exposure to the cue and going to the food.

Hunter (1918) also developed the temporal maze and the idea of the double-alternation problems. In most maze-learning, so long as the left turn could signal a right turn, and the right turn could signal a left turn, solution of the problem could be handled by simple conditioning theory even when various sensory cues were eliminated. On the other hand, in double-alternation, when a right turn first signals another right turn, and then signals a left turn, while the left turn signals first a left turn and then a right turn (symbolized as RRLL), the meaning of right and left turns becomes ambiguous unless the animal can do something comparable to counting, or unless there is some kind of central process which is the equivalent of counting. Hunter (1924) was inclined toward the hyothesis that some response of the organism comes to have some symbolic value in the learning process. His studies showed that while rats cannot learn double-alternation, cats and dogs will learn at least a single series of RRLL. Cats and dogs, however, could not extend the series, but chimpanzees and human children could generalize it readily to new series. Out of such problems, greatly extended in variety, has come agreement among many investigators that something more is going on between the ears than a mere switchboard connection between afferent processes, arising from stimuli, and efferent processes, observed as responses.[2]

---

[2] There are exceptions to this agreement. Guthrie (1935), Estes (1950), and Estes & Burke (1953) have developed theories of complex learning based strictly on connection between stimulus-response, and Skinner (1950) has argued that theories of learning are unnecessary in either physiological or logical form.

On the other hand, investigators have not agreed concerning the nature of what is going on. Some, notably Hunter (1924), Hull (1943), and Dollard & Miller (1950), have conceived of these mediational activities as peripheral responses, such as language. Another group, e.g., Tolman (1932, 1937), Krechevsky (1932), and Tolman & Brunswik (1935), have argued in favor of central processes.

The first group of behavior theorists have largely based their conceptions of responses mediating between stimulus and response in complex activities upon Hull's (1930, 1952) idea that an act could have stimulus value and thereby lead an organism into making finer discriminations or more complex generalizations than it could have ever made before. This conception of "pure stimulus acts" has been elaborated by Miller & Dollard (1941). They have pointed out how counting permits a discrimination between two piles of objects which could not be discriminated by any global perception. They have also pointed out how a variety of different people or objects which are designated by the same term may come thereby to elicit the same response. Thus, people who look very different can all elicit aggressive responses if they are termed *enemies*. Dollard & Miller (1950) have elaborated this theory in an intriguing way to account for planning and reasoning, to show how neuroses may be learned, and also to conceptualize why psychotherapy can have effects.

The other group, which has insisted that mediational processes are central in nature, has taken its lead from Tolman (1932), who conceived of learning as the formation of hypothetical "sign-Gestalt-expectations" or "expectancies." These are "expectations of what leads to what," and they have been conceived to conform to the probabilities of signs leading to what they signify (Tolman & Brunswik, 1935). Krechevsky (1932) has used the term *hypotheses* for these central mediational processes. He has argued that even the rat with a persistent tendency to go to one special position is showing evidence of a central process which might, in a human being, be termed a belief. Krechevsky (1933a) conceived these hypotheses to be innate, in the sense that the animal's repertoire depends upon his somatic and cerebral structures, but he (1933b) also conceived them to be docile, in the sense that the hypotheses which survive within the situation are those which correspond with reality and are confirmed by successes in goal achievement. In the case of more complex problems, Tolman (1948) has argued that the combining and recombining of these expectancies derives from the animals' nurture, and past experience permits organisms to infer new expectations, or even to invent new knowledge of the relationships among perceived portions of the stimulus field.

In discussing such conceptual systems, Spence (1942) has written:

Until the process of inventive ideation is linked up by assumed principles or postulates with the manipulative experimental variables, or with other theoretical constructs which themselves are tied up with experimental operations, it remains merely a duplicate description of the behavior phenomena it purports to explain. This same criticism holds for the very similar concept "insight" which the German Gestalt psychologists have introduced in similar connection (p. 297).

With this criticism one can heartily agree.

A THEORY OF MEDIATIONAL PROCESSES. On the theoretical side, considerable rapprochement between S-R theory and cognitive theory has been affected by Osgood (1953, pp. 392–412) with his theory of mediational processes. This is a two-stage theory of behavior. It elaborates upon the Hullian (1930) conception of pure stimulus acts and the Miller-Dollard (1941) theory of response-produced cues and response-produced drives in order to make more explicit formulation of the origin, nature, and function of Tolman's (1932, 1938) sign-Gestalt-expectations. According to Osgood's mediational theory,

. . . stimulus-objects (e.g., either salty taste in the mouth or rubber ball in the hand) typically elicit a complex pattern of reactions from the organism, some of which are dependent upon the sensory presence of the object for their occurrence and others of which can occur without the object being present . . . When other stimuli occur in conjunction with the stimulus-object, they tend to be conditioned to the total pattern of reactions elicited by the object; when later presented without support of the stimulus-object, these other stimuli elicit only the "detachable" reactions (1953, p. 396).

These two propositions provided Osgood with the basis for distinguishing between *stimulus objects* ($\dot{s}$), defined as those stimuli capable of eliciting instrumental responses without any mediation, and *signs* ($\boxed{S}$), defined as those stimuli which come to elicit the mediational processes or "detachable" reactions. Although the mediational hypothesis does not force a decision on the matter, Osgood (1953) assumes that

. . . both instrumental sequences and representational mediating reactions are selectively developed and eliminated on the basis of some reinforcement principle . . . [Furthermore], of the total pattern of "detachable" reactions conditioned to a sign, some fraction becomes the stable mediational process . . . Mediating reactions tend to become as reduced as possible, while retaining their distinctive cue functions. The mediating reactions evoked by a sign give rise to self-stimulation . . . to the extent that this self-stimulation is distinctive, it can participate in the selection of instrumental behaviors, or to the extent that it energizes the organism, this self-stimulation can have motivational and reinforcing properties (pp. 396–98).

Osgood notes that the typical learning experiment utilizes behaviorally mature organisms as subjects. Mature organisms bring to each experimental situation, which is new to them, systems of representational mediating mechanisms and systems of instrumental skill-sequences presumably derived from a combination of maturation and previous experience. For these mature organisms, learning typically consists of two types: "(A) modification in the mediation process elicited by particular stimulus pattern, or (B) modification in the instrumental sequence elicited by a particular mediator" (see Figure 4–1).

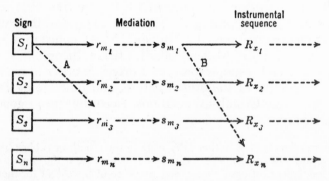

Fig. 4–1. Diagram of the loci or types of modification in the behavior of mature organisms in typical laboratory experiments on learning. Type A, indicated with the broken arrow labeled A, depicts a modification of the significance of the sign ($\boxed{S_1}$) from the mediational response (r_{m_1}) to another mediational response labeled (r_{m_3}). For the Pavlovian experiment described in the text (p. 70), this is illustrated by the change in the meaning of the moving card ($\boxed{S_1}$) from "something to look at" (r_{m_1}) to "there's meat-powder coming on table 1" (r_{m_3}). Type B, indicated with the broken arrow labeled B, depicts a modification of the instrumental-act sequence. In the experiment by Miller (1948) described in the text (p. 71), this type of modification is illustrated by changing from running (R_{x_1}) to escape from the white chamber ($\boxed{S_1}$) to turning a ratchet (R_x) to escape from the white chamber. After Osgood (1953, p. 404).

Type A is illustrated by the classical conditioning situation of Pavlov. Learning consists of a change in the mediation process without any particular change in the instrumental sequence which is fixed. For instance, the sound of the metronome does not signify meat powder to the dog at the beginning of training, but with regular association with this stimulus object, the sound of the metronome in acquiring the capacity to evoke some of the "detachable" reactions elicited by the meat powder, acquires a new significance. What is learned is not merely a stimulus substitution for the salivary response. Such an interpretation, as Zener (1937) pointed out, was tenable only so long as the behavioral restrictions imposed upon the subject in the Pavlovian laboratory go unnoted. Zener permitted freer conditions for the dog's response in order to get evidence to demonstrate a mediational mechanism. A dog, fastened in the usual harness, was first conditioned to salivate to a conditional stimulus (CS)—here, a moving card. The dog was then placed on another table in the same room but without harness. The very first time the CS card was moved, this dog jumped off the second table, ran up the stairs onto the first table, and took an "expectant" posture over the food pan. Such a complex sequence of behavior can hardly be predicted from Pavlov's theory of stimulus-substitution, but it makes sense if one views the process of conditioning as the establishment of of a new *meaning* for the CS. This is depicted as Type A (broken arrow labeled *A*) in Figure 4–1.

Type B, or change in instrumental sequence, may be illustrated by Miller's (1948) classic experiment on acquired drive. First, rats were shocked in a white compartment. To escape the shock, they were permitted to run into an adjacent black compartment. With the shock eliminated, the white compartment had come to signify danger. Presumably, various "fear" responses which had been part of the rat's total response to shock continued to be elicited by the white compartment. When a barrier was placed between the white and black compartments, the rats promptly shifted from running to leaping. This modification of the instrumental sequence came promptly presumably because leaping as well as running are alternate locomotor responses which have typically been associated repeatedly with danger situations in the past experience of mature rats. At the next stage, Miller inserted a wall between the two compartments. The wall had a door which could be operated by turning a rachet device. When the wall kept the rats from running or leaping to escape the white compartment, they tried a variety of responses one after another, until they hit upon pawing the rachet. This opened the door. With repetition it became a prompt response to being put in the white compartment. Such modification in the instrumental sequence to a mediational process ($r_{m_1} \rightarrow s_{m_1}$) is depicted as Type B (broken arrow labeled *B*) in Figure 4–1.

One of the advantages of Osgood's (1953) theory is the way in which it ties mediating reactions to the responses which the organism has made to the concrete situation. The theory explicitly makes the representational mediation-process evoked by a sign of an object some portion of the total reaction to that object. An organism acquires these mediational processes as fractional anticipatory reactions through the mechanism of generalization. They are modified through the combined processes of *short circuiting* (object-tied versus detachable reactions) and *reduction* (selective modification resulting from such factors as interference, conditionability). The antecedent conditions under which signs will come to elicit portions of the reactions originally elicited by objects are the same as those which Hull (1943) formulated for the acquisition of overt responses. They include (*a*) contiguity between sign and object, (*b*) reinforcement, and (*c*) the observable characteristics of the response to the object but including even those characteristics observable only by physiological techniques. With Hull, Osgood presumes that the strength of those mediating reactions is a function of the same factors that determine the strength of overt responses, namely, the number of reinforced repetitions, the amount of reinforcement, temporal delay of the reinforcement, etc.

Although Osgood conceives that these mediational processes derive from overt behavior, he also presumes them to be more or less central. He says little about the development of these mediational processes in the life history of organisms or persons, which development is the central topic of this whole discussion of the experiential roots of intelligence. He attempts merely to illustrate the process with the imaginary development of an instrumental skill. The illustration gives his theory concreteness. He writes as follows:

When the experienced shoe salesman whips through the sequence [of tying one's shoes], looking at *you* and conversing all the while, the speed and effortlessness of the operation defies description. So we shall imagine the process as it might appear in very slow motion film. We could also observe the fumbling and painfully slow attempts of the five-year-old. We would observe that a fairly stable series of stimulus-situations in the physical world (S_1, S_2, etc., [in A of Fig. 4–2]) is being paralleled by a fairly stable series of movements on the part of the organism (R_1, R_2, etc.). Let us assume that the stimulus pattern initiating shoe-tying is the sight of the loose strings. This stimulus (S_1), must be associated with the response (R_1) of grasping the strings in a certain way with both hands. Making this response changes the situation for the child; his hands appear in a new position and the strings are seen in a new relation. This second stimulus (S_2) must now be associated with the second response in the series (R_2), the movement of crossing and twisting the strings. Again, this movement changes in the situation to S_3 which must in turn be associated with the third response— and so on throughout the shoe-tying sequence.

How is it that this disjointed series of isolated habits becomes a skill? Careful introspection indicates that although external cues (mainly visual) initially control and direct the sequence of acts, they lose their importance at later stages and, as in the case of the shoe salesman, the skill seems to run itself. Let us look at the stimulus pattern more closely: after the child has made the initial response of grasping the strings in a certain manner, not only has the external stimulus situation changed because of this movement, but this movement itself has produced the distinctive input of stimulation to the central nervous system. Whenever a part of the body is moved, receptors in the muscles, tendons, and joints are activated and deliver their characteristic impulse patterns to higher centers. There are many other response-produced cues, such as the changes in locus and intensity of cutaneous sensations in the present shoe-tying illustration. Now if these response-produced stimuli are present at the time of the next response when the sequence is made as they must be once the child can perform the sequence with sufficient rapidity and in the right order—then, following ordinary learning principles, they will also become conditioned to these responses [See $R_1 \rightarrow S_{p1} \rightarrow R_2 \rightarrow S_{p2}$ etc., in B of Fig. 4–2]. In other words, *the cues produced by preceding movements must become conditioned to succeeding movements.* When these new habits become sufficiently strengthened, *these* stimuli will elicit the movements in the sequence and, since their occurrence is immediately contingent upon each movement, there is a reduction of delay and the behavior sequence "telescopes" in time. Once the shift-over to control by response-produced cues is established, the skill sequence truly runs itself. Each movement produces the distinctive cues that initiate the next (1953, p. 400).

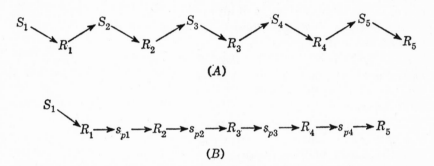

(A)

(B)

Fig. 4–2. Two stages in the development of an instrumental skill. In the early stage (A), the occurrence and sequence of component responses depends upon the presence of exteroceptive cues for each successive component. At a later stage (B), control of the behavior sequence has shifted to proprioceptive cues; i.e., each response produces the necessary cues for the next. After Osgood (1953, p. 400).

This is the traditional behavioristic explanation of learning an instrumental skill. It may well be true in part, especially for the early stages, but, as Osgood asserts, it is certainly not a sufficient explanation. Anyone who has observed a child or an adult in the early stages of learning to play the piano has seen the stimuli of musical notation giving rise to specific motor responses on the keys of the piano. As this skill develops with practice, one can see the learner perceiving a measure or two of notation and then reacting in terms, possibly, of one movement cuing the next one, and so on. In the case of the highly skilled pianist, however, a look at the notation takes in a number of measures. This look may serve to direct the playing of a swift cadenza. At this point the chaining theory breaks down because it relies upon peripheral "feedback" from receptors in the responding muscles. As Lashley (1917) pointed out long ago, the rate of such piano playing does not allow time enough between movements to permit such peripheral feedback. It follows that at the higher levels of skill in such a performance as piano playing, the sequential ordering of motor patterns must be controlled centrally. Moreover, in the case of the expert pianist who reads musical notation with facility, the skill includes the processing of the information coded in notation and transforming it into organizations of rapid manual movements that produce music. Such a highly developed skill illustrates the logical demand for the existence of central processes which can organize information derived from receptors and transform them into action. On the other hand, the conditions for the development of such capacities for information-processing go back to repeated practice of fairly rapid sequences of movements which are, at first, guided by the distance receptors, then by muscular feedback, and only ultimately by central processes.

Although the skill of the concert pianist has sometimes been looked upon as a motor skill, it is fairly obvious from even such casual considerations as these just made that a highly developed system for information-processing is also involved. This system for information-processing is of the order of the central processes involved in much of intelligent behavior. Certain structural characteristics of the human brain may well be important factors in determining a person's potential for acquiring a facile technique of reading musical notation and performing it, but what these characteristics may be is quite unknown. Lore has it that a connection exists between musical and mathematical abilities. This connection may not be accidental. On the other hand, it is obvious that the technique of processing musical notation into performed music does not come automatically with maturation even in the most natively talented. Since it is not one of the components commonly taken for granted in intelligence, the technique of processing musical notation may serve as a useful paradigm of a complex skill demanding control by central processes. At any rate, this conception of an habituated, central technique for information-processing both exemplifies and extends Osgood's theory of mediational processes and illustrates the important role of experience in their development.

FROM MEDIATIONAL PROCESSES TO CENTRAL SYSTEMS. The term *system for information-processing* is borrowed from Newell, Shaw, & Simon (1958), who have described the elements of the theory of human problem-solving. Their theory is the result of an attempt to specify what would be required in a program of information-processing to generate the behavior of a human problem-solver handling specified tasks. Their theory assumes that an organism consists of receptors, which take in information in coded form, of effectors, which engage in action, and of a control system joining these. They make three postulates concerning the nature of the control system: (*a*) It has a number of memories containing symbolized information that are interconnected by various ordering relations; (*b*) it has a number of processes which operate on the information in the memories; and (*c*) it has a definite set of rules for combining these processes into programs of processing. At the level of theorizing with which Newell, Shaw, & Simon (1958) are concerned, as

. . . an explanation of an observed behavior of the organism is provided by a program of primitive information processes that generates this behavior . . . A program viewed as a theory of behavior is highly specific; it describes one organism in a particular class of situations . . . it can be used . . . as a predictor of behavior in two ways. First, it makes many precise predictions that can be tested in detail regarding the area of behavior it is designed to handle . . . Second, there will be important qualitative similarities among the programs that an organism uses in various situations, and among the programs used by different organisms in a given situation (pp. 151–52).

The ability to specify programs to infer accurately what problem-solving behavior they will produce derives from experience in the use of high-speed electronic computers. Once specified, however, these programs of information-processing need have nothing to do with computers. A program is rather "a specification of what the organism will do under varying environmental circumstances in terms of certain elementary information processes it is capable of performing" (p. 153). Electronic computers do come into the picture, but only because they can be programmed to execute systems of information processes that human beings are presumed to utilize when they are solving problems.

The empirical side of such an approach comes from devising a program capable of solving problems in some domain, and then instructing the computer to print out its intermediate results. Asking the computer to work its problems on paper approximates having a human subject proceed to solve his problem out loud. Newell, Shaw, & Simon (1958) call the program utilized the *logic theorist* because it is designed specifically for discovering proofs of theorems in elementary symbolic logic. In symbolic logic, "a proof is a sequence of statements such that each statement: (*a*) follows from one or more of the others that preceded in the sequence, or (*b*) is an axiom or previously proved theorem. Here 'follows' means 'follows by the rules of logic' " (p. 157). They gave their logic theorist four rules of inference: substitution, replacement, detachment, and syllogism or chaining. These rules of inference constitute the particular combination of methods or strategies for information-processing used by the logic theorist to achieve a link in a proof. In addition to these method processes, the logic theorist got an executive process to coordinate the use of the methods, and to select the subproblems and theorems upon which the methods operate. The method processes also utilize such common subprocesses in carrying out their activity as the matching process and the similarity task. From the data provided by the computer concerning the methods employed, the sequence of these methods, and the theorems employed, the procedure of the logic theorist shows phenomena resembling "set, insight, concept formation, and structure of the problem-subproblem hierarchy" (p. 159).

This notion of strategies for information-processing goes considerably beyond Osgood's (1953) mediational processes. These strategies may be conceived as habits in the sense that they depend upon experience for their acquisition. Although they are required to explain not only human problem-solving but also such skills as playing a complex piece of music at sight from notation, they lose the nice tie, maintained by Osgood for his mediational processes, to the overt behavior from which they have presumably been distilled or internalized. On the other hand, evidence exists to indicate that these processes may get built essentially out of looking and listening rather than out of motor action. Moreover, the studies of the effects of early experience on intelligence indicate that it may be rewarding to investigate the degree to which perception and action are both important in the experiential roots of the strategies of information-processing. This is the question of the roles of S-S relationships and S-R relationships. Furthermore, as will be pointed out below, approximate counterparts of the various portions of the control system conceived by cyberneticists like Newell, Shaw, & Simon (1958) are apparently being discovered within mammalian brains.

EVIDENCE FOR EXPERIENTIAL ROOTS OF INFORMATION-PROCESSING STRATEGIES. Osgood (1953) claims as one of the advantages of his mediational theory that it makes a clear distinction between old learning—or "primary learning," to use Hebb's term—and the new learning of most experimental situations. The same goes for this extension of mediational theory to include strategies for information-processing. These strategies probably derive in large part from primary learning, much of it very early learning. An attempt will be made to show this shortly in a review of Hebb's theorizing and of the empirical investigations of the role of early experience in intelligent behavior that stem from his theorizing. But first consider evidence from investigations with mature animals.

Some evidence comes from the studies of Jackson (1942) and of Birch (1945) already cited in Chapter 3. These studies show that chimpanzees use tools in the process of solving problems only if they have already learned to see those tools as instruments for reaching, etc. In the case of Jackson's (1942) study, joining sticks to reach an object too far away to get with one stick depended upon having already joined sticks in play. In the case of Birch's (1945) study, the only one of six chimpanzees that succeeded in securing food with the hoe-like tool, consisting of a stick which had attached at its far end another stick at right angles, was the animal which had been observed to use sticks regularly in its spontaneous play.

Further suggestive evidence comes from Bingham's (1929) study. This study found that chimpanzees which had been taught to stack one box on top of another and also to get on top of a square box to reach a banana could quickly discover how to stack four boxes, one on another, for use as a platform from which they could reach a banana. This behavior (sudden discovery of a solution to a problem) had been reported by such Gestalt psychologists as Köhler (1925) and termed *insight*. Bingham (1929) argued, however, that insight consists in the relatively sudden regrouping, not of innate brain patterns, but of skills acquired in former situations.

HARLOW'S "LEARNING SETS." Especially interesting is the evidence coming from Harlow's (1949) investigations of "learning to learn." Harlow's "learning sets" may be seen as analogues of strategies for information-processing acquired by rhesus monkeys from repeated experiences with a given kind of problem. The results of Harlow's research are highly significant for the issue of whether or not intelligence is fixed.

Harlow (1949) used the object-quality discrimination problem in which the monkey is required to choose one of two objects which differ in some way. In any one problem, the monkey is presented with a situation like the following (see apparatus in Figure 4–3). There are two cups with covers. The cover of the one may be red and the other yellow. A grape is placed regularly under the yellow cover without the monkey's seeing the placement. The yellow cover is sometimes on the right and sometimes on the left. The order of placement is predetermined but random. In learning such a discrimination problem, the naive monkey tends to look first to the position in which he last found a grape. The procedure, however, associates the reward ambiguously with the place cue, and regularly with the cover cue. The monkey learns gradually to neglect the place cue, and to respond to the cover cue, in this particular instance the yellowness. One of these discriminations may take many trials for a naive animal, before it responds regularly to such a cover cue.

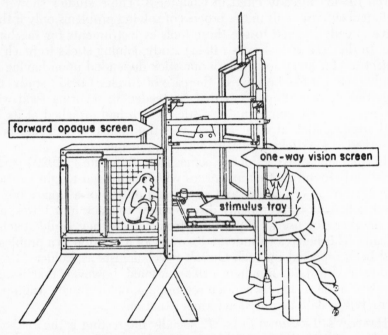

Fig. 4–3. The Wisconsin general-test apparatus used by Harlow in his studies of "learning sets" in monkeys. After Harlow (1949, p. 52).

In one of Harlow's experiments eight monkeys were given a series of such problems. They were given 50 trials on each of the first 32 problems. This means that they were given 50 trials in which to discriminate the yellow cover from the red cover, and then another 50 to discriminate something like a white cover from a black cover, 50 more for a square cover and a round cover, etc., through the first 32 problems. Next came 200 such problems on which the eight monkeys got six trials each, and then 112 more on which they got an average of nine trials.

Figure 4–4 depicts the results. Each point on these various curves describes the percentage of correct responses on the trial of that number for the group of discrimination problems indicated in the legend. The lowest curve depicts the percentage of correct responses on the first six successive trials for the first eight problems learned. Since a 50-50 chance exists of the subject being right on any trial, it may be seen that this lowest curve does not rise appreciably above chance during the first three trials. Moreover, the animals were getting only about 75 per cent of their responses correct on the sixth trial. Contrast this with the curve for the last 55 problems. These start after the animals have already had training on 256 such problems (see top curve of Figure 4–4). The monkeys make only 50 per cent correct responses on the first trial, of course, but on the second trial they are correct 97 per cent of the time. The marked rise in the percentage of correct responses on the second trial, from about 51 per cent on problems one to eight to 97 per cent on problems 257 to 312, is the evi-

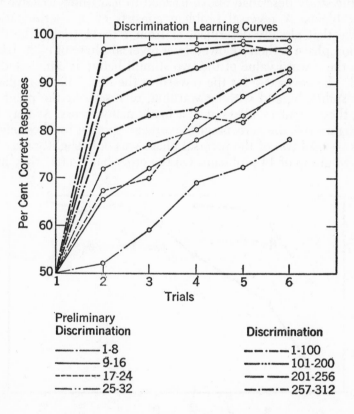

Fig. 4–4. Discrimination learning curves for successive blocks of problems. Each of the points on the various curves represents the percentage of correct responses from eight monkeys on trials from one to six in a consecutive set of discrimination problems, i.e., 1–8, 9–16, etc. The evidence of learning to utilize the information from the characteristics of the cover under which the reward was placed may be seen in the rising percentage of correct responses on trial two for the successive groups of consecutive problems. After Harlow (1949, p. 53).

dence that the monkeys have learned to learn this kind of discrimination problems. All such an "educated" monkey needs is a single trial in which to discover under which of the two differently marked covers his reward is hidden. He can then go directly to it on the next trial. One can properly say that he has *acquired* insight, or that he has acquired a capacity to utilize the information given in the characteristic marking of the cover as a cue to the location of the reward in the second trial.

Such results have been repeated by Braun (Harlow, 1951, p. 202). Moreover, Harlow (1949) has shown that the same eight monkeys used in the study described above learned to learn how to solve reversal problems. A reversal problem consists of a discrimination phase, like that already described, of from 7 to 11 trials. The discrimination phase is then followed by a reversal phase of eight trials in which the reward value of the two stimuli being discriminated is switched. The cover cue for the reward in the discrimination phase becomes suddenly, and without warning, reversed. At the point of reversal, these eight monkeys at first made many errors. As may be seen in Figure 4–5, the percentage of correct responses for these eight monkeys on trial two of the reversal phase was only slightly over 50 for the first group of 14 problems. On the other hand, after they had

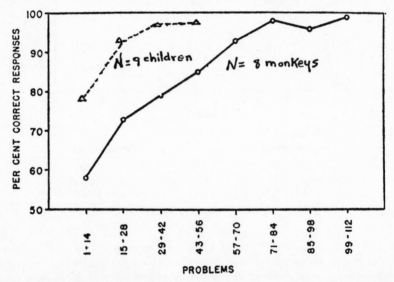

Fig. 4–5. Discrimination-reversal, learning-set curves. Each point on the lower curve represents the percentage of correct responses for eight monkeys on trial two of the reversal phase for the successive groups of problems indicated. After Harlow (1949, p. 57 for monkeys, p. 59 for children).

got training on 98 such problems, the percentage of correct responses on trial two for the last 14 problems (99-112) rose to 97. This is to say that after training on several groups of such reversal problems, these chimpanzees learned something akin to a "concept" of reversal. After a single reversal trial, their responses were correct nearly 100 per cent of the time on trial two.

Harlow (1951) has applied the learning-set approach to the somewhat more complex oddity problem. In the oddity problem, the subject is presented with three cups. Two of the covers are alike; the third is different. As with the discrimination problem, place cues are randomized. But the oddity problem contains a further complication. Not only is position rewarded ambiguously, but the perceptible characteristics of the objects are also rewarded ambiguously. In a series of trials, only the single representation, i.e., the odd object, is regularly rewarded. Thus, both position and object cues must come to be disregarded by the animal. Monkeys typically take upwards of 400 trials to reach a criterion of 90 per cent correct responses on a given oddity problem. In the course of training on 60 such oddity problems, however, they showed progressive interproblem tranfer. Each of these problems utilized a different set of three objects; and the monkey got 24 trials with each set. At the end of this training, the four monkeys had reached the point of making 90 per cent correct solutions on the very first trial (Harlow, Meyer, & Settlage, 1951). One might say that these monkeys had learned the "concept" of oddness.

Harlow (1949) has also shown that such learning sets may operate as if they were relatively isolated central units. This is illustrated in an experiment on six monkeys with previous experience on discrimination learning, but with no previous training on positional discriminations. The monkeys were given seven blocks of 14 problems each. They started with a block of 14 problems involving object discriminations, each consisting of 25 trials. This was followed by a block of 14 problems involving 25 trials of position discriminations that alternated left position and right position. In the remaining five blocks of 14 problems, each block of object-discrimination problems was alternated with a block of right-left position-discrimination problems. Figure 4–6 presents curves showing the percentage of correct responses on the total number of trials (14 x 25 = 350) for each of these alternate blocks of antagonistic discrimination problems. The learning-set curve for a positional discriminations shows progressive improvement throughout the series. On the other hand, the curve for the object-quality discriminations begins at a high level of accuracy. It shows decrement on the second block, presumably from the interference from the first block of positional discriminations, then returns

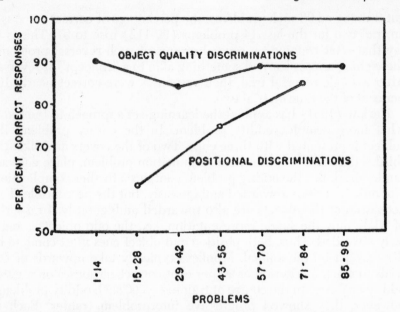

PROBLEMS

Fig. 4–6. Learning-set curves for problems with alternating discriminations of objects and positions. The curves show the percentage of correct responses for alternate blocks of 14 problems, each consisting of 25 trials. After Harlow (1949, p. 62).

to normal. By the end of the program of training, these two originally antagonistic learning-sets were operating in succession with a minimum of interference. Harlow (1951) writes as follows:

Between these two blocks of object-discriminations there were 350 trials in which no object was differentially rewarded, and between these two blocks of position-discriminations there were 350 trials in which no position was differentially rewarded. Despite this, the monkeys learned to shift from one type of problem to the other with amazing ease and efficiency. This relative functional isolation of learning-sets is undoubtedly a basic mechanism in facilitating solution of complex problems . . . Man possesses this ability to try out alternate problem solutions (techniques of processing information) to a far greater degree than other animals, but the mechanism is also apparent in monkeys (pp. 206–7).

In this program of investigation, Harlow (1949) chose a primate as subject because primates are more similar to man in psychological capacities than are the lower creatures. He utilized what he terms *multiple-sign learning* because it is roughly analogous to the problems which children face in learning to use such words as "I" and "you." As Harlow puts it:

The meanings of these words change according to the speaker. When the child is talking, "I" refers to himself, "you" to the person addressed. When the child is addressed, he is no longer "I" but "you" . . . there is a vast difference between a girl who is "awful pretty" and one who is "pretty awful" . . . Multiple-sign responsiveness so pervades human behavior that it is accepted as a natural and automatic way of behaving. Recognizing the infinite number of multiple signs and their vast complexities gives some appreciation of the degree of separation of the human being from the sub-human primate, and at the same time stresses the importance of analyzing such behavior in the animal laboratory if we are to comprehend the learning of significance for man (1951, p. 199).

These "learning sets" appear to approximate analogues of the operations for processing information thought by Newell, Shaw, & Simon (1958) to underlie human problem-solving. Harlow's investigation demonstrates that such techniques of information-processing as learning-sets make insight possible. Moreover, they also indicate that these information-processing techniques which underlie intelligent behavior do not come ready-made, as Köhler (1925) and other Gestalt psychologists have contended. They must apparently be acquired. Once they are acquired, however, they supply a basis for insightful problem-solution. They also increase the capacity of the organism to solve at least certain classes of problems.

On the other hand, Harlow's work certainly does not deny that an inherited factor sets limits upon the potential an organism has for acquiring complex techniques of information-processing. A rat could not live long enough to learn the first oddity problem let alone acquire the oddity-problem learning set. Innate factors undoubtedly control the facility with which learning sets are acquired. In Figure 4-5, above, the learning-set curve for discrimination-reversal from nine children aged between two and five years with IQ's between 109-151 has been drawn in for comparison with that of the monkeys. The children have reached the final level of the monkeys by only the third block of 14 problems. Three more blocks were required by the monkeys to reach this level. Moreover, Kaufman (1956) and Peterson (1956) have shown that mentally retarded children (IQ's ranging from 50 to 75) require more blocks of problems to reach a criterion of perfection in learning-sets than do normal children (IQ 90–109) and House & Zeaman (1959) have found that imbeciles with IQ's ranging between 14 and 48 do not acquire learning sets. Nevertheless, early experience may also be a factor in the facility with which individuals acquire learning sets. It is conceivable that the kind of stimulus deprivation, such as that in the orphanage observed by Dennis (1960) in Teheran, might damage an individual's facility in acquiring learning sets. Little is known concerning how much and in what way later learning depends upon early learning. What is known comes largely from the work stimulated by the theorizing of Hebb (1947, 1949).

INFORMATION-PROCESSING STRATEGIES AND
EARLY EXPERIENCE

Hebb (1949) built his theory in an attempt to bridge the gap conceptually between what is known from physiology and neurology about the operation of the nervous system on the one hand, and what is known from psychology about human and animal behavior on the other hand. Central to this theory is the problem of thought. This is the problem of accounting, in terms of what is known about neural functioning, for the relatively autonomous activities of organisms which may be attributed to processes going on within the cerebrum.

HEBB'S NEUROPHYSIOLOGICAL THEORY OF THOUGHT. Hebb's (1939) concern with brain function turned on his failure to find any diminution of intelligence with standard tests in patients following removal of upwards of 20 per cent of the mass of cerebrum. On the other hand, he also noted that the presence of cerebral lesions in infancy resulted in considerable retardation and also a feebleminded pattern of performance in which scores on verbal tests lag behind those on performance tests. From these two facts, he got the idea that brain tissues needed for the development of intellectual function might not be so necessary for its maintenance (Hebb, 1942).

This fact suggested that amount of tissue, especially of associative brain tissue as distinct from the tissue of the primary sensory and motor areas of the cortex, might set limits on the acquisitions underlying intelligence. It has been commonly observed that the associative areas of the cortex show a relative increase in size up the phylogenetic scale from reptiles and amphibians to man. Moreover, the higher mammals like primates and men can learn more complex relationships and appear to be less directly controlled by external stimulation than are lower animals like the reptiles. Such considerations led to the conception of the A/S ratio, the ratio between the area of the cortex with presumed associative function and the area of the cortex concerned directly with either receptor input or motor output.

Hebb (1949) was most concerned with that behavior which occurred in the absence of external stimulation or direct stimulus-control. The ubiquitous notions of attention, attitude, set, expectancy, hypothesis, intention, vector, need, perseveration, and preoccupation (Gibson, 1941) all recognize that behavior is determined by something besides the immediately preceding receptor input. Various investigators of behavior had inferred the existence of central processes which are relatively independent of afferent stimuli.[3] These Hebb

[3] See, for example, Hilgard & Marquis (1940), Beach (1942), Morgan (1943).

(1949, p. 5) termed *autonomous central processes*, and he presumed they underlie perception, attention, perceptual learning, and, in short, thought. Presumably these autonomous central processes that underlie thought account for intelligence, and presumably they have their locus in the associative areas of the brain. Such an inference derives support from studies made of learning in animals (Hebb, 1945). Hebb (1949, p. 116) reviewed these to show that: "(1) more complex relationships can be learned by higher species with large A/S ratios at maturity; (2) simple relationships are learned about as promptly by lower as by higher species; and (3) the first learning is slower in higher than lower species." The slowness of the first learning in higher species implied that autonomous central processes must have to be established within the associative areas before receptor inputs can gain extensive control over motor action. On the basis of such considerations, Hebb distinguished between what he called *primary* learning and *later* learning. This is a distinction like the one made later by Osgood (1953) between *old* and *new* learning, but there is also a difference. Where Osgood conceived old learning in terms of stimulus-response relationships with central mediating processes consisting of portions of the early responses, Hebb conceived of *primary* learning in terms of perceptual experience. Contrary to Gestalt theory, von Senden's (1932) review of published reports on the vision of the congenitally blind given sight abruptly by surgical operation indicated that it takes a great deal of learning in order to be able to perceive simple figures. Riesen's (1947) studies, to be reviewed below, confirm von Senden's in showing that it takes a great deal of perceptual experience for chimpanzees reared in darkness to come to recognize objects. Hebb asked what the neurophysiological basis is for these autonomous central processes that presumably get established in the associative areas through early, primary learning.

The key concept in his answer is the *cell assembly*. This is conceived as a closed system in which neural firing can "reverberate" after the receptor input has ceased. The physiological possibility of such reverberatory circuits was established by Lorente de Nó (1938a, 1938b). The cell assembly presumably corresponds to the common or redundant aspects of the receptor inputs from a given object. It is these common or redundant aspects of the receptor inputs getting "fixed" within the cell assembly that give the perceived object its constancy of shape and size even when it is seen from various angles and at various distances. Thus, the cell assembly corresponds to an image. It is a representative process. Forming connections among assemblies is, as Hebb conceived it, the mechanism of association.

Cell assemblies made up of single neurones, or connections among such assemblies, get established in the course of repeated stimulation. Hebb postulated that when one neurone is near enough to a second one to have any possibility of firing it, and does take part in firing it, a metabolic change takes place which increases the capacity of the first cell to fire the second one. Some kind of synaptic resistance is presumably reduced. A given assembly is conceived to consist of numerous neurones spread over a considerable portion of the association areas. It is this spread of the assembly over a large portion of the brain which presumably accounts for the fact that lesions in adult brains do not destroy abilities. Similarly, various cell assemblies also get functionally connected through the redundancy or repetitiousness of stimulation conditions operating through the receptor inputs. The stimulating conditions may be a visual contour or change in illumination as the eye moves from a lighter to a darker area; repeated exposure to a particular vowel sound; a series of tactual stimulations, say from an infant's bottle, etc.

Hebb proposed that these representative cell assemblies, each of which corresponds to some property of environmental stimulation, gradually form connecting links with each other and with concurrent motor activities. The basis for such connection is also the postulated reduction of "synaptic resistance." Since most assemblies would presumably get established along with concurrent motor activities,

. . . each would therefore establish neural connections with, and tend to produce its own motor activity. However, actual muscle contraction would often not occur, because some other assembly activity occurring at the same time might inhibit the motor path, or simultaneously active assemblies might have motor effects that were physically incompatible with each other (e.g., flexing and extending a limb at the same time). Overt movements would result whenever such inhibition or conflict was absent (Hebb, 1959, p. 628).

Experience goes on in time. It is sequential. Cell assemblies, once established, get connected in sequences. Such organizations Hebb termed *phase sequences*. Each phase sequence corresponds to one current in a stream of thought. As Hebb writes:

. . . each assembly activity in the series might be aroused (1) sensorily, (2) by excitation from other assemblies, or (3) in both ways. It is assumed that the last, (3), is what usually happens in an organized flow of behavior. Each assembly must establish connections with a number of other assemblies, at different times; which of these others it will arouse on any specific occasion will depend on what other activity, and especially what sensory activity, is going on at that moment. Assembly A tends to excite B, C, and D; sensory activity tends to excite D only, so A is followed by D. At each point in time, behavior would thus be steered both sensorily and centrally, jointly controlled by the present sensory input and immediately prior central activity (1959, p. 629).

Since two or more phase sequences may run concurrently, there is the possibility that one may conflict with another and thereby produce uncoordinated behavior. This, Hebb assumes, is what happens in the case of gross emotional disturbances.

In this conceptual scheme, Hebb sees the phenomena labelled *attention*, or *set*, as evidence of the influence of an ongoing central activity. When an organism is presented with a situation that can arouse various activities, each controlling a different motor response, which one will occur depends in part upon the assemblies already active when the receptor inputs from that situation arrive.

Intelligent invention or insight is explained by fresh combinations of phase sequences. When a situation arouses one or more phase sequences which have never happened together before, these may produce new combinations of overt action with adaptive value in that situation. The new combination of assemblies in sequence also means seeing the situation in a new way. One of the salient characteristics of adult learning is the promptness with which complex but familiar systems of association can be established. For instance, "experiments on learning have shown again and again that nonsense syllables like *tob, del, rec,* and *til,* are harder to memorize than the more complicated (but more familiar) items *tob*acco, *del*ights, *rec*ommend, and hear*tily*; and that this unconnected list of words is still harder than the sentence 'I recommend the delights of tobacco heartily'" (1949, p. 128). Adult learning of this sort depends upon having available for connection well-organized cell assemblies and phase sequences for combination. Invention and insight also depend upon previously organized processes, and having these assemblies and sequences very tightly organized might conceivably interfere with their formation of fresh combinations required for insight.

NEWER DEVELOPMENT IN THE THEORY OF BRAIN FUNCTION. Although it is Hebb's theorizing which has prompted most of the recent investigations of the effects of early experience (primary learning) on intelligence in adulthood, the theory of brain function has been changing since Hebb (1949) formulated his theory. In considerable degree this theory has been influenced by what has been learned about programming electronic computers to solve various kinds of problems. Although von Neumann's (see 1956) attempts to determine how probabilistic logics can synthesize reliable organisms from unreliable components have led him (1958) to wonder if "organismic mathematics" may not be basically different from that which mathematicians have thus far invented and have used for the programming of electronic computers, the apparent similarities of problem-solving processes in man and in computer has suggested new terminology for theorizing about brain functioning and has also suggested a search for the counterparts of the programming art within neuropsychological processes. Newell, Shaw, & Simon (1958), for instance, have inferred the following about neural processes from programming their logic theorist:

The picture of the central nervous system to which our theory leads is a picture of a more complex and active system than that contemplated by most associationists. The notions of "trace," "fixation," "excitation," and "inhibition" suggest a relatively passive electro-chemical system (or, alternatively, a passive "switchboard"), acted upon by stimuli, altered by that action, and subsequently behaving in a modified manner when later stimuli impinge upon it.

In contrast, we postulate an information-processing system with large storage capacity that holds, among other things, complex strategies (programs) that may be evoked by stimuli. The stimulus determines what strategy or strategies will be evoked; the content of these strategies is already largely determined by previous experience of the system. Ability of the system to respond in complex and highly selective ways to relatively simple stimuli is a consequence of this storage of programs and this "active" response to stimuli. The phenomena of set and insight that we have already described and the hierarchical structure of the response system are all consequences of this "active" organization of the central processes (p. 163).[4]

The changes, as Pribram (1960) reviews them, have not interrupted the trend which Hebb (1949) set but have made the brain appear to be more and more active. Moreover, approximate counterparts of components of the control systems for processing information are being found within the complex anatomy of the brain.

First of all, the traditional conception of brains as inert masses of specialized tissue sensitive to excitations brought by receptor inputs and carried away through motor outlets is no longer tenable. Although an isolated slab of cortex becomes quiescent (Burns, 1958), the application of a few electrical stimuli produces neural activity that endures for many minutes after stimulation stops. Inasmuch as receptor organs, especially the eye, fire spontaneously and thereby sustain the neural activity of the brain-stem reticular system (Granit, 1955), external stimulation may be seen as having the role of modulating this ongoing intrinsic activity.[5]

Second, a neural mechanism for the line of feedback postulated by communication engineers from the control system or interpreter to receptors to govern which aspects of stimulation are sensed and

[4] Other papers in the series, of which this one quoted is the first, are the following: Newell, Shaw, & Simon (1959a, 1959b) and Newell & Simon (1959).

[5] There have also been reports of spontaneous activity in isolated brain tissue (Echlin, Arnett, & Zoll, 1952; Gerard & Young, 1937; Henry & Scoville, 1952). I am originally indebted to a conversation with Carl Pfaffmann for making me aware, during the late 1940's, of this conception of stimulation as a modulator of ongoing, intrinsic activities within the brain.

transmitted (Hake, 1957, p. 35) appears to exist within the brain (Granit, 1955; Bruner, 1957).

Third, the notion of cortical association areas as the place where the receptor inputs to the receiving areas are appropriately mixed transcortically and sent to the motor areas for transmission to muscles and glands is giving way for several reasons. Contradicting the notion are such facts as (1) the existence of sensory inputs to motor areas and motor outputs from sensory areas (Pribram, 1958b), and (2) the lack of functional deficit from either circumsecting or crosshatching these cortical areas (Wade, 1952; Chow, 1954). Functional deficit occurs when fibers connecting the so-called associational cortex with subcortical centers are cut. The various systems of the brain appear, thus, to be concentrically arranged.

Because the thalamic fibers of these association areas derive from nuclei which receive no input from receptors, Rose & Woolsey (1949) have termed these areas *intrinsic* to distinguish them from the *extrinsic* areas which are connected with the thalamic nuclei that relay inputs from the eyes, ears, etc. Pribram (1958b, 1960) has inferred from such facts that there are two classes of cerebral systems, the *intrinsic* one and the *extrinsic* one which correspond in considerable degree to the classical conception of the brain as a receiver of receptor inputs and an emitter of motor outputs. The intrinsic system becomes an analogue of the computer's memory with the strategies for information-processing stored there, probably in large part as a function of past experience.

The intrinsic system consists of two portions. The anterior portion consists in considerable portion of medial thalamic nucleus and frontal cortex with numerous connections to the subcortical centers of the limbic system (Pribram, 1958b; Rose & Woolsey, 1949). Pribram (1960) believes that this anterior portion mediates *intentions*, and that it is the integrative mechanism for the motivational processes of the limbic systems (Pribram, 1958b). He believes this because lesions in the tracts of this frontal intrinsic system interfere with the execution of complex sequences of action. Lesions in these tracts under the frontal lobes, for instance, interfere with such functions as delayed reaction and double alternation in monkeys (Jacobsen & Nissen, 1937). Moreover, such lesions appear to interfere with what must occur at the time the delay task is set in the delayed-reaction type of experiment and not with recall per se (Mishkin & Pribram, 1956; Pribram & Mishkin, 1956). Thus, this confusion of intention appears to result from an inability to arrange and utilize the information coming from a task in the absence of persistent and detailed external instructions.

Such lesions also damage the ability of human beings to carry out sequences of action. For instance, Milner (1958) has reported evidence that patients with surgical resections of the medial structures of the temporal lobe, the amygdala, and the hippocampal formations show such an effect in striking degree. Sent to the grocery store with a list, a patient with such lesions can purchase the items on the list, but once the purchases are completed, he does not recall what to do next and he is completely incapable of finding his way home. In the laboratory, such patients react with appropriate emotion to difficult situations, and they can sometimes undertake complex sequences of action. If distracted, however, they are unable to continue where they left off, and may not even recall the task at all. Yet, at the same time, their memory for the events of their lives prior to their surgery appears to be normal, and also their immediate memory is intact; they can repeat a series of digits heard for the first time. In this same connection, Nichols & Hunt (1940) found that a highly educated man, who had suffered the loss of about 20 grams of brain tissue from each frontal pole but who still exhibited an IQ of 130, failed on the double-alternation task and also on continuing such an arithmetic progression as 39-38-36-33-29. He showed in many situations an inability to deduce the implications of the concrete cues deriving from his ongoing activity for his future activity. Moreover, in the case of the arithmetic progression, he was incapable of keeping separate and utilizing the fact that the main series was decreasing while the series of differences between the consecutive numbers in the main series was increasing. In eight years of class demonstrations, he repeatedly failed on this item. It is from such evidence that Pribram (1960) concludes that the frontal intrinsic system mediates intentions, and that the deficit which follows frontal lobe lesions may be attributed to a defective representation of intentions.

The posterior portion of the intrinsic system consists of the posterior dorsal nucleus (pulvinar) of the thalamus with its connections to cortex in the parietal, temporal, and occipital lobes and their connections to various subcortical nuclei (Pribram, 1958b). Lesions in the fiber tracts of this system interfere with the identification of objects and with the acquisition of learning sets (Rosvold, 1959). For this reason, Pribram (1960) concludes that the projection systems of this posterior portion make it possible for the organism to respond to those invariant and most redundant properties of receptor inputs. Here, then, presumably, are located the neuronal patterns of representation for objects and events that underlie object perception and discrimination. These are analogues of the strategies for information processing. Pribram (1960) does not decide whether the neuronal patterns underlying these representations should be conceived after the fashion of Hebb's (1949) cell assemblies, with the additional inhibitory properties proposed by Milner (1957), or after the fashion of Beurle (1956), who bases his suggestions on the cytological work of Sholl (1956) and takes into account the new finding that cortical neurones can fire in degree according to the "all-or-something" law rather than the "all-or-none" law (see Li, Cullen, & Jasper, 1956).

Fourth, as the basic functional unit in the control of action, Miller, Galanter, & Pribram (1960) have been formulating the concept of the Test-Operate-Test-Exist (TOTE) sequence to take the place of the static notion of the reflex arc. (The reflex arc has served as the traditional unit for considerably more than half a century [Sherrington, 1906]; John Dewey was finding fault with such a unit before the turn of the century). The TOTE sequence is conceived to operate much as do the "similarity" or "matching" routines of Newell, Shaw, & Simon (1958). It presumes two reciprocally connected neuronal systems. One of these, analogous to the intrinsic system of the brain, performs the test functions. When receptor inputs arrive, a search is made among the hierarchically arranged store of representations either of action systems (frontal portion) or of perceived objects and events and processes (posterior portion) to find one that matches the input. When incongruity persists between input and representation, Miller, Galanter, & Pribram (1960) presume that control is shifted to the extrinsic system. This system then operates on either the receptor mechanisms or on the environment, or on both, until the incongruities of the test are resolved.[6] Thus, Pribram (1960) has combined anatomical and behavioral evidence to come up with a conception of brain function which is fairly consonant in many ways with the picture of the problem-solving logic theorist of Newell, Shaw, & Simon (1958), which was originally conceived from the experience of developing programs for an electronic computer.

Such developments in brain functions have elaborated considerably over Hebb's (1949) formulations. They tend, if anything, to reinforce the necessity for the distinction between primary learning, through which the presumed representations within the intrinsic systems are established, and the later learning and problem-solving,

---

[6] Other ways of resolving the incongruity of such tests must be learning in which (1) what Pribram (1960) calls the bias of the homeostats becomes altered and (2) the representations of the invariant properties of objects are changed over time. Presumably even the "rules" which constrain the otherwise random properties of the neural networks must also be changed gradually, as Pribram notes, with repeated experiences of incongruity of some given kind. It is interesting to consider what Piaget's conception of *accommodation* (see Chapters 5, 6, 7) would mean in the terms of such neuropsychological processes.

which profit from the fact that the programs for processing information are already largely established when such problem-solving takes place. Consider next the evidence from the behavioral investigations of the effects of variations in early experience on, first, perception, and second, intelligence.

EFFECTS OF VISUAL DEPRIVATION IN INFANCY ON VISUAL PERCEPTION. The first study depriving a developing organism of visual experience was made by Mowrer (1936) in connection with the issue of maturation versus learning. What Mowrer did was to close the eyelids of newly hatched pigeons by sutures and to keep them closed until the pigeons were about six weeks old. When the sutures were removed, the vestibular nystagmus could be observed immediately, i.e., the movements of the eyes which accompany bodily movements were as prominent in the deprived birds as in birds of the same age reared under normal conditions. On the other hand, visual fixation did not appear until three days after the sutures were removed, and even then it appeared to be shaky. At that time, Mowrer concluded that maturation alone was sufficient to account for vestibular nystagmus but not sufficient to account for coordinated visual fixation.

Another of the early studies was done by Hebb (1937a, 1937b). The experiment was originally expected to demonstrate the truth of the Gestalt theory of perception and to embarrass learning theory. Eighteen rats were reared in complete darkness until they were 60 days of age. Then, following the precedure and using data from a study done earlier but published later by Lashley (1938), these rats were trained on a jumping stand to discriminate horizontal from vertical lines. The results already obtained from the Lashley (1938) experiment served as control data. Lashley's normal rats had averaged 21 trials to learn this discrimination. Those Hebb (1937a) reared in darkness averaged 129 trials with a range from 40 to 190. In later tests, these rats reared in darkness behaved like normal animals, thus showing that the slow learning of this discrimination was not a matter of structural defects. This ratio of six to one sharply contradicted the expectations from Gestalt theory. This was among the various pieces of evidence that prompted Hebb (see 1949, p. 81) to develop the theory outlined on pages 84–87.

Although the rats Hebb reared in darkness took six times as many trials to learn a visual discrimination as did rats normally reared, the fact that it was only a short time before those reared in darkness behaved like ordinary rats suggests that the effects of visual deprivation may be quite temporary, at least in rats. The A/S ratio[7] of the rat

[7] One is tempted to substitute Pribram's (1960) terminology here and to speak of an I/E ratio, i.e., the ratio of the intrinsic portion of the brain to the entrinsic portion.

brain, however, is relatively small (see Woolsey, 1958). If the effects of infantile experience increase as this ratio increases, visual deprivation during infancy might well have a relatively more marked and more lasting effect upon the behavior of higher animals. The fact that human patients operated on for congenital cataract take a long time to learn to recognize objects tends to confirm this inference (von Senden, 1932). Such individuals can neither name objects familiar to them by touch when they see them nor can they give a description of the shape of the object seen. They learn first of all the name of the color, but from this point on, progress is typically slow and highly discouraging. While these results from human subjects are exceedingly interesting, they are, unfortunately, complicated by extraneous factors. For instance, considerable variation occurs in the degree of optical correction that is possible when the lens of the eye is absent. Better data are needed.

With the danger of serious damage likely, experimental deprivation of vision in human subjects cannot be justified. On the other hand, anthropoid subjects approach human beings in the size of the A/S ratio. If primary learning in an animal with a high A/S ratio is highly important for the development of the strategies for processing visual information, as Hebb's theory demands, then depriving primates of vision during infancy should result in disturbances in visual function.

The relevant data came from the work of Riesen (1947), who removed two newborn chimpanzees, one male and one female, from their mothers and housed them for 16 months in a completely darkened room. The only light experienced by these animals during these 16 months was an electric lamp which was turned on for about 45 seconds several times daily to facilitate their care and feeding. When they were first tested at the age of 16 months, a time at which the young chimpanzee has typically developed locomotor and postural skills roughly equivalent to those of a two-year-old child, they exhibited an extreme degree of visual incompetence. Present from the beginning, however, were constriction of the pupil to light and startle responses to sudden changes in the level of illumination. The animals also turned their eyes in the direction of a light in the darkened room and made crude following motions as the light was moved, but these following motions were jerky. On the other hand, the majority of responses typical of seeing-chimpanzees of this age were absent. They could not fixate any object, still or moving. An object rapidly approaching the eye failed to evoke the blink response. This blink response began to appear only after some 48 days when the animals had been in light for a total of some 570 hours. Although the feeding-bottle was highly familiar once it was touched, such signs of visual recognition as reaching toward it when it was held out before the infant's face did not appear for some 11 days of life in light. Even after this point, reaching responses were grossly inaccurate for both animals. These young chimpanzees failed also to respond to play objects and many hundreds of trials were required to learn to discriminate large signs differing in color or pattern. The vision of these chimpanzees was also inferior in acuity. Lines and spaces had to be wider than three millimeters to permit discrimination of horizontal and vertical stripes at 45 inches distance from the eye. Normal chimpanzees typically discriminate lines of one-third millimeter.

At first, as the theory dictated, these visual deficiencies were attributed to lack of primary learning, or to the absence of the central neural processes typically acquired in the course of living and performing in a lighted place. As Riesen (1951) has written:

It was therefore an entirely unexpected finding when ophthalmoscopic examination of the eyes was made, that the retina and optic disc, especially the latter, did not reflect as much light as do normal chimpanzee eyes. This observation remains unexplained, but it is of interest in connection with changes in light reflectance with shifts in visual attention reported to occur in human children (Gesell & Thompson, 1929) . . . So far as was previously known, light stimulation is not essential to the normal growth of the primate retina or optic nerve. Yet this seems to be one possible explanation of the present lack of visual function and the pallor of the optic discs in the chimpanzee subject named Snark.

Brattgård (1952) has reported a similar finding in rabbits. Total light deprivation produced atrophy in the retinal ganglion cells and also disappearance of the pentose nucleoprotein fraction as estimated from X-ray microradiography. Perhaps such maturational disturbance is related to metabolic insufficiency associated with drastic reduction of stimulation (Riesen, 1958). Piaget (1936) has spoken of light as the "aliment of the visual system." Perhaps this is more than a figure of speech.

On the other hand, failure of normal growth for the primate retina and optic nerve in the chimpanzees reared in darkness does not explain all of the findings. Later studies by Riesen (1958) and others demonstrate quite clearly that the speed with which particular classes of visual inputs can gain control over behavior depends upon the degree of prior exposure to this class of inputs. Patterned visual experience appears to be essential for the development of visual perception. The evidence for these statements comes from several studies. In one, Riesen, Chow, et al. (1951) reared three infant chimpanzees from birth in a dark room for a period of seven months. One of these three was kept in complete darkness for this duration.

Another was allowed an hour and a half of light daily through a white plexiglass mask which admitted only diffuse, unpatterned light. During the remaining hours of each day this infant chimpanzee lived in darkness. A third was allowed an hour and a half of patterned light each day. A light was turned on so that this third infant chimpanzee could observe the edges of his crib, the variations in pattern introduced by movements of his own body and limbs, and the accompaniments of bottle feeding. When these infants were tested in the light at seven months of age, the behavior of the one reared in complete darkness and of the one reared with only diffuse unpatterned light resembled very much the behavior of the chimpanzees which had been kept in darkness for 16 months. While the optic discs again showed the failure to reflect the normal amount of light in ophthalmoscopic examination, this pallor disappeared after transfer to daylight surroundings. Thus, with only seven months in darkness, the physiological effects appear to have been reversible.

The number of days required to acquire various typical skills of visual perception were determined. For the infant reared in total darkness and the infant allowed only unpatterned light, these were, respectively, as follows: blink to objects moving across the field of vision, 15 days and 6 days; visual pursuit of a moving person, 30 days and 13 days; visual pursuit of the feeding bottle, 16 days and 20 days (a reversal); mouth approach toward a feeding bottle only seen, 27 days and 20 days; fixation of a person, 30 days and 13 days. These are all items of visually determined behavior which can be taken for granted in a chimpanzee infant of seven months of age. Moreover, the infant chimpanzee allowed an hour and a half of patterned light each day showed immediately all of these responses except that of avoiding a strange object. This he acquired in two days, whereas it took some four months for the other two chimpanzees that had experienced only unpatterned vision or darkness to acquire this. The behavior of the infant chimpanzee allowed an hour and a half of patterned vision each day was hardly distinguishable from that of normally reared chimpanzees, according to the tests used.

Maturation as well as experience plays a role in the acquisition of these visual responses. This is indicated by the fact that the two animals reared in darkness for seven months took only from six to 30 days to begin to show responses that normally reared chimpanzees do not achieve until approximately two months after birth.

Even more spectacular evidence exists to show that patterned light is necessary for the development of normal visual perception. Human beings without special visual defects see with either eye the scene before them. It looks the same to one eye as to the other. Moreover, any discrimination that can be made with one eye readily transfers to the other so long as the other eye shows no defect in acuity. This well-known fact has always been conceived to be a consequence of the way the eyes and the brain were built. On the other hand, Levine (1945) and Siegel (1953) have shown that pigeons must have experienced patterned vision with both eyes during development if what is seen by the two eyes is to be similar. Moreover, Riesen, Kurke, & Mellinger (1953) have shown that this is true for cats, and Chow & Nissen (1955) have shown that it is true for chimpanzees.

Consider the method of investigation. One cannot ask pigeons, cats, and chimpanzees whether the picture seen by the right eye is like the picture seen with the left. On the other hand, it is quite feasible to raise any of these animals in darkness. The procedure has been to give one eye a period of patterned vision each day while the other gets only the kind of diffuse light that would come through the shell of a ping-pong ball. For a perceptual test, such animals can then be trained while using the pattern-experienced eye to obtain food by going to a container marked by such a sign as a black triangle as distinguished from another container marked by a black circle. As soon as such a discrimination is well learned, the pattern-experienced eye can be covered and the eye which has been permitted only diffuse light can be uncovered. The animal then goes back into the same situation with only the diffuse-light eye in use. If this eye gets the same picture as the eye which experienced patterned light, the animal should immediately make the discrimination on which he has been trained. Such a transfer does occur immediately in cats reared under ordinary conditions. But this transfer does not occur in animals which have been deprived of patterned vision in one eye. Instead, Riesen *et al.* (1953) found that it takes from 100 to over 500 trials of training to achieve this transfer. Essentially this same picture holds for chimpanzees and pigeons.

It should also be noted that these experiments confirm those described earlier showing that all of the experimental animals reared in darkness were much inferior to normally reared animals in the original acquisition of such a discrimination. A background of primary visual learning is apparently necessary before visual discriminations can be acquired. It is also interesting to note that kittens that have experienced patterned vision in each eye on alternate days are capable of transferring a habit learned with one eye to the other (Riesen & Mellinger, 1956). That the capacity and the readiness of stimulation to influence behavior depend upon appropriate past experience fits nicely the notion that such past experience is the source of the strategies for processing information which underlie intelligence.

How permanent and irreversible the effects of visual deprivation are is still unknown as long as no defects within the visual apparatus itself complicate the picture. The cats and chimpanzees in the Riesen experiments appear in time to catch up in efficiency with those animals which suffered no infantile deprivation. Whether or not they retain some degree of permanent deficit is unclear. How important the permanent deficit may be, if one exists, also remains unclear. The existence of a deficit may be a matter of the precision of measurement. For instance, in von Senden's (1932) reports, human beings who have been operated on for congenital cataracts may gradually learn to identify objects. In ordinary circumstances their readiness for identification appears as efficient as that of normal people. On the other hand, when such subjects are given only a very short time to scrutinize objects, as when objects are exposed through a camera shutter that opens but for a fraction of a second or through a tachistoscope, identification fails, but it does not fail in the normal subject.

An experiment by Wolf (1943) is also pertinent in connection with the issue of the permanence of deficit. Wolf deprived one group of albino rats of hearing and another group of vision for a 10- to 15-day period during infancy. After these rats had reached sexual maturity and had been given suitable training, Wolf placed sex-matched litter mates in competition for food. They competed first in response to a visual signal and subsequently in response to an auditory signal. Those animals which had been deprived of auditory experience won more often under a visual signal, and those which had been deprived of visual experience won more often under the auditory signal. Although Wolf gave quite a different interpretation for this experiment, it appears to indicate that a relatively brief period of receptor deprivation in infancy leaves even the lowly rat with a lessened readiness to utilize information from the deprived receptor modality. Gauron & Becker (1959) have repeated the essential features of this study with similar results, but they note that during the last four days of the second competition, whether the stimulation be visual or auditory, the disadvantage of the deprived animals becomes hardly noticeable. Apparently, even under conditions of competition, the strategies within the intrinsic systems for utilizing information continue to improve. To what degree animals with high A/S ratios can recover from various degrees and durations of deprivations remains to be determined.

RICHNESS OF EXPERIENCE AND LATER INTELLIGENCE. The conception of intelligence as problem-solving ability, being based upon either systems of cell assemblies and phase sequences (Hebb, 1949) or strategies for processing information within the intrinsic cerebral

systems (Pribram, 1960) which have been established in the course
of previous experience, leads not only to the expectation that deprivation of experience would diminish ability, but also to the expectation that an enrichment of experience would improve ability. The
first studies done to test such deductions from Hebb's position were
made by Hebb himself. A group of seven rats were blinded in infancy
while a group of seven litter mates were blinded at relative maturity
(30 days of age). Both groups were handled frequently, and were
given equal opportunity to run outside their cages in a large space
where there were a number of objects. The question to be answered
was this: "Would the group with vision growth learn something
about finding their way around that they would retain after being
blinded in maturity?" (Hebb, 1949, p. 297). For these groups, and
the first tests, the answer was negative. When the rats were compared
in their ability to find food in one of four containers in an open field
two months after the second group were blinded, there was no difference. The problem selected, however, was poorly calculated to use
the relative enrichment of experience obtained by the rats blinded
at maturity over those blinded in infancy. At this point, what remained of the two groups were tested on an "intelligence test" for
the rat (Hebb & Williams, 1946). In this test, after 10 to 14 days of
preliminary training in which the animals got used to being handled,
got familiar with the test situation, and had experienced the daily
change in route required to get food, the animals were tested on a
series of from 20 to 24 problems. On each of these they were given
from 6 to 10 trials. Each problem consisted of a different route from
the starting point to the food when both starting position and food
position were continuously fixed. In this preliminary study, the four
remaining rats in the early-blinded group all made more errors than
did any of the three remaining late-blinded rats. Moreover, the
difference was substantial, suggesting, in spite of the small number
of animals, that the extra experience gained from being blinded late
facilitated shifting from one route to another.

This study suggested another mode of attack (Hebb, 1949, p. 298).
The ordinary experience of rats reared in small cages in laboratories
is limited. Would rats of the same strain reared at home as pets show
the same kind of advantage over laboratory-reared pups in the ability
to shift routes to food in the Hebb-Williams "intelligence test?" They
did. All seven of the home-reared pups scored in the top third of the
total distribution for cage-reared pups. The better scores of the
pets might be attributed to the fact that they were tamer, were less
distracted emotionally, or had better rapport with the experimenter.
If such an explanation were true, the cage-reared animals should

come to score closer and closer to the level of the pets as testing continued. This, however, was not the case. The pet rats actually improved their relative standing during the last 10 days of testing following 10 days of preliminary training and 11 days of testing. Hebb writes: "This means that *the richer experience of the pet group during development made them better able to profit by new experience at maturity*—one of the characteristics of the 'intelligent' human being" (Hebb, 1949, p. 299). Perhaps it should be noted that this observation implies that the deficit is permanent and that it also contradicts the findings concerned with infantile experience and visual perception.

By themselves, these exploratory studies may be relatively unconvincing, but they have now been bolstered by a variety of repetitions in which the richer of two early experiences is regularly associated with a higher level of ability in problem-solving. This is true, however, only so long as the problem to be solved in the test makes use of the enriched experience, and so long as the enriched experience does not complicate finding a solution.

Perceptual versus motor experience. Although Hebb's (1949) conception of the development of cell assemblies and phase sequences emphasizes perceptual experience, other investigators, such as Piaget (1936; to be discussed in Chapter 5) and Osgood (1953), have argued that it is motor behavior which structures the central processes. Repetitions of the early studies on the effects of infantile experience on problem-solving ability, measured by the Hebb-Williams (1946) intelligence test for rats, were done by Hymovitch (1952). The intelligence of rats brought up in a "free environment" was compared with that of rats brought up in cages with wooden walls which diminished variety of visual experience but did not eliminate patterned vision. A "free environment" meant living in a large box, four feet square, provided with simple wooden and metal structures which the growing rat pups could see and about which they could scramble. In the tests made when the animals were five months of age, the superiority of the rats reared in the "free environment" over those reared in the restrictive boxes was substantial. Hymovitch (1952) found, however, that animals reared in mesh cages placed within the free-environment gave performances on the tests indistinguishable from those reared in the free environment. Inasmuch as the mesh cages restricted the motor experience of these animals, but did not prevent their seeing the wooden and metal structures placed outside their cages, Hymovitch (1952) argued that it is perceptual experience rather than motor experience that is important in the establishment of the central processes that facilitate problem-solving.

This may well have been a premature conclusion. Forgays & Forgays (1952) made a special issue of the role of motor activity in environments both with and without special playthings. In this study, the animals allowed the motor experience of the free environments, either with or without playthings, were superior in problem-solving to any of the groups reared in mesh cages. This superiority was found regardless of the nature of the environment surrounding the mesh cages. Since this superiority was substantial and highly significant, it appears that motor experience may be an important factor. Moreover, so long as the animals have motor experience with playthings, the presence of the playthings also makes a significant contribution to the problem-solving scores. Repetitions of this study by Forgays & Forgays[8] have confirmed these results, and further confirmation has come from studies by Forgus (1954, 1955a, 1955b).

INTERACTION BETWEEN EARLY EXPERIENCE AND SUCCESS IN SOLVING VARIOUS TYPES OF TEST-PROBLEMS

Where the infantile experience is arranged to make a certain class of perceptual cues especially prominent and the test problem is so chosen that this class of cues stands in the way of finding the correct solution, enrichments of infantile experience may increase the number of errors in the test problem and slow the rat's learning. What this means can best be seen in concrete illustrations. In a study by Forgays & Forgays (1952), the investigators got the idea that those animals reared in a free environment were making more use of visual distance-cues than were the animals reared in the board cages. If this hypothesis be true, they reasoned, turning the maze, which served as the Hebb-Williamson intelligence test, by a quarter turn to the left from the standard position and then later to the right from the standard position should result in a greater increase of errors for those animals reared in the free environment, where they had opportunity to fixate distant objects, than for those reared in the board cages. This turned out to be precisely what occurred. In fact, the free-environment animals made approximately three times as many errors as did the animals reared in the board cages, where they had never had an opportunity to see anything beyond 10 inches from their eyes. Those animals reared in the mesh cages placed within the free environment also made more errors than did those reared in the board cages.

In an experiment with somewhat similar implications, Forgus (1954) found that in tests where visual cues were important for suc-

[8] Personal communication.

cess, rats allowed only visual experience during infancy performed as successfully as rats allowed both visual and exploratory experience. In tests where visual cues were less important for success, the animals allowed only visual experience were not as successful as those allowed both kinds. In the tests, both of these groups were superior to a group reared with a minimum of both visual and exploratory experience. What Forgus did was to compare various samplings of adult behavior in three groups of animals. One of these groups was allowed to range freely in a large plywood box four feet by four feet with walls 60 inches high. The walls of this box were painted black, and the 16 square feet of area contained a fairly large number of blocks, alleys, tunnels, elevated platforms, and inclined planes which were painted white. The animals in this first group were, thus, permitted both visual and exploratory motor-experience in this environment. A second group of rats was reared in a small transparent plastic cage which, during the course of their rearing, was placed in various positions within the larger box just described. They got only the visual experience. A third group was reared in a small box walled with black plywood but illuminated by a 100-watt bulb to equalize its illumination with that of the others. The animals of the first two of these three groups differed little when, in performance as adults, they were put on an elevated maze where visual cues are presumably especially important. On the other hand, both groups made their responses more quickly, were more active, were less emotional, and showed greater variety of response than did the animals reared in the small black box. In another test involving latent learning, the animals were allowed, while satiated, to explore three paths through a tunnel maze, where visual cues are presumably unimportant, to a food box. These paths differed in length. When the animals were tested at a later time when hungry to see if they "got the relationship," the group allowed both visual and motor experience proved most superior. The group allowed only visual experience was intermediate, and nearly all of the group reared in the black-walled box failed.

In still another approach to this problem of the interaction between type of infantile experience and the type of later problem in effects on ease of solution, Forgus (1955a) has shown that the effects of richness of experience can be offset by giving special emphasis in the test-situation to that class of cues emphasized in the infantile experience of the animals with the less rich experience. Here Forgus (1955a) compared the maze-learning scores of one group of rats which had been allowed to range freely in the large area well stocked with objects, with the scores of another group reared in small transparent plastic cages placed within the same large area. Later, in a test maze with no special visual cues for the correct and incorrect turns, the group with both visual and manipulative experience during infancy learned with substantially fewer trials. On the other hand, when the correct choices were marked by horizontal striations, and the incorrect by vertical striations, any difference between these two groups in the number of trials required to achieve the criterion of learning disappeared. Similar results were obtained in another modification of this study by Forgus (1955b).

More recently, investigations of the effect of perceptual experience on the readiness with which discriminations are learned by rats have shown that the effects are not entirely general. Gibson & Walk (1956) compared the discrimination learning in adulthood of two groups of rats. The control group had been reared in ordinary mesh cages surrounded by cardboard walls. The experimental group had been reared in a similar environment, but black metal cut-outs were hung on each of the four walls: circles on the two sides, triangles on the two ends. The group of animals exposed to the cut-outs learned to discriminate the circle from the triangle in substantially fewer trials than did the controls. Gibson, Walk, *et al.* (1958) extended this experiment to test situations in which the forms used in the discrimination tests varied in degree from those to which the rats were exposed during the first 75 days of their lives in their nesting cages. The facilitation of discrimination learning resulting from the experience of exposure to the visual forms on the cage walls was found again. This exposure to visual patterns also facilitated the learning of a discrimination between patterns similar to but not identical with those exposed. On the other hand, when the cage patterns and the test patterns were made very different, the facilitation of discrimination disappeared. Forgus (1958a), in a similar study, has found that exposure to perceptual forms facilitates learning a visual discrimination between the forms. He has also found that exposure to truncated triangles (triangles with corners cut off) for rats during their early development markedly facilitates their learning a discrimination between a triangle and a circle. Forgus accounts for this additional facilitation, however, on motivational grounds. To rats which have been exposed to a triangle with the corners absent, the presence of the corners is presumably novel. The novelty presumably draws attention. When attention is drawn to the corners of the triangle, it becomes easier to discriminate the triangle from the circle. In a second study, Forgus (1958b) confirmed this result and drew the conclusion that the positive effects of early experience are based not only on familiarity and reinforcement, but also on the extent to which the relationship between the forms to which the animals have been exposed leads to selective responding to the differences between the forms used in the test problem. Thus, these experiments have gone just far enough beyond the exploratory stage to permit the generalization that enriched experience improves the capacity of an organism to profit from the experience *unless* the test situation is so rigged as to make special use of the particular kind of experience which the more impoverished organisms have had or to make no use of the experiences which the more enriched organisms have had.

EFFECTS OF INFANTILE EXPERIENCE ON INTELLIGENCE AND THE A/S RATIO. It is exceedingly interesting that variations in the richness of early experience can be shown to influence later ability even in the lowly rat, where the A/S ratio is so small. Presumably, the larger this ratio between the sizes of the intrinsic and extrinsic regions of the brain, the larger the effects of variations of enrichment in infantile experience. Such a presumption is based on the notions (*a*) that problem-solving capacity is dependent upon the strategies for information processes stored within the intrinsic systems of the brain, (*b*) that the larger these intrinsic regions, the more complex the strategies, and (*c*) that the more complex the strategies, the more important the role of the primary learning through which they are acquired.

Unfortunately, except for Riesen's studies of the effects of rearing chimpanzees under various kinds of visual experience on their visual perception, studies of the effects of deprivation and enrichments of early experience on later functions using as subjects animals with a large A/S ratio have been rare. To the writer's knowledge, the only one concerned with effects of early experience on later ability to solve problems is that one using dogs as subjects by Thompson & Heron (1954). These investigators compared the "intelligence" of 13 Scottish terriers from a sample of several litters which had been deprived of early experience with the "intelligence" of 13 of their litter mates which had been given rich early experience. The results from this one experiment lend support to the three theoretical propositions just stated.

Thompson & Heron (1954) submitted their Scottish terriers to three degrees of restriction in early experience. Two of the pups were reared in cages with complete isolation in which they never encountered either other dogs or human beings from weaning till they were eight months old. Eight were reared from weaning to eight months in ordinary laboratory dog-cages but the wire-mesh fronts and sides of the cages were covered with cardboard. The experience of the remaining three was restricted only by their being reared in the laboratory in the regular open wire-mesh cages. Each of these 13 cage-reared pups had a litter mate in the group that received enriched early experience. These 26 subjects came from several litters, but they were inbred. All litters were decendants of a single litter of Scottish terriers. The enriched experience of the latter group came in the form of their being reared as pets in homes from their weaning till they were eight months old. The differences in problem-solving behavior in the tests to be considered here are, thus, differences between the cage-reared dogs and their pet-reared litter-mates at about 18 months of age after both groups had shared 10 months of living in the laboratory.

The tests were of several types. In orientation tests, the animals were fed in a square room. After several trials of finding the food behind a screen in one corner, the food was then placed, while the dogs were watching, behind screens in other corners of the room. Whereas the pet-reared dogs almost always followed the food to the new corner immediately, the cage-reared returned to the corner where they had found the food before as soon as it went out of sight. In the cage-reared dogs, apparently, central processes aroused by such visual inputs as seeing where the food had been placed could not dominate the habit of going to the usual corner.

In one barrier test, depicted in Figure 4–7A, each dog was first given five trial runs to food placed at F, which was approximately six feet along the wall from the starting-box marked S. After these trial runs in an empty room, a chicken-wire barrier, five feet in length and four feet high, was introduced immediately in front of the food. An error zone was marked with chalk extending from one end of the barrier to a point on the wall two feet from the other end. Each dog was then given 10 test runs, and the score was the number of runs which did not involve entry into the error zone. The pet-reared dogs averaged nearly three times as many errorless runs (6.75) as did the cage-reared dogs (2.40), a difference which was highly significant ($t = 6.13$, $p<.001$). As in the orientation test, the cage-reared dogs appeared to have more difficulty in modifying their already established habit of running directly to the food.

In a second barrier test, the chicken-wire barrier was placed at right angles to the wall, as in Figure 4–7B, but close to S, and a second chicken-wire barrier two feet by four feet was placed at a right angle to form a starting enclosure. Each dog was placed in this enclosure and shown the food through the barrier at about the place labeled F. Getting to the food demanded that the dog turn his back on the food, exit through the rear of the enclosure, and run around the barrier to it. Each dog got five trials, and the score for each trial was the time required to reach the food. The cage-reared dogs averaged 72.1 seconds while the pet-reared dogs averaged only 29.4 seconds. All but one of the eight pet-reared dogs reached the food more quickly than did any eight cage-reared dogs, and the difference is statistically significant ($t = 2.26$, $p < .05$). Again, it would appear that turning away from the food, which would presumably require autonomous central processes to dominate the receptor-inputs of the moment, is more difficult for the cage-reared than for the pet-reared dogs.

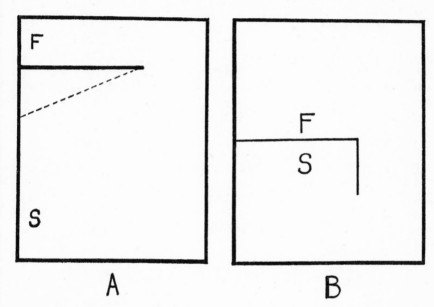

Fig. 4–7. Diagrams of the floor plans of the barrier tests A and B. After Thompson & Heron (1954).

In the delayed-reaction test, the dogs were given a chance to observe the placement of food and then forced to wait for various periods of time before being released to go to the food. The capacity for the pet-reared and cage-reared dogs to delay their reactions differed markedly. All five of the pet-reared dogs used in this test went to the correct place for food after delays as long as 300 seconds, and they learned in many fewer trials than the maximum of 255 used. Of the seven cage-reared dogs used, however, only one achieved any delay within 255 trials, and that delay was of only 25 seconds. Inasmuch as delayed reaction is one of the functions most damaged by lesions in the frontal intrinsic system (see Pribram, 1960), this finding is exceedingly interesting. It suggests that the effect of restricted experience is similar to lesions in the frontal intrinsic system. If, as Pribram (1960) suggests, this frontal intrinsic system contains the programs which control "intentions," these results suggest that such programs, or the central processes on which they are based, are acquired in the course of early experience.

Thompson & Heron (1954) also tested these groups of dogs on the Hebb-Williams (1946) test of "intelligence." The restricted animals made more errors than the pet dogs on all 18 problems. Only one of the restricted animals got a score above the lowest score obtained by a pet dog. This is interesting because these tests were made when the dogs were from one to one and a half years of age. The two groups had thus had similar experience for a period ranging from four months to a year. The fact that the pet-reared animals remained so markedly superior at this age suggests that the effects of restricted experience on problem-solving may be relatively permanent in animals with a high A/S ratio.

In each of these tests above, the difference between the restricted cage-reared dogs and the pet-reared dogs is highly significant ($p<.001$). The impression is certainly created that the effect of restricted experience on the dog is greater than that on the rat, thus tending to confirm the contention that the degree of effect of infantile experience on problem-solving behavior increases with the A/S ratio. More experiments on dogs and monkeys and chimpanzees like this one of Thompson & Heron (1954) are needed, however, to establish this point.

SUMMARY

Conceptions of the development of intelligence and its dependence, or lack of dependence, upon experience have been in large part a function of the concurrent theories of psychology in general. No sooner had Lloyd Morgan (1894), Thorndike & Woodworth (1901), and Watson (1919) eliminated the traditional mental entities and left the void of an empty organism, conceptually speaking, between stimulus and response, than stimulus-response method, as distinct from stimulus-response theory, began to refill the void. Since behavior is not immediately dependent upon external stimulation for its control, observation of animals and human beings behaving in controlled situations soon implied that something was going on between the ears. The new constructs differed from the traditional ones, however, in being better, if not perfectly, tied to both the stimulus history of the organism and to its responses.

Even though Hunter (1912, 1918) introduced symbolic processes and Hull (1930) introduced the pure stimulus act and a variety of other intervening variables which were elaborated into response-produced cues and drives by Miller & Dollard (1941) and into mediation theory by Osgood (1953), the behavioristic theory continued to emphasize peripheral receptor and motor processes in the control of ongoing behavior and in the origins of the central mediational processes. Moreover, intelligence, perceiving, and complex problem-solving were all off the center of interest of the behavior theorists, who were concerned chiefly with the learning process. Finally, in the behavioristic tradition, the brain continued to be at least implicitly conceived as a sensitive but static organ serving the switching function.

The opposing theory of Gestalt (Köhler, 1925, 1929) emphasized central processes and criticized the switchboard conception of brain function, but denied an important role to past experience in the origins of these central processes. Tolman (1932) accepted such central processes as sign-Gestalt-expectations without neurologizing them. Lashley (1917) destroyed the explanatory value of stimulus-response chaining as an explanation of complex skills and also the notion of the brain as a simple switchboard, but he allowed no role for experience in the development of central processes.

People who program electronic computers (e.g., Newell, Shaw, & Simon, 1958) have developed formal conceptions of the requirements for problem-solving. These include memory and strategies for the processing of information, since evidence exists that such phenomena as insight do not occur in organisms that lack in their memories the representations required for the insight. Moreover, Harlow's (1949) work on learning sets indicates that counterparts of strategies for the processing of information can be learned in the course of repeated experiences with a given class of problems.

It was Hebb (1949) who gave us a new conceptual synthesis of developments in neurophysiology with behavioral knowledge to provide a conception of central processes which could be helpful in accounting for perceiving and problem-solving. This conceptual scheme derives these central processes, cell assemblies, and phase sequences, from experience, and distinguishes sharply between primary learning, through which they get established, and later learning and problem-solving where they achieve their explanatory value. The potential of an organism for complex problem-solving is seen as a function of its A/S ratio, i.e., the size of the associative areas, where the central processes are presumably located, relative to the size of motor and sensory areas of the cortex.

Pribram (1960) has reviewed recent developments in the theory of brain function to show that something approximating counterparts of the various components required in electronic computers to solve complex problems may actually exist within the complex anatomy of the brain. Although von Neumann (1958) has called attention to what may be fundamental differences between brain functions and computer functions, the fact that their apparent similarities have stimulated a search for counterparts has helped to stimulate some interesting modifications of neuropsychological theory. The association areas, for instance, give way to intrinsic systems in which are stored the approximate counterparts of the computer's memory with its representations and strategies for processing information. The reflex arc gives way to a Test-Operate-Test-Exist sequence that operates after the fashion of an analogue computer. Such developments tend to elaborate and extend the directions set by Hebb (1949) but not to alter implications for behavior and intelligence.

The empirical studies of early experience on later perceptual and problem-solving capacity have been prompted by Hebb's theorizing. Studies by Riesen (1947, 1958) and others of the effects of rearing animals in darkness indicate that perceptual capacities do indeed demand a background of perceptual experience. In fact, even normal physiological development of the optic apparatus may require at least a minimal experience of light stimulation.

Moreover, even though the rat as a species would be expected from its small A/S ratio to show little effects of early experience, the studies of the effects of depriving or enriching the experience of developing rats appear to indicate that these deprivations and enrichments do affect the rat's later capacity for solving problems. Finally, the one existing study of the effects of variations in early experience on later capacity for problem-solving in an animal with a larger A/S ratio, the dog, appears to indicate that, as expected, the effects may be more marked and perhaps more permanent than those in the rat.

CHAPTER 5

Piaget's Observations:
The Sensorimotor Period

A conception of intelligence as problem-solving capacity based on a hierarchical organization of symbolic representations and information-processing strategies deriving to a considerable degree from past experience, has been emerging from several sources. These sources include observations of human behavior in solving problems, the programming of electronic computers, and neuropsychology. It is interesting, therefore, to find such a conception coming also from Piaget's observations of the development of intelligence in children. The various lines of evidence appear to be coalescing to flow in one direction, a direction that makes interaction between the environment and the organism continuous. Piaget's observations of the homely interactions of the child with his everyday environment demonstrate empirically the formation of a vertical hierarchy of operations for the processing of information to guide action. His observations begin to show what these concepts of a vertical hierarchy of information-processing operations and a continuous interaction between the organism and the environment mean empirically in human development, where they most need to be understood.

For more than 30 years, Piaget and his collaborators at the Rousseau Institute in Geneva, Switzerland have been studying the development of intellectual functions and logic in children. Although

he has not typically done "experiments" in the American manner,[1]
Piaget is a master at developing the theoretical implications of his
observations. Moreover, his life's program constitutes research in the
grand manner, both in scope and implications.

In his early studies of the child's language and thought (1932),
judgment and reasoning (1924), conception of the world (1926),
conception of physical causality (1927), and moral judgment (1932),
Piaget based his observations almost completely on the language behavior of pairs of children in free-school situations. Out of this
method came the well-known distinctions between egocentric and
social language, between prelogical thinking and reasoning, and
between animistic and symbolic forms of thinking. This portion of
his work, and especially his propositions about the prevalence and
ages of egocentric thought in children, have been severely criticized,[2]
and Piaget (1953a) has admitted that "my method of studying logic
in the child was much too verbal at first, dealing particularly with the
relation between thought and language" (p. 32).

Beginning, however, with his observation of the early origins of intelligence and reality constructions in his own children, Piaget (1936,
1937) revised his method of observation to focus on the child's actions in manipulating objects. He varied the objects and their arrangement to check his own interpretation of what central processes
were implied by the child's actions. With older children he has set
practical tasks and asked precise questions about the events taking
place or about their own action. Piaget writes:

This study of the child's actions brought me to the conception of logic based on
operations—an operation being considered as internalized action which becomes
reversible, that is to say, can be carried out in both directions, and links up with
others. In the sphere of intelligence, operations always constitute whole structures, rather like the Gestalt in the sphere of perception; the structures being,
however, larger, more mobile and essentially reversible, and capable of coordination (1953a, p. 32).

It is Piaget's "operations" or "structures" that appear to correspond
to the strategies for information-processing and the representations

[1] What Piaget (1936, 1937) commonly calls "experiments" consists of making variations in the situation to check his inference of the implication of a child's action for
theory. On the other hand, in the work on the differences between perception and
thought with Lambercier (1942, 1943a, 1943b, 1944, 1946, 1953), they have done
typical psychophysical experiments, and in his work on the thinking of children and
adolescents he and his collaborators, especially Bärbel Inhelder and Alina Szeminska,
have devised exceedingly ingenious procedures for getting children to solve problems
while they are interrogated about how and why. For a review of the developmental
studies of perception, see Wohlwill (1960).

[2] For these criticisms, see Isaacs (1930), McCarthy (1930; and for review, 1954,
pp. 562 ff.), Curti (1938), Valentine (1942), Huang (1943), and Russell (1956).

that those who design programs for electronic computers put into the "memories" of their instruments (see Wiener, 1948; Newell, Shaw, & Simon, 1958). This is a conceptual correspondence which Piaget (1953b) himself recognizes. This later work of Piaget is relatively little known in America. Although Berlyne (1957) has provided an excellent brief review, it hardly makes the nature of Piaget's empirical observations clear. It is his observations that give concrete human significance to his conceptions, that show the nature and origins of operations for information-processing, and eradicate the preformationism which still often lingers in psychology, just as Wolff's (1768) demonstrations of epigenesis of embryological forms undid preformationism for morphology. For these reasons, Piaget's work will be given enough space to make clear his method, the nature of his data, and the basic theoretical implications of his work.

PIAGET'S GENERAL CONCEPTIONS

Although the observations themselves are what make Piaget's work clear, it may be wise to outline first his general approach and conceptions. Inhelder (1953) has characterized Piaget as "a zoologist by training, an epistemologist by vocation, and a logician by method. Accordingly, his conceptions and unusual terminology derive from this triple orientation—biological, epistemological, and logico-mathematical" (p. 75).

For Piaget (1936, 1947) the zoologist, intelligence is a special instance of adaptation. Life is a continuous creative interaction between the organism and the environment. This interaction functions outwardly as adaptive coping and inwardly as organization. Adaptation and organization are complementary aspects of a single cyclical mechanism (1936, p. 7). The process of living is thus a continuous creation of increasingly complex structures of body and of behavior. It is the structures (e.g., epigenesis of the heart in embryology) which change; the functions (e.g., assimilation and accommodation) remain invariant. Piaget the epistemologist is at continuous pains to show that epigenesis is as true for the structures of the mind (i.e., of behavior and thought) as for the structures of the body. He conceives of adaptive coping as continually reorganizing the structures of mind, and this is a conception maximally dissonant with the preformationism that has lingered since Plato in philosophical accounts of such logical structures as the notions of the object, of space, of causality, and of time.

Piaget (1936, 1947) conceives the adaptive interaction between organism and environment to involve two complementary processes, corresponding to inner organization and outer adaptation, which he calls *assimilation* and *accommodation*. Although such inclusiveness may be questioned, Piaget conceives these processes as common to both the physiological and psychological domains.

Assimilation occurs whenever an organism utilizes something from the environment and incorporates it. In the biochemical domain, it is exemplified by the ingestion of food which gradually transforms the somatic structures. In the psychological domain, assimilation operates whenever the organism sees something new in terms of something familiar, whenever it acts in a new situation as it has acted in other situations in the past, whenever it invests anything with familiarity (recognition), importance, or value. Thus, assimilation includes the phenomena which Pavlov (1927) called "conditioning," and also those which Hull (1943) and others have termed "stimulus generalization" and "response generalization." But where these terms have referred to associative or connective relations between observed stimuli and responses, Piaget takes the quite different view that the organism always acts in terms of the centrally organized, Gestalt-like structures which it has present (analogue of Hull's [1943] response repertoire). Moreover, these structures, which are observed as repeatable and generalizable pieces of behavior termed *schemata* and which are presumably mediated by neurophysiological processes of no immediate concern to psychology, warp receptor inputs to their own pattern and nature. It is thus that Piaget (1947) speaks of assimilation as "the action of the organism on surrounding objects, insofar as this action depends on previous behavior involving the same or similar objects" (p. 7).[3]

Accommodation, the process complementary to assimilation, operates as the variations in environmental circumstances demand coping which modifies existing schemata. It is thus that the environmental circumstances act upon the organism, not by merely evoking a fixed response, not by getting a passive submission to circumstances, but rather by modifying the action or *schema* affecting them.

[3] Piaget's starting points in psychological theorizing, e.g., his viewing of reflexes as Gestalt-like sensorimotor schemata and his coordinations, ring of Dewey's (1896) famous paper on the concept of the reflex arc in psychology that launched the Chicago school of functional psychology. This is hardly surprising when one notes that Piaget's tutelage in psychology came in association with Edouard Claparède, who was the successor in the Geneva chair of psychology to his teacher and elder cousin, Theodore Flournoy. Flournoy was a long-time friend and correspondent of William James, whose pragmatism was the forerunner of functional psychology. Although Claparède was reared intellectually in the functional tradition, he remarks (1930) how encouraged he was to find his functional conception of mental processes in the books by John Dewey apparently without realizing that both were part of the same stream of psychological thought.

In the course of this dual adaptive process of assimilation and accommodation the ready-made reflexive schemata of the newborn infant become progressively transformed through differentiations and coordinations into the logical "organizations" (or operations for information-processing) of adult intelligence. This is the epigenesis of mind. As it proceeds, the child becomes capable of taking account of stimuli more and more remote from him in space and time, and also of resorting to more and more composite and indirect modes of solving problems.[4] In this sense, "life is a continuous creation of increasingly complex forms and a progressive adaptation of these forms to the environment" (1936, p. 3).

The picture of the development of intelligence which emerges from the observations and experiments of Piaget and his collaborators is one of continuous transformations in the "organizations" or "structures" of intelligence.[5] At birth the only "organizations" available are the congenital sensorimotor schemata, reflexes or instincts. The first period of intellectual development, the *sensorimotor*, lasts from birth till the child is roughly between 18 months and two years old. The reflexive sensorimotor schemata are generalized, coordinated with each other, and differentiated to become the elementary operations of intelligence which begin to be internalized and which correspond to the problem-solving abilities of sub-human animals. During this

[4] Although Piaget (1947, p. 6) agrees that affective life can be distinguished from intellectual life, he regards them as inseparable because "all interaction with the environment involves both a structuring and a valuation . . . we cannot reason, even in pure mathematics, without experiencing certain feelings, and conversely, no affect can exist without a minimum of understanding or of discrimination." He concentrates on the intellectual aspect in his writings. These are the subject matter of this review, but elsewhere the writer (1960) attempts to utilize the implications of Piaget's observations for a theory of motivation.

[5] The picture outlined in what follows in this chapter and the next is based chiefly on Piaget's (1936, 1937, 1945, 1947; Piaget & Szeminska, 1941; Piaget & Inhelder, 1948; Inhelder & Piaget, 1955) translated writings. Here the dates refer to the original publication in French. All the translations of Piaget's later works have been done since 1950. Of those listed, *The psychology of intelligence* (1947) is the briefest survey, but it gives too little of the observational material to provide one with a grasp of the nature of the empirical side of Piaget's work. The picture outlined here is also supplemented by papers by Berlyne (1957), Inhelder (1953), and by some degree of examination of some of the untranslated works (Piaget, 1941, 1942, 1946, 1949a, 1949b, 1954b). Collaborators have clearly had a hand in Piaget's tremendous output. The work on the development of the concept of conservation of quantity and of number appears to have been done with Alina Szeminska (1935, 1939, 1941) and with Bärbel Inhelder (1936, 1941), that on space with E. Meyer (1935) and Inhelder (1948), that on spontaneous geometry with Inhelder and Szeminska (1948), that on probability with Inhelder (1951). No attempt is made to include Piaget's work on the development of perception and the difference between perception and thought (1949, 1950; Piaget & Albertini, 1950; Piaget & Lambercier, 1942, 1946) nor his reinterpretation of Weber's law in terms of "coupling probability" (Piaget, 1954a, 1955), but these works should both be of considerable interest to students of perception and to psychophysicists.

period, the child creates through his continual adaptive accommodations and assimilations, in six stages, such operations as "intentions," "means-end" differentiations, and the interest in novelty (Piaget, 1936). On the side of constructing reality, the child also develops the beginnings of interiorized schemata, if not actual concepts, for such elements as the permanence of the object, space, causality, and time (Piaget, 1937).

The second period of concrete operations in intellectual development, beginning when the child is about 18 months or two years old, lasts till he is 11 or 12 years old. It contains, first, a *preconceptual* phase during which symbols are constructed. This lasts to about four years of age, and during it the child's activity is dominated by symbolic play, which imitates and represents what he has seen others do, and by the learning of language. The accommodations forced by the variation in the models imitated along with the assimilations resulting from repetitions of the play-activities gradually create a store of central processes which symbolize the actions imitated (Piaget, 1945). As the images are established, the child acquires verbal signs for those which correspond to the collective system of signs comprising language. At this point the child comes under dual interaction with the environment, i.e., with the world of things and the world of people. The child's action-images greatly extend the scope of his mental operation beyond the range of immediate action and momentary perception, and they also speed up his mental activity, for the sensorimotor action is limited by the concrete sequence of perceptions and actions. This period contains, second, an *intuitive* phase.[6] This is a phase of transition that lasts till the child is seven or eight years old. In the course of his manipulations and social communications, he is extending, differentiating, and combining his action-images and simultaneously correcting his intuitive impressions of reality (space, causality, and time). It contains, third, the phase of *concrete operations.* As the child interacts repeatedly with things and people, his central processes become more and more autonomous. Piaget (1945, 1947) speaks of his thought becoming "decentred" from perception and action. With greater autonomy of central processes come both differentiations and coordinations, or groupings, of

---

[6] This terminology of *periods, phases,* and *sub-stages* does not quite correspond to that of Piaget and his collaborators. They, however, have been inconsistent with both terms and numberings. Each successive book has its own. Here the three *major divisions* of the course of intellectual development are termed *periods.* The first, *sensorimotor* period is here divided into six *stages* following Piaget. The second *period* (see Chapter 6) is divided into three *phases:* I—*preconceptual;* II—*intuitive;* and III—*phase of concrete operations.* Each of these *phases* will be divided into two *sub-stages.* The third *period* is that of formal operations.

the action-images into systems which permit classifying, ordering in series, numbering.[7] These "concrete groupings" bring to the child's thought the properties of logical "groupings" or mathematical "groups" (see Poincaré, 1906). Piaget (1953) sees logic as the reflection of thought, and he finds in logical operations the models that serve to explain what the child can and cannot do at various levels of development. The acquisition of these "concrete operations," which may be seen as analogues of both Harlow's (1949) "learning sets" and the operations for information-processing (Newell, Shaw, & Simon, 1958), bring a distinctive change in the child's concrete conceptions of quantity, space, causality, and time. This phase, and with it the second period, ends as the child spontaneously masters the multiplicative compensations that underlie the proportionality schema and the conservation of volume at about 11 or 12 years of age (Inhelder & Piaget, 1955).

The third period of *formal operations* starts at about 11 or 12 years when the child begins to group or systematize his concrete operations (classifications, serial ordering, correspondences, etc.) and thereby also to consider all possible combinations in each case. This period is marked by the beginning of ability to classify, order, enumerate, etc., in verbal propositions. In the period from age 11 or 12 to age 15 or 16, the child achieves the final steps of "decentring" and "reversibility" as his central processes become sufficiently autonomous to permit him to operate with the sum total of possibilities rather than merely the empirical situation. The child, become essentially adult, can now operate with the *form* of an argument while ignoring its *empirical content*. He can use systems of operations (e.g., the logician's INRC group [see Chapter 7 or Piaget, 1953a] in which each operation has two distinct opposites) which permit him to deal with proportionality and probability. He can also use combinatorial analyses based on the logical structures which mathematicians call *lattices*. With these new-found thought structures, he need no longer confine his attention to existing reality. Not only do the hypothetico-deductive procedures of science and logic open to him, but he becomes concerned socially with seeing the world as it might better be and enters the roles of critic and social reformer.

It should be noted that in this picture of the epigenesis of the behavioral and thought structures comprising intelligence, those of each phase become incorporated and reorganized in the subsequent phase. The result is something analogous to the hierarchical arrangement of information-processes that have been postulated by the

7 See Piaget (1941, 1942a, 1945, 1947), Piaget & Inhelder (1948), and Inhelder & Piaget (1955).

programmers of electronic computers (Newell, Shaw, & Simon, 1958) and that are beginning to be found within the brain (Pribram, 1960). Consider now the observational basis for this developmental picture.

THE DEVELOPMENT OF INTELLIGENCE IN
THE SENSORIMOTOR PERIOD

As is true for organ structures in embryology, the transformations of sensorimotor schemata in the earlier periods are more radical and remarkable than those which come later. Piaget's (1936) observations begin at birth. The newborn human infant arrives with a number of sensorimotor organizations ready-made.[8] He sucks, looks at lights, vocalizes, listens to sounds, waves his limbs, and grasps what touches the palm of his hand. These are the ready-made schemata listed by Piaget, but he makes no pretense that it is a complete picture of the newborn's repertoire (see Pratt, 1954). The list need not be complete, for Piaget's concern centers in showing how the invariant adaptive functions combine with maturation to transform such reflexive schemata into intelligent actions.

Piaget's (1936, 1937) observations of development during the sensorimotor and symbolic periods were made on his own three children, Lucienne, Jacqueline, and Laurent. He finds six stages during the sensorimotor period:

1. Exercising the ready-made schemata (age range roughly 0 to one month).
2. Primary circular reactions: coordination of ready-made schemata to form motor habits and perceptions, no response to vanished object (age range roughly one to 4.5 months).
3. Secondary circular reactions: coordination of motor habits and perceptions to form intentional acts, development of prehension, beginning search for vanished objects, magico-phenomenalistic causality, and subjective time series (roughly 4.5 months to 8 or 9 months).
4. Coordination of secondary schemata: application of familiar schemata in new situations as means and as ends, active search for vanished object but no account of the sequence of visible displacements, elementary objectification of causality and time, beginnings of imitation of auditory and visual models (age range roughly 8 or 9 months to 11 or 12 months).
5. Tertiary circular reactions: discovery of new means through active

[8] Piaget is not concerned with the development of these ready-made schemata, but the observations of the development of behavior in chick embryos by Kuo (1932a to 1932e), to be reviewed in Chapter 8, indicate that a continuous organism-environment interaction is also involved during the still earlier phases of foetal and embryological development.

experimentation, interest in novelty, object permanence through sequences of visible displacements, systematic imitation of new models, appreciation of objective, spatial, causal, and temporal sequences (age range roughly 11 or 12 months to between 18 months and two years).

6. Internalization of sensorimotor schemata: invention of new means through mental combination, object permanence through invisible sequences of displacements, representative spatial, causal, and temporal series, beginnings of symbolic imitation (age range roughly 18 months to two years as the new preconceptual phase begins).

STAGE 1. EXERCISING THE READY-MADE SENSORIMOTOR SCHEMATA

The first transformation of the ready-made sensorimotor schemata consists in a shift from their passive release by stimulation to active groping on the part of the infant. This shift is most dramatic in the case of the sucking schema. Piaget observed sucking-like movements in his own three children almost immediately after birth. As soon as the infant's hand accidentally rubbed his lips in the course of activity, sucking was released. As children have long been observed to differ in their adaptation to the first meal at the breast, Piaget observed differences in his children. For Lucienne and Laurent contact of the lips with the nipple sufficed to release sucking, but Jacqueline was slower. The shift from passive response to active search shows most prominently in the sucking of Laurent. On the day after birth, he seized the nipple as soon as it touched his lips. By the third day, all he needed in order to begin groping actively with an open mouth for the nipple was to touch the smooth skin surrounding the nipple with his lips. On the other hand, when the nipple touched one cheek, he groped on the wrong side as well as on the correct side. By the twentieth day, although Laurent might attempt to suck the skin of the breast, he soon withdrew, began to cry, and then groped actively with his mouth for the nipple. By this time, he no longer made errors; a touch on the cheek immediately guided his groping toward the side touched, and he persisted in groping until he found the nipple and began swallowing.

These changes illustrate the first accommodations of the sucking schema that occur with practice and with variations in circumstances. The passive release of the sucking reflex by each contact changes to discriminative functioning. In the experienced child, as soon as sucking is not followed by swallowing, he stops sucking and begins an active search that goes on until his mouth finds the nipple and swallowing begins. The shift from passivity to active groping is thus accompanied by a crude response-based discrimination between breast and not-breast and a crude recognitory assimilation of the nipple which derives from this discrimination.

Such early changes are also characteristic but less dramatic for the other ready-made sensorimotor schemata. In the case of looking, perception of light exists from birth, as evidenced by the pupillary and eyelid reflexes. During the first week after birth, Piaget observed changes in Laurent's expression as luminous objects happened within his line of sight. The shift from passive release of looking to active search came early for him. From the sixth day, Laurent turned his head toward the window when he moved away from it as though seeking to continue the stimulation. By the end of the third week, Laurent followed a lighted match in a dimly lit room, and at 25 days of age, his head described an angle of 180 degrees as he followed the movement of a handkerchief brought within his view. Jacqueline and Lucienne also showed changes of expression at the sight of light, but they exhibited active following only toward the end of their first month.

Vocalizing and hearing are likewise present from birth. The newborn child cries almost immediately upon waking, but reflexive crying is complicated by the digestive rhythm and by the fact that the voices of others waken the child. The effects of adaptive accommodations and assimilations appear, however, as soon as it becomes possible to differentiate among hunger cries, anger cries, and the wailing which appears to be maintained for its own sake. Evidences of hearing come from changes in expression and from the cessation of crying as sounds occur.

Prehension, in the form of the grasping reflex, is likewise present at birth in the sense that the newborn closes his hand on anything that lightly touches his palm. At first grasping is unaccompanied by any search, but after use, as the child closes his hand around an object which touches his palm, he reveals the changes of expression that betoken interest. For instance, at 12 days of age, Laurent stopped crying when Piaget put his finger inside Laurent's palm. While prehension does not lend itself to systematic use immediately, impulsive movements of the arms, hands, and fingers are almost continuous during the first weeks. Yet Piaget observed no accommodation to objects or even any systematic continuity during the first month.

Piaget asks what accounts for this shift from passive responsiveness to active exercising of these ready-made schemata. His answer is assimilation, which he considers to be the fundamental fact of development. Various stimuli become assimilated into the reflexive schemata. Piaget (1936, p. 43) speaks of light as an aliment of the visual apparatus and of the looking schema. Riesen's (1947, 1958) discovery that the visual apparatus does not develop properly in chimpanzees that are reared in darkness suggests that Piaget's contention is no mere figure of speech. But beyond this physiological assimilation of light, Piaget argues that the assimilated exercise of functions brings its own inherent satisfaction and reinforcement of the function. He takes issue with the theoretical distinction between "need" and "function," and argues that a need for function, which is seen in an increasing tendency to repeat the action, increases as the organism exercises any schema. Such a conception of intrinsic reinforcement approximates the concept of "function pleasure" suggested by Karl Bühler (1928).

Important as is assimilation from Piaget's point of view, he argues that the environment is also indispensable to this development, for it is the groping search occasioned by varying circumstances that promotes the transformation of schemata, a point which is highly consonant with the concept of the TOTE unit of Miller, Galanter, & Pribram (1960) and its operation in the reinforcement. As Piaget writes, "without the previous contact with the nipple and the experience of imbibing milk, it is very likely that the eider-down quilt, the wool coverlet, or the parental index finger, after setting in motion the sucking reflex, would not have been so briskly rejected by Laurent" (1936, p. 32). These two complementary processes are not distinguishable at this first stage.

STAGE 2. PRIMARY CIRCULAR REACTIONS[9]

The second stage of sensorimotor development emerges in continuity with the modifications of the reflexive sensorimotor schemata in the first stage. The second stage is marked, first, when variations in the schemata themselves begin to appear as an increasing variety of stimuli become assimilated to them. Secondly, reciprocal coordinations among these schemata appear as the hand movements become coordinated with sucking, things heard become something to look at, things seen become something to reach for and grasp, and things grasped become something to suck. Third, repeated stimulation leads to perceptual recognitions.

[9] Piaget appears to have borrowed the concept of the "circular reaction" from J. Mark Baldwin (1906), whose observations of his own children also served as the basis for his theorizing about development and whose influence is apparent at several points in the work of Piaget. More descriptive than "circular reaction," however, is the term "reciprocal coordination" of schemata, and in the text below, the latter term has usually been used.

COORDINATIONS OF READY-MADE SCHEMATA. At about the beginning of the second month, Piaget observed variations in the sucking of his children. These activities occurred while the child manifested an expression of contentment. They included such acquired elaborations of sucking as the systematic protrusion of the tongue, which was accompanied later with licking the lips, actions with the saliva, and the sucking of the thumb. For instance, when Laurent was 30 days of age, Piaget observed him lying awake making sucking-like movements. Three days later, Laurent alternated between a sucking-like movement and passing his tongue over the lower lip. Two weeks later, his skill in this activity had increased, and he added grimacing as well as making a clapping sound when quickly closing his mouth after such exercises. Three more weeks, and Laurent added playing with his saliva, "letting it accumulate within his half-open lips and then abruptly swallowing it" (1936, pp. 51–52). A reciprocal coordination of arm movements and sucking came gradually. As the thumb and fingers came in contact with Laurent's face, his mouth grasped them. As thumb and fingers were thus discovered and rediscovered, a coordination between the arm movement and the sucking gradually emerged. In this process, the head could be observed to turn toward the hand, while the hand, in turn, moved irregularly toward the mouth. With repetition this coordination was perfected, and a circular response had resulted in an accommodative coordination of arm motion and thumb-sucking.

In the course of repeating routines, various positional, tactile, acoustic, and visual stimuli became assimilated into the ready-made schemata. These assimilations correspond to the phenomena of conditioning and stimulus generalization. For instance, by his ninth day, Laurent, who lay asleep in his crib, opened his mouth and began sucking the moment he was placed on his mother's bed. Later, being picked up by the nurse started both sucking and groping behavior. At three months of age, both Laurent and Lucienne stopped crying and made sucking motions at the sight of their mother unfastening her dress for nursing. At approximately five months, Jacqueline opened her mouth as soon as she saw the bottle. By seven months, she opened her mouth in one fashion at the sight of a bottle and in another fashion at the sight of a spoon. An accommodative differentiation was clearly evident.

A similar course of development appears for looking and its coordinations. Shortly after the child can follow a moving light by turning his head in coordination with his eye movements, objects of moderate brilliance are followed. At this point, Piaget observed his children staring at one object and then another for minutes at a time.

When such staring behavior was in evidence, sucking-like movements and arm movements were absent. Just as the sucking schema generalizes from the breast to assimilate various other objects and signals, the looking schema generalizes. When several objects were hung from the hood of the bassinet, Piaget's children alternately examined one after the other. When new sights appeared, such as having the toys on the hood of the bassinet shaken, they looked with excited expressions, and they would actively look again and again as if attempting to repeat the experience by returning their gaze to the hood.

Reciprocal coordination between looking and hand movements grew directly out of these acquired elaborations and generalizations of looking to new objects. Such watching coordinations came about gradually, as is illustrated in the following quoted observation:

Observation 62: At age two months and four days, Laurent by chance discovers his right index finger and looks at it briefly. At two months and 11 days, he inspects for a moment his right hand, perceived by chance. At two months 14 days, he looks three times in succession at his left hand and chiefly at his raised index finger. At two months 17 days, he follows the spontaneous movement of his hand for a moment, and then he examines it several times while it searches for his nose or rubs his eye. At two months 19 days (please note for subsequent reference), he smiles at the same hand after having contemplated it 11 times in succession. I then put his hand in a bandage; as soon as I detach it (half an hour later) it returns to the visual field and Laurent again smiles at it. The same day he looks very attentively at his two clasped hands. At age two months and 21 days, he holds his two fists in the air and looks at the left one, after which he slowly brings it towards his face and rubs his nose with it, and then his eyes. A moment later the left hand again approaches his face, he looks at it and touches his nose. He recommences and laughs five or six times in succession while moving the left hand to his nose. He seems to laugh before the hand moves, but looking has no influence on the movement. Age two months and 24 days: at last looking acts on the orientation of the hands which tend to remain in the visual field (1936, pp. 96–97).

In the course of this development, the visual schema has assimilated the manual schema. This is to say that the eye tries to follow what the hand does, but the hand appears not to realize what the eye sees. Gradually, the accommodative effort of trying to see the hand brings the hand under visual control, and the child is thereby enabled to grasp the objects he sees. Something looked at becomes something to grasp. Similarly, as arm movements and the sucking become coordinated, as already noted, anything grasped becomes something to suck.

A similar coordination occurs between hearing and looking. Sounds heard gradually become something to look at. Consider the following abridged course of observations of Jacqueline:

Observation 43: At age one month, Jacqueline still limits herself to interrupt-
ing her crying when she hears an agreeable voice or sound, but she does not try
to mark the sound. At one month, six days, same reaction. At one month 10
days, on the other hand, Jacqueline begins to smile at the voice . . . At two
months 12 days, Jacqueline turns her head to the side whence the sound comes.
For example, on hearing my voice behind her, she turns in the right direction.
At two months, 26 days, she localizes the source of sound quite accurately with
her glance. She searches until she finds the person who is speaking, but it is
difficult to say whether she identifies the source of the sound or whether this is
simply accommodation to the sound (1936, pp. 80–81).

REPETITION AND PERCEPTUAL RECOGNITION. These primary circular
reactions, which result in the generalizations of the ready-made schemata to new situations and into such habitual coordinations, result
also in complementary discriminations which Piaget calls *recognitory
assimilations*. A kind of recognition was observed early in connection
with sucking when non-nipple was differentiated from nipple as sucking was followed or not followed by swallowing. For the visual
schema, what begins as looking for the sake of looking gradually becomes transformed into "looking-in-order-to-see." As various objects
appear over and over, their assimilation to the scheme of looking is
evidenced by the fact that the child smiles when they appear (see
observation of Laurent and Jacqueline above), or shows through
some other variation in gesture or expression some evidence of the
coupling of perception with the differentiation of familiarity. Piaget
contends that although the smile may perhaps be a reflexive response
to pleasurable stimulation in general, it is a dependable sign of
recognition, which may itself be pleasurable at this stage. Although
various investigators have contended that the smile is strictly a social
reaction (Bühler, 1930, 1933; Spitz, 1946), Piaget records many instances in which his children smiled for other than social stimulation.
They smiled when the fringe on the hood of the bassinet shook even
though no person was in view. They smiled when familiar objects
were hung from the hood. They smiled at the sight of their own hands
coming before their eyes, and Laurent smiled after repeatedly finding
his nose with his fingers. In each of these instances, however, the
smile appeared only after the event had been repeated many times.
Recognition, thus appears to be a product of the familiarity which
derives from repetition, and at this stage, the recognitive familiarity
appears to give pleasure.

REALITY STILL SUBJECTIVE. At this second sensorimotor stage,
reality exists only as components in the child's functioning. Objects
have no permanence. For instance, the nipple endures no longer than
the process of sucking, as indicated by the fact that the child makes
no search for objects which have disappeared.

No general space exists. Piaget (1937) bases his organization of the spatial field upon the mathematical concept of the group, i.e., a closed circle of operations that returns to the point of departure through operation of the group as a whole. Geometrically, the concept of the group has been essential to the interpretation of space ever since Poincaré (1906) analyzed space into changes in the external world that can be corrected by movements which lead a perception back to its initial status. He thus distinguished changes of position from changes of state, for the latter cannot be corrected in this fashion. While Poincaré had considered such a distinction to be elementary, Piaget points out that a change of position may be distinguished from a change of state, first, only if the subject, in this case an infant under four-and-a-half months old, conceives of the external world as composed of permanent objects, and second, only if the subject distinguishes the external universe from personal activity, and third, only if the subject locates himself in a spatial field conceived as external to his body and independent of action. At this stage, none of these three conditions is present, so there must be a "buccal" or "oral" space, a visual space, an auditory space, a tactile space, etc. No basis for a general space exists.

Causality can hardly be more than a diffuse feeling of efficacy at this stage because the child is just beginning actively to follow objects with his eyes and to seek the source of sounds with his eyes, and to reach for what he sees. Piaget (1937) contends that this feeling of effort from such actions probably supplies the point of departure for causality.

Finally, time also has its point of origin in sequential expectation. Since the child turns to look for things heard and begins anticipatory sucking upon being picked up by the nurse, it is implied that he has at least some expectation that one perception will lead to another. On the other hand, the child has no appreciation of the past or the future; there is for him no "before" and no "after."

EXPERIENCE AND THE HAND-WATCHING SCHEMA. From its ongoing character during these first two stages, it is easy to see how various observers have considered development to consist of an automatic unfolding of response systems. In a sense, Dennis & Dennis (1941) are correct in speaking of these early coordinations as *autogenic*. Inasmuch as the child can move its arms and catch a view of its hands as they move by, the gradual development of visual control as prehension can occur without accommodations to outside variations in stimulation. On the other hand, this does not mean that development cannot suffer environmental interference or facilitation. For instance, Piaget comes near experimentation when he points out that Lucienne and Laurent began exhibiting the primary circular reaction of hand-watching at two months and four days, and two months and 16 days, respectively, whereas Jacqueline failed to exhibit this behavioral landmark until something after six months of age. Piaget contends that the delay in the case of Jacqueline is no matter of limited potential on her part. It was due simply to the fact that Jacqueline was born in the winter. She was kept out of doors in the sun as much as possible, and, for protection, her arms had to be encased in mittens and covers. She had, thus, no opportunity to develop the eye-hand coordination. Lucienne and Laurent, on the other hand, were born in the early summer when their hands could be free for exploration by the eyes, and father Jean was on hand to conduct his many "little experiments."

It is interesting to note what this temporal displacement of hand-watching would mean if it were used as an item for computing a developmental quotient (DQ). Inasmuch as approximately 75 per cent of babies show this hand-watching schema at about four months of age, it might properly be considered a four-month item. From this standpoint, one can readily see that the DQ for summer children, based on this schema, would be nearly 200 for Laurent ($DA/CA = 4/2 \times 100 = 2 \times 100 = 200$), and for Lucienne 160 ($DA/CA = 4/2.5 \times 100 = 160$). On the other hand, for winter-born Jacqueline, the DQ would be approximately 67 ($DA/CA = 4/6 \times 100 = 67$). Thus, the opportunities for functioning associated with such an accidental factor as season of birth may be seen as the basis for a very substantial variation in DQ (see also Pintner & Forlano, 1943). Moreover, opportunities for spontaneous exercise in these autogenous functions can be seen at any testing to make a tremendous difference. How permanent such differences may be is another matter.

In summary, the circular reactions of the second stage generalize the reflexive schemata, elaborate them, bring about their reciprocal intercoordination, or combination, and, through repetitive exposure to the same circumstances, bring about recognition which is marked by such changes of expression as the smile. Moreover, as the child continues to function, he becomes less and less engaged in passive responding and more and more engaged in active functioning.

STAGE 3. SECONDARY CIRCULAR REACTIONS

Although the exercise of the ready-made schemata during the first and second stages increases the child's tendency for active repetition of these activities, he remains basically a responder to stimulation. The earliest coordinations of arm movements with sucking, of vision with arm movements, of hearing with seeing, etc., are still but joint reciprocal coordinations of these reflexive schemata. On the other hand, as the movements which satisfy the sucking schemata come gradually to be sustained by the primary circular reactions of the second stage, and, as the child comes to recognize visually such phenomena as objects in motion and to discover a connection between these old activities and those motions, a reversal transformation takes place in which the child begins to show some anticipation of the consequences of his own acts. This reversal transformation arises from the fact that the coordinations of the schemata from the second stage become dissociated and regrouped in various ways. They acquire thereby much of the independence of the learning sets reported by Harlow (1949). Thus, two important developments occur at this third stage: first, the anticipation of effects, which epitomizes the beginnings of intentionality, and second, the beginnings of a distinction of means from ends. Moreover, from these developments, new bases for recognition appear. In the place of the reflexive smile, recognitive perceptions come to be acknowledged by schemata (action patterns) which have in the past been associated with the objects recognized.

INTENTION: A REVERSAL TRANSFORMATION. The first signs of this reversal transformation, which appears in what Piaget calls the secondary circular reactions, occurs when the child focuses upon some result produced in the external environment. At the beginning, intention appears in an apparent attempt to prolong or repeat the interesting perception. This is illustrated in the following quoted observation of Lucienne:

Observation 94: At age three months and five days, Lucienne shakes her bassinet by moving her legs violently (bending and unbending them, etc.), which makes the cloth dolls swing from the hood. Lucienne looks at them, smiling, and recommences at once. These movements appear simply to be the concomitants of joy . . . The next day, I present the dolls: Lucienne immediately moves, shakes her legs, but this time without smiling. Her interest seems intense and sustained. There also seems to be an intentional circular reaction . . . At age three months eight days, I find Lucienne swinging her dolls. An hour later I make them move slightly: Lucienne looks at them, smiles, stirs a little, then resumes looking at her hand as she was doing shortly before. A chance movement disturbs the dolls: Lucienne again looks at them and this time shakes herself with regularity. She stares at the dolls, barely smiles and moves her legs vigorously and thoroughly . . .

At three months 13 days, Lucienne looks at her hand with more coordination than usual. In her joy at seeing her hand come and go between her face and the pillow, she shakes herself in front of this hand as when faced by the dolls. Now this reaction of the shaking appears to remind her of the dolls which she looks at immediately as though she foresaw their movement . . . Her attention attaches itself to the dolls which she then shakes with regularity . . . At age three months 16 days, as soon as I suspend the dolls she immediately shakes them, without smiling, with precise and rhythmical movements with quite an interval between shakes . . . At four months four days, Lucienne in a new bassinet: she moves her loins violently in order to shake the hood. At four months 13 days, she moves her legs very rapidly while looking at the festoons on the bassinet hood: as soon as she sees them again, after a pause, she begins once more . . .

At four months 27 days, Lucienne is lying in her bassinet. I hang a doll from the hood over her feet. This immediately sets in motion the schema of shaking. Her feet reach the doll and give it a violent movement, which Lucienne surveys with delight. Afterwards she looks at her motionless foot for a second, then recommences . . . At four months 28 days, as soon as Lucienne sees the dolls she moves her feet. When I move the doll toward her face, she increases her movements . . . At five months and one day, when I raise the doll a little she resumes foot movements and even seems to regulate them. She gropes until she has felt contrast between her naked foot and the doll, then she increases the movement . . .

At five months 18 days, I place the doll at different heights, sometimes to the left sometimes to the right: Lucienne tries to reach it with her foot, and then, when she has succeeded, she shakes it. This schema is therefore definitely acquired and begins to be differentiated through accommodations to various situations (1936, pp. 157–59).

Thus, the secondary circular reactions become no longer a utilization of advantageous circumstances, but rather they bring definite actions to bear upon circumstances. In such illustrative items of behavior, which Piaget supplies with profusion, he sees the beginnings of the reversal transformation which provides the basis for *intention*. The specific accommodation of these secondary circular reactions is apparently the search of the child to rediscover what produced the interesting spectacle. With repetition, he comes to anticipate this interesting spectacle. It thereby becomes a kind of end or goal, and his own action becomes a kind of means. It is in this sense that end and means begin to be differentiated. This transitional pattern is familiar to everyone who has ever dandled an infant on his knee and felt the infant-initiated jouncing that starts whenever one's knee stops moving.

RECOGNITION AS OUTLINED ACTS. At this third stage, an advance occurs in recognition. Various objects have been assimilated into the secondary circular reactions which Piaget (1936) also calls habits. As in observation 94, quoted above, the sight of dolls hanging from the hood of Lucienne's bassinet has been assimilated into her leg-shaking in order to bring back the spectacle of the moving dolls. Whereas recognition is evident during the first two stages only in the sense that various circumstances evoke their characteristic responses (being picked up evokes sucking, a sound starts looking) or a smile, at this third stage various impressions come to be recognized by brief responses that merely outline the nature of the more complex habitual schemata into which they have been assimilated. Thus the meaning of an object has become assimilated. Recognition is manifested, not yet implicitly or mentally, but by a fore-shortened motor act. Consider the following series of observations of Lucienne which tie back to the one quoted immediately above:

Observation 107: At age five months three days, Lucienne tries to grasp a spool suspended above her by means of elastic bands . . . She manages to touch but not to grasp them. Having shaken them fortuitously, she then breaks off to shake herself a moment while looking at them, but then she resumes her attempts at grasping . . . Why has she broken off in order to shake herself a few seconds? It was not in order to shake the spool because she did not persevere and because she was busy with something else at the moment; neither was it in order to facilitate her attempts at grasping. Is it a question of a purely mechanical movement started by the sight of their chance swinging? It would seem so, but the rest of the observation shows that this behavior pattern was renewed too often to be automatic: it therefore certainly has a meaning . . . Everything transpires as though the subject, endowed for a moment with reflection and internal language, had said to herself something like this: "Yes, I see that this object could be swung, but it is not what I am looking for." But, lacking language, it is by working the schema that Lucienne expresses this "thought," before resuming her attempts to grasp. In this hypothesis, the short interlude of swinging would thus be equivalent to a sort of motor recognition.

Such an interpretation would remain completely hazardous when confronted by a single fact, but its probability increases along with the following observation. At age five months 10 days, Lucienne again relapses into states identical to those with the dolls. At age six months five days, she shakes herself several times in succession . . . It is an outline of some action suggested by this sight . . . At six months 12 days, Lucienne perceives from a distance two celluloid parrots attached to a chandelier. These she had sometimes had on the hood of her bassinet. As soon as she sees them, she definitely but briefly shakes her legs, but without trying to act upon them from a distance. This can only be a matter of motor recognition . . . At six months 19 days, she catches sight of her dolls from a distance (these are dolls which she had previously learned to swing with her hands) and it suffices for her to outline the movement of swinging them with her hand . . . At seven months 27 days, certain highly familiar situations no longer set in motion secondary circular reactions, but simply outlines of the schemata. Thus, when seeing a doll which she actually had swung many times, Lucienne limits herself to opening and closing her hands or shaking her legs, but very briefly and without real effort . . . It is only a sort of acknowledgment (1936, pp. 186–87).

This delightful series of observations appears to imply that the recognitory response becomes less and less complete and less and less overt as central processes take the place of peripheral motor processes. In his discussions of the origins of meaning, Osgood (1952) has hypothesized that such recognition by motor outline must occur in the development of the young. This need not necessarily mean that Piaget's observations favor Osgood's (1953) theory of mediational responses, which holds that they derive entirely from the overt responses which an organism has made to a situation, in preference to Hebb's (1949) hypothesis that central processes become established through repetitive perceptual experience. What Piaget's observations do suggest is that many of the recognitions manifested at the second stage by the smile may well be a product of repeated perceptual experience, while those of later stages which are manifested by brief motor responses derive from the schema into which the recognized object has been assimilated. Probably both kinds of processes go on continuously during these early stages of development but with the Hebbian perceptual process dominating the earlier stages and with the short-circuiting of motor responses predominating in later stages.

RECOGNITION AND BEGINNINGS OF RESPONSE TO THE STRANGE. With the motor recognition of various objects becoming fairly common at this third stage, the child begins to show some appreciation of strangeness, limited, however, to a kind of surprise and distress at the presence of unknown objects. Unless the discrepancy between the unknown object and familiar ones is too marked, the child attempts very shortly to employ it, like familiar objects, in one of his habitual schemata. An example of such a generalization may be seen in Laurent's behavior the first time he saw a paper knife. For Laurent at this point, all objects were something to be swung, shaken, or rubbed against the wicker side of his bassinet. Consider the following series of observations:

Observation 110: At three months and 29 days, Laurent sees for the first time the paper knife. He grasps and looks at it, but only for a moment. Afterwards he immediately swings it with his right hand as he does all objects grasped. He then rubs it by chance against the wicker of the bassinet and tries to produce the sound heard as though the knife were the rattle he has used for this purpose. It then suffices that I place the object in his left hand for him to shake it in the same fashion . . . The novelty of the object is therefore in no way interesting to the child except for that brief glance at the beginning. The paper knife from the onset was used as an aliment for the habitual schemata . . .

At four months eight days, I place a large rubber monkey in front of Laurent; the mobile limbs and tail as well as its expressive head constitute an absolutely new entity for him. Laurent reveals, in effect, lively astonishment and even a certain fright. But he calms down and then applies to the monkey some of the schemata which he uses to swing hanging objects; he shakes himself, strikes the monkey with his hand, etc., graduating his effort according to the result attained . . . At five months 25 days, I place an unfolded newspaper on the hood of Laurent's bassinet. He looks at it and immediately begins to pull the strings hanging from the hood, to shake himself, or his feet and arms. On seeing the movements of the newspaper, he bursts out laughing just as he frequently does when the rattle shakes (1936, pp. 197–98).

In these illustrations, the procedures acquired to repeat or prolong interesting spectacles are now generalized to each new, if not too discrepant, object that comes within the infant's purview. Inasmuch as these objects vary, each calls for an accommodation on the part of the infant, and this accommodation becomes assimilated as a variation in the schema. At this phase of development, the extent to which the child's secondary schemata become generalized and differentiated is a function of environmental opportunity. The greater the variety of objects and events there are to cope with, the more widely do the child's habitual schemata become generalized and the more differentiated do they become for purposes of recognition. In the sense that all these new objects are what Piaget terms aliments for the existing schemata, the stronger the habit organizations become, the more reinforcement there is for spontaneous activity, which, in turn, motivates the coordination of these secondary schemata and their application to new situations. This coordination then leads to the next stage. It is thus that environmental variety during the age period from three to eight or nine months can make for either slow or rapid development. Since tests can only sample the presence or absence of such schemata as exist at the moment of testing, this would mean that decrements and increments in variety of stimulation should be correlated with similar variations in DQ and IQ. So much for the story of intellectual operations.

ELEMENTARY CONSTRUCTIONS OF REALITY.

Object permanence. In the construction of reality, this third stage is also important. Objects begin to acquire permanence, for when they vanish, the infant exhibits an active search for the vanished object.

Such search may be merely a visual search, following the disappearance of an object from sight. Consider the following series of observations:

From Observation 6: At five months and 24 days, Laurent makes no attempt to follow with his eye any of the objects I drop in front of him . . . At six months three days, with Laurent lying down, I drop a box 5 cm. in diameter vertically and too fast for him to be able to follow the trajectory. His eyes search for it at once on the sofa on which he is lying . . . At seven months 29 days, Laurent searches the floor for everything I drop above him, if he has in the least perceived the beginning of the movement of falling (1937, pp. 14–15).

Such search indicates that the child imputes to the object an existence beyond his own immediate perception of it. On the other hand, at this stage the permance of the objects depends essentially on the child's own action. Although the series of illustrations just quoted shows Laurent searching for objects his father has dropped, at the beginnings of the stage the child responds with search more commonly when the child himself has lost an object he was grasping.

From Observation 14: At eight months 20 days, Jacqueline takes possession of my watch which I offer her while holding the chain in my hand. She examines the watch with great interest . . . I pull the chain; she feels the resistance and pulls back with force, but ends by letting it go. She does not try to look but holds out her arm, catches the watch again and brings it before her eyes . . . I recommence the game; she laughs at the resistance of the watch and still searches without looking. If I pull the object progressively, she searches further and further, but if I pull it back abruptly, she is content to explore the place where the watch departed, touching her bib, her sheet, etc. This permanence is solely a function of prehension. If, before her eyes, I hide the watch behind my hand, or behind the quilt, she does not react and forgets everything almost immediately (1937, p. 21).

Space as subjective groups. In the construction of the spatial field, stage 3 sees the development of subjective groups in the place of the various spaces (visual, buccal, tactile-kinesthetic, etc.). The coordination of looking with grasping and with sucking brings about the elaboration of a subjective group of displacements. Two acquisitions result: (*a*) In learning to use his hands to act upon things, the child begins to utilize the relationships among things themselves in place of the simple relations of things to his functioning organs; (*b*) as the child produces spatial displacements in the course of his manipulations of objects, he begins to watch himself act, and he observes his hands, his arms, and the contact of his hands with objects grasped. The evidence derives from the fact that the child tries to adjust the movements, or displacements, of his hand to those of the object. At the same time, he attempts to watch what he is doing. The following series of examples shows the development of such a subjective group:

From Observation 69: At six months, when Laurent lets a box escape him, he looks to left and right of his head, while searching for the object with his hand. But as he does not succeed in touching the box, he does not coordinate his glance with the movements of his hand . . . At six months and 30 days, Laurent lets go of a toy as he raises his arm (he is lying down). The toy falls to the level of his waist; he searches for it at once with his hand, lowers his forearm without displacing his arm (knocks the object as it happens to be located in the trajectory of his hand). Throughout this whole search his glance is aimed in the right direction, but he does not succeed in seeing the object. Next, Laurent loses the object on his left at the level of his hair; he searches for it simultaneously with his hand and by looking. But in trying to grasp it he gradually pushes it above his head. Although he is the cause of this movement, it does not occur to him that the object has been displaced. He continues to look for it where he saw it just before . . . At seven months 12 days, Laurent also coordinates his glance and his tactile search, the latter remaining independent of the former when the child cannot see the object but being oriented by it when the object is visible (1937, pp. 115–16).

At this third stage, the child also shows some appreciation of depth. In familiar situations, this shows in the child's discrimination between that which he can and that which he cannot grasp. When she was between six and seven months of age, Piaget confronted Jacqueline, lying on her back, with her favorite toy at a distance well beyond her reach. He then brought it closer to her gradually. Repeatedly, she stretched out her hand to grasp it only as the object entered the field of prehension. On the other hand, in unfamiliar situations the child may reach for things well beyond the limits of prehension. Piaget describes Jacqueline, at nine months 17 days, stretching out her hands toward the moon when she was carried out on the balcony in the evening. The space beyond the limits of the child's prehension Piaget (1937) considers analogous to the celestial space of an uninformed adult to whom the sky appears as a big spherical cover on whose surface the sun comes and goes and the moon and the stars move without depth. Historically, it was only through patient observation, interrelating the movements of these celestial objects from the fashion in which they masked each other, that men elaborated various subjective groups for the heavens. It was not until Copernicus formulated his image of the earth and the solar system that a constitution of objective groups was possible.

Causality as "magico-phenomenalistic efficacy." The concept of causality has its beginnings at this third stage, according to Piaget, as a kind of "magico-phenomenalistic efficacy." When Lucienne shook herself in her bassinet in order to sway her dolls hanging on the hood, the fact that she looked with anticipation at the dolls as she shook her legs indicates some appreciation of connection between her shaking and her perception of the doll's swaying. On the other hand, it implies no appreciation of how the shaking produces the swaying. In many instances, Piaget observed his children repeating acts associated with interesting spectacles, with no appreciation of the nature of the relationship:

From Observation 112: At seven months two days, Laurent is in the process of striking a cushion (striking is one of his favorite schemata) when I snap my middle finger against the ball of my thumb. Laurent then smiles and strikes the cushion again, but while staring at my hand rather than the cushion. As I no longer move, he strikes harder and harder, with a definite expression of expectation and, at the moment when I resume snapping my fingers, he stops as though he had achieved his object (1936, p. 202).

Similarly, Jacqueline pulled the strings hanging from the hood on her bassinet to continue the movement of a book or bottle that Piaget would swing at the proper time (1936, p. 202). Piaget argues that causality of this kind can be interpreted "only through the union of efficacy with phenomenalism.[10]

The time concept. Temporal appreciation remains completely subjective at this stage, yet there is some anticipation of future events and memory for past events. For instance, as Lucienne discovered that she could move the dolls on her bassinet by shaking her legs, she regulated these movements in time. She did not look at the dolls as if she expected them to move before she shook her legs. The movement of the dolls is therefore appreciated as a sequent of the shaking. Moreover, the first evidences of the permanence of the object implies some memory for localization in time. Piaget describes eight-month-old Laurent's reaction to seeing his mother enter the room and take a seat behind him. He resumed his playing, but turned around several times in succession to look at her again. Inasmuch as there was no sound to remind him of her presence, this behavior implies the beginning of memory. On the other hand, it is not a memory for objective sequences. This is shown by the fact that when Laurent's mother left her seat behind Laurent and disappeared through a door across the room, Laurent watched her disappear, yet turned immediately to look behind him in the place where she had been sitting. Thus, while there is memory for the place where he had seen her, there is no appreciation of the objective sequence of her crossing the room and disappearing through the door.

The beginnings of imitation. Imitation, or at least pseudo-imitation, appears first at this third stage, and it figures in the child's construction of causality. The first imitations occur with a kind of training as follows:

From Observation 18: At five months and nine days, Lucienne put out her tongue several times. Each time, I also did so. She then showed great interest, put out her own as soon as I pulled mine back, and so on. She behaved as though her action (of which she was aware through the sensations of her lips and tongue) constituted an "effective device" for making my action, of which she was only aware visually, continue. It was thus a case of pseudo-imitation based on perception of a connection between her action and mine . . . After a moment's interruption, when I resumed my suggestion, Lucienne again began putting out her tongue . . . but on the next day my stimulus produced no reaction whatever . . .

At five months and 21 days, Lucienne made a noise with her saliva. I imitated the noise, and she imitated me in her turn, again putting out her tongue

[10] Dr. Rogers Elliott objects to characterizing such phenomenalistic efficacy as *magical.* In striking the cushion to get father Jean to snap his fingers, he says, Laurent is using the only probabilities to which he has access. Only after experiencing many incongruities will he gradually build a more articulated conception of causal relations; his present one may be immature but it is not magical.

. . . but an hour later, as well as on following days, nothing remained of the association (1945, p. 28).

In such instances of pseudo-imitation, the child is apparently using the imitated schema to prolong a spectacle because it corresponds to what the child is already doing.

Persons often constitute interesting spectacles. As the child develops schemata that he utilizes to prolong and repeat spectacles, he tries them out on people. Whenever an adult whistles, sings, or snaps the finger, the cessation of such action tends to start the infant's repertoire of procedures. In this sense he may cause the other person to continue with his interesting action. From the standpoint of causality, therefore, both his imitative efforts and his procedures involve the same mixture of efficacy and phenomenalism already described. This is magico-phenomenalistic causality.

Thus, the reversal transformation which brings about the beginning of intention brings with it also these several elementary constructions of reality.

STAGE 4. COORDINATION OF THE SECONDARY SCHEMATA

SEPARATION OF MEANS AND ENDS. At eight or nine months of age, the child typically begins to show behavior in which means are definitely differentiated from ends. Piaget's (1936) discovery of this fact provides a correction for the widely held belief that means and ends are inherently separate. Such a belief is common to most modern psychological theories. The functional school (Dewey, 1896; Angell, 1907) always distinguished between the organism's need and the action taken to meet that need. Freud (1915) clearly distinguished the aim from the mode and the object of his *Trieben*. Modern behavior theory distinguishes between goal and instrumental act and also between the constructs of drive and habit (Hull, 1943; Sears, 1944). Although these distinctions are constructions by observers, they have led to the presumption that a functional separation exists inherently from the beginning. One of the merits of Piaget's observations of his first two stages is the showing that a schema is indeed an organized, Gestalt-like unit. Beginning in the third stage, a separation of means and end begins to become apparent in the child's action, but the end lies outside him and is fortuitous. Only the means lies within his own action. On the other hand, with intercoordination of the secondary schemata into action systems wherein one schema serves as the end and the other schema serves as the means, this separation is definite and complete. This transformation marks the beginning of the fourth stage. Thereafter, the child's action is no longer a simple repetition of either ready-made schemata or coordinated schemata. It is rather the subsuming of a series of schemata which serve as means, under one schema which serves as the end. Very commonly the earliest goal schema is prehension. Here are several of Piaget's illustrative observations. First, a transitional example which differs but slightly from those of stage 3:

> *From Observation* 120: At six months one day, Laurent tries to grasp a piece of paper that I offer him. I finally place it on the hood of his bassinet. Laurent begins by stretching out his hands. As soon as the object is placed, he reacts as he always does in the presence of distant objects: he shakes himself, waves his arms, etc. I regulate the situation by removing the paper from the hood for a few seconds in order to move it progressively closer and further away. It is when the paper seems inaccessible to the hand that Laurent shakes himself. After having thus behaved for a moment, he seems to look for the string hanging from the hood with which he had learned to shake various objects. He pulls it harder and harder while staring at the paper. At the moment when the paper is ready to fall from the hood, Laurent lets go of the string and reaches for the paper of which he immediately takes possession. Several subsequent attempts yielded the same result. It goes without saying that it cannot be demonstrated that Laurent pulled the string in order to grasp the paper, but the whole behavior pattern gave me the impression of being performed with this end in view, and of being perfectly coordinated (1936, p. 214).

Another illustration for which the interpretation is clearer:

> *Observation* 121: At age eight months 20 days, Jacqueline tries to grasp the cigarette case which I present to her. I then slide it between the cross strings which attach her dolls to the hood. She tries to reach it directly. Not succeeding, she immediately looks at the strings which are not in her hands and of which she sees only the part in which the cigarette case is entangled. She looks in front of her, grasps the strings, pulls and shakes them. The cigarette case falls and she grasps it . . . Second experiment: same reactions but without trying to grasp the object directly (1936, p. 215).

This means-end distinction within pattern of action becomes even clearer when an obstacle is placed between the child and the goal object. Consider the following series of observations in which Laurent learns to strike an obstacle in order to grasp an object, and then modifies his striking schema to one of pushing the obstacle away.

> *From Observation* 122: When he is six months of age, I present Laurent with a match box, extending my other hand laterally to make an obstacle to his prehension. Laurent tries to pass over my hand or to the side, but he does not attempt to displace it . . . Same reactions at age six months eight days, six months 10 days, six months 21 days, and seven months 10 days . . .
> Finally, at seven months 13 days, Laurent reacts quite differently. I present a box of matches above my obstacle hand, but behind it, so that he cannot reach the matches without sending the obstacle aside. After trying to take no notice of it, Laurent suddenly hits my obstacle hand as though to remove or lower it. I let him lower the hand, and he grasps the box . . . I recommence to bar his

passage, but I use as a screen a sufficiently supple cushion to keep the impress of the child's gestures. Laurent tries to reach the box, and, bothered by the obstacle, he at once strikes it, definitely lowering it until the way is clear . . .
With Laurent seven months and 17 days old, I resume the experiment without previous intervening attempts. I present my watch 10 cm. behind the cushion (the watch of course being visible). Laurent tries at first just to grasp the watch, then pauses to hit the cushion . . . With Laurent age seven months 28 days, instead of simply hitting the things which intercede between his hand and the object, Laurent applies himself to pushing them away or even to displacing. I present him a little bell 5 cm. behind the csuhion. Laurent first strikes the cushion, as previously, but then depresses it with one hand while he grasps the object with the other. He shows the same reaction when I use my hand as an obstacle. At age seven months 29 days, he immediately depresses the cushion with his left hand in order to reach the match box with his right. At eight months one day, when my hand intervenes with the obstacle, I definitely feel that he depresses it and pushes harder and harder to overcome my resistance . . . At eight months 28 days, he pushes my hand away with his left hand while pulling at the rattle I hold with his right (1936, pp. 217–19).

As pushing proves more effective in eliminating obstacles than striking, Laurent accommodates his striking to pushing. Moreover, the means-end distinction and the fact of intention are clear.

Thus, in thousands of repetitious variations of this class of behavior, the child gradually adapts or accommodates his old schemata as means to achieve other, also old, schemata which, in various instances, become ends. In the process, the accommodations modify the old schemata. They are generalized to new situations, and the means-end relationships become more and more sharply differentiated. In such behavior, Piaget points out that the adaptive accommodation is always double because it involves a relationship between at least two acts of assimilation. The first of these is the choice and pursuit of the end or goal; the second is the adjustment of the means to the goal involved. This is the beginning of truly intelligent behavior as Piaget (1936) conceives it.

NEW EMPHASIS ON ACCOMMODATION. The fact that even this primitive intelligent adaptation is always double brings about something distinctly new in the developmental process. It increases the emphasis on accommodation. So long as means and ends are one, as in the case of the exercise of the ready-made schemata and the primary circular reactions (bringing the hand to the mouth for sucking, reaching for what is seen, and looking toward what is heard), accommodation has a relatively minor role. It occurs only as the schemata must be modified to variations in the situation. Inasmuch as the objects are part of the act, the child makes little effort to put things themselves into relationships. Such an effort derives from the fact that obstacles arise between the intended goal and its realization.

The obstacle requires the use of intermediate means, and the means must be adapted to both the goal of the action and the nature of the obstacle. It is thus that obstacles become assimilated to familiar schemata in the same fashion that the object of the action is assimilated to the schema of the goal. Piaget (1936) illustrates this double adaptation as follows:

> *From Observation* 130: At age 10 months and three days, Laurent utilizes as a "means" or a transitional schema, a behavior pattern which he discovered the previous day . . . In manipulating a tin for shaving cream he learned to let this object fall intentionally. Now, I give it to him again. He at once begins to open his hand to make it fall and to repeat this behavior a number of times. I then place a large wash basin 15 cm. from Laurent and I strike the interior of it with the tin in order to make Laurent hear the sound of the metal against this object. Already at nine months, Laurent had, while being washed, by chance struck a small pot against such a basin and immediately played at reproducing the sound by a simple circular reaction. I therefore wanted to see if Laurent was going to use the tin to repeat the phenomena and how he was going to go about it . . . Now, at once, Laurent takes possession of the tin, holds out his arm and drops it over the basin. I move the basin, as a check. He nevertheless·succeeded, several times in succession, in making the object fall on the basin. Hence this is a fine example of the coordination of two schemata of which the first serves as "means" whereas the second assigns an end to the action: the schema of "relinquishing the object" [serves as means] and that of "striking one object against another" [becomes the goal] (1936, p. 225).

The repeated business of directing the fall of objects in a particular way in order to make them strike something or pushing obstacles away in order to grasp other objects, supplies one basis for the elaboration of "kinds" or classes of objects. For instance, it is these groupings and regroupings of objects in connection with such means-end operations which gradually yield such relationship concepts as "like" and "opposite." Moreover, in such a context, the child begins to discover the universe independent of himself, and thereby to discriminate the "me" from the "not-me."

In addition to these discriminations whose importance is central for the construction of reality, this grouping and regrouping of objects as means and as ends brings a substantial increase in capacity for intelligent behavior. Such capacity depends upon the readiness of a child's schemata to be differentiated and intercooordinated into new patterns. Such readiness Piaget (1936) conceives to be a function of the mobility of the schemata; that is to say, in their becoming detached from their limited contents to become applicable to a growing number of objects. The repeated dissociations and regrouping of intentional means-end operations promote differentiation and mobility. The degree of differentiated mobility is largely a function of the number of repetitions which the various schemata have had in a variety of situations. The correspondence between Piaget's conception of a mobile schema and Harlow's (1949) conception of a "learning set" is striking.

DEVELOPMENT IN RECOGNITION. Recognition becomes, at this fourth stage, a genuine recognition of sign meanings. Each of Piaget's stages brings a characteristic type of meaning. At the first reflexive stage, the child recognizes whether he is merely sucking the skin of the breast or is really nursing the nipple by whether or not he is getting milk and swallowing. At the second stage, the recognition of sensory impressions is indicated by their evoking the act which they signify or by a smile. At the third stage, the recognition of an object may be shown by the child merely outlining the schema with which it is assimilated. At this fourth stage, the child's behavior indicates that he foresees an event which is quite independent of his own action. Consider these illustrations:

> *Observation* 134: At age nine months 16 days, Jacqueline discovers complex signs in connection with her meal. She likes the grape juice in the glass, but not the soup in a bowl. She watches her mother's activity. When the spoon comes out of the glass she opens her mouth wide, whereas when the spoon comes from the bowl, her mouth remains closed. Her mother tried to lead her to make a mistake by taking a spoon from the bowl and passing it by the glass before offering it to Jacqueline. But she is not fooled . . . At age nine months 18 days, Jacqueline no longer needs to look at the spoon. She notes by the sound whether the spoonful comes from the glass or the bowl and obstinately closes her mouth in the latter case . . .
>
> At age 11 months 15 days, Jacqueline cries as soon as her mother puts her hat on. This is not due to fear of the strangeness of seeing mother in a hat, but is due rather to the fact that "mother in a hat" signifies that mother is departing (1936, pp. 249–50).

In both of these instances, Jacqueline's behavior indicates that she recognizes what is coming even though the spoon and mother-in-a-hat have nothing to do with her own actions-in-progress at the time these signs are perceived.

The child's behavior in relation to phenomena which are new to him changes at this fourth stage. Whereas, at the beginning of the third stage a new obstacle only served to arrest his activity until such time as the child could find a way to utilize the object as an aliment for his habitual schemata, the child now not only looks at new objects for a much longer time, but he also engages in a series of exploratory movements relating to the object rather than to himself. Consider these illustrations from Laurent's behavior:

> *From Observation* 137: At eight months and 29 days, Laurent examines at length an (unfamiliar) notebook which he has just grasped. He transfers it from one hand to the other while turning it in all directions, touches the cover, then

one of the corners, then the cover again and finally the edge. Afterwards, he shakes himself, shakes his head while looking at it, rubs it against the side of the bassinet. He then observes that in rubbing against the wicker, the notebook does not produce the usual effect (sound? consistency?) and examines the contact most attentively while rubbing more gently.

At nine months six days, Laurent examines a series of new objects which I present in sequence: a wooden figure of a man with movable feet, a wooden toucan 7 cm. high, a match box case, a wooden element (10 cm. long) and a beaded purse. I observe for quite constant reactions. In the first place, a long visual exploration: Laurent looks at the objects which are at first immobile, and then looks at them very rapidly while transferring them from one hand to the other. He seems to study their various surfaces or perspectives . . . Second, after the visual exploration a tactile exploration begins. He feels the object, especially the toucan's beak, the little man's feet, and gently passes his finger over the unevenness of the object . . . he scratches certain places. Third, he slowly moves the objects in space: chiefly movements perpendicular to his glance but already perhaps desired displacements in depth. Fourth, only at last does he try the various familiar schemata, using them each in turn with a sort of proof as though studying effects produced. He shakes them, strikes them, swings them, rubs them against the bassinet, draws himself up, shakes his head, sucks them, etc. (1936, pp. 254–55).

In this last observation, Laurent feels and explores the surface and possible uses of the unfamiliar objects as if they represented an external reality. Such unfamiliar objects are now something to which the child accommodates himself; they are no longer simple aliments for his own ready-made activities.

CONTRIBUTIONS TO THE CONSTRUCTION OF REALITY

Object permanence. The groupings and regrouping of objects in connection with the various means-end operations, with their focusing of the child's attention on the reality external to himself, lead him to several new constructions of reality. The groupings and regroupings yield gradually such relationship concepts as "like" and "opposite." This discovery of a universe independent of himself in turn leads gradually to a discrimination between the "me" and the "not-me." Here, at about eight or nine months of age, the object begins to have a permanence of its own. This is indicated by the fact that the child begins to search for objects which depart from his perceptual field. This search for the vanished objects is limited. Piaget has devised a special procedure to test the persistence of search in a sequence of object displacements. He hides an object at a point A and allows the child to search for it and find it. After the child has found it twice at A, the object is hidden in a second spot B. The movements of the object to both A and B are perfectly visible to the child. At this stage, even though the child watches the object and sees it disappear at *B*, he nevertheless immediately tries to find it at *A*. Consider the following observations:

From Observation 44: At nine months and 17 days, Laurent is placed on a sofa between a coverlet *A* on the right and a wool garment *B* on the left. I place my watch under *A*; he gently raises the coverlet, perceives part of the object, uncovers it, and grasps it. The same thing happens a second time. I then place the watch under *B*; Laurent watches this maneuver attentively, but at the moment the watch has disappeared under garment *B*, he turns back toward the coverlet *A* and searches for the object under that screen. I again place the watch under *B*; he again searches for it under *A* . . . (1957, p. 53).

From Observation 40: At age 10 months, 18 days, Jacqueline is seated on a mattress without anything to disturb or distract her (no coverlets, etc.). I take a parrot from her hands and hide it twice in succession under the mattress, at her left, in *A*. Both times Jacqueline looks for the object immediately and grabs it. Then I take it from her hands and move it very slowly before her eyes to the corresponding place on her right, under the matress, in *B*. Jacqueline watches this movement very attentively, but at the moment when the parrot disappears in *B* she turns to her left and looks where it was before in *A* . . . During the next four attempts I hide the parrot in *B* every time without having first placed it in *A*. Everytime Jacqueline watches me attentively. Nevertheless each time she immediately tries to rediscover the object in *A* . . . (1957, p. 51).

It is interesting to note that this test of Piaget's corresponds almost precisely to the "orientation tests" employed by Thompson & Heron (1954) with their dogs. The behavior of adult dogs reared in the relative isolation of laboratory cages corresponds closely to that of Piaget's children at stage 4. The permanence and unity of the object is limited. Occasionally this may lead to curiously inconsistent behavior. In another instance, Lucienne and her mother were in the garden. As Piaget arrived, Lucienne saw her father and smiled. Lucienne's mother then asked, "Where's papa?" Even though her father stood almost within reach and Lucienne was smiling at him in recognition, the question prompted her immediately to turn back toward the house, and she pointed toward her father's office where she was accustomed to seeing him. At this fourth stage of development, even though the child appreciates that the object has disappeared and searches for it, it lacks unity. Thus, for Lucienne, there can both be "papa-approaching" and "papa-in-his-office" at the same time.

The concept of space. The construction of space shows progress. As objects in various positions participate, now as means and now as ends, in the child's various schemata, the child's central processes become sufficiently autonomous to give objectivity not only to the perceived object itself, but also to permit the child to form the beginnings of objective groups of spatial placements. The evidence for the objective groups lies in a pattern of behavior characteristic of the child of between nine and 10 months of age. It consists in his moving his head laterally in front of an immobile object so as to examine its various perspectives. These are some of Piaget's observations:

From Observation 88: At age eight months and 26 days, Laurent is in his bassinet. He leans to the side in order to look at the corner of the room. He remains motionless for a few seconds, and then straightens up very slowly . . . In his hammock, he pauses to lean over and from that position to examine the chandelier, the big table, etc. . . . But he does not yet seem to vary the perspective; he merely leans to the right and the left and remains motionless while looking at the object. At nine months 16 days, on the other hand, Laurent leans alternately to the left and right with a pause between the two positions. This reaction becomes increasingly frequent during the following weeks . . . (1937, p. 159).

From Observation 89: At nine months eight days, Lucienne looks at the objects (hanging rattles, bassinet hood, etc.) and bends her head slowly from side to side while studying in detail the effect produced . . . (1937, p. 159).

From Observation 91: At 11 months 23 days, Jacqueline is in her baby swing and perceives her foot through one of the two openings for the use of the legs. She looks at it with great interest and visible astonishment, then stops looking to lean over the edge and discover her foot from the outside. Afterwards she returns to the opening and looks at the same foot from this perspective. She alternates this five or six times between the two points of view. [Apparently the child is discovering a reversible process: by moving he can make an object look one way and by moving back he can retrieve the original perspective.] (1937, pp. 159–60).

At this fourth stage, the child can also reverse the side of an object. For instance, when Laurent, aged eight months and six days, is handed his bottle upside down, he makes no attempt to turn the nipple in toward him. But, by age nine months and 10 days, he no longer tries to suck the wrong end, but "immediately displaces the wrong end with a quick stroke of his hand, while *looking beforehand in the direction of the nipple*" (1937, p. 163). Thus, the child has discovered a reversible operation for his manipulation of objects as well as for visual positions. In these reversible operations, the child emerges, as Piaget puts it, from his solipsism. Even so, he cannot recognize positions and displacements as relative to one another, but only relative to himself. In this sense, his spatial field remains egocentric.

The concept of causality. An implicit conception of causality emerges also which is separate from the effort and phenomenalism of personal activity. For instance, when Jacqueline pushes away her father's hand that stands as an obstacle to her grasping her duck, the behavior indicates that external objects are appreciated, after a fashion, as sources of action. This is also implied when Lucienne pushes away the hand that offers unpleasant soup. Similarly, the fact that the child of this age begins to look to someone else to obtain what interests him indicates that his own actions are no longer the sole source of causality. Moreover, through the coordination and progressive adjustment of means and ends, the child comes to objectify causality in the sense that he no longer participates at the outset in actions he is watching but rather waits to let things happen, as if he considered them as unpredictable and even fearful.

Piaget (1937) finds an elementary appreciation of objective temporal sequence at this fourth stage. This is implicit in the child's searching for vanished objects which he has seen hidden. Moreover, this is the first evidence of memory for a sequence in which the child has played no active role.

IMITATION, PLAY, AND THE ORIGINS OF SYMBOLIC IMAGERY.

Symbolic imagery, along with the development of intelligence and the construction of reality, is a third product of the child's continuous interaction with the environment. Piaget (1945) has been led from his observations to conceive of symbolic imagery as deriving from imitation, seen as almost pure accommodation, and from play, seen as almost pure assimilation. During the first two sensorimotor stages, accommodation and assimilation are inseparable. Accommodation occurs as the child must modify his schemata to incorporate into them the various objects that his environment contains. How much he must accommodate is a function of the richness of his environment. Assimilation occurs simultaneously with his accommodations and with repetition of the modified schemata. During the second stage, the beginnings of imitation appear as the child becomes capable of coordinating the movements of his hands with his vision, and then simultaneously gets the power of imitating certain movements of other hands. Such pseudo-imitation also occurs for vocalization and vision. In the case of the former, as an adult imitates a sound which the child has made, the child redoubles his effort in making that sound. Similarly, in the case of vision, the child may repeat movements which have occurred while he was following an object with his eyes. Play likewise has beginnings during these first two stages in the sense that the child repeats various schemata over and over without making any effort at accommodation and, apparently, merely for the inherent pleasure of exercising his capacities, i.e., the "function-pleasure" of Bühler (1928). At stage 3, however, imitative accommodation and playful assimilation begin to be differentiated in the child's activity. Pseudo-imitation becomes more common as the child begins to repeat after others those sounds and movements which he has already made and seen. Similarly, playful assimilations of the "procedures for prolonging an interesting spectacle" come to be carried out merely for the amusement of what Piaget (1945, p. 92) characterizes as the "pleasure of being the cause."

Imitation. The differentiation of imitative accommodation and playful assimilation becomes more complete at this fourth stage. Genuine imitation appears. The child begins to imitate movements which he has already made but has, of course, never seen. In such cases, the child must match his own familiar movements that he has never seen to those which he sees in the model. Piaget (1945, pp. 41 ff.) finds such a coordination mediated by way of what he calls "indices." Indices are mobile signs, "detached from the action underway, which make it possible for the child to anticipate the immediate future and to reconstruct the recent past." Consider the following observation, in which Jacqueline learned to imitate a certain movement of the lips through hearing the sound of saliva which served to mediate matching her own movements to those of her father:

From Observation 19: At eight months and four days, Jacqueline was moving her lips as she bit on her jaws. I did the same thing, and she stopped and watched me attentively. When I stopped, she began again. I imitated her, she stopped again and so it went on. In contrast to what occurred earlier (the pseudo-imitations of stage three) Jacqueline again began to imitate me an hour later, and on the next day without her having made the movement immediately before . . .

In order to understand this new development, two circumstances must be noted. Firstly, for some days she had not merely imitated sounds for their own sake, but had watched the mouth of the model with great attention . . . Secondly, as she moved her lips, Jacqueline began by making a slight noise with her saliva as a result of the friction of her lips with her teeth, and I had imitated this sound at the onset. Her interest in the movements of the mouth was thus clearly due to interest in the production of sound. Later, I resumed the experiment without making any sound, and without Jacqueline herself having made the movement beforehand. She watched my lips moving, and then distinctly imitated me three times, keeping her eyes fixed on my mouth. The same evening there was a similar reaction. She showed the same interest and was obviously "trying to see what would happen." She moved her lips, at first slowly and timidly, and then more boldly as if she were testing the efficacy of the procedure. On the following days, the suggestion of the model continued to be effective (1945, pp. 30–31).

At stage 4, the child also begins to imitate new auditory and visual models. In these imitations, the child responds to the model with a schema only roughly analogous to that exhibited by the model as is shown by the child's mistakes. In successive attempts at imitation, the child's accommodation shows as his responses become gradually more similar to those of the model. Consider the following observations of imitative vocalizations by Jacqueline and Lucienne:

From Observation 32: At eight months eight days, i.e., a few days after she first imitated movements not visible to herself, Jacqueline reacted for the first time to a sound which was new to her . . . When I said the sound "gaga" it gave rise to a sustained effort. Jacqueline said "mama," then "aha," then, "baba," "vava," and finally "papa." . . .
During this stage, at nine months and 28 days, Lucienne also made quite definite efforts, but with little success, to reproduce sounds new to her. For instance, she reacted to the phoneme "papa" with the following sounds "aha" . . . "dada" . . . "gaga" . . . "tata." She needed many tentative efforts in order to arrive at "papa." On the following days, her reaction to the model was almost always "atata." It was only at ten months eight days that she made a serious effort to react correctly (1945, p. 46).

Similarly, Piaget put out his tongue, part of his mouth, and Jacqueline assimilated the model to her own schema involving the same organ, namely, by biting her lips. When Piaget opened and closed his eyes, Lucienne got the motion by opening and closing her mouth, but missed the organ. In such attempts to imitate, the child's mistakes illustrate the mechanism, but his progressive approximation of the model shows the accommodative nature of imitation.

Imitation and interest in the novel (curiosity). Piaget (1945) takes pains to point out that the child's interest in new models is part of his beginning differentiation between the subjective and the objective. At stage 3, and early in stage 4, his interest in objects is subjective in the sense that they are merely to be incorporated into his habitual schemata; "interest is merely the affective aspect of assimilation" (1945, p. 50). As the child's schemata become more and more differentiated and mobile, however, and as the objects and models that confront the child become at least partially independent realities, new models become interesting. This interest appears to be a kind of conflict between the resemblance, which prompts the child to assimilate what he perceives, and the difference between the model and his own schema that attracts his attention the more because it is an obstacle to immediate reproduction (1945, p. 51). Models too remote from the child's experience leave him indifferent. It is thus that interest in new or novel models is a continuation of the pseudo-imitation of the familiar. It is also thus that the child's interest in the novel is increased by the degree to which he has been forced to accommodate to a variety of stimuli during his first six or eight months of life. The early actions of the environment on the organism thereby carry over into the spontaneous motivations of later states. How permanently they do remains as a problem for investigation.[11]

Play. Playful assimilation becomes marked, at this fourth stage, by the absence of either imitative accommodation or intelligent efforts to define objects by their use. Once the child has applied a known schema to a new situation, he may continue it "for the pleasure of the activity and without any effort at adaptation to achieve a definite end." Consider the following observation:

> *Observation 61:* At seven months and 13 days, Laurent, after learning to push away an obstacle in order to gain his objective, began to enjoy this kind of exercise. When several times in succession I put my hand or a piece of cardboard between him and the toy he desired, he reached the stage of momentarily forgetting the toy and pushed aside the obstacle, bursting into laughter. What had been intelligent adaptation had thus become play, through transfer of interest to the action itself, regardless of its aim (1945, p. 292).

Moreover, the increased mobility of schemata at the fourth stage permits the child to form playful combinations. The child goes from one schema to another without any effort of adaptation. He no longer tries them out successively on a new object, but merely indulges in a "happy display of known actions." Consider the following observation:

> *Observation 62:* At nine months and three days, Jacqueline was sitting in her cot and I hung her celluloid duck above her. She pulled a string hanging from

[11] Although the problem of the development of motivation as such lies outside the scope of this discussion and has been left for another book now in preparation, Piaget's (1945) observations indicate that the motives of interest and curiosity are inherent in intelligent activities. Moreover, his observations of the origins of the child's interest in the novel are strikingly close to those upon which Hebb (1949) based his notion that it is those central processes which are as yet "incomplete that dominate attention." Piaget's observations are also strikingly similar to Berlyne's (1960) conflict theory of curiosity and attention. What Piaget (1936, 1945) adds is a picture of the developmental origins of such motivation in the continuous interaction of the child with his environment. Piaget's theory of interest in the novel as the motive for imitation, however, differs markedly from the motive for imitation assumed by Miller & Dollard (1941) and that which Mowrer (1950) developed as the mechanism for imitative talking in birds. These latter investigators have conceived the motivation for imitation to be extrinsic to the action imitated and to derive from dependency needs which have developed as the model became a sign that homeostatic needs are shortly to be satisfied. Because the model has been associated with being fed, it is presumed to have maximum capacity for secondary reinforcement. The imitator's first approximations become gradually more and more like the model in order to maximize this anticipation of satisfaction. On the contrary, Piaget's conception of the basic motivation for imitation puts that imitation inherently in the child's developing sensorimotor patterns themselves, yet he also notes (1945, chap. iii) that the child typically imitates those people to whom he is emotionally attached. As in the case of sucking, noted above in connection with the discussions of stage 1, it would appear that both of these kinds of motivation, one inherent in the use of schemata themselves and one which derives extrinsically from gratification, are genuine factors.

the top of the cot and in this way shook the duck for a moment, laughing. Her involuntary movements left an impression on her eiderdown; she then forgot the duck, pulled the eiderdown towards her and moved the whole of it with her feet and arms. As the top of the cot was also being shaken, she looked at it, stretched up and then fell back heavily, shaking the whole cot. After doing this some ten times, Jacqueline again noticed her duck: she then grasped the doll also hanging from the top of the cot and went on shaking it, which made the duck swing. Then noticing the movement of her hands, she let everything go, so as to clasp them and shake them . . . Then she pulled a pillow from under her head, and having shaken it, struck it hard and struck the sides of the cot and the doll with it. As she was holding the pillow, she noticed the fringe, which she began to suck. This action, which reminded her of what she did everyday before going to sleep, caused her to lie down on her side in a position of sleep, holding the corner of the fringe and sucking her thumb. This, however, did not last for half a minute, and Jacqueline resumed her earlier activity (1945, p. 93).

In the latter portion of this observation, Jacqueline goes from aimless combinations to "ritualization." She goes through the ritual of actions that she usually uses when going to sleep (lies down, sucks her thumb, holds the fringe). In such ritualizations, Piaget sees the preparation for symbolic games.

Stage 4, then, contains another major set of transitions. Means and ends are separated; objects acquire permanence; space, causality, and time begin to have objectivity; interest in the new or novel begins, which, in turn, motivates imitation of unfamiliar models; these new achievements are assimilated in playful repetitions. At this fourth stage, moreover, imitative accommodation becomes differentiated from playful assimilation, and in combination these two processes lead to the development of images, i.e., central processes symbolizing concrete actions.

STAGE 5. THE TERTIARY CIRCULAR REACTIONS

Beginning about the end of the first year, Piaget observed in his children that the secondary circular reactions of the third stage and their intercoordinations of the fourth stage become, in turn, intercoordinated in what he calls the "tertiary circular reactions." In these reactions, some new spectacle is not only reproduced and prolonged, but the infant also begins to modify his movements, and to modify them in progressively more deliberate fashion. In the course of this process, two major landmarks of transition appear in the structure of the child's behavior, and these distinguish the fifth stage. One is the shift of attention from the spectacle *per se* to the movements that the child initiates in the objects he manipulates and to the variations in these movements that he can produce. This discovery appears to bring about an interest in novelty for itself. In turn, the developing interest in novelty gives rise to the curiosity that motivates a continuing process of growth and change in the child's central processes and in his relationship to his environment. The discovery of deliberate variation also leads gradually to the groping of trial and error, or to what Piaget calls "a discovery of new means through active experimentation." With these developments the child begins to imitate unfamiliar models and to repeat his imitations in ritualistic games that approach "make believe" play. As these modifications take place, the elaboration of reality continues. Objects become more permanent, and space, time, and causality begin to achieve some objectivity.

This transformation comes about through gradual transitions among secondary circular reactions, tertiary circular reactions, and, finally, active experimentation. The following series of observations of Laurent's play with the white metal case for soap illustrates these transitions:

From Observations 141, 140: This first example will make us understand the transition between secondary and "tertiary reactions": that of the well-known behavior pattern by means of which the child explores distant space and constructs his representation of movement, the behavior pattern of letting-go or throwing objects in order subsequently to pick them up (1936, p. 268).

At age 10 months and two days, Laurent examines an empty white metal case for shaving soap which he sees for the first time. He begins by turning it in all directions while passing it from one hand to the other as he does characteristically with objects. But the object, being slippery and hard to handle, slips from his hand two or three times. Then, struck by this phenomenon, Laurent applies himself to reproducing it a certain number of times. At first I had some difficulty in deciding whether it was indeed an intentional act for Laurent began each time by holding the case for a moment and turning it over before letting it go. But then it fell more and more frequently and above all systematically . . . What interests Laurent at the beginning of this behavior pattern is not the trajectory of the object—that is to say the objective phenomenon of its fall—but the very act of letting it go. Sometimes Laurent delicately opens his hand, and the case rolls along his fingers, sometimes Laurent turns his hand over and the case falls backward between the thumb and index finger which are separated, sometimes Laurent simply opens his hand and the object falls . . .

For several days, Laurent only utilized this schema of relinquishing in connection with the same object, the case for shaving soap, but on the fifth day, he twice lets fall a small bottle (new to him) which falls from his hand fortuitously at first, then he begins to throw everything to the ground . . . (1936, p. 258).

At 10 months 10 days (after some 10 days of such behavior), the reaction changes and becomes "tertiary." That day Laurent manipulates a small piece of bread (without any alimentary interest) and lets it go continually. He even breaks off fragments which he lets drop. Now, in contradistinction to what has happened on the preceding days, he pays no attention to the act of letting go, whereas he watches with great interest the body in motion; in particular he looks at it for a long time when it has fallen, and picks it up when he can . . . Next day, Laurent is lying on his back but nevertheless resumes his experiments of the day before. He grasps in succession a celluloid swan, a box, etc., stretches out his arm and lets them fall. He distinctly varies the positions of the falls. Sometimes he stretches out his arm vertically, sometimes he holds it obliquely, in front of or behind his eyes, etc. When the object falls in a new position, he lets it fall two or three times more on the same place, as though to study the spatial relation; then he modifies the situation. At a certain moment the swan falls nears his mouth: now, he does not suck it (even though this object habitually serves this purpose) but drops it three times more while merely making the gesture of opening his mouth . . . Next day, Laurent lets go of a series of objects while varying the conditions in order to study their fall. He is seated in an oval basket and lets the object fall over the edge, sometimes to the right, sometimes to the left, in different positions. Each time he tries to recapture the object, leaning over and twisting himself around, even when the object falls 40 or 50 cm. away from him. He especially tries to find the object again when it rolls under the edge of the basket and hence cannot be seen [implying permanence of the object] (1936, pp. 268–69).

In these observations, Laurent starts by applying his available schemata to the new object, discovers accidentally the new means of "letting-go," becomes interested in the motion of the object which is dropped, and then varies the dropping act until it becomes throwing, while he observes with growing interest the effects of his throwing efforts upon the trajectory of the object. This throwing schema is well known. It is a landmark in children's development much like the hand-watching of stage 2 and the procedures to continue and repeat interesting experiences at stage 3. Dropping and throwing, which in the terms of Dennis (1941) may be seen as autogenous in the sense that they require no teaching from other people, appear to be useless activity to mothers concerned with the orderliness of their habitation, but to the child they provide a new surge of interest. Through them, he learns about the relationship between variations in his own effort-of-action and what happens in space to the object dropped or thrown. Dropping and throwing constitute but one of the child's various manipulative schemata, of course; he can also roll objects, slide them, press them, and mouth them.

Origin of Interest in Novelty (*Curiosity*). What marks the onset of this fifth stage is the shift in the child's attention to what happens to the object. This transition is but a gradual continuation of the trends toward greater autonomy and spontaneity in the child as he assimilates more and more objects and toward the differentiation of subjective assimilation of objects and objective accommodation to them and their relationships. In the early stages, external objects are only something to be seen, heard, grasped, etc. The child's activity is thus essentially conservative, and environmental novelties are accommodated only as they are imposed. The primary and secondary circular reactions are progressively coordinated and differentiated only by the variety of stimulation imposed by the environment acting upon the child. As the infant's schemata become more and more differentiated and more and more mobile, however, he tries to prolong and repeat objective spectacles (stage 3) and then to understand them by fitting them into his repertoire of procedures. As this effort to assimilate leads to the discovery of object properties and relationships which cannot be reduced to his own schemata, accommodation becomes differentiated from assimilation (1) as an interest in novelty or curiosity (Berlyne, 1960), (2) as search for new means, and (3) as imitation of the unfamiliar.

The correspondence here between the observations of Hebb and Piaget should be noted. Hebb (1946) has noted that chimpanzees are quite uninterested in objects with which they have had no experience, especially if those objects are unlike any they know. Moreover, from noting the monotony that derives gradually from repetition of given interactions with the environment, and also the evidences of interest in change or novelty, Hebb (1949, p. 229) derives the principle that one "would find behavior dominated always by the thought process that is not *fully* organized—one that is achieving a new organization or one in which synaptic decay makes it necessary that organization be reachieved." Correspondingly, Piaget (1936, pp. 274 ff.) has noted in the behavior of his children that new objects or phenomena with no connection with schemata already assimilated were of no interest. They could arouse nothing in the child because they have never been assimilated. But objects or phenomena which are almost assimilable arouse an interest and an attempt at accommodation which is greater than if they were assimilable immediately (1936, p. 276). It is thus that the variety of objects and phenomena experienced during the first four stages influences the rate with which intelligence develops at this fifth stage. As Piaget puts it:

The more complex this system of schemata of assimilation, the greater the interest in novelty in general. New events have the more opportunities of animating at least one particular schema according as the ensemble of the schemata formed is large . . . We have already stated something similar in connection with vision: the more objects the child sees the more new ones he wishes to see. But, in the latter case, accommodation only forms one entity in the generalizing extension of an assimilatory schema, whereas henceforth accommodation exists before every true assimilation, and this accommodation is simply set in motion by earlier assimilations without being directly derived from them. With regard to interest in the external result of acts, characteristic of the secondary circular reactions, it is also sooner or later a source of accommodation for the sake of accommodation (1936, pp. 276–77).

Such considerations explain how variety of stimulation during the early months of infancy can have an enduring effect upon development later. They explain nicely the apathy in orphanage children who have experienced minimal variety of stimulation during their early months (Skeels & Dye, 1939; Spitz, 1945, 1946; Dennis, 1960). Piaget's conceptions go beyond those of Skeels & Dye in explaining the meaning of "richness of the environment" and its action on the infant human being. His conception of the nature of the causal factor also differs markedly from that of Spitz. It is not so much a lack of a personal relationship with a mother figure, as emphasized by Spitz, but rather the fact that such institutional children have been confined to narrow limits of space, have had few objects to examine and explore, and have had little variety of external stimulation thrust upon them to force early accommodations during the first several months of life; hence their failure to develop and differentiate that variety of schemata which contain inherently within them the basis for interest. Almost anything outside their small range of familiar circumstances is so foreign to the schemata that these orphanage children have developed that they can show only apathy or fear.[12]

DISCOVERY OF NEW MEANS THROUGH ACTIVE EXPERIMENTATION. Active experimentation is commonly motivated by the child's developing interest in novelty, and it leads to the discovery of new means. This process is to the tertiary circular reactions what the application of familiar means to new situations was to the secondary circular reactions. In these activities, the child begins to manifest the constructive, original element characteristic of intelligence, an element that is completely missed in the assumption of predetermined development and that is also largely missed in the stimulus-response theory of behavior.

One of the first manifestations of this original, constructive, discovering intelligence that Piaget observed in his children was what

---

[12] It is interesting to use Piaget's conception to account for the resistance met by such observations as those of Skeels & Dye (1939) on the improvement in intelligence-test performance of the children from orphanages who were put into feebleminded institutions and taken care of by adult moron inmates. So long as the conceptual scheme of intelligence holds that it is fixed, that it develops as an automatic consequence of the unfolding of neural and somatic structures, such observations cannot be assimilated. Moreover, insofar as a theory, or conceptual schema, acquires value in itself, effort toward what Piaget calls accommodation is inhibited, and the observer either ignores or denies the facts themselves. This is to say that skepticism becomes so rigid that it approximates denial. It is also interesting in this connection to recall Conant's (1951) point that negative evidence, by itself, seldom destroys a theory. A theory in science is only destroyed when a new one is created to take its place. This implies that the trick in fostering the development of new knowledge in science is to find evidence that is just close enough in its implications to an existing theory to suggest modifications in it and thereby to become assimilated. Evidence too contradictory can only be ignored or denied.

he calls "the behavior pattern of the support." Consider the following series of observations:

From Observation 148: Until age 10 months and 16 days, Laurent has not understood the relation "placed upon," hence the relation existing between an object and its support . . . Numerous experiments repeated between ages seven months and 29 days and 10 months and 16 days have revealed that Laurent, until the later date, has remained incapable of utilizing it systematically. At seven months and 29 days, he succeeded, once in four attempts, in drawing a cushion toward him in order to grasp a box placed upon it; at eight months and one day he behaves in the same way . . . But there it is still only a question of a coordination of schemata, analogous to that of the fourth stage. Being unable to grasp the box directly, the child instead takes possession of the first object encountered, while subordinating this act to the persisting desire to attain the objective. The proof in this case is the existence of the following reactions: . . . when I hold the objective in the air, 20 cm. above the support, Laurent pulls the latter toward him just as though the object were placed upon it . . .

At age 10 months 16 days, on the other hand, Laurent discovers the true relations between the support and the objective and consequently the possibility of using the former to draw the latter toward him. Here are the child's reactions:

(1) I place my watch on a big red cushion and place the cushion directly in front of the child. Laurent tries to reach the watch directly and not succeeding, he grabs the cushion which he draws toward him as before. But then, instead of letting go of the support at once, as he has hitherto done, in order to try to grasp the objective, he recommences with obvious interest, to move the cushion while looking at the watch. Everything takes place as though he noticed for the first time the relation for its own sake and studied it as such. He thus easily succeeds in grasping the watch.

(2) I then immediately attempt the following counterproof. I put two colored cushions in front of the child, of identical form and dimensions. The first is placed as before, directly in front of the child. The second is placed behind, at an angle of 45 degrees, that is to say, so that the corner of the cushion is opposite the child. This corner is placed on the first cushion but I manage to flatten the two cushions at this place, where one is partially superimposed on the other, so that the second does not protrude and is not too visible. Finally I place my watch at the other extreme end of the second cushion. Laurent, as soon as he sees the watch, stretches out his hands, then grasps the first cushion which he pulls toward him by degrees. Then, observing that the watch does not move, he examines the place where the one cushion is superimposed on the other, and he goes straight to the second one. He grasps it by the corner, pulls it toward him over the first cushion, and takes the watch. The experiment, when repeated, yields the same result the second time.

(3) I now place the two cushions next to each other, the proximal side of the second parallel to the distal side of the first. But I superimpose the first on the second on a strip about 20 cm. wide, the watch of course being at the extremity of the second cushion. Laurent immediately pulls the first cushion but, observing that the watch is not displaced, he tries to raise this cushion to reach the second one. At a certain moment he has succeeded in raising the first cushion, but without removing it, and he holds it against his chest with his left hand while trying to pull the second one with his right hand. He finally suc-

ceeds and takes possession of the watch, thus revealing his perfect comprehension of the role of the support.

(4) Finally I place the second cushion as in (2) but sidewise, the proximal corner of the second superimposed on one of the distal corners of the first. Laurent does not make a mistake, and at once tries to reach the second cushion. These four reactions combined reveal that the relationship between the objective and its support has been acquired (1936, pp. 282–84).

This observation epitomizes what Piaget means in his own methodology by an "experiment," namely, the varying of circumstances to make certain that a given interpretation is correct.

In his observations of such groping behavior wherein various schemata are subordinated as means to other schemata as ends, Piaget (1936) notes repeatedly how those elements which have no connection with the end are gradually eliminated. This observation corresponds to Thorndike's (1911) observation of the gradual elimination of unsuccessful responses in his chickens and cats in puzzle boxes and to Osgood's (1953) point that the "heavy" elements of response are gradually eliminated. It also corresponds to Hebb's (1949) short-circuiting among phase sequences as actions become autonomous central processes. Although Piaget sometimes uses the term *trial-and-error* to describe such groping behavior, he rejects the concept of trial-and-error because, in his observations of his children in past situations, he has seen that the so-called "error responses" are actually schemata which they have used in a variety of earlier situations. The trying of one already assimilated response after another on unfamiliar objects, which Piaget terms *groping accommodation,* was characteristic of the fourth stage. From the developmental perspective, in addition to the view of the change in an organism's behavior while seeking one given end, Piaget sees this groping directed by the schemata already established, as did Krechevsky (1933) in his conception of rat "hypotheses."

Related patterns commonly discovered through such groping behavior are the "pattern of the string," in which the child learns to pull and lift objects by means of string when they lie outside his reach, and the "pattern of the stick," which involves the use of an instrument. Consider the use of the stick in the following example:

From Observation 157, 158: At age 12 months and five days, Lucienne already possesses the "behavior pattern of the support," and I try to determine, the same day, if she is capable of that of the stick . . . Lucienne is playing with a very elongated cover which can fulfill a stick's function; with it she hits the tiers of her table, the arms of her chair, etc. Then I place before her, but out of reach, a small green bottle for which she immediately has a strong desire. She tries to grasp it with outstretched hands, struggles vigorously, wails, but does not have the idea of using the cover as a stick. I then place the cover between her and the bottle; same lack of comprehension. Then I place the bottle at the end of the cover; Lucienne pulls the cover to her and grasps the bottle. Then I again put the bottle out of reach, but this time I place the cover next to the object and at the child's disposal; nevertheless it does not occur to Lucienne to use it as a stick.

At 13 months seven days, Lucienne happens to make a notable discovery: while playing at hitting a pail with a stick she is holding (all this without preliminary goals) she sees the pail move at each blow and then tries to displace the object. She strikes it more or less obliquely to augment the movement and does this many times, but she does not utilize this finding to bring the pail toward her nor to move it in a certain direction.

At 16 months, Lucienne is seated opposite a sofa on which is placed a small aluminum flask. Next to it lies the same stick as before with which she amused herself in recent weeks, using it to hit objects and the floor, but without progress since she was 14 months and seven days old. At first, she tries to grasp the flask directly, with her right hand. Not succeeding she takes the stick. This behavior constitutes an important novelty: the stick is no longer only utilized when it is already in hand, it is sought for its own sake. Moreover, having grasped it by the middle and observing, after trying it out, that it is not long enough, Lucienne switches it to her other hand, and then takes it again in her right hand, this time by the end. But the rest of the observation shows that the stick is not just grasped with the purpose of pushing the flask; Lucienne merely hits the object and this does not authorize us to envisage that as prevision of its falling. The flask, however, falls and Lucienne picks it up. It is clear that the desire to obtain the flask aroused the schema of striking by means of the stick, but one cannot therefore see in this behavior pattern a procedure already adapted to the particulars of the situation.

A moment later, on the other hand, I place the flask on the floor, 50 cm. away from Lucienne. She begins by wanting to grasp it directly, then she takes the stick and hits it. The flask moves a little. Then Lucienne, most attentively, pushes it from left to right by means of the stick. The flask is thus brought nearer. Lucienne again tries to grasp it directly, then takes the stick again, pushes it once more, this time from right to left, always bringing the object toward her. Delighted, she grasps it, and succeeds in all subsequent attempts . . . (1936, pp. 297–99).

Similar observations are described for Jacqueline.

It will be recalled that Birch (1945) and Jackson (1942) found that this behavior of the stick does not appear in chimpanzees who had not previously been observed to play with sticks and who had not exhibited the behavior before they were presented with a problem in which it was required (see Chapter 4). Like the "behavior of the support" and the "behavior of the string," the "behavior of the stick" here emerges gradually as a differentiation of earlier schemata in the course of groping and active experimentation. It is not a sudden reconstruction such as the Gestalt psychologists have claimed. On the other hand, in children or chimpanzees who have learned several such schemata as the "relation of support" and "the behavior of the string" and who have also definitely internalized them as autonomous central processes, the "behavior of the stick" might well be invented as a kind of generalization of such previously "learned sets" (see Laurent's invention below).

IMITATION OF UNFAMILIAR MODELS; VERBAL IMITATION. With the development of an interest in novelty comes a systematic imitation of new models. Moreover, just as the child becomes capable of experimenting in order to discover new means, his imitation of new models goes beyond mere application and accommodation of existing schemata to accommodation through systematic groping. This shows in both the imitation of movements and in the field of verbal imitation. Consider this example of verbal imitation, for it is precisely at this fifth stage that children begin actively to imitate meaningful sounds that are new to them and which are typically words in adult speech.

From Observation 41: At 15 months and 18 days, for instance, in response to the word *parti*, Jacqueline said *papeu*, perhaps through analogy with *papa*. Afterwards, on her own account, she said *papeu*, when people went out of the room or when things came to an end, and gradually she corrected it to *pati* (1945, p. 54).

Especially interesting are imitations of new movements connected with parts of the body which are not visible to the child. In the case of such invisible movements, it is no longer sufficient for the child to try out various known schemata. The child proceeds by experimentation, and imitation thus becomes a kind of systematic and differentiated accommodation which tends to modify schemata with respect to objects as distinct from accommodations which are inherent in intelligent activities. Consider the following series of observations:

Observation 43: Jacqueline has succeeded in imitating certain familiar movements connected with the mouth, nose, eyes, and ears because she had a tactual knowledge of these organs, and was thus able by means of a system of "indices" to make her own movements correspond with those of the model. During the same period (stage 4), I tried to make her imitate new models. The simplest movement I attempted was to make her put her hand on her forehead, either anywhere, or at certain precise spots. This does not seem to be one of the actions the child makes spontaneously . . . Up to 11 months and 11 days, there was no attempt to imitate any movement connected with the hair or forehead. On that day, however, when I put my hand on my head, Jacqueline raised her hand and seemed to be feeling in the right direction. There was no reaction as far as the forehead was concerned.

At 11 months and 20 days, Jacqueline watched me with great interest when I touched my forehead with my forefinger. She then put her right forefinger on her left eye, and moved it over her eye brow, then rubbed the left side of her forehead with the back of her hand, but as if she were looking for something else. She reached her ear, but came back towards her eye.

At 11 months and 23 days, she rubbed her right eye doubtfully when I touched my forehead, watching me carefully as she did so. Once or twice she went a little above her eye brow, but then came back to her eye. At 11 months and 24 days, same reaction. At 11 months and 26 days, she three times touched the sides of her forehead above her eyes, but never the center. The rest of the time she merely rubbed her eye.

At 11 months and 28 days, Jacqueline, confronted with the model, continued merely to rub her eye and eye brow. But afterwards, when I seized a lock of my hair and moved it about my temple, she succeeded in imitating me. She suddenly took her hand from her eye brow which she was touching, felt above it, found her hair and took hold of it, quite deliberately.

At 11 months and 30 days, she at once pulled her hair when I pulled mine. She also touched her head when I did so, but when I rubbed my forehead she gave up . . . At 12 months and 16 days, Jacqueline discovered her forehead. When I touched the middle of mine, she first rubbed her eye, then felt above it and touched her hair, after which she brought her hand down a little and finally put her fingers on her forehead. On the following days she at once succeeded in imitating this gesture . . . (1945, pp. 55–56).

Thus the imitation of the fifth stage, compared to that of the previous stages, shows analogous progress. The reproduction of new movements of invisible portions of the body demands systematic experiment and something analogous to the discovery of new tools. In the case of Jacqueline attempting to locate her forehead, she started from her eye, which she knew, and then groped about, touching first her ear, then her hair, realizing that she had not reached her objective. Presumably it was acquaintance with the smooth surface of her cheeks that gave her a guide for recognizing her forehead. It was probably acquaintance with silky and woolly objects that enabled her to recognize the correspondence between feeling her hair and seeing her father's hair.

ELABORATIONS OF REALITY.

Object permanence through sequential displacements. The increased interest in novelty, the "discovery of new means through experimentation," and imitative groping all lead to an increasingly rapid elaboration of reality as the child experiments actively with the new. Objects acquire an increasing degree of permanence as shown by the fact that the child begins to take full account of sequential displacements that he can observe. For instance, in the standard test situation of hiding an object twice in the first position (*A*) and then shifting to a second position (*B*), the child of approximately 12 to 14 months of age readily takes account of a varied series of the visible placements of objects. Consider the following observation:

From Observation 54: At 11 months 22 days, Laurent is seated between two cushions, *A* and *B*. I hide my watch alternately under each: Laurent constantly searches for the object where it has just disappeared, that is, sometimes under

A, and sometimes under B, without remaining attached to the first, privileged position as during the fourth stage . . . At 12 months and 20 days, he also searches sequentially in both my hands for a button I am hiding. Afterward he tries to see behind me when I make the button roll on the floor (on which I am seated), even though, to fool him, I hold out my two closed hands (1937, p. 67).

On the other hand, at stage 5 the child does not succeed in following displacements if any one of them is invisible. For instance, when Jacqueline is 18 months old, Piaget takes a potato with which she is interested in playing. He puts it into an empty box, then turns the box upside down under the rug. He leaves the potato hidden under the rug without letting the child see the maneuver. He then hands the empty box to Jacqueline and asks for the potato. She searches for the potato in the box, looks at her father, looks again at the box, looks at the rug, but it fails to occur to her to raise the rug in order to find the potato underneath. Thus, she and her brother and sister, at this stage, succeeded in keeping track only of the visible displacements. This following of sequences of displacements implies an increased degree of permanence of the object over that found in stage 4. Presumably this increased permanence results from central processes becoming more autonomous with experience. This conclusion is implied by the fact that the pet-reared dogs of Thompson & Heron (1954) also followed sequences of displacements of food objects whereas those cage-reared in relative isolation returned repeatedly to the first placement as do children at the fourth stage.

The child's attempts to discover new means through active experimentation serve at once to bring out other limitations in the child's conception of the object at this stage and also to show how these are in the process of being corrected. Consider one example, that of Jacqueline trying to find how to draw sticks and other objects through the bars of her playpen. The varied attempts correspond in many ways to the so-called trial-and-error behavior of animals in laboratory problems. This observation is interesting in that it illustrates her lack of appreciation of the qualities of resistance and substantially in the vertical bars of her playpen; it illustrates also how the attempts to discover new means through active experimentation gradually correct these defects of Jacqueline's perception.

From Observation 162: At 15 months and 12 days, Jacqueline is seated in her playpen whose four sides are formed by vertical bars connected at base and summit by horizontal bars. The bars are six cm. apart. Outside the pen, parallel to the side where Jacqueline is, I place a stick 20 cm. long which takes up the distance of about three spaces between the bars. We shall call these spaces *a, b,* and *c,* and space *b* corresponding to the middle part of the stick . . . (1) Jacqueline begins by grasping the stick through space *b.* She raises it along the bars but holds it horizontally and parallel to the frame so that the harder she pulls the less it moves. She then extends her other hand through c, but holds the stick horizontally and does not succeed in making it come through. She finally lets go of the object which I put back in its initial position.

(2) Jacqueline begins over again by graping the stick at c. In raising it, she tilts it up a little, by chance, and so makes it slightly oblique. She immediately takes advantage of what she perceives and, passing her hand through c, she tilts the stick until it is sufficiently vertical to pass through. She then brings it into the playpen through b. Why did she tilt it up? Was it through foresight or did she simply extend the movement which was due to chance so as to see what would happen?

(3–4) This time Jacqueline grasps the stick through space c at one of its ends. She draws it horizontally against the bars, but encountering resistance from them, she quickly makes it vertical and passes it through without difficulty. The speed of this adaptation is due to the fact that the stick was grasped by one of its ends.

(5) Jacqueline grasps the stick by the middle, at b. She raises it, puts it horizontally against the bars as in (1). She pulls and seems very surprised by a failure. It is only after a while that she tilts it and succeeds in bringing it in.

(6–10) Same reactions. At each new attempt, she begins by trying to make it penetrate horizontally . . . Only after this initial failure does she tilt up the stick, still quite slowly.

(11) This time Jacqueline turns the stick more rapidly because she grasps it at c.

(12–15) She again grasps it at b and recommences to try to bring it through horizontally. Then she tilts it up, more slowly than at (11) and succeeds.

(16) She continues to take it at b and to try to pull it through horizontally, but this time she does not persist and tilts it up immediately.

(17) For the first time Jacqueline tilts the stick before it has touched the bar, and no longer tries to bring it in horizontally even though she grasped it at the middle.

(18–19) She begins by trying to bring it through horizontally, but it seems that this was due to automatism and she tilts it up immediately afterwards.

(20 et seq.) She finally turns it systematically before it touches the bars.

At 15 months and 13 days, Jacqueline, in the same experiment, but complicated by a stick 55 cm. long: too long to pass vertically between the bars of the play pen which is 50 cm. high. Ten attempts were enough to enable her to solve the problem: (1) Jacqueline grasps the stick at b, raises it horizontally and pulls against the bars with all her strength and then displaces it unsystematically, raises it and all at once brings it through by chance without having understood how she did it.

(2) This time she grasps the stick at a, pulls it horizontally against the bars as hard as she can . . . then gives up.

(3–5) In each case she begins by pulling horizontally, and ends by bringing it through accidentally.

(6) Same beginnings. The stick is held at the top by the edge of the frame and at the bottom by Jacqueline's dress which is pressed against the lower edge of the pen. Jacqueline then watches both ends of the stick attentively, then raises it gently to disengage it from her dress. She then brings it in slowly by the bottom part and then pulls until she has been completely successful.

(7) First she grasps the stick at a, applies it horizontally and pulls. Then she

grasps it with the other hand at c and brings it through by raising it first and then pulling it by the lower part as before (6).

(8) Jacqueline succeeds at once this time, almost without pulling the stick against the bars.

(9) She grasps it with the wrong hand (too high to be able to pull it through the lower part). She immediately switches to the other hand and succeeds at once.

10) Immediate success without groping and without first touching the bars.

At 15 months 15 days, Jacqueline fails at the first attempt with the 50 cm. stick, but on the second attempt, she rediscovers the combined two acts of tilting up the stick and bringing it in by the lower part.

At age 16 months, after an interruption of several days, she relapses into her former mistakes, but then succeeds (1936, pp. 305–7).

Piaget continued this experiment, presenting Jacqueline first a book and then a doll too wide to push through the bars, and a cardboard rooster. In each case she proceeded by pulling against the bar and only through a gradual process of successive modifications did she learn to bring the object through, but, as is the case with Harlow's (1949) various "learning sets," in each instance the discovery of the correct procedure was more rapid than the previous one. Presumably she gradually learned to attribute resistance and substantiality to perceived bars.

In observing Jacqueline pulling sticks through bars of the playpen, Piaget asks whether the solution comes (1) by the chance selection of trial-and-error, the Thorndikian hypothesis; (2) by reorganization of the perceptual field, the Gestalt hypothesis; or (3) by an assimilation of a modification in the structure of activity which did not exist from the start. Piaget rejects the first alternative because he sees in such behavior as Jacqueline's a progressive, creative comprehension analogous to that which can be observed in adults who grasp little by little the essentials of a problem and who come to a clear picture only after considerable groping. False solutions reappear only because the outline of the correct solution remains too weak to counterbalance the influence of the old schemata being applied in the new situation. He rejects the second, Gestalt alternative on the ground that it is by functioning that the schema becomes structured; this solution is no mere reorganization of natively given brain fields. Visual perception, for instance, plays only a secondary role in such behavior patterns at the beginning because sensorimotor experience has not yet conferred upon the child's perception of vertical bars those qualities of resistance and substantiality which later permit the child to anticipate that pulling against them would be to no avail. It is thus that Piaget considers it wrong to speak of a sudden reorganization of the perceptual field independent of restructuring assimilatory activity, because "it is the action which fashions the field of perception and not the reverse" (1936, p. 314).[13] It is presumably through such experiences as Jacqueline's in Observation 162 that central processes are created which mediate the permanence, substantiality, and other characteristics of objects just as it is presumably also the central processes derived from such experiences that permit a child or a dog to see an object as permanent through a sequence of displacements.

Elaborations of causality. The very existence of imitation implies a new level of objectification of causality. Moreover, acts of imitation foster the objectification of causality. In trying to repeat what others do, the child both discovers his own limitations and learns to attribute to others the power that he lacks. This is indicated by the fact that Piaget's children began at this fifth stage to request that their parents do various things for them (e.g., opening boxes, reaching objects, pushing things away) that they could not do for themselves. Some of the various new means discovered are basically causal in character. The "relation of an object to its support," the "behavior of the string" and of the stick all imply that the child no longer "assumes" that his own activity is the center of the world. They indicate rather that the child takes account of at least some of the relations between the body and things and some of the relations among things.

Elaborations of time. During the fifth stage, time also ceases to be merely a necessary aspect of an action or a perception, and, interconnected with physical causality, space, and the permanence of the object, time becomes an objective sequence of external events. Similarly, since the child structures his activities in sequences, the implicit concepts of *before* and *after* are no longer limited to his acts but are applied also as displacements which are perceived, foreseen, and remembered (1937, pp. 341–45).

DIFFERENTIATION OF PLAY. Play becomes more obviously differentiated as essentially pure assimilation which insures the transition from the "happy display of aimless actions" of stage 4 to symbolic or make-believe play of stage 6. The "happy displays" become

---

[13] At this point, Piaget's statements are dissonant with Hebb's (1949) conception of cell assemblies and phase sequences being established by way of the redundant aspects of receptor inputs. In part the difference is fundamental; Piaget starts with the sensorimotor schema, including a motor output as well as a receptor input in all looking and hearing, whereas Hebb (1949) appears to see receptor inputs producing only cerebral firing processes without making any clear place for a motor output. Beyond this, the difference may appear larger from the language used than it really is, for the building of cell assemblies may well be predominantly a matter of redundant perceptions in stages 1 and 2, whereas by this fifth stage it may well be that action is both modifying the cell assemblies and linking them into phase sequences which serve to represent symbolically such characteristics of objects as hardness and substantiality.

"rituals" which approach make-believe. Consider the following observations:

From Observation 63: At 10 months and three days, Jacqueline put her nose close to her mother's cheek and pressed, which forced her to breathe much more loudly. This phenomenon at once interested her, but instead of merely repeating it or varying it in order to investigate it, she quickly complicated it for the fun of it: she drew back an inch or two, screwed up her nose, sniffed and breathed out alternately very hard (as if blowing her nose), then again thrust her nose against her mother's cheek, laughing heartily. These actions were repeated at least once a day for more than a month, as a ritual . . .

At 15 months 11 days, Jacqueline asked for her pot and laughed a lot when it was given to her. She indulged in a number of ritual movements, playfully, and the game stopped there, to be taken up again on following days (1945, p. 94).

Thus, stage 5 brings another major transformation. Instead of merely using his schemata to make interesting phenomena last or to apply them as familiar means to new situations, the infant begins through adaptive groping to modify the schemata that he employs as means to achieve his ends. Modifying his schemata attracts the infant's attention to their results. This shift of attention to external results promotes an interest in objects which gradually becomes an interest in the new or novel as such. This interest in the novel constitutes curiosity. It motivates the creative discovery of more new means through active experimentation as accommodation becomes differentiated from assimilation. This curious, accommodative interest in the novel leads also to overt imitation and further differentiation of the infant's schemata. Through repetition of the modifications in his schemata and through ritualized play, the infant gradually assimilates the differentiations of his schemata and his imitations of reality as central processes. Objects thereby acquire an increased degree of permanence and space, causality, and time become objective.

STAGE 6. INVENTION OF NEW MEANS THROUGH MENTAL COMBINATION

At the sixth stage, which Piaget found beginning in his children toward the middle of the second year, occurs another transformation marked by the invention of new means through mental combination. This new, implicit level of operation makes its first appearance, as Piaget (1936) notes, long before it becomes characteristic, and long before the secondary and tertiary circular reactions disappear. At this new level, inventions begin to occur by rapid internal and implicit coordination of schemata which have already been internalized as central processes which can run off independently of receptor inputs and motor outputs. This is imaginal operation. Piaget (1945, 1949a) considers images to be not static representations but rather active central neural processes which represent or symbolize actions. Henceforth in the course of the child's development, the sensorimotor schemata achieve completion as internalized or imaginal actions which permit invention through mental combination.

The contrast between the "discovery of new means through active experimentation" of stage 5 and the "invention by mental combination" of stage 6 is illustrated by a comparison of the manner in which Lucienne came to the "pattern of the stick" in Observations 157 and 158 (see above) and the manner in which Laurent came to it at an older age. Laurent's "invention" is also to be contrasted with Jacqueline's learning to bring a stick through the bars of her playpen (see Observation 168 above).

From Observation 177: In contrast to Jacqueline and Lucienne who were submitted to numerous experiments during which they had opportunity to "learn" to use the stick, Laurent only manipulated it at long intervals until such time as he knew how to use it spontaneously. In order to characterize that moment, it is worthwhile to retrace briefly the ensemble of Laurent's earlier behavior patterns relating to the stick.

As early as four months and 20 days of age, i.e., at the beginning of the third stage, Laurent is confronted by a short stick which he assimilates by shaking it, rubbing it against the wicker of his bassinet, etc. In general, he makes it the equivalent of the paper knife . . . At four months and 21 days, when Laurent is holding the stick, he happens to strike a hanging toy and immediately continues. But during the next hours, Laurent no longer tries to reproduce this result even when I put the stick back in his hand. This is not, then, an example of "the behavior pattern of the stick." . . . The following days I give him the stick again and try to make him associate it to the activity of the various schemata, but Laurent does not react then or in the following weeks . . . In the course of the fourth stage, characterized by the coordination of the schemata, the use of the stick makes no progress. During this stage, however, Laurent comes to use the hand of another person as intermediate to act upon distant objects, thus succeeding in spatializing causality and preparing the way for experimental behavior. But when, at eight months or even nine months, I give Laurent the stick he only uses it to strike around him and not to displace or to bring to him the objects he hits . . .

At 12 months, i.e., well into the fifth stage, when Jacqueline and Lucienne succeeded in "discovering" the utilization of the stick, Laurent manipulates a long wooden ruler for a long time, but arrives at only the three following reactions: (1) turning the stick over systematically while transferring it from one hand to the other, (2) striking the floor, his shoes and various objects with it, (3) displacing it by pushing it gently over the floor with his index finger. Several times I place at certain distances from Laurent some attractive object to see whether he, already holding the stick, will know how to use it. Each time Laurent tries to attain the object with his free hand without having the idea of using the stick . . .

At 14 months and 25 days, I give him back the stick because of his recent progress. He has learned to put objects on top of one another, to put them in a cup and turn it upside down, etc.: the relationships which belong to the level of the behavior of the stick [in the sense that they presume a grasp of objective spatial and causal sequences—see: 1937, pp. 271 ff.]. Laurent grasps the stick and immediately strikes the floor with it, then strikes various objects placed on the floor. He displaces them gently, but it does not occur to him to utilize this result systematically . . . I put various desirable objectives 50 cm. or one meter away from Laurent, but he does not realize the virtue of the instrument he holds . . . If I had repeated such experiments at this period, Laurent, like his sisters, would have discovered the use of the stick through groping and apprenticeship. But I broke off the attempt and only resumed it during the sixth stage.

At 16 months and five days, Laurent is seated before a table and I place a bread crust in front of him, well out of reach. Also, to his right I place a stick about 25 cm. long. At first Laurent tries to grasp the bread without paying any attention to the instrument, and then he gives up. I then put the stick between him and the bread; it does not touch the bread but nevertheless carries with it an undeniable visual suggestion. Laurent again looks at the bread, without moving, looks very briefly at the stick, then suddenly grasps it and directs it toward the bread. But he grasped it toward the middle, and not at one of its ends, so that it was too short to attain the objective. Laurent then puts it down and resumes stretching out his hand toward the bread. Then, without spending much time on this movement, he takes up the stick again, this time at one of its ends (chance or intention?), and draws the bread to him. He begins by simply touching it, as though contact of the stick with the objective were sufficient to see the latter in motion, but after one or two seconds at most he pushes the crust with real intention. He displaces it gently at first, but then draws it to him without difficulty. Two successive attempts yield the same results . . . An hour later, I place a toy in front of Laurent (out of his reach) and a new stick next to him. He does not even try to catch the object with his hand; he immediately grasps the stick and draws the toy to him. Thus, it may be seen how Laurent has discovered the use of the stick almost without any groping when, during the preceding stages, he handled it without understanding of its usefulness. This reaction is therefore distinctly different from that of his sisters (1936, pp. 333–36).

Like Köhler's (1925) adult chimpanzees, Laurent, at 16 months, has "invented" the use of the stick quite suddenly. In view of the other relatively similar causal relationships that Piaget had observed Laurent "discover" by groping, however, this sudden invention implies no such discontinuity from restructuring the cortical field as Köhler assumed. In fact, when it is seen from the vantage point of Piaget's observations of the development of his own children, the continuity-discontinuity controversy (see Hilgard, 1956, pp. 434 ff.) appears to have taken place chiefly for lack of scope in the data being interpreted. In a longitudinal, developmental setting the data used to support the discontinuity hypothesis fail to support it.

In certain ways, Laurent's quick invention of the "pattern of the stick" compared with the slow, groping discovery by Jacqueline and Lucienne corresponds to the findings in the experiments by Gesell & Thompson (1929) and Hilgard (1932, 1933) where older children achieved the same degree of skill in various performances with much less practice than had been required by younger children. These findings were considered to confirm the assumption of predetermined development and to indicate that giving a child practice in a skill for which he is maturationally unready is useless. The latter point may be correct, but this does not mean that experience is unessential for the development of such behaviors as stair-climbing, cutting with scissors, and buttoning. What these investigators appear to have missed was the role of apparently unrelated experience, i.e., the establishment and differentiation of central processes in related learning sets derived from the great variety of accommodations demanded in the child's spontaneous activities.

NEW CONSTRUCTIONS OF REALITY WITH MENTAL COMBINATION. The construction of reality reaches a new level as the child internalizes sensorimotor schemata. The object acquires a new degree of permanence and the spatial field becomes objectified to a degree which permits the child to follow an indefinite sequence of displacements, including even hidden displacements. Moreover, the child becomes oriented in an objective spatial field in the sense that he keeps track of where the various objects and persons in his experience are located.

Object permanence through hidden displacements. Consider first the evidence concerning the increasing permanence of the object. At 18 months, Jacqueline could find objects hidden in a series of places so long as she could see where they were hidden. On the other hand, she made no effort to search for a potato that was put in a box, which was, in turn, emptied under a rug. But a month later, after many "search-games" with her father, Jacqueline was able to follow even invisible displacements.

From Observations 64, 65: At 19 months and 20 days, Jacqueline watches me as I put a coin in my hand, then put my hand under a coverlet. I withdraw my hand closed; Jacqueline opens it, and then, finding no coin, she searches under the coverlet till she finds the object. I take back the coin at once, put it in my hand and then slip my closed hand under a cushion situated at the other side (on her left and no longer on her right); Jacqueline immediately searches for the coin under the cushion. I repeat the experiment by hiding the coin under a jacket; Jacqueline finds it without hesitation.

I complete the test as follows: I place the coin in my hand, then my hand under the cushion. I bring it forth closed and immediately hide it under the other coverlet. Finally I withdraw it and hold it out, closed to Jacqueline. Jacqueline then pushes my hand aside without opening it (she guesses there is nothing in it, which is new), she looks under the cushion, and then directly under the coverlet where she finds the object . . . During a second series (cushion and jacket) she behaves in the same way . . . I then try a series of three displacements: I put the coin in my hand, and move my closed hand sequentially from A to B and from B to $C;$ Jacqueline sets my hand aside, then searches in A, in B, and finally in C.

At 19 months 23 days, Jacqueline is seated opposite three object screens, A, B, and C (a beret, a handkerchief, and her jacket), aligned equidistant from each other. I hide a small pencil in my hand, saying, "Coucou, the pencil." I hold out my closed hand to her, put it under A, then under B, and then under C (leaving the pencil under C); at each step I again extend my closed hand, repeating, "Coucou, the pencil." Jacqueline then searches for the pencil directly at C, and finds it and laughs. I repeat this experiment nine times in succession, always taking the following precautions: (1) I show the child my closed hand every time I withdraw it from under one of the three screens, and especially after having brought it out of the third one. (2) I vary the order in each experiment; A, B, C, then C, A, B (the pencil being in B), then C, B, A, etc. (3) Each time I move the object screens; sometimes the beret is on the left, sometimes in the middle, sometimes on the right. (4) Each time the pencil is left under the last screen under which I pass my hand. During the first eight experiments, Jacqueline constantly searches for and finds the pencil under the last object screen under which I put my hand. At the ninth attempt, she searches for it under the next to the last one, and at the tenth she recommences without hesitation to investigate under the last one . . . Clearly there is definitely a system here. These facts cannot be explained by chance alone, given the modifications I introduced each time in the order followed. Moreover, it is impossible to state that the child remembers the third position only; her hesitations often reveal that she mentally retraces the order followed (1937, pp. 79–81).

Many similar observations are recorded for the other children.

Space and imagery. The representative elaboration of the spatial field at the sixth stage shows both in the capacity of the child for detours and in the memory of relationships between changes in location. First, illustrations of detours, which are exceedingly difficult for animals below the dog and the monkey to learn:

From Observation 123: At 18 months and eight days, Jacqueline throws a ball under a sofa. Instead of bending down at once and searching for it on the floor, she looks at the place, realizes the ball must have crossed under the sofa, and sets out to go behind it. There is a table at her right and the sofa is backed up against the bed on the left; therefore she begins by turning her back on the place where the ball disappeared, goes around the table, and finally arrives behind the sofa at the correct place. Thus, she has closed the circle of displacements by an itinerary different from that of the object and has thereby elaborated a group through representation by the invisible displacement of a ball and of the detour to be made in order to find it (1937, p. 205).[14]

[14] Piaget (1937) takes the term and the concept of the *group* from Poincaré's (1906, chaps. iii, iv) analysis of the concept of space wherein he considers as elementary the distinction between changes of position and changes of state. Some changes in the external world can be corrected by body movements which lead perception back to its initial state, e.g., looking down to see something that has dropped out of sight; while other changes cannot. The first constitute changes of position, or displacements; the second, changes of state. The *group* is any set of operations which can be neutralized by a corresponding set of reverse operations (see pp. 102 ff.).

From Observation 125: With Laurent, the first obvious detour was observed at 15 months and four days. Laurent is standing in the garden. He clings to me with his left hand and with his right tries to pull an iron gate toward him (the gate is solid and without any grill work). He succeeds to a slight degree, but does not succeed in opening it wide. He stops, then suddenly leads me to the other side of the wall; there, without any hesitation or false move, he pushes the gate with both hands and thus succeeds in opening it. Hence he has gone around the object representing to himself ahead of time the path to follow since the gate is not transparent (1937, p. 206).

Consider next an illustration implying memory for relationships among changes of location or displacements:

Observation 126: At 19 months 27 days, Jacqueline follows me about 100 meters away from a mountain chalet on a path leading to the plain, a path which her grandfather took on his departure three days earlier. I ask Jacqueline: "Where is mother?"; "Where is grandpa?" etc., alternately naming the members of the family who remain in the chalet and those who have gone down to the plain. Each time Jacqueline points in the correct direction.

At 23 months 10 days, we follow a straight road about one kilometer from the house. I ask Jacqueline where the house is; she turns around and points in the correct direction. On the return trip, I repeat my question. Jacqueline begins by pointing behind her systematically (which is wrong). But after a few meters, she changes her mind and points in front. Now, this correction does not come from seeing the house in the distance, but only from noticing that she is on the return trip (1937, p. 207).

Causal reconstructions and foresight. With the development of images or representative processes, the child becomes capable of reconstructing causes in the presence of their effects alone. Just as the permanence of the object is extended by the image of absent objects, the objectification and spatialization of physical causality come gradually to entail the symbolic representation of sequences not directly given in the perceptual field. Consider the following illustration of a child reconstructing the cause mentally from a perceived object:

Observation 157: At 18 months 8 days, Jacqueline sits on a bed beside her mother. I am at the foot of her bed on the side opposite Jacqueline, and she neither sees me nor knows that I am in the room. I brandish over the bed a cane to which a brush is attached at one end and I swing the whole thing. Jacqueline is very much interested: she says "Cane, cane" and examines the swinging most attentively. At a certain moment, she stops looking at the end of the cane and obviously tries to understand. She tries to perceive the other end of the cane, and to do so, leans in front of her mother, and then behind her, until she has seen me. She expresses no surprise, as though she knew I was the cause of the sight . . . A moment later, while Jacqueline is hidden under the covers to distract her attention, I go to the foot of the bed and resume my game. Jacqueline laughs, says "Papa," looks for me in the place where she saw me the first time, then tries to find me in the room, while the cane is still moving. She does not think of finding me at the foot of the bed (I am hidden by the foot board), but she has no doubt that I am the cause of the phenomenon (1937, pp. 295–96).

The invention of new means often implies a foresight for effects starting from a considered cause.

Observation 160: At 16 months 12 days, Jacqueline has been wrested from a game she wants to continue and placed in her playpen from which she wants to get out. She calls, but in vain. Then she clearly expresses a certain need, although the events of the last ten minutes prove that she no longer experiences it. No sooner has she left the playpen than she indicates the game she wishes to resume! Thus, we see how Jacqueline, knowing that a certain appeal would not free her from her confinement, has imagined a more efficacious means, foreseeing more or less clearly the sequence of actions that would result from it (1937, p. 297).

From these illustrations, it becomes clear that causality is no longer merely objective; it is also imaginal, i.e., based on representative central processes.

Temporal elaborations. When the representative central processes have become liberated to some degree from external support, the objective time series becomes extended into both the future and the past as memorial anticipation and memory. In the following illustration, a perception reminds Jacqueline of events several days past.

From Observation 173: At 19 months and 25 days, Jacqueline picks up a blade of grass which she puts in a pail as if it were one of the grasshoppers a little cousin brought her a few days before. She says "Totelle (sauterelle, or grasshopper), totelle, jump, boy (her cousin)." In other words, perception of the grass reminds her symbolically of a grasshopper and enables her to evoke past events and reconstruct them in sequence (1937, p. 346).

Similarly, Jacqueline's crying "toilet" in order to get back to the game she wished to continue implies an imaginal anticipation of the future results. Thus, at about a year and a half, Jacqueline's behavior implied appreciation to some degree of both a past and a future on an imaginal or representative basis.

"DEFERRED IMITATION" AND PLAYFUL MAKE-BELIEVE. Empirical intelligence becomes invention through mental combination presumably as central processes become more and more autonomous and can represent overt actions. This representational capacity shows also in those activities where accommodation is primary (imitation) and in those activities where assimilation is primary (play). The evidence for this assertion comes, first, from the fact that the child can immediately imitate new models, and second, from the appearance of "deferred imitation." In "deferred imitation," the child reproduces the actions of a model that is no longer present. Consider the following illustrative observations:

Observation 52: At 16 months and three days, Jacqueline had a visit from a little boy of 18 months whom she used to see from time to time, and who, in the course of the afternoon, got into a terrible temper. He screamed as he tried to get out of a playpen and pushed it backwards, stamping his feet. Jacqueline stood watching him in amazement, never having witnessed such a scene before. The next day, she herself screamed in her playpen and tried to move it, stamping her foot lightly several times in succession. The imitation of the whole scene was most striking. Had it been immediate, it would naturally not have involved representation, but coming as it did, after an interval of more than 12 hours, it must have involved some representative or pre-representative element (1945, p. 63).

Observation 54: At this same period of the behavior of her little friend, Jacqueline began to reproduce certain words, not at the time they were uttered, but in similar situations, and without having previously imitated them.

Thus, at 16 months and eight days, Jacqueline said *in step* as she was walking, although she had never uttered these words and they had not been said in her presence immediately before. It must thus have been a case of virtual imitation becoming real imitation in an active context . . . At 16 months and 10 days, Jacqueline pointed to her mother's nose, and said *nose*, again without having uttered the word before and without hearing it immediately before (1945, p. 63).

It should be noted that these instances of deferred imitation are either independent of language, as in the case of Jacqueline's imitation of her friend's tantrum, or else actually participate in the acquisition of language. This is an important fact for the issue of whether implicit speech is the basis for all thought (see Watson, 1914; Carnap, 1942; and Skinner, 1957; also Chapters 6 and 7).

With this progress of representational processes, which are presumably autonomous central neural circuits, the ritualistic patterns of action become genuine playful make-believe, and the child acts out patterns he has either lived through or observed. It is clear, moreover, that the child recognizes the representative character of these playful actions. Consider the following illustration:

Observation 64: Jacqueline first manifested playfully symbolic actions with every appearance of "make-believe" at 15 months and 12 days . . . She saw a cloth whose fringed edges vaguely recalled those of her pillow; she seized it, held a fold of it in her right hand, sucked the thumb of the same hand, and lay down on her side, laughing hard. She kept her eyes open, but blinked from time to time as if she were alluding to closed eyes. Finally, laughing more and more, she cried *Nene* (nono). The same cloth started the same game on the following days. At 15 months and 13 days, she treated the collar of her mother's coat in the same way. At 15 months and 30 days, it was the tail of her rubber donkey which represented the pillow! And from 17 months onward, she made her animals, a bear and a plush dog, also do "nono."

Similarly, at 18 months and 28 days, she said *avon* (savon = soap), rubbing her hands together and pretending to wash them (without any water).

At 20 months and 15 days and following, she pretended she was eating various things, e.g., a piece of paper, saying "very nice" (1945, p. 96).

It is the application of schemata to inappropriate objects coupled with expressions of pleasure that characterizes the beginnings of this playful make-believe. There is "symbolism along with pretense of assimilating object to schema without accommodation." Again it should be noted that such playful make-believe comes before speech in the development of children, another fact that is relevant to the issue of whether it is implicit speech that underlies thought.

Thus, at stage 6, the human child completes the development of his sensorimotor schemata in the sense that they reach what Piaget (1947) calls a mobile equilibrium. The child can reverse his actions; he can reach a given goal by various routes. Moreover, he has achieved the beginnings of symbolic processes such as appear in the chimpanzee (Köhler, 1925; Hebb & Thompson, 1954): he has begun to invent by mental combination; to him objects have acquired permanence even through sequences of displacements which are invisible; he keeps track of himself as an object among objects in an objective spatial field, and his symbolic representational capacities are beginning to show in deferred imitation and in playful make-believe.

SUMMARY

An attempt has been made to synopsize Piaget's accounts (1936, 1937, 1945) of the development of intellectual processes during the sensorimotor period in sufficient empirical detail to permit an understanding of what Piaget saw concretely in the changing behavior of his three children and of how he derived his theoretical picture from what he saw. The two main themes which dominate his story should now be clear. The first of these themes concerns the invariance of organismic functions which, in their operation, produce a continuously changing set of behavioral structures. In connection with this theme, Piaget describes the epigenesis of the behavioral structures of intelligence, the implicit constructions of reality, and the gradual changes and differentiation of imitation and play. During the first stage, the ready-made schemata are extended with the assimilation of new objects. During the second stage, these various ready-made schemata are coordinated so that something heard becomes something to look at, something looked at becomes something to grasp, and something grasped becomes something to suck, etc. At this stage appears the behavioral landmark of hand-watching, one of the "primary circular reactions," wherein the child brings the movements of his hands and arms under visual control. With the third stage come the "secondary circular reactions" wherein appear the first "intentions" when the child attempts to prolong or repeat fortuitous spectacles that attract his interest. It is also at this stage that interest in the objective world begins, and the child begins to look or feel for objects lost from view or grasp, thereby attributing to them at least a degree of constancy. These "intentional" activities of stage 3 provide another behavioral landmark. With stage 4 the differentiation of goal and instrumental act becomes evident in the child's behavior as the schemata derived from the secondary circular reactions become coordinated now as means and now as ends. Objects which vanish evoke active search, and accommodation and assimilation begin to be differentiated as imitation and play. With stage 5 comes the interest in novelty and the discovery of new means through active experimentation; the child systematically imitates new models and indulges in playful rituals; he follows objects through sequences of placements, and his behavior implies objective space, causality, and time. With stage 6 comes the invention of new means through mental combination, the capacity for detours, object constancy through invisible sequences, deferred imitation, and symbolic play. These stages are transition points in a process of continuous change.

Piaget's second theme concerns the continuous interactions of infant and environment through the invariant functions of assimilation and accommodation. It is this second theme which makes Piaget's picture of development so different from that of Gesell. Both have placed behavioral landmarks against the background of chronological age, but in Gesell's normative schedules, which are based upon the assumption of predetermined development, normative description is conceived to be the equivalent of explanation. Piaget, on the other hand, has been continually mindful of how assimilation and accommodation operate in a continuous process to produce the epigenesis of the behavioral structures. His observations of the development of his three children are like observing the learning of an experimental animal in a consecutive series of situations with the observer giving a theoretical commentary. Out of these observations come a number of principles or hypotheses. First, the persistence of a reflexive schema depends upon an opportunity to use it. Second, the schemata develop continuously through use and through stimulation demanding accommodative modifications. Third (more implicitly than explicitly), accommodative modifications depend upon a proper match between existing schemata and objects encountered. Fourth, the greater the variety of situations to which the child must accommodate his behavioral structures, the more differentiated and mobile they become, the more rapid is his rate of intellectual development, and the greater is his range of interests in the novel and the new. Fifth, the behavioral landmarks of the successive stages appear, for these sensorimotor structures, to form a natural ordinal scale (see Guttman, 1941, 1944) for measuring intelligence, although Piaget makes no such explicit claim. Finally, Piaget emphasizes continuity. Gradualness of change in structures as a consequence of the continuous organism-environment interaction summarizes both themes.

Even in this gradual process of transformation, the hierarchical nature of the developing organization, noted at the opening of this chapter, is evident. The reflexes of the first stage are incorporated into the primary circular reactions of the second. The primary circular reactions of the second period are incorporated into the secondary circular reaction of the third period. Moreover, the secondary circular reactions, after being coordinated now as means and then as ends in the fourth period, become incorporated into the tertiary circular reactions of the fifth stage, and these, in turn, become short-circuited and internalized as images, which, again, become generalized and differentiated as the "concrete operations" to be discussed in Chapter 6.

CHAPTER **6**

Piaget's Observations: From Sensorimotor Schemata to Formal Operations

Although genuine intelligence emerges at the sixth sensorimotor stage, the gap between the sensorimotor intelligence of the infant aged between a year and a half and two and the reflective intelligence of adults is wide indeed. In fact, this gap is approximately equivalent to that between the intelligence of the dog, the monkey, or the chimpanzee and the intelligence of adult man.

As Piaget (1945, 1947) notes, this gap is based upon a number of factors. Where sensorimotor intelligence consists only in coordinating successive perceptions of actual objects and overt movements from one place to another through relatively brief anticipations and memorial reconstructions, reflective thought arrives at an all-embracing representation of the relationships within the universe. As Piaget puts it: "Sensorimotor intelligence acts like a slow-motion film, in which all the pictures are seen in succession but without fusion, and so without the continuous vision necessary for understanding the whole" (1947, p. 121). Where sensorimotor intelligence aims only at success in achieving goals, reflective intelligence becomes concerned with explanation, with understanding the relationships among things, or with knowledge and truth as such. Where the speed of sensorimotor operations is limited to the speed with which concrete events transpire, adult thought is exceedingly rapid. Through the neural processes of short-circuiting, the central processes of thought come to operate like a speeded film which can go through an outline of action in an exceedingly brief period of time. Where sensorimotor intelligence proceeds only in one direction as the actual sequence of events transpire in either perception or motor action, the central processes of thought are reversible in the sense that they are analogous to a film which can be rapidly wound in either direction as the short-circuited representations of events are played now forward and now backward. Furthermore, where sensorimotor intelligence is essentially private and egocentric, the central processes of thought, so socialized through the collective signs of language, permit intersubjective communication and cooperation. Finally, where sensorimotor processes are centered or focused on specific portions of objects and places as a matter of chance with distorting and illusory consequences, reflective intelligence is general and has built into it the five properties of logical "groupings." These are combinativity, reversibility, associativity, nullifiability, and tautology, all of which will be considered in some detail below (Piaget, 1947, 1953b).

Piaget (1947) sees three essential factors in the transition from the sensorimotor level of intelligence to the reflective level. First, an increased speed of thought is required in order to allow knowledge of the successive phases of action to be molded into a simultaneous whole. Second, an increase in scope is required which will permit the concrete actions affecting real entities to be expanded by symbolic representations in order to carry the individual beyond the role of the immediate and local in perception and action into a universe extended indefinitely in both time and space. Third, the individual must develop a concern not only for the results desired of action but also for the actual mechanisms by which results are obtained so that the search for solutions may be combined with the development of knowledge of their nature. Thus, the development of thought is no mere translation of sensorimotor schemata into symbolic form, even though this is the first step. The development demands also a continuation of the hierarchical integration of sensorimotor schemata for perception and action into images of action in order to speed them up, then the grouping of these images into ensembles (*Gestalten*) of operations with logico-mathematical properties for dealing with concrete material, and finally the regrouping of these "concrete groupings" into ensembles of "formal operations" with their logico-mathematical properties of the lattice and the group INRC (Piaget, 1953b). This development takes place in the second and third periods already outlined at the beginning of Chapter 5. The second period, lasting from roughly 18 months or two years of age until the child is 11 or 12, contains a "symbolic or preconceptual" phase, an "intuitive" phase, and the phase of "concrete groupings." [1] The third period of "formal operations" begins at age 11 or 12 years and lasts through adolescence as the child takes the final steps of "decentring" and "reversibility" as, presumably, his central processes become sufficiently differentiated and autonomous to permit him to operate with the sum total of possibilities rather than with merely the empirical situation.

THE PRECONCEPTUAL PHASE AND THE ORIGIN OF THE SYMBOL

The preconceptual phase begins when the child is about 18 months or two years of age and it lasts till the child is about four years of age. So far as the development of intelligence is concerned, this is the period during which the child develops his "symbolic function" or imagery. It is also concerned with the acquisition of language. For this phase, Piaget's observations concern both his own children and the pre-school children at the Maison des Petits of the Rousseau Institute in Geneva. His observations are concerned with the development of imitation, play, and the preconcepts shown in language behavior. On the side of theory, he is concerned with the relation of the development of imagery to imitation and play, and also with the issue of whether thought is based on internal language, as many have contended, or whether the use of verbal signs depends upon experience and the exercise of a more basic symbolic function.

IMITATION AND THE IMAGE. The beginnings of deferred imitation and playful make-believe (symbolic play) at the sixth sensorimotor stage, when the child also begins to invent new means by mental combination, have already been noted. Piaget (1945) asks whether it is representational capacity that comes to the support of imitation at this stage, thereby producing deferred imitation, or whether the

[1] Perhaps it should be noted again that this terminology of *periods, phases,* and *sub-stages* does not quite correspond to that of Piaget and his collaborators. It has been adopted to overcome the inconsistencies that appear as one goes from book to book. Here the three major divisions are termed *periods.* The first, *sensorimotor period,* with its six *stages,* was described in Chapter 5. The second period is here divided into three *phases:* I—*preconceptual;* II—*intuitive;* and III—*phase of concrete operations.* Each of these *phases* is further divided into two *sub-stages* (A and B). For the third *period* of formal operations, this numbering will be continued as IV-A and IV-B even though Inhelder & Piaget (1955) start their numbering of the consecutive phases in their study of the growth of logical thinking with I-A and I-B at the *intuitive phase* and use III-A and III-B for dividing the *period* of formal operations into what they call *stages.*

representative image itself may not be the interiorized product of imitation. Although it would appear unnecessary to answer such a question categorically, Piaget contends that "the image is the result of a construction akin to that which produces the schemata of intelligence but which takes its material from the 'world of sensation.' But we must add that this material is motor as well as sensorial . . . The image is as it were the draft of potential imitation . . . just as interior language is the draft of words to come and the interiorization of acquired exterior language" (1945, p. 70).

Imagery as internalized imitation. As this quotation implies, Piaget denies the long-established notion that images are reactivations of the traces of past experiences which have been passively recorded on inert nervous tissue. Like such programmers of electronic computers as Newell, Shaw & Simon (1958), Piaget sees the image as an interiorization of actions made or observed. In the language of behavior theory, imagery consists of "implicit" responses. Presumably, images represent autonomous central processes, which have been developed as the actions they symbolize have been short-circuited in the course of repetition.

Overt imitation in the role of imagery. As evidence for his contention that the image is interiorized imitation, Piaget cites several observations in which overt imitation often plays the part of the interior image before the behavior implying imagery appears in the course of development. At sensorimotor stage 3, for instance, when the child recognizes objects by motor outlines of the schemata into which those objects have been assimilated, he is expressing something analogous to imitation. At stages 4 and 5, as imitative accommodation becomes differentiated from playful assimilation, the pursuit of novelties and their reproduction also involves imitation, as in the instance when a baby uses his hand to make hanging objects swing. This act imitates and represents the motion of the object previously observed that the baby is attempting to reproduce. Moreover, at the transition between the "discovery of new means by groping" and the "invention of new means by mental combination," imitation appears to play the role analogous to that of imagery both in understanding and in intelligent planning. Consider first an illustration of imitation as an aid to understanding:

From Observation 58: At age 12 months and 10 days, Laurent was looking at a box of matches which I was holding on its end and alternately opening and closing. Showing great delight, he watched with great attention, and imitated the box in three ways. (1) He opened and closed his right hand, keeping his eyes on the box. (2) He said *tff, tff* to reproduce the sound that the box made. (3) He opened and closed his mouth [see Lucienne below]. It seemed to me that these reactions were much more concomitants of perception than attempts to act on the object, since the child's movements were unobtrusive, not deliberate "devices" varying in intensity as a result of success or failure (1945, p. 66).

In the following observation, which Piaget is fond of using for illustrative purposes, Lucienne used overt imitation of an anticipated action after the fashion of imaginal planning.

From Observation 180: At age 16 months, [an imitative action, equivalent to] a mental invention permitted Lucienne to discover an object inside a match box . . . I play at hiding the chain inside the same match box into which Lucienne has learned to put the chain. I begin by opening the box as wide as possible and putting the chain into its cover (where Lucienne herself had put it, but deeper). Lucienne, who has already practiced filling and emptying her pail and various receptacles, then grasps the box and turns it over without hesitation. No invention is involved, of course. It is the simple application of a schema acquired through previous groping . . . Then I put the chain inside an empty match box, then close the box leaving an opening of 10 mm. Lucienne begins by turning the whole thing over, then tries to grasp the chain through the opening. Not succeeding, she simply puts her index finger into the slit and so succeeds in getting out a small fragment of the chain. She then pulls it until she has completely solved the problem.

Here begins the experiment we want to emphasize. I put the chain back in the box and reduce the opening to 3 mm. Lucienne is not aware of the opening and the closing of the match box and has not seen me prepare the experiment. She possesses only the two preceding schemata: (1) turning the box over in order to empty it, and (2) sliding her finger into the slit to make the chain come out. It is of course this last procedure that she tries first, but fails completely. A pause follows during which Lucienne manifests a curious reaction bearing witness not only to the fact that she tries to think out the situation and to represent to herself through mental combination the operations to be formed, but also the role played by imitation in the genesis of representation. Lucienne mimics the widening of the slit.

She looks at the slit with great attention; then, several times in succession, she opens and shuts her mouth, at first slightly, and then wider and wider! . . . Due to inability to think out the situation in words or clear visual images, she uses a simple motor indication as "signifier" or symbol. Now, as the motor reaction which presents itself for filling this role is none other than imitation, that is to say, representation by acts, which, doubtless earlier than any mental image, makes it possible not only to divide into parts the spectacles seen but also to evoke and reproduce them at will. Lucienne, by opening her mouth thus expresses, or even reflects her desire, to enlarge the opening of the box . . . There is doubtless added to this an element of magico-phenomenalistic causality or efficacy . . . Soon after this phase of plastic reflection, Lucienne unhesitatingly puts her finger into the slit and, instead of trying as before to reach the chain, she pulls so as to enlarge the opening. She succeeds and grasps the chain. During subsequent attempts, with the slit always 3 mm. wide, the same procedure is immediately discovered. On the other hand, when the box is completely closed, Lucienne is incapable of opening it (1936, pp. 337–38).

Here Lucienne's mouth-opening appears to imitate and to symbolize her later action of opening the box. Such reactions make it clear that representative imitation does not follow the image in development, but precedes it. The interior symbol may thus be conceived to be a product of the short-circuiting which occurs with repeated imitations of the actions of persons and things. In a similar fashion, Piaget (1933) observed earlier that interior, or imaginal language, occurs only after the child has had long practice with soliloquies, monologues and collective monologues. The apprenticeship in talking out loud thus prepares the way for implicit speech.

The image and language. On similar grounds, Piaget takes his stand against those who consider thought to be the implicit speech of a "well developed language" (see Watson, 1914; but especially Carnap, 1942). First of all, within the life of the individual, symbolic actions precede speech. Second, both deferred imitation and playful make-believe make their appearance before language. Third, behavior implying a symbolic function appears in a number of animals which, of course, cannot talk. The raccoon, the dog, the monkey, and the chimpanzee can all learn Hunter's (1924) double-alteration problem. Köhler (1925) and Hebb & Thompson (1954) describe deceitful behaviors in the chimpanzee which imply a high level of symbolic behavior without language. Finally, the studies of Wolfe (1936) in which chimpanzees learned to work for poker-chip tokens and the cooperative behavior demonstrated by Nissen & Crawford (1937) in the chimpanzee attest further that symbolic capacities come before the development of language. Instead of the language underlying thought, both Piaget (1945) and Hebb & Thompson (1954) suggest the opposite, namely, that language can only occur in organisms which have already developed autonomous central processes which can symbolize actions and events.

Classes of symbols exist within the general symbolic function. Piaget distinguishes between "symbols" and "signs," as one class, and "indices" and "signals," as another. In the case of either the index or the sign, the signifier is either some objective aspect of the signified or is perceived as an objective antecedent of the signified. In the case of the symbol and the sign, on the other hand, the differentiation between the signifier and the signified is made by the subject himself. When Lucienne, aged 19 months, pretended to drink out of a box and then held it to the mouths of all those who were present, for instance, she surely recognized the pretense in which the action signifies drinking real water from a real glass. Piaget (1947) also differentiates between a symbol, which is based on individual experiences and therefore egocentric or idiosyncratic, and the sign, which is arbitrary and social. Thus, whereas the symbol represents the subject's own actions or imitates actual actions he has seen—for example, when the child feeds her doll with a spoon as she has been fed or sits and pretends to be reading a newspaper, as she has seen her father doing—the collective signs of language are standardized with respect to both the signifier and what is signified.

The acquisition of language, then, follows closely on the formation of the image in the course of human development. As soon as the child begins to indulge in symbolic play in which he projects his symbolic schemata onto new objects, thereby going beyond playful make-believe in his own actions, the child then begins to make rapid strides in the acquisition of language. Thus, Piaget conceives language development to depend upon the development of images and thought processes (see also pp. 185–90)

PLAY AND THE TYPES OF GAMES. Play is important in these acquisitions. Imitation, intelligent adaptation, and play represent three separate emphases in activity. In intelligent adaptation, there is a balance between assimilation and accommodation. In imitation, accommodation predominates. In play, assimilation predominates. The objects of reality are subordinated to playful action in such a degree that they are distorted. Piaget (1945) synopsizes this set of relationships graphically (see Figure 6–1).

Piaget (1945) examines critically the various classifications of playful behavior. He first shows that children's games cannot be classified sensibly in terms of their content, in terms of the functions they are supposed to be pre-exercising (Groos, 1905), or in terms of the instinct that gives rise to them (Claparede, 1910). He then attempts a classification based upon an analysis of the underlying behavioral structures called for by each game. Out of these underlying structures come his categories of (*a*) *practice games,* (*b*) *symbolic games,* and (*c*) *games with rules.* These make their appearance in the order named. Practice games are especially characteristic of the sensorimotor period; symbolic games are characteristic of the pre-conceptual phase under discussion, and games with rules arise later as the "grouping structures" develop. Constructional games correspond to no definite stage, but rather occupy a position intermediate between play and intelligent work or between play and imitation. Thus, when the child instead of playfully using a chip of wood to represent a boat in his play, makes something approximating a boat by hollowing out the wood and putting on a sail, he is moving from the realm of playful assimilation toward that of imitation and work.

Practice games. Practice games appear almost throughout the sensorimotor stages described in Chapter 5. Nearly all of the sensorimotor schemata give rise to a playful repetition marked by the smile

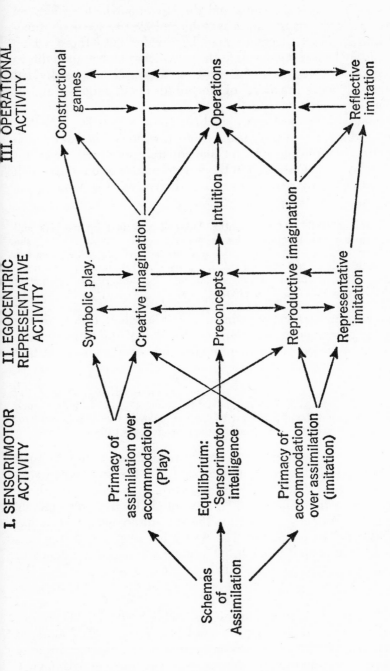

Fig. 6–1. The relationships among play, intelligence, and imitation in the course of development from the sensorimotor stage to the stage of concrete operations. From Piaget (1945).

and by laughter. It is the smile and the laughter which, at least in part, have led such investigators as Bühler (1928) to speak of "function pleasure." Practice games may be divided into those which remain purely sensorimotor and those which involve thought to some degree. In turn, each of these two categories can be divided into games of "mere practice," of "fortuitous combinations," and of "intentional combinations."

The games of *mere practice* include those repetitive activities which reproduce, out of their usual context, various schemata which are new for the child and as yet inadequately mastered. They include the play of stages 2 to 5 in the sensorimotor period, but which "mere-practice" play continues long thereafter. Consider these observations:

> *From Observation* 66: At 27 months, Jacqueline picked up pebbles and threw them in a pond, laughing a lot as she did so . . . At 32 months, she filled a pail with sand, overturned it, demolished the sand pile with her spade and then began again, and she did this for more than an hour . . . At three years eight months, she laced and unlaced her shoe, looked very pleased, having just learned how to do it (1945, p. 113).

Here follows an observation which, even though it occurs in the fourth year, corresponds essentially to the play of the third sensorimotor stage in which the child prolongs and repeats an interesting experience.

> *From Observation* 67: At three years and seven months, Y scraped the ground, made little heaps of dust and moved them about. He collected as much dust as he could in his hand and let it trickle out, enjoyed the sensation it produced as it flowed through his fingers, and then began again (1945, p. 115).

Although the play appears to have an aimless quality in such games of mere practice, when a given skill is in the process of being organized, Piaget (1936, 1945) has noted that practicing may have a quality of intentional urgency. He has noted also that this urgency and even the tendency to practice the skill disappears once it has been "mastered" or organized. The writer has observed in his own children what appeared to be an intentional and urgent tendency to repeat, sometimes *ad nauseam* for the adult concerned, skills in the process of organization. For instance, when one of his daughters was between nine and eleven months of age and beginning to stand alone, she took an intense interest in "being walked." The writer started the practice of holding her hands while she walked along in front of him with this support. For about two months her appetite for this game was almost insatiable. Daddy need only get within view to elicit from her activities designed to get him to play this game of mere practice. Once she had begun to walk alone, however, this stopped, and she no longer wanted to play this game at all.

Piaget (1936, 1945) has also noted that it is at a stage of the process of development when the organization of a new skill has well begun, but is also well short of completion, that such evidences of delight as the smile and the laugh, which justify the term "function pleasure," are most predominent. In such situations, games of mere practice also give rise to the pleasures which Piaget (1945) has characterized as that of "being the cause" and that of "feeling the power." The significance of these observations for motivational theory should be noted (see Hendrik, 1943; Hebb, 1949; White, 1959; also Chapter 7, pp. 252–54, 260–62).

Fortuitous combinations are but an extension of games of mere practice. They are marked by the new combinations which sometimes appear in the course of such apparently aimless activity. Here are examples:

From Observation 68: At three years and two months, Jacqueline arranged ninepins in a line two at a time and finally (by accident) had one row perpendicular to the other; she then made single rows with no apparent purpose. At three years and six months, she put some pebbles in a pail, took them out one by one, put them back, transferred them from one pail to another, etc. Then the game became symbolic (she pretended to be drinking tea, with the pailful of pebbles) (1945, pp. 115–16).

From Observation 69: The educational games at the Maison des Petits always produce among the three-to-four-year-olds play activities without any specific aim before the appearance of constructions properly so-called . . . At three years and 11 months, T spent a long time threading the beads onto the rods of a counting-frame, mixing the colors without rhyme or reason. He also molded and broke up the modeling clay without making or portraying anything. He aimlessly piled up the boxes of a game of volumes and knocked them down again (1945, p. 116).

Included in this class of "fortuitous combinations" is destruction of objects, which Piaget sees motivated by the mere matter of "trying out for the fun of the activity." It is interesting to note that monkeys in their avid concern with taking puzzles apart also manifest such destructive activity.

Intentional combinations are activities often only a shade removed from fortuitous combinations. The removal appears to lie in the degree and persistence of absorption with the particular combination. Whenever some special combination like that in skating or in the skills of various games is involved, the tendency to return to the combination takes on the quality of *intention* as did the mere practice of being walked in the writer's daughter. Moreover, it should be noted that it was in the destructive activity of disassembling six-device puzzles that Harlow (1953, p. 32) observed two monkeys "still working enthusiastically" during the last of 10 consecutive hours of testing.

Games of *mental exercise* show these same three categories of variation: mere practice, fortuitous combinations, and intentional combinations. Asking such questions as "What's that?" or "Why?" may at first be an act of reflective intelligence, but the child then continues to practice asking questions for fun. He may also combine by chance words and concepts, or he may make up a story for the pleasure of making it. The combinations which occur, although intentional, are unstable.

Symbolic games. Symbolic games play an especially prominent role in the child's activity during the preconceptual phase. The earliest instances of such games have already been illustrated. In these early instances, the play is symbolic chiefly of the child's own activities: recall Jacqueline laying her head on the fringed shawl and imitating sleep. As Piaget (1945, p. 121) sees it, it is through symbolic play that the child consolidates his imaginal schemata that represent the various aspects of all reality. Symbolic play is for representational assimilation what practice play has been for functional assimilation. Piaget (1945) finds justification for this principle in his classification of symbolic games, consisting of three major types, each with its sub-types.

The transition from sensorimotor stage 6 to the "preconceptual phase" occurs when the child begins to project symbolic schemata onto new objects. This constitutes Type I-A. Thus, Jacqueline, after having played for two months at pretending to sleep (see Observation 64 quoted in Chapter 5), began to make her bear and her dog sleep. This "projection of symbolic schemata onto new objects" is continuous with "playful make-believe" inasmuch as the projection constitutes merely a generalization of these behaviors. Consider the following:

From *Observation* 75: At 19 months, Jacqueline said "cry, cry" to her dog and herself imitated the sound of crying. On the following day, she made her bear, a duck, etc., cry. Next day she made her hat cry . . . [For some two months Jacqueline had playfully bitten her mother's cheek in make-believe], at 20 months, instead of biting her mother's cheek herself, she pressed her bear's face on the same spot and said "oh! oh!" . . . (1945, p. 121).

Symbolic games of Type I-B consist of projecting imitative schemas onto new objects. In these games, the symbolic schemata are again projected, but they are also borrowed from models which have been imitated rather than coming from the child's own activities.

From Observation 76 (b): At 15 months and 20 days, a quarter of an hour after I blew a hunting-horn in his presence, Laurent picked up a doll's chair a couple of inches high, put it to his mouth and pretended to sound it: *Tantara.* He was unaware that he was being watched . . . (1945, p. 122).

In such projection of imitative schemata, both the action and the object to which it is applied are "symbolizers" of the action represented and the object represented. Here, Laurent's action of lifting the little chair to his mouth and vocalizing symbolizes his father's action of blowing the hunting-horn. The doll's chair, of course, stands for the hunting-horn. Laurent's vocalization represents the sound made by the horn. These few illustrations quoted may fail to show the continuity emphasized by Piaget in the course of development from functional practice-play through playful rituals to the projection of imitative schemata. In this instance, the imitative aspect of the play has a functional resemblance to those actions which attempt to prolong and to repeat interesting spectacles that were characteristic of sensorimotor stage 3. What is added here is Laurent's new-found representative capacity to hold "in memory" the pattern of action observed in his father's blowing the hunting-horn and to use it as a draft for his own imitative action, which, as it were, imitates his memory image.

Symbolic games of Type II are characterized by the identification of one object with another. There is also identification of one object with another in the symbolic games of Type I, but the identification is inseparable from the actions which give rise to it. In the examples to follow, it is the identification which gives rise to the game. In Type II-A, illustrated first, the identification is object with object.

From Observation 77: At 21 months, Jacqueline saw a shell and said "cup." After saying this, she picked it up and pretended to drink. (She had often pretended to drink with various objects but in these instances the object was assimilated to the drinking schema. Here the identification of the shell with the cup preceded the action.) The next day, seeing the same shell, she said "glass," then "cup," then "hat," and finally "boat in the water." Three days later she took an empty box and moved it to and fro saying "motycar." . . . At 24 months and 22 days, she moved her finger along the table and said: *finger walking . . . Horse trotting.* . . . At three years four months, Jacqueline was talking to a safety-pin: *She's going into her house: she's a grandmother.* But already at this stage, the symbols, apart from a few residual exceptions, tended more and more to be used in varied combinations. For instance, at 47 months and 24 days: *I see a dead frog*—"Where?"—*Here, you can see its eyes and its mouth. Look, there's a big hole in its back.*—"No, I can't see anything."—*I was only joking; it's a basket* (1945, p. 124).

The games of Type II-B involve the identification of the child's own body, or self, with that of other people or with things. It is these

games which have been traditionally called "games of imitation."
Consider the following:

Observation 79: In the case of Jacqueline, the assimilation of the ego to others
was achieved directly through games of type I-B. At 23 months, she pretended
to be playing hide and seek with a cousin who had been away for two months.
Then she herself became her cousin: *Clive running, Clive jumping, Clive
laughing,* and she imitated him, strutting up and down. At 26 months and 23
days, she pretended to be ironing like the washer woman, but a moment later
she became the washer woman: *It's Mrs. Sechaud ironing* (1945, p. 125).

Although such games involve imitation, the imitation itself is subordinated to playful assimilation because the child does not merely
copy others while continuing to be himself; he actually identifies
himself with the others.

Symbolic games of Type III develop immediately into a variety of
symbolic combinations. The subtypes A, B, C, and D show increasing complexity. In Type III-A, the combinations are simple. They
begin with the transposition of real scenes and gradually develop
more widely, and they are continuous with the games of Type II.

From Observation 81: At 25 months and nine days, Jacqueline put her doll's
head through the balcony railings with its face down towards the street, and
began to tell it what she saw: *You see the lake and the trees. You see a carriage,
a horse,* etc. The same day she seated her doll on a sofa and told it what she
herself had seen in the garden . . . At 25 months 13 days, she fed her doll,
talking to it for a long time in the way used to encourage her to eat her own
meals: *A little drop more. To please Jacqueline. Just eat this little bit.* . . . At
27 months 25 days, she set her doll astride a gate and pulled its hair back
from its ears to make it listen to a musical box.

At 29 months and 25 days, she prepared a bath for Lucienne. A blade of
grass represented a thermometer. The bath was a big box and she merely stated
that the water was there. Jacqueline then plunged the thermometer into the
bath and found the water too hot. She waited a moment, and then put the
grass in again: *That's all right, thank goodness.* She then went up to Lucienne
(this she actually did) and pretended to take off her apron, her dress, her vest,
making the movements but not touching the clothes. . .

It was at about 32 months that the complex combinations become quite distinct from the games of type II-A and II-B, the transition from these to the
latter types being made possible by activities such as those just quoted. At 32
months, for instance, two weeks after Jacqueline had visited a cousin whom she
had not since mentioned, suddenly everything became "cousin Andree": the
cat, a lid, herself, her mother, her dolls, etc. She talked about her all day long
and made her do everything . . . At about 33 months, the same cycles were
followed with "Marceline," another cousin, but one whom she had only heard
talked about and had never seen . . . The private nature of these cycles is
noteworthy. One day when I saw her lying down and I went up to her, Jacqueline called out: *Go away, I'm Marceline.* On other occasions she wanted to be
her as when she enacted conversations between her parents: *Yes, my dear* . . .
No, John (1945, pp. 127–28).

Piaget (1945, p. 130) argues that it takes "a large dose of theoretical belief to see in such games a continuous tendency to pre-exercise" genetically predetermined patterns such as Groos (1905) had seen. Moreover, contrary to G. Stanley Hall's recapitulation theory, which had seen successive stages of behavioral recapitulations in the *content* of play, Piaget notes that the "motycar," often figuring in Jacqueline's play, could not possibly have been in the content of the lives of primitive men. The content of these symbolic games derives from the child's own experience. And it is thus that Piaget (1945, p. 130) concludes that "just as practice play reproduces through functional assimilation each new acquisition of the child, so 'imaginative' play reproduces what he has lived through, but by means of symbolic representation."

The complications in Types III-B, III-C, and III-D are essentially motivational. Piaget characterizes Type III-B as *compensatory combinations*. Consider the following example:

From Observation 84: At 28 months and eight days, Jacqueline, not being allowed to play with the water being used for washing, took an empty cup, went and stood by the forbidden tub and went through the actions, saying *I'm pouring out water.* . . .

At 32 months and six days, Jacqueline was angry with her father, tried to hit him, etc., and since this seemed likely to have unfortunate consequences, she suddenly cried: *It was much nicer when Carolyn* (a friend of her godfather) *was cross with godfather.* She then related, drawing on her imagination (note that it is a displaced imitation of the present situation), how Carolyn had struck godfather and she began to mime the scene in detail. When later on her mother spoke to her about her original anger, Jacqueline would have none of it: *No, it was Carolyn.* At 32 months and seven days, when she was on a diet, she made up a whole scene about a meal of things she would like to have (1945, pp. 131–32).

Related to these compensatory combinations are those in which the child neutralizes a fear through play (catharsis).

From Observation 85: At 33 months and 14 days, Lucienne was afraid of a tractor in the field next to the garden. She then told her doll that *Dolly told me she would like to ride on a machine like that.* . . . At four years and two months, she did not dare, like Jacqueline, to go alone to a neighboring barn where some children were making a theater. She then organized with her dolls a big theater game, both as compensation and to "purge" her fear (1945, pp. 132–33).

In the same vein, after the present writer's daughter had a tonsillectomy at four years of age during which she was traumatized by a nurse, a large share of her doll play for more than a year concerned this episode in which she played the part of the nurse, had a nice nurse, re-enacted the experience of the anesthesia, etc.

Type III-C is characterized by *liquidating combinations*. With difficult or unpleasant situations, the child may accept the difficulty, compensate for it, or alter it symbolically so that the unpleasantness is removed from the context. Some of the difficulty in utilizing these sub-types, interesting as they are, is epitomized by the fact that perhaps the present writer's illustration, given above, belongs in this class rather than in Type III-B. Here are a couple of examples of liquidating combinations:

> *Observation* 86: At 31 months and two days, Jacqueline had fallen down and cut her lip. After the usual scene, she consoled herself by projecting it all onto "cousin Andree" who took the form of a doll: *Oh! It's cousin Andree. We're washing her because she fell down and hurt her lip. She made a little hole in it. She cried.* The next day again she played at falling down, pretending to be with her cousin Francoise, and the "juice from her lip" made a stain on the wall (1945, p. 134).

Anticipatory symbolic combinations characterize Type III-D. In these there is symbolic anticipation of the consequences that would ensue should a certain event transpire.

> *Observation* 87: At four years and seven months, Jacqueline was walking on a steep mountain road: "Mind that loose stone."—*Marecage once trod on a stone, you know, and didn't take care, and she slipped and hurt herself badly . . .* Three days later, on another rather precipitous path, I pointed out to Jacqueline the rushing stream at the foot of the mountain and told her to be careful: *Do you know what my little negress friend* (imaginary) *did? She rolled right to the bottom of the mountain into the lake. She rolled for four nights. She scraped her knee and her leg terribly. She did not even cry. They picked her up afterwards. She was in the lake. She couldn't swim and was nearly drowned. At first they couldn't find her and then they did*—How do you know all that?—*She told me on the boat* (the boat on which Jacqueline first saw a negress who gave rise to this imaginary cycle) (1945, p. 134).

In this fashion, the anticipatory symbolic combinations of the game facilitate the assimilation of anticipated consequences.

Games with rules. Games with rules do not appear during either the preconceptual phase or the later intuitive phase. They do not make their appearance, according to Piaget's observations, until the third phase of this second period of development, when the reversible "concrete operations" become implicitly evident in many other of children's activities. At this point the child becomes able to appreciate the point of view of others and can therefore share it. With the development of this capacity to share points of view, games with rules not only appear but rapidly become dominant in the play of children who have the capacity. This occurs because even the "fortuitous combinations" that may occur in the course of shared activities lead, through the fact that they are jointly appreciated, to a game with rules. The rules may be evanescent inasmuch as they may operate only for the duration of the game, but they control the behavior and the interaction of the young players. At this point, with their new-found release from what Piaget (1926) early termed "egocentrism" that comes with this new-found capacity to share points of view in social interaction and communication, children resent the intrusion of those younger, who still lack this capacity for appreciating the point of view of others, and flock to the group-activities which utilize their new-found capacity. But this gets ahead of the developmental story.

TRANSITIONAL PRECONCEPTS AND THE ACQUISITION OF LANGUAGE AND LOGIC.

Images and semi-verbal signs. Images are idiosyncratic symbols depending upon the child's own private and active interactions with the environment. Piaget's observations with the development of verbal schemata indicate that these also are at first idiosyncratic in the sense that they depend upon the child's own special imitative approximation of what he has heard. Moreover, this approximation of the verbal sign typically signifies something quite different from that which is signified by the standard verbal sign.

The first of these semi-verbal signs signify the child's own sensorimotor schemata. Consider the following observations:

From Observation 101: At 13 months, Jacqueline used the conventional onomatopoeic sound *tch tch* to indicate a train passing her window, and repeated it each time a train passed, probably after the suggestion had first been made to her. But she afterwards said *tch tch* in two quite distinct types of situation. On the one hand, she used it indiscriminately for any vehicle she saw out of another window, cars, carriages, and even a man walking. At about 13 months and six days and on the following days, any noise from the street, as well as trains, produced *tch tch*. But on the other hand, when I played bo-peep, peering and disappearing without speaking, Jacqueline also said *tch tch* probably by analogy with the sudden appearance and disappearance of the trains . . .

At about 13 months 20 days, Jacqueline said *bow-wow* to indicate dogs. At 13 months and 29 days, she pointed from her balcony to the landlord's dog in the garden and said *bow-wow*. A few hours later, she made the same sound as she pointed to the geometrical pattern on the rug, and three days later, on seeing a horse from her balcony, she looked at it attentively and finally said *bow-wow* . . .

At about 18 months, Jacqueline was becoming more and more skillful in using adults in order to obtain what she wanted, and always grizzled [complained in a fussy vocal gesture] when they refused or pretended not to hear. One of her grandfathers was the person she found most accommodating, with the result that at 18 months and 13 days she began to use the term *Panana* not only to call her grandfather but also to indicate that she wanted something, and even when he was not present. She would indicate what she wanted by saying its name, give a definite grizzle and add *Panana*. At 18 months and nine days, she even said *Panana* when she was finding it boring to be washed. *Panana* was merely an indication that she wanted something to amuse her (1945, pp. 216–17).

Semi-verbal signs are legion. Their interest lies in the fact that they have the same kind of relationship to sensorimotor schemata that the first forms of deferred imitation have to immediate imitation and that the first symbolic schemata have to practice play. They lie intermediate between sensorimotor intelligence and conceptual schemata. Moreover, these semi-words are also intermediate between idiosyncratic imitative symbols and true signs, which are collective or social in character in the sense that what is signified is agreed upon generally. In fact, the semi-words illustrated are closer to the sensorimotor than to the conceptual. *Tch tch* applies to vehicles of all kinds and also to things appearing and disappearing. *Panana* (a corruption of grandpa) refers not only to this gentleman, but also to any desire for something he might have got for her had he been present. Similarly, *daddy* typically refers to all men and to various actions; and *mommy* may signify all women and also various actions done for the child.

One of the first three semi-words of one of the present writer's daughters was *maia-ma* (a corruption of mailman). She got this semi-word at about 11 months of age when she was just learning to walk and was allowed to go through the living room to the front door with her mother whenever the mailman rang. *Maia-ma* signified many things: the mailman, the door bell ringing, a noise on the front porch leading to an excited excursion to the front door, a letter or any piece of white paper, and a newspaper or a magazine. These formed an undifferentiated constellation of things and actions in this baby's life, and one semi-word *maia-ma* signified the whole constellation or any part of it indiscriminately.

Corresponding orders in the acquisition of images and language. Once the child is in the possession of such semi-verbal signs, he quickly learns to speak. His progress follows the familiar order of word-sentences, sentences of two words, then complete sentences which soon come to be linked one with another (see McCarthy, 1954). In his vocabulary development, he first acquires chiefly nouns. Verbs come later. At first blush this fact that nouns are acquired before verbs might seem to contradict Piaget's contention that images are the sensorimotor actions internalized, but it must be recalled that the definitions that younger children give to nouns are in terms of use. 'Use" signifies the sensorimotor actions into which the objects are most commonly incorporated. Thus, a chair "is to sit on"; a glass "is to drink from."

Although the first semi-words are little more than accompaniments of the sensorimotor activities, they often function as expressions of desire. Presumably as central processes become more independent of receptor inputs and motor action, imagery develops and these semi-words become signs of actual objects and actual actions. Consider the following:

Observation 104: The first time we had verbal evidence of recall in the case of Jacqueline, she was talking to herself. At 19 months and 13 days she was in bed in the evening when it was quite dark, and was sitting up talking to herself, unaware that I was listening. *Look, look, Uncle G., Aunt A., Uncle G.* Then she stopped and lay down, saying to herself *No, no.* After that she sat up and began again, going on for fully ten minutes . . .

At 19 months 28 days, Jacqueline told her mother about a grasshopper she had just seen in the garden: *Hopper, hopper jump boy*, meaning that the grasshopper jumped as a boy had made her jump. A boy cousin had in fact made her jump two days earlier (1945, p. 222).

Such behavior illustrates a transition. The verbalizations cease to be mere expression or accompaniment of actions in progress. In this observation, they serve rather the functions of re-presentation and recognition. Now, following this transition, verbalizations not only accompany action as did semi-words, they also describe the action. This descriptive aspect gives the action a new degree of objectification which is part of the business of communication and which takes part in the socialization of thought. This transition is typically marked also by the emergence of the question, "What's that?"

Observation 105: At about 21 months to 24 months, Jacqueline felt the need to introduce things and people by name to anyone who came into the room: *Daddy, mama, nose* (of her doll), *mouth,* etc. She would often bring a doll to her parents and say *little man* or bring some object, calling it by name as if she wanted to share her knowledge . . . But she behaved in exactly the same way when she was alone, and oddly enough it was during one of her monologues that we observed her first *what's that?* At 21 months and 24 days, for example, I heard her say to herself: *What's that, Jacqueline, what's that?* (1945, p. 223).

This question, "What's that?" Piaget (1945, pp. 223–33) sees as referring to both the name of the object and its placement among things (the class to which it belongs). It appears to imply that the child has a new grasp of the significance of communication. His verbalization is no longer a matter of obtaining wants; rather the child joins with adults in a common orientation toward "things that have names." That this is a generalization from experience rather than a pattern that unfolds automatically through maturation is attested by the fact that Helen Keller (1903), who had been both blind and deaf following an illness in her first year of life, did not hit upon this generalization until the critical water-pump incident that came in her eighth year after a tedious period during which Teacher (Anne Sullivan) had repeatedly associated the various forms of the touch alphabet with objects. At the pump, however, Helen suddenly discriminated, with Teacher's help, the signs for the water that overflowed onto her hand from the cup that she held in her hand, and to discriminate the signs of both of these from the sign for the act of drinking. The result was a generalization closely akin to one of Harlow's (1949) learning sets.

The acquisition of this "learning set" in the development of language puts the child into a dual system of relationships: (1) that which he sustains in his interaction with concrete objects and events, and (2) that concerned in his communications with other people (see also Rogers, 1951, chap. xi). While the child's images are based upon his private assimilative generalizations, the answers to his question "What's that?" continually correct his private generalizations and edge them toward the collective, agreed-upon relationships between verbal signs and their referents. It is not so much language that is being acquired in this process as the concept of the general class itself. Many of the collective verbal signs signify conceptual schemata which the child must gradually construct.

The preconceptual confusions of early childhood are a perennial source of amusement. Here are several examples from Piaget's daughters.

From Observation 106: At 26 months and 12 days, Jacqueline was in the garden walking on the landlord's flower-beds. Her mother stopped her from doing so and Jacqueline at once replied: *Me spoil Uncle Alfred's garden,* i.e., she was identifying this situation with another, very similar, but which she had experienced in another town and in the garden of an uncle who had no connection with the landlord in question . . .

At 31 months and 12 days, Jacqueline, seeing Lucienne in a new bathing suit, with a cap, asked: *What's the baby's name?* Her mother replied that it was a bathing costume, but Jacqueline pointed to Lucienne herself and said *But what's the name of that?* (indicating Lucienne's face) and repeated the question several times. As soon as Lucienne had her dress on again, Jacqueline exclaimed very seriously: *It's Lucienne again,* as if her sister had changed her identity in changing her clothes.

As an illustration of the reality attributed to pictures, Lucienne, at 32 months and 14 days, said spontaneously: *It's very heavy* (the picture book) *because there's a little girl in it.*—"Is the little girl in it?" . . .

When Lucienne was 38 months and 20 days old, we passed a man: *Is that man a daddy?*—"What is a daddy?"—*It's a man. He has lots of Luciennes and lots of Jacquelines.*—"What are Luciennes?"—*They're little girls and Jacquelines are big girls.* . . . At 51 months, Lucienne seeing a mountain stream in a village: *It's the same one we bathe in* (in another village).—"But where does it come from? Look!" (We could see it coming down from the mountain)—*From the stream we bathe in.*—"And the stream we bathe in?"—*From that one.* (1945, pp. 224–25).

The following illustration indicates the jumbled unevenness of progress in the formation of concepts during this phase of development:

Observation 107: At 30 months and three days, Jacqueline remarked: *That's not a bee, it's a bumble bee. Is it an animal?* But also at about 30 months, she used the term *the slug* for the slugs that we went to see every morning along a certain road. At 31 months and two days she cried: *There it is!* on seeing one, and when we saw another one 10 yards further on she said: *There's the slug again.* I answered: "But isn't it another one?" —Jacqueline went back to see the first one. "Is it the same one?" *Yes*—"Another slug?"—*Yes*—"Another or the same?"— . . . The question obviously had no meaning for Jacqueline . . . At 39 months, Jacqueline was playing with a red insect which disappeared. A quarter of an hour later when we were out for a walk, we tried to look at a lizard, which darted away. Ten minutes afterwards we found another red insect. *It's the red animal again.*—"Do you think so?"—*Where's the lizard then?* (1945, p. 225).

The preconcepts of this stage have, as particular objects, less individuality, and as classes less comprehensiveness than they will have in later stages. Slugs, for example, are all "the slug" reappearing in various forms. The same is true of "the red animal," with the interesting addition that once it had been connected with the lizard, it was expected to be accompanied by the lizard when it reappeared. This expectation derives from the fact that the child's thought is not reversible. Two features, the absence of individual identity and the absence of general class, are characteristic of these preconcepts. These two characteristics are basically one and the same. Piaget (1945) says they result "because a stable general class does not exist, and the individual elements, not being assembled within the framework of a genuine whole, partake directly of one another without permanent individuality." These characteristics are especially prominent in the following illustration in which Jacqueline's father is making an attempt to correct her preconcept.

Observation 108: At 38 months and 23 days, Jacqueline could not understand that Lausanne was *all the houses together* because for her it was her grandmother's house, *Lecret* that was *the Lausanne house.* For instance, talking about a lizard climbing up the wall, *It's climbing up the Lausanne house.* The next day I wanted to see if my explanation had been understood. "What is the Lausanne house?"—*It's all these houses* (pointing to all the houses around). *All these houses are Lecret.*—"What's Lecret?"—*It's granny's house, it's Lausanne.* . . . "All these houses" thus constituted a complex object depending on one of its elements which was seen as representing the whole (1945, pp. 225–26).

It may be well to contrast the preconcepts and questions of these preceding illustrations with the concepts and the self-corrective questions, well beyond the stage of "What's that?", manifest in this conversation of Jacqueline at nearly seven years of age.

Observation 110: At six years and seven months of age, Jacqueline said: *They're all called mushrooms, aren't they? Are fuzz-balls* (for which we were looking in the field) *mushrooms?* . . . The same day, referring to a hamlet of four or five houses: *Is that a village?*—No. It's still LaSage.—*Then it's part of LaSage?* (1945, p. 229).

Preconceptual reasoning: Transduction. It is instructive to look at the reasoning efforts of children in this preconceptual phase. The distortion of reality in the first deductive efforts resembles that in symbolic play except for the fact that there is no make-believe. The child believes seriously his deductions. Here are examples:

From Observation 111: At two years and 14 days, Jacqueline wanted for her doll a dress that was upstairs. She said *Dress,* when her mother refused it, *Daddy get dress.* As I also refused, she wanted to go herself *To mommy's room.* After several repetitions of this she was told that it was too cold there. There was a long silence, and then: *Not too cold.*—"Where?"—*In the room.*—"Why isn't it too cold?"—*Get dress.* Thus the judgment originated from the practical end in view. This is another example of what we [1936] called elsewhere sensorimotor reasoning (coordination of schemas for a definite end), but with the inclusion of representation which transformed reality and served as a means to obtaining the end . . .

At 34 months and eight days, Jacqueline had a fever and wanted oranges. It was too early in the season for oranges to be in the shops, and we tried to explain to her that they were not yet ripe. "They're still green. We can't eat them. They haven't yet got their lovely yellow color." Jacqueline seemed to accept this, but a moment later, as she was drinking her camomile tea, she said: *Camomile isn't green, it's yellow already . . . Give me some oranges!* Her reasoning here is clear: if the camomile is already yellow, the oranges can also be yellow:—a case of "active" analogy or symbolic participation (1945, pp. 230–31).

In such transductive reasonings, the child proceeds from the particular to the particular. He cannot proceed from the particular to the general, as in induction, nor from the general to the particular, as in deduction, because he is reasoning without genuine concepts, "without the reversible nestings of a hierarchy of classes and relations." He is rather coordinating schemata which are "the product of assimilation that is direct and distorting because it is centered on the individual elements which interest the subject" (1945, p. 237). It is in this sense that the preconcepts with which the child deals are "egocentric."

In some cases, when the reasoning involves only practical schemata, such transduction may lead to correct conclusions. Thus, at 30 months and 27 days, Jacqueline, in the bath room, remarked: "Daddy's getting hot water, so he's going to shave." Such an inference is only one step removed from the association by contiguity of ordinary Pavlovian conditioning, the coordination of the contiguous elements, i.e., "Daddy's getting hot water" and "Daddy's going to shave," being sufficient. It should be noted however, that the "bath room setting" is an important limiting cue. This limiting cue is analogous to those conditioning situations in which a buzzer signifies "food-coming" when the dog is in the "harness situation" and "shock-coming" when the dog is in the "situation of a two-compartment box." Dogs can readily acquire different responses to the same signal when that signal comes in different situations (Hilgard & Marquis, 1940). In such instances, transduction may lead to correct conclusions, but on the other hand, consider the following illustration:

From Observation 112: At 25 months and 13 days, Jacqueline wanted to see a little hunchbacked neighbor whom she used to meet on her walks. A few days earlier she had asked why he had a hump, and after I had explained she said: *Poor boy, he's ill, he has a hump.* The day before Jacqueline had also wanted to go and see him, but he had influenza, which Jacqueline called "being ill in bed." We started out for our walk and on the way Jacqueline said: *Is he still ill in bed?*—"No. I saw him this morning, he isn't in bed now."—*He hasn't a big hump now* (1945, p. 231).

Here "nestings" or categories are involved, and they are beyond Jacqueline. The class "illness" includes both "influenza" and "hunchback." For Jacqueline, who appears to be dealing with the verbal signs of these categories transductively, eliminating the *illness of influenza* must also eliminate the *illness of hunchback.* In applying the verbal response "illness" to both of these afflictions, an instance of the Miller-Dollard (1941) category of response-produced generalization, Jacqueline generalizes from influenza-illness to hunchback-illness without recognizing that these two "illnesses" are of two quite different orders. Chance focus of the items of her interest, uncollected by autonomous central processes that represent an appropriate hierarchy of categories, leads to the error. It is argument by simile: A is like B in one respect; therefore, A must be like B in all respects. Only after Jacqueline has found her transductions unconfirmed many times, has asked many questions about categories (e.g., "Are fuzz-balls mushrooms?"), and has been asked many questions will she fill in her still meager imagery of the world with the "learning sets" that correct her perceptions and mediate categories.

That this is a learning process rather than something which comes automatically through maturation is attested by the fact that such transductive formulations of causality are found among adult primitive people who are confronted with phenomena outside their ken. During a field investigation in Australia, for instance, Porteus (1937) awakened one morning to find a group of the aborigines surrounding one of the trucks that served the expedition. This truck was an old Reo. The sound made by the starter was distinctive and readily identified. A medicine-man chief sat at the wheel of the truck holding his arms and body after the fashion of the native driver. At this chief's signal, the group of natives surrounding the truck began in chorus to make a noise resembling that made by the Reo starter. Then following another signal from the medicine-man director, they altered the sound to one which approximated that of the engine. When Porteus asked his native interpreter what these people were doing, the interpreter answered, in somewhat abashed fashion: "They're trying to make the truck go. They think the sound moves the truck." Thus, just as the object acquires permanence as the infant acts upon it in more and more situations, and as shapes and sizes acquire constancy as the child develops autonomous central processes representing imitative perceptions of shapes seen from many different points of view, categories and variables come into being as "learning sets" which generalize individual objects and relationships.

CONSTRUCTIONS OF SPACE. Beginning at this preconceptual level, Piaget and his collaborators have supplemented their observational method with a method of getting the child to deal with concrete objects in various ways while the investigator directs questions designed to bring out the child's intentions or conceptions of what he is doing. This method of interrogating the child while he is manipulating concrete things has typically been employed with children who are four years old or older, but in the case of the studies of the conception of space, Piaget & Inhelder (1948) have found it possible to utilize this method with children under four, and in some cases at three.

TOPOLOGICAL CONCEPTS BEFORE EUCLIDEAN CONCEPTS. One of the merits of this approach is to bring out the way in which the child's constructions of space and imagery fall short of his sensorimotor capabilities. Even though the child of 18 months can keep track of himself as an object among objects which are located in various directions, he cannot image such relationships. This approach also brings out the fact that images of topological space are acquired long before images of either projective space or Euclidean space.

Topological relationships include (1) *proximity* (a point belongs to each of its neighbors), (2) *separation* (elements which are distinguished or separated), (3) *order* (which Piaget & Inhelder see as a synthesis of proximity and separation), (4) the relationships of *surrounding* or *enclosure,* and (5) *continuity* and *discontinuity.* These topological principles are primitive in the sense that they are purely internal to a particular figure whose intrinsic properties they express. Except for the factor of continuity and discontinuity, they do not express the relation among figures in a more complex field. Projective space deals with the problem of locating objects or their configurations relative to one another in accordance with principles of perspective or projective systems or of coordinate axes. Euclidean space involves the conservation of straight lines, angles, curves, distances; Piaget & Inhelder (1948) see such constructions beginning to be considered as the child incorporates within his image systems the capacity to take imaginally a point of view.

Evidence from the manipulation of objects. In one of these studies, Piaget & Inhelder (1948, chap. i) had children attempt to recognize various kinds of objects through manual manipulation without vision. They placed the child before a screen behind which he felt the objects handed to him. This permitted the investigator to observe the child's method of tactile exploration while keeping the child from seeing the objects manipulated. The objects presented for recognition consisted of (1) familiar solids (brush, ball, scissors, etc.), (2) flat geometrical shapes cut from cardboard or plastic sheets (squares, circle, triangle, trapezoid, swastika), and (3) a number of topological forms (irregular surfaces pierced by one or two holes, open or closed rings, two intertwined rings, etc.). They tested the child's recognition by having the child indicate which object he was feeling either by naming it or by picking it out of a group presented. This method proved unfeasible for children below about three, but at three years of age, the children readily recognized such familiar objects as a brush, a pencil, a key, and scissors. On the other hand, they failed completely to recognize either the geometric or topological figures and the level thus characterized is sub-stage A of phase I. Beginning at between three and three-and-a-half years of age, children begin to recognize, not the geometric figures, but the topological figures. Although they cannot distinguish a circular piece of cardboard from a square piece of cardboard, they easily distinguish an open figure from a closed figure, a surface with one or two holes from one without holes, a ring from a circle, intertwined rings from separate rings, etc. This is sub-stage B of phase I.

Observation of the manner in which the children manipulated the objects brought out a reason why topological figures are more readily identified than Euclidean figures, which are more familiar to adults.

Older children actively explore the figures, tracing the edges, feeling around them in an effort to "make something" of them. These younger children of the preconceptual phase have not yet acquired the "learning set" of trying to find out what the object is. They are content to grasp it, and pass it from hand to hand. Thus, Piaget & Inhelder (1948) point out that, while these younger ones are quite capable of the purely receptive perception which centers the child's hand on one or another part of the object, they do not undertake the sensorimotor activity which changes these "centrations" and supplies the child with a variety of impressions which he can coordinate to construct the unseen shape or to make the identification. The topological principles of proximity and separation and especially of continuity and discontinuity are easier to construct from a limited amount of manipulation than are the straight lines and curved lines and angles of Euclidean figures.[2]

Evidence from children's drawings. Drawings were also used as a source of evidence. The spontaneous drawings of the child between three and four show what Piaget & Inhelder call "synthetic incapacity." These drawings represent an image. Although the child may lack the motor capacity to execute his image, the fact that he draws a man in the shape of a large head to which he appends four strokes, two representing arms and two legs and a small trunk separate from these limbs, is not to be referred alone to this motor incapacity. The fact that the child represents the nose as above the eye is probably not a function of his motor incapacity but rather a function of his failure to synthesize in imagery the topological relationships which he sees in perception. This relationship between nose, eyes, and mouth, and that between limbs and trunk are matters of order in which proximity and separation are synthesized, and it is this order that the three year old has not yet generalized.

Piaget & Inhelder (1948) got support for this interpretation when they had children of this stage attempt to draw geometrical figures. During sub-stage 0, up to about two years six months to three years of age, no purpose nor aim could be discerned in the attempts the children made to copy figures. The scribbles they made in copying the cross were indistinguishable from those they made in copying a circle. In phase I-A, roughly from 2.5 years to 3.5 years, the scribbles begin to vary according to the model being copied. The scribble made for the cross differs from the scribble made for the circle, but,

[2] The principle that objects which are most rapidly identified by topological principles are recognized earlier by haptic perception than Euclidean shapes gets support from the studies of Page (1959) and Lovell (1959). Lovell, however, has found that rounded shapes are recognized as early as topological shapes, and he suggests that it is the straight-sided shapes that are difficult to recognize.

curiously enough, it is only the topological relationships which are indicated. In the copy of the cross, the lines tend to be close together while the copy of a circle is drawn as an irregular closed curve. At phase I-B, beginning in the second half of the fourth year, it is possible to speak of real drawings, but even yet the child draws circles for both triangles and squares which are indistinguishable from his copy of a circle. He manages to get more or less intersecting lines for a cross. When he copies either a circle with a triangle drawn in it or a triangle with a circle drawn in it, he gets only the topological principle of inclusion by drawing one circle within another.

Evidence from seriations. Piaget & Inhelder (1948) have studied order or sequence, the third basic topological relationship, by showing the child a model consisting of from seven to nine vari-colored beads on a rod and asking the child to reproduce this order of colored beads on another rod. Following this, they present two "washing lines" one strung out a few centimeters above the other. Between seven and nine paper imitations of pieces of washing are arranged to hang on the first line. After the child has named the colors, he collaborates with the examiner in hanging them on the line which supplies the model. Then the child is asked to reproduce the order of pieces of washing on the lower line. When children between two and three are asked to reproduce such series of objects in a particular order, they are completely unable to understand the request. At phase I-A, during roughly the first half of the fourth year, the child manages to match items, but is unable to match order. In the terms of mathematics, the child can *combine* a group of objects or events, but he cannot *permute* their order.[3] After matching the items on the wash line, dress with dress, and shirt with shirt, he simply puts the matching items on the second line without any appreciation of the fact that the dress is not next to the shirt on his line as it is on the model line. When asked if his reproduction is just like the model, he discovers no errors. At phase I-B, although the child again fails to copy the order, when he is asked if his reproduction is just like the model, he finds errors and he can correct the order in specific given pairs, but he is still unable to coordinate successive pairs.

Evidence from tying knots. Asking children of this age to tie simple knots around a stick brings out the fact that children in phase I-A cannot copy knots even when they watch a model tie them because they cannot grasp the principle of intertwinement. They either wind one end of the string around the other without managing to insert either end in the loop, or else they insert one end in a half loop without

[3] A point suggested by Dr. Rogers Elliott.

superimposing it. Either way, the child misses the necessary "surrounding" and thereby gets no knot. During phase I-B the child learns how to copy the simplest knots, but he cannot follow the various sections of a slack knot with one finger, nor can he distinguish false knots from true knots. On the other hand, these children of phase I-B can bring the opposite ends of a string together, cross them, and then pass one end through the loop so formed. Thus, they have some appreciation of the topological relationship of "surrounding." On the other hand, they are unable to apply it generally, and even though they may succeed in the tying act, the lack of the concept shows in the fact that they cannot distinguish a true knot from a false one by merely looking at it or by tracing it. It is such evidence that leads Piaget to contend that, at this preconceptual stage, imagery lags behind sensorimotor action.

Evidence from ordering objects in lines. Straight and curved lines are also readily recognized, but children of this preconceptual phase have no clear idea of what constitutes a straight line. By having children arrange match-sticks stuck into bases made of plasticine, with the child told that each match represents a telegraph pole that he must arrange to form a perfectly straight line running along a road, Piaget & Inhelder (1948) show that these children can readily arrange the match sticks along the edge of a table when they can put the match sticks very close together. On the other hand, if two endposts are set up across a round table or diagonally across a square table, children of the preconceptual phase are completely incapable of arranging the matches in a straight line between such pairs of points. From such performances, Piaget & Inhelder infer the absence of the representation of a projective line despite the fact that it is well appreciated perceptually. On the representational level, however, these performances indicate that the representation of a line is limited to the topological proximity.[4]

SUMMARY: PRECONCEPTUAL PHASE

A major series of transformations of behavior and presumably of central processes occur during the transition between sensorimotor

---

[4] In his monograph on the development of transitivity, Braine (1959, p. 37) states that there is "a hiatus in Piaget's studies of child development. In his works on infancy he leaves the child at 18 months to two years; in his studies of 'operational' thinking the youngest subjects are about four years old. The intermediate period of development has not—at least not yet—been extensively studied by Piaget." Since Piaget (1945) does not appear in his list of references, it appears clear that Braine has missed *Play, Dreams and Imitation in the Child.* At any rate, perhaps this extensive synopsis of Piaget's work for the period between the ages of two and four will correct the impression that Piaget has left any such hiatus.

activity and preconceptual thought. Representation appears when new objects and events are assimilated not merely to schemata which are activated by perceptible stimuli but also to those which are evoked by means of "signifiers." The connection between "signifiers" and "signified" is mediated by images that intervene in the development of imitation, play, and even cognitive representation. The symbolic function, or imagery, is essential for the construction of representative space and the various other "real" categories of thought, and it makes possible the acquisition of language or collective "signs." This development of imagery involves a differentiation between the signifying schemata and the signified schemata. Piaget sees this differentiation becoming possible through the differentiation between accommodation and assimilation, e.g., between imitation, where accommodation predominates, and play, where assimilation predominates. This differentiation is depicted graphically in Figure 6–1 (p. 177) which synopsizes the course of development between the activity of sensorimotor stage 6 and the operational activity of the child from age seven or eight to 11 or 12.

"Signifier" and signified" are undifferentiated during the sensorimotor period, since the only "signifiers" consist of "indices" or "signals," which are merely aspects of either the object or the schema. But as the imitative process becomes internalized, presumably through both maturation and the gradual short-circuiting that comes with repeated imitating, it becomes capable of evoking absent models and thereby of supplying the "signifiers" for assimilative activities. Just as the differentiation between means and ends at the fourth sensorimotor stage permitted a new level of coordination of schemata, this differentiation of accommodation and assimilation permits the integration of new systems which are more complex than sensorimotor schemata. Inasmuch as the images can run off more rapidly than sensorimotor actions, they serve to speed up representative processes. Moreover, inasmuch as images can represent what is not present, they increase the scope of the child's activity.

"Cognitive representation" at this level takes the form of the preconcept because the highest adaptive thought of which the child is capable in this phase of development still remains close to either imitative representation or symbolic play. The preconcepts which are superimposed on sensorimotor schemata as a function of the image and language lack both true generality (what Piaget calls "a hierarchy of nestings") and true individuality in the sense of constancy of the object outside the immediate field of action. They are also irreversible in the sense that they follow the course of the perceptions and actions represented.

"Transductive" reasoning, which involves the coordination of these preconcepts, therefore remains half-way between the combining or coordination of actions and deductive reasoning. Adaptive equilibrium between assimilation and accommodation is impossible when the child goes beyond the sphere of immediate, practical activity. The new universe which symbolic processes open to the child compels him to repeat much the same evolution he has already completed on the sensorimotor plane. This he does by devoting most of his time to imitation and symbolic play. This means that the rate at which the child develops and the degree to which his imagery is differentiated is to a considerable degree a function of the variety of models, appropriate to his already acquired schemata, that the child has an opportunity to imitate.

Appropriateness of models depends upon the match between the model and the schemata already acquired. This matching is a dynamic affair. The child is bored with those models which he has already fully assimilated, and those which are beyond his accommodative grasp are meaningless. In their studies of the development of representational space, Piaget & Inhelder (1948) make a substantial contribution to this matching by pointing out that the topological aspects of space become representative before the projective and Euclidean aspects.

FROM PRECONCEPTS TO CONCRETE OPERATIONS

When the child reaches the age of approximately four years, Piaget and his collaborators change both their method of study and their emphasis in theory. Although no dramatic transformation in the structures of thought appears here at the beginning of the intuitive phase, the fact that the child can communicate with language and has a somewhat expanded span of attention and a level of interest which permits directions makes it possible to change from the observational method, with occasional experiments to test the accuracy of interpretations, to a method in which the child is presented with concrete tasks and is interrogated with questions designed to bring out what he can and cannot do with the material supplied. One form of this method has already been described in connection with the studies of the recognition of objects by manual manipulation with vision by Piaget & Inhelder (1948). On the side of theory, the primary emphasis shifts to the relationship between the structures of thought and the operations of symbolic logic.

INTUITIVE PHASE: OUTLINE OF THE THEORY. Consider first the theory in outline. Phase II, the intuitive phase, is one of growing conceptualization. Piaget (1949) sees this conceptualization occurring as central neural processes become more and more autonomous with repetitions of various kinds of overt actions. Just as he (1945) conceives images to arise in the child from the internalization of imitation, the "regulations" of intuition appear as the central processes arising from the child's activity provide him with the basis for feedback from internalized standards. So also does Piaget (1942) see the three fundamental "operations" (classes, relations, and numbers) develop as the internalization of overt activities. Classifying derives from the action of grouping objects together according to some aspect in which they are perceived to be similar. Asymmetrical relations (A is longer than B; X is the mother of Y) derive from the act of comparing and ordering objects according to some aspect in which they are perceived to differ. Numbers arise from the combining of classifying and ordering (Piaget & Szeminska, 1941). At the close of the intuitive phase these operations become grouped into Gestalt-like structures (*structures d'ensemble*) which Piaget (1947) terms "concrete operations" or "groupements." The development of "concrete operations" at approximately age seven or eight marks the beginning of a new phase of operational intelligence which lasts till the child is about eleven or twelve years old.

Organism-environment interaction. It is in the continuous organism-environment interaction and through the invariant processes of assimilation and accommodation that this development takes place. During the preconceptual and intuitive phases, Piaget (1947, pp. 38–39) notes that thought is in disequilibrium or in a state of unstable equilibrium. The child attempts to solve each new problem with the "anticipatory schemata" or "expectations" from past assimilations at his disposal for new situations. These expectations frequently meet with contradiction. Contradiction is a matter of the organism-environment interaction, which is still poorly understood. It is apparently the functional equivalent of the "disconfirmation" of Miller, Galanter, & Pribram (1960). If the child has the conceptual wherewithal to appreciate the contradiction, the contradiction results in either accommodative modification or emotional disturbance analogous to that which Festinger (1957) has termed "cognitive dissonance." Which result occurs appears to be a matter that Hebb (1949) and McClelland *et al.* (1953) have attempted to encapsulate in the "discrepancy hypothesis." One way of putting the relationship is the following. If the child has the wherewithal to appreciate the contradiction and can cope with it, accommodative modification in the conceptual structures (revised expectations, attitude changes, etc.) occurs. If the child can appreciate the contradiction but cannot cope with it, the consequence is emotional disturbance. If the child cannot appreciate the contradiction, his interaction with that situation has no more effect upon his conceptual structures than does the proverbial "lecturing a pig about Sunday." In this sense, if corrective modification is to occur, it is essential that the problem should be appropriately matched to the schemata available in the child to permit the accommodation.[5] In Piaget's (1947) theorizing the solution may be found by "extending, subdividing or differentiating, or combining" the existing structures.

As the central processes or thought structures become more and more autonomous, and as they come to correspond with a larger and larger portion of reality, their efficiency of operation increases. They acquire what Piaget (1947, p. 40) terms a "mobile equilibrium." This is no static state of rest, but rather a "system of balanced interchanges, alterations which are continually compensated by others. It is the equilibrium of polyphony and not that of a system of inert masses, and has nothing to do with the false stability which sometimes results in old age from the slowing down of intellectual effort." Thus, the two themes (1) of continuous organism-environment interaction through the invariant processes of accommodation and assimilation and (2) of the gradual transformation of the structures of intelligence are continued. It is the problem of explaining the "mobile equilibrium" of the "concrete operations" that brings the increased emphasis on the relations between thought and logic.

Thought and logic. Piaget (1947, chap. ii) reviews the studies of "imageless thought" by Külpe and his students of the Würzburg school (see Titchener, 1909) as a springboard for relating logic and thought. These introspective studies indicated (1) that the role of images is accessory rather than essential, as associationism would have it, (2) that intellectual feelings and attitudes can be reported, and (3) that thought itself consists of "anticipatory schemata" such as "intentions," "rules," and relationships like "$A < B$," "X is subordinate to I," and "E is in front of F." Thus, these anticipatory schemata could be seen as logic-like. Moreover, Selz (1922) found that solution-searching could not be reduced to sensorimotor schemata, but consisted rather of "filling in the gaps in complexes of ideas and relations." Duncker (1945) has extended this concept further in his "search model." This "filling in the gaps" is claimed to be always oriented by anticipatory schemata or "search models," and they obey precise laws. These laws are the laws of logic. Thus, these investiga-

[5] The importance of a proper match between the schemata already acquired and the circumstances encountered in determining the effect of an encounter has been demonstrated by Greco (1959b), Goustard (1959), and Matalon (1959).

tions of adult problem-solving by the introspective method have tended "to make thought the mirror of logic." Because such anticipatory schemata as intentions are absent until the child is about six months old, and schemata of rules and relationships are typically absent until children are about seven years old, Piaget (1947) has reversed this verdict to make "logic the mirror of thought."

Piaget's problem is to formulate the properties of the "concrete operations" or "groupements" in a fashion that will permit explaining both their "mobile equilibrium" and their ontogenetic formation. He attempts to discover the properties by observation or experiment, and to formulate these properties in terms of the operations of logic and mathematics. In this connection, he observes that the languages of both mathematics and logic reflect action. In such an expression as $(x^2 + y = x - u)$, for instance, Piaget (1947, 1953) notes that "each term refers to a specific action: the sign $(+)$ refers to combining, the sign $(=)$ expresses a possible substitution, the sign $(-)$ a separation, the square (x^2) the action of reproducing 'x' x times, and each of the values u, x, y, and z the action of reproducing unity a certain number of times." Similarly, he observes that two classes (vertebrates and invertebrates) can be added like numbers (to constitute all animals). Here the word *and* (or the logical sign $+$) represents the action of *combining*. Classifying may itself be either an overt act of sorting objects or an implicit operation. Moreover, two asymmetrical relations $(A<B; B<C)$ may be arranged in a series; the double relation permits the inference that $C>A$, and the inference could be acted out by placing A, B, and C in a series of increasing size. Again, classifications may be made from several points of view. Thus, animals may be divided into vertebrates and invertebrates, and they may be distributed according to their habitat on land (terrestrial) or in water (aquatic). By combining these two classification systems (an operation termed logical multiplication in symbolic logic) one gets: (1) vertebrates terrestrial, (2) vertebrates aquatic, (3) invertebrates terrestrial, and (4) invertebrates aquatic. It is thus that the operations of logic and mathematics may be said to correspond to overt actions and to the operations of thought. The properties of thought-operations which have achieved "mobile equilibrium" are four in the case of "groups" of a mathematical order, and five in the case of "groupings" of a qualitative or logical order.

(1) *Combinativity or transitivity.* Any two classes may be combined into one comprehensive class which embraces them both, e.g., $2 + 3 + 5 = 10$; *all boys and all girls = all children.* Moreover any two relations $(A>B)$ and $(B>C)$ may be joined into the one relation $(A>C)$ which contains them both. Thus, from a psychological

standpoint, this first property of operations showing a mobile equilibrium corresponds to the coordinating of actions.

(2) *Reversibility.* Every logical or mathematical operation is reversible in the sense that there is an opposite operation which cancels it (e.g., 3 + 5 = 8, but also 8 — 5 = 3; *all boys and all girls = all children,* but *all children except girls = all boys*). These are examples of subtraction as the converse of addition. Similarly, division is the converse operation for multiplication (e.g., 3 × 5 = 15; but 15 ÷ 5 = 3). Piaget (1947) emphasizes reversibility as the most clearly defined characteristic of mature thought or intelligence. Although motor habits and perceptions are capable of combination, they remain irreversible. Motor actions become reversible when the child (sensorimotor stage 6) can retrace his steps, but such reversibility of action goes beyond habit and requires intelligence as Piaget (1947) defines habits and intelligence. Images, like the habits and perceptions from which they derive, lack reversibility. It is only gradually, as central processes become more and more autonomous, that thought acquires this property of reversibility. The younger the child, the less reversible are his thought processes, and the more they resemble the sensorimotor patterns out of which they develop.

(3) *Associativity.* When several operations are to be combined, it makes no difference which are combined first, e.g., (2 + 3) + (4 + 5) = 2 + (3 + 4) + 5; *all vertebrates and all invertebrates = all mammals and all non-mammals; A is the aunt of B and B is the mother of C = A is the sister of D and D is the grandmother of C.* Associativity is analogous to the capacity for detours which makes its original appearance at sensorimotor stage 6. Neither perception nor motor habits show this property. In perception, two distinct paths lead to different results,[6] and motor habit tends to be relatively stereotyped. Associativity reaches an especially high level in the identities of trigonometry and of symbolic logic.

(4) *Identity.* Any operation can be nullified by combining it with its opposite (e.g., + 3 — 3 = 0, or x 5 ÷ 5 = x 1; *all Alaskans except those who are Alaskans = nobody; I move 10 steps to the north then I move 10 steps to the south = I stand where I started*). In the thought of the adult, making an hypothesis and subsequently rejecting it alters nothing, but the child cannot do this; the original data of a problem tend to be somewhat distorted by his having formulated an hypothesis even though he may discard it.

---

[6] Here Piaget (1947) is referring to the kind of phenomena Helson (1959) has treated under adaptation-level theory. These include the effects of anchoring a scale. Thus, water of 80 degrees feels warm after one has become adapted to water of 65 degrees, and cold after one has become adapted to water of 95 degrees.

(5) The fifth property has two versions, one for qualitative logical classes and relations and another version for numbers. (*a*) *Tautology* holds for logical classes. Repeating a proposition, a classification, or a relation leaves it unchanged. Repeating a message may permit a listener to absorb the information, but the repeated message contains no more information than is contained in its first statement (e.g., *all mammals and all mammals = all mammals;* A>B, A>B, = A>B). (*b*) *Iteration* holds for numbers. When a number is combinded with itself, the result is a new number (e.g., $3 + 3 = 6$, and $3 \times 3 = 9$).

INTUITIVE PHASE: PIAGET'S METHODS AND RESULTS. The facts which this theory was designed to explain derive from experiments in which children between four and eight years of age, in phase II, were presented with a variety of materials which they examined or manipulated in some fashion and were interrogated to bring out what they did and did not understand. A full protocol will be given for one of these test situations. For the various other selected situations, the evidence will be synopsized.

Conservation of continuous quantities. In one of the first kinds of experiment, one concerning the conservation of quantities of liquid, Piaget & Szeminska (1941) give the child-subject two beakers of equal dimensions (see A_1 and A_2 in Figure 6–2). They contain the same quantity of liquid as shown by the levels in the beakers. The liquid in A_2 is then poured into two smaller beakers of equal dimensions (B_1 and B_2). The child is then asked whether the quantity of liquid poured from A_2 into B_1 and B_2 is still equal to that in A_1. If the child answers yes, the liquid in B_1 is poured into two smaller containers (C_1 and C_2), and that in B_2 is poured into containers. (C_3 and C_4), identical with C_1 and C_2. As the liquid is divided in this fashion, the problem concerning the conservation of its quantity is put to the child in form of a question as to the equality or nonequality with that in one of the original containers. Moreover, as a check on the child's answers, he is commonly asked to pour the liquid into a container of a shape differing from that of the original beaker. Again the problem is to see if he judges the quantity to remain the same or to be changed thereby.

Here is the record of the experiment with Clairette Blas, a four year old.

Blas (4:0). "Have you got a friend?—*Yes, Odette.*—Look, we're giving you, Clairette, a glass of orangeade (A_1, three-fourths full), and we're giving Odette a glass of lemonade (A_2, also three-fourths full). Has one of you more to drink than the other?—*The same.*—This is what Clairette does: she pours her drink into two other glasses (B_1 and B_2, which are thus half-full). Has Clairette

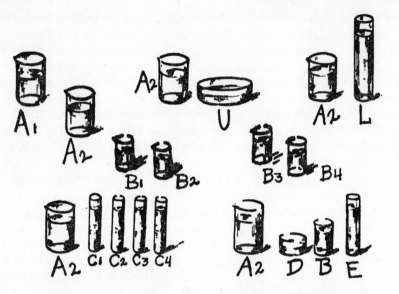

Fig. 6–2. The containers used to investigate the conservation of continuous and discontinuous quantities. From Inhelder (1953, p. 80), with modifications.

the same amount as Odette?—*Odette has more.*—Why?—*Because we put less in* (she pointed to the levels of B_1 and B_2, without taking into account the fact that there were two glasses).—(Odette's drink was then poured into B_3 and B_4). *It's the same.*—And now (pouring Clairett's drink from B_1 and B_2 into L, a long thin tube which is almost full)?—*I've got more.*—Why?—*We poured it into that glass* (pointing to the level in L), *and here* (B_3 and B_4) *we haven't.*—But were they the same before?—*Yes.*—And now?—*I've got more.*" Clairette's orangeade was then poured back from L into B_1 and B_2: "Look, Clairette has poured hers like Odette. So is all the lemonade (B_3 and B_4) and all the orangeade (B_1 and B_2) the same?—*It's the same* (said with conviction).—Now Clairette does this (pouring B_1 into C_1 which is then full, while B_2 remains half-full). Have you got the same amount to drink?—*I've got more.*—But where does the extra come from?—*From in there* (B_1).—What must we do so that Odette has the same?—*We must take that little glass* (pouring part of B_3 into C_2).—And is it the same now? Or has one of you got more?—*Odette has more.*—Why?—*Because we poured it into that little glass* (C_2).—But is there the same amount to drink, or has one got more than the other?—*Odette has more to drink.*—Why?—*Because she has three glasses* (B_3 almost empty, B_4 and C_2, while Clairette has C_1 full and B_2)" (Piaget & Szeminska, 1941, p. 6).

Phase II-A: Early sub-stage of the intuitive phase. Although the child of less than two years of age attributes permanence to an object, this child of four, and she is typical, attributes no permanence to the quantity of liquid that she sees poured from one container into several or from a container of a given shape into a container of another shape. Her criteria of quantity are perceptual. In the language of Piaget & Szeminska (1941), her criteria derive from the aspects of the containers on which her attention is "centered" or focused. These include the number of containers, the height of the column of liquid, and the thinness or thickness of the column of liquid. In the performance illustrated here, the child's thought processes have not yet developed to a point where they can correct what Heraclitus noted long ago as the "illusory flux of appearances." These appearances predominate because the child's central or thought processes still lack the logical property of *reversibility*. With her attention "centered" on what she sees, Clairette does not think of reversing the pourings, nor, when they are reversed by the examiner, does she see the implications of the reversal for the "conservation of quantity." Thus, although the object has permanence for her, quantity does not. Moreover, she can no more appreciate the contradictions derived from reversibility than, to be repetitious, can the proverbial pig appreciate a lecture about Sunday. The discrepancy between her central processes and what she sees happening is so great that it fails to produce the emotional disturbance of Festinger's (1957) cognitive dissonance. The match between this environmental situation and Clairette's intellectual structure is so poor that the interaction between them is irrelevant to any intuitions she may have about the quantity of liquid.

If one thinks of Piaget's observations in physiological terms as Piaget (1949) himself has, it would appear that one important factor in the reversibility of thought may be the autonomy of central neural firing-systems. Presumably this autonomy is a function of both the experience of living and of maturation. But perhaps autonomy is merely another name for reversibility. Perhaps the effect of experience on the autonomy of central neural processes depends upon the factor of the relevance or upon the appropriateness of the match between the central processes and the environmental situations with which the organism must cope.

Phase II-B: later sub-stage of the intuitive phase. At any rate, after about a year and a half or two years when children have reached the later sub-stage of the intuitive phase, such pourings as those Clairette observed above do become relevant to a child's conceptions of quantity, for some appreciation of contradiction becomes evident. Here is one of those intermediary performances. Edi, aged six years and four months, considers the quantity unchanged when the liquid is poured from A_1 into the two beakers B_1 and B_2. Yet, when it is poured into three or four beakers, Edi's perceptual appearances predominate and he relinquishes his belief in "conservation."

Edi (6:4). "Is there the same in these two glasses (A_1 and A_2)?—*Yes.*—Your mommy says to you: instead of giving you your milk in this glass (A_1), I give it to you in these two (B_1 and B_2), in the morning, and one at night. (It is poured out.) Where will you have the most to drink, here (A_2) or there (B_1 and B_2)?— *It's the same.*—That's right. Now, instead of giving it to you in these two (B_1 and B_2), she gives it to you in three (pouring A_2 into C_1, C_2, and C_3), one in the morning, one at lunch time and one at night. Is it the same in the two as in the three, or not?—*It's the same in the three as in the two . . . No, in the three there's more.*—Why?—(B_1 and B_2 were poured back into A_1). And if you pour the three ($C_1 + C_2 + C_3$) back into that one (A_2) how far up would it come?—(He pointed to a level higher than that in A_1.)—And if we pour these three into four glasses (doing so into $C_1 + C_2 + C_3 + C_4$, with a consequent lowering of the levels) and then pour all back into the big one (A_2), how far up will it come? (He pointed to a still higher level.)—And 5?—(He pointed to a still higher level.)—And with 6?—*There wouldn't be enough room in the glass"* (Piaget & Szeminska, 1941, pp. 13–14).

Such intermediary reactions, characteristic of the second sub-stage of the intuitive phase (II-B), are methodologically as well as theoretically important. The fact that the child gives a correct answer when the liquid is poured into two containers (discrepancy relatively slight) but fails to assume conservation of quantity when it is poured into three or four (discrepancy increased) demonstrates that he *does understand* the question. Moreover, his answers indicate that he appreciates the contradiction. A kind of conflict is developing between the import of his thought processes and the import of the appearances deriving from his perceptual centrations. A long series of variations exists between responses like those of four-year-old Clairette and those of the six-year-old Edi. It would be interesting to see how the relative dominance of central processes and perceptual centrations changed longitudinally in a given child.

In the following Edi is faced with a slightly different problem.

"(Glass A_1 was 1/5 filled.) Pour as much orangeade (from a pitcher) into this one (L) as there is in there (A_1).—(He filled L to the same level as that in A_1.)—Is there the same amount to drink?—*Yes.*—Exactly the same?—*No.*—Why not?—*That one* (A_1) *is bigger* (= wider than L) [see Fig. 6–2]. What must you do to have the same amount?—*Put some more in* (filling L).—Is that right?—*No.* —Who has more?—*Me* (pouring some back).—*No, the other one has more* (A_1). —(He continued to add more and then pour some back, without reaching a satisfactory conclusion)" 'Piaget & Szeminska, 1941, pp. 15–16).

In this situation, Edi discovers by comparing the two columns in height, that A_1 is wider than L. He decides therefore that A_1 contains more than L *because it is bigger*. This illustrates what Piaget means by the "regulations" of the intuitive phase. In this fashion, Edi is beginning to consider both the height of the column of liquid and the circumference of the container, but not quite simultaneously. This is the beginning of logical multiplication.

Phase III: concrete operations. The onset of Phase III and the "concrete operations" is marked by *necessary conservation* of quantity. This comes at approximately seven or eight years of age, but sometimes considerably younger or older, when children state almost immediately that the quantities of liquid are "the same" even though they are sub-divided indefinitely or they are poured into containers of widely varying shape. In the following, AES, aged six years and six months, appears to be on the threshold of necessary conservation.

AES (6:6). A_1 and A_2 were ¾ filled, and then A_1 was poured into P_1 which was wide and low [like U in Fig. 6–2]. "Is there still as much orange juice as there was in the other glass?—*There is less.*—(A_2, which is supposed to be his glass, was poured into P_2 [also wide and low but not pictured in Fig. 6–2]). Will you still have the same amount to drink now?—*Oh yes! It's the same, it just seems as if there's less because it is bigger* (= wider), *but it's the same.*—(P_1 and P_2 were poured back into A_1 and A_2, and A_1 was poured into B_1 plus B_2.) Has Roger got more than you now?—*He's got the same* (definitely stated).—And if I were to pour yours into four glasses (A_1 into $C_1 + C_2 + C_3 + C_4$)?—*It'll still be the same*" (Piaget & Szeminska, 1941, p. 17).

Here AES is at first apparently fooled by the "appearances," but one "disconfirmation" is enough to make the import of his thought processes dominate over the import of the appearances from his perceptual "centrations." Similarly, Bert, aged seven years and two months, began by filling L to the same level as A_2, then added some more "*because the glass* (L) *is smaller: you think it's the same, but it's not true*" (Piaget & Szeminska, 1941, p. 18).

Such comments in the situation provided demonstrate that these children recognize the difference between "appearance" and "reality." They assume the conservation of quantity. In doing so their remarks show both reversibility of thought and a capacity for logical multiplication. They take account of both the height of the column of liquid and the width of the container simultaneously. It is these logical operations which make it possible for them to justify conservation of quantity in spite of the variations in appearance.[7]

Conservation of discontinuous quantities. The same set of beakers depicted in Figure 6–2 are used with beads which provide discontinuous quantities that can be globally evaluated. In this case, however, the child is asked to put beads into one beaker, one by one, at

[7] Confirmation of the existence of these stages in the development of conservation of quantity has come from studies outside Piaget's laboratory by Lovell & Ogilvie (1960) and Smedslund (1959).

the same time as the experimenter puts beads, one by one, into the other beaker. The child is then asked whether the total quantities are the same, with or without identity in the shape of the two containers. Children of all ages agree that the two quantities are the same.

Phase II-A. As soon as the beads are poured from a container of one shape to a container of a different shape and dimension, however, children of four or five, the first sub-stage of the intuitive phase, think that the quantity either increases or decreases depending upon his perceptual criterion of quantity. As was true for the liquids, the quantities are estimated from perceptual centrations or criteria which are uncoordinated one with another, and the children do not think of reversing the act of pouring.

Phase II-B. Again, at the later sub-stage of the intuitive phase, there is evidence of a conflict between appearances, on the one hand, and the child's knowledge of equality based upon the fact that he himself dropped the same number of beads into one of the containers that the experimenter dropped into the other container. In the following case of Von, aged five years and 10 months, the instability of his thought stands out.

Von put one pink bead into A_2 each time I put a blue one into E. "Who has the most?—*It's the same in both.—*Why?—*We put them in together.*—And if we make two necklaces?—*Both the same.*—Well, why is the level in there (E) higher than the level in the other (A_2)?—*Because here* (E) *is round and long, and there* (A_2) *it's round and bigger* (= wider) *and we put in the same amount.*— (The beads in A_2 were then poured into D which was then full.) Now what about this (E) and that (D)?—*They're the same.*—Why?—*Because that one* (D) *is smaller* (= lower) *and this one* (E) *is longer;* [Reader, note!] *it's bigger and so there's more.*—More what? (E and D were both full to the brim, so Von was not therefore distinguishing between the volume of the glasses in the quantity of the beads.)—*More beads. There are more beads in there* (E).—And if we made two necklaces?—*You* (E) *would have more; the blue necklace would be longer.*—And what about the pink one(D)?—*Shorter, because there are less beads"* (Piaget & Szeminska, 1941, pp. 31–32).

Here the instability of Von's thought processes show in his midstream switch from a judgment that the two containers hold the same number of beads, because "we put in the same amount," to a perceptually-centered judgment that there are more blue beads in the tall thin test-tube than pink ones in the broad flat dish. Even though Von knows that the same number of beads were put into the two containers, the fact that he cannot take account of both the height of the column and the width of the container at the same time (logical multiplication) does not permit him to justify the conservation of quantity, and his perceptual centrations predominate. It is attractive to think of this instability of thought-processes as weakness in the terms of Hull's (1943) conception of "habit strength."

Phase III. Again, Phase III and the concrete operations bring necessary conservation. For instance, when Lee, aged seven years and seven months, compared E and D (each containing 16 beads), he remarked: "Here (E) it's not so wide, but it's higher. That one (D) is wider, but it's smaller." This multiplication of relations permits a justification of the equating of the apparent differences and eradicates the contradiction between "appearances" and "the known."

Conservation of numerical correspondence. In another experimental situation, Piaget & Szeminska (1941, chap. iii) presented children with a row of egg cups and an equal number of eggs (see Figure 6–3). The children were asked to take just enough eggs for the egg cups, not more not less, one egg for each cup. The child is then asked to check his selection by putting one egg in each egg cup. This provokes a one-to-one correspondence. Next, the eggs are taken out of the egg cups and bunched, and the child is asked whether there is the same number of eggs as egg cups.

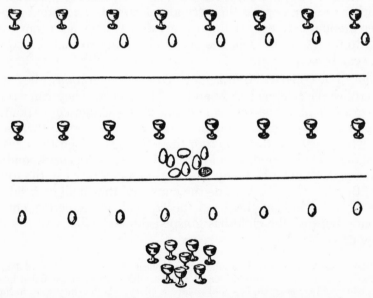

Fig. 6–3. Egg cups and eggs used to provoke numerical correspondence in the study of the conservation of number. From Inhelder (1953, p. 79).

Phase II-A. Children of the first sub-stage of the intuitive phase cannot make the one-to-one correspondence by themselves. Instead they tend to arrange a series of eggs before the egg cups which extends the same distance but may have either more or fewer eggs. They are typically surprised, when they are asked to put an egg in each cup, to find that they have either too many or too few. When the eggs are removed from the egg cups and clustered and the child is asked whether they are the same, he typically sees more egg cups than eggs. Or if the egg cups are clustered he sees more eggs than egg cups. Inasmuch as his thought is not reversible, it does not occur to him that the action of clustering the egg cups can be reversed, and that since none has been added or taken away, he can readily again put one egg in each cup and thereby prove the equality of the numbers. Lacking this, he tends to focus (or center) on the amount of space covered by either the eggs or the egg cups, and the amount of space covered determines which appears to be more.

Phase II-B. In the latter portion of the intuitive phase, children spontaneously make the one-to-one correspondence, but they cannot see that the correspondence implies lasting equivalence of the sets of eggs and egg cups regardless of their arrangement. In some instances, when the arrangement of eggs is a row only slightly shorter than the row of egg cups, the child reports equivalence, but as soon as either the egg cups or the eggs are clustered, perceptual appearances predominate over thought processes. It does not occur to the child to reverse in thought the act of clustering so that the equivalence can be conserved.

Phase III. Once children achieve concrete operations, they grasp the equivalence immediately and insist upon it. They can arrange the eggs in one-to-one correspondence with the egg cups spontaneously. They show great confidence that they can prove their selection when they put the eggs into the egg cups. When the eggs are taken out and clustered, a child of this level sees the correspondence unchanged. When asked *why*, he answers something like the following: "Because they were inside the cups, and they'll all go inside the cups again." Thus, at this level the equivalence is permanent, apparently because the child has grasped the reversibility of the clustering procedure.[8]

---

[8] Estes (1956) has reported an attempt to replicate these observations of Piaget & Szeminska (1941) on the conservation of number which she supposed failed because "if a child could count at all, he could count the blocks whether they were in line, in a pattern, or piled up." What appears to have failed is her understanding of what is meant by conservation of number and of the Piaget testing procedures. Confirmation of these observations has come from studies by Churchill (1958) and by Wohlwill (1959), whose chief concern, however, was whether conservation of number develops from operations of adding and subtracting by inferential means or from direct reinforcement.

Composition of classes: Mobility of part-part and part-whole relationships. In order to study the composition of classes, Piaget & Szeminska (1941, chap. vii) presented children with a box containing about 20 wooden beads [superordinate class = wooden beads (B)]. Most of these 20 beads were brown (subordinate class A), but two of them were white (subordinate class A'). The child was then asked whether the box contained *more wooden beads* or *more brown beads.* This question concerns the elementary form of the additive composition of classes: A + A' = B, and therefore A = B − A' and A' = B − A, and A<B. In order to make the problem interesting for the children, Piaget & Szeminska (1941, p. 164) asked them whether a necklace made with the brown beads would be longer, shorter, or equal in length with a necklace made from the wooden beads. Furthermore, to be sure the children grasped the difference between A and B, before asking this question, they put two empty boxes beside the box of beads and asked the child-subject: "If we take out the brown beads and put them here (first empty box) will there be any beads left in this one (the full box)?" Children of all ages above four years regularly answered that the white beads would be left. The examiners also asked: "If we take out the wooden beads and put them there (in a second empty box) will there be any left in this one (the full box)?" The children readily understood this question too, answering *no.* On the other hand, understanding these two questions did not imply a correct solution to the problem of the length of the necklaces.

Phase II-A. At the early sub-stage of the intuitive phase, children could not understand that there would be more wooden beads than brown beads. Although they agreed that all the beads are made of wood, the answer to the question "Would there be more wooden beads or more brown beads?" was regularly answered: "More brown ones." Piaget attributes this confusion to the child's inability to think simultaneously of both the whole (wooden beads) and the parts (brown beads and white beads). As a result, the child cannot regard wooden beads as resulting from the addition of brown beads *and* white beads. Once his attention is focused upon the subordinate classes, he can grasp only the part-part relationship of the brown beads to the white beads; the part-whole relationship escapes him because his thought lacks reversibility.

Phase II-B. At the more advanced sub-stage of the intuitive phase, children discover that there are more wooden beads than brown beads by a kind of trial-and-error process. Thus, Gale, age six years, at first answered the question "Which would make the longer necklace, the brown beads or the wooden beads?" by saying that the necklace of brown beads would be longer. When asked why, she answered, "Because there are more brown beads." When the question is then asked "Are there more wooden beads than brown beads?" Gale answered, "More brown beads . . ." Then suddenly she says, "No, more wooden beads . . . no, they're the same." Apparently the part-whole relationship between brown beads and wooden beads is as yet too tenuous to predominate over Gale's focus on the part or subordinate classes of brown beads and white beads (Piaget & Szeminska, 1941, p. 175). Tail, aged seven years and two months, also answers at first that there would be more brown beads than wooden ones. When asked whether the white beads are made of wood, he answers *yes*, and similarly for the brown ones. When the examiner asks the leading question "Then there are more wooden beads or more brown ones?" Tail answers "More wooden ones, because there are two white ones as well [as the brown ones]." In spite of this answer, when Tail is asked which necklace would be longer, he answers that one made with brown beads would be longer, and only when the leading questions are repeated does he discover that the necklace made of wooden beads would be longer because of the two additional white ones (Piaget & Szeminska, 1941, p. 175).

Phase III. At the level of concrete operations children answer immediately, spontaneously, and with strong confidence that the necklace made of wooden beads would be longer than the one made of brown beads "because there are more wooden beads than brown beads." Thus, at this operational level, the child's thought moves readily back and forth between the parts and the whole. He can simultaneously take into consideration both kinds of classes because, in the language of Piaget, his thought has been "decentred" and has become "reversible."

Seriation and ordinal correspondence. Comparing two objects in terms of some perceptible property is a primitive activity, but ordering a number of objects in terms of such comparison is another matter. In order to study this process, Piaget & Szeminska (1941, chap. v) present children with 10 wooden dolls of the same thickness, which can either stand up or lie down, but are clearly of varying heights; the tallest is twice as tall as the shortest. The children are also presented with 10 sticks, and these also vary in length but with less variation among them. In this situation, the children are told that the dolls are going for a walk, and each doll has his own walking stick. The child is asked to arrange the dolls and the sticks so that each doll can easily find his own stick.

Phase II-A. At the early sub-stage of the intuitive phase, this task is nearly meaningless and impossible. Children of four and five years of age put together only uncoordinated pairs of dolls and sticks. One might think of the double seriation as more difficult than ordering of single series would be, but Piaget & Szeminska (1941) find that if a child cannot produce the serial correspondence called for here, neither can he order either the sticks or dolls alone according to height. For instance when a child at this level is asked to make a staircase of the sticks, he does so, but he attends only to the ends of the sticks that make the staircase. The other ends are left irregular. Children at this early sub-stage of the intuitive phase (II-A) are unable to conceive of either double or single seriation. Piaget attributes this failure to lack of appreciation that each item in a series is both greater than the preceding item and smaller than the one which is to follow. Although the child can say with confidence that any item is longer than any one other (A>B) and that the shorter of these is longer than any given third item (B>C), he is incapable of combining these two perceived relations to form the inference that A>C. It is this lack of logical transitivity to which Piaget attributes the inability of the child at the early stage of the intuitive phase to order items into an ordinal series.[9]

Phase II-B. At the later sub-stage of the intuitive phase, children are capable of constructing a series correctly, after a certain amount of trial-and-error. They can also solve in part the problem of serial correspondence by actually carrying out overtly the act of double seriation. Thus, when a child of this later stage is asked which stick belongs to a given doll, he can answer the question but only by actually arranging the dolls and the sticks into corresponding series. On the other hand, if the two series are reversed, the dolls being arranged from left to right and in order of increasing height while the sticks are arranged from left to right in order of decreasing height, the child fails completely. In such cases, he frequently makes mistakes of direction by picking that stick which happens to be placed in the same position as the doll in question. In some instances, the child may adopt the technique of counting aloud, but this also leads to error. The error derives from the fact that the child counts the number of dolls which are shorter than the reference doll. Thus,

[9] Smedslund (1960) has found that not one of 40 children aged 5–4 to 7–5, with only three above 7 years, showed capacity for transitivity when the criteria were four correct predictions and sufficient explanations for all of them, but 8 showed the beginnings of this capacity by passing a weaker criterion of all four predictions correct and/or at least one partial explanation. Such results appear to indicate that transitivity must be acquired and that inferences about psychological phenomena are structured no earlier than those about physical phenomena.

when he counts the sticks upward from the shortest to the one corresponding in the cardinal series of numbers to the number of dolls shorter than the reference doll, he misses by one. He misses because he failed to count that doll for whose stick he is searching, and he gets the stick corresponding to a doll. Thus, while children of this later stage of the intuitive phase have some grasp of ordering, they remain dependent upon overt actions and perceptions and they are unable to coordinate ordinal and cardinal correspondences.

Phase III. Again, the third phase and the concrete operations bring a change in the child's mode of ordering the dolls and sticks according to size. The trial-and-error are gone. He proceeds by picking out the shortest stick or doll and places it; then he picks out the shortest stick or doll among the remainder and places it beside the former, etc. It is clear from this mode of performance that at this stage the child envisages the whole series from the beginning. Moreover when one of the series is reversed, and the child is asked to pick out the stick for a given doll, he proceeds by counting the preceding elements each time, but without error. Moreover he can proceed from either end of the series. Thus, when asked to pick out the stick for doll seven in a series of 10, he notes that there are three dolls larger than doll seven, so he proceeds to count down three sticks from the larger end of the stick series but picks out the fourth stick. He recognizes that he has counted only the three larger and that the reference is the largest one smaller than any of these. The child with concrete operations may not even count aloud. When asked how he knows, he may reply: "I counted in my head." Thus, at this level the coordination between order and cardinal number is completed, and the child can take into account in his thought both series, noting that any given doll or any given stick takes a position in which there are so many smaller and so many larger. Moreover, he can reverse these processes without confusion.

It is from the fact that the child at the level of concrete operations coordinates both cardinal and ordinal relationships that Piaget concludes that numbering, as an operation, is based upon a combination of classifying and ordering. A child at the later stage and sometimes at the early stage of the intuitive phase can count. If he fuses saying the numbers with pointing, he can count. In counting objects he implicitly considers them equivalent. They belong to a class, and he can count the items in a class. In so doing, he ignores the differences. Thus, when he counts the number of dolls below the one for which he is to find the proper stick, he considers them equivalent and ignores the difference (decentration). In spite of their variations in height, they form the class of dolls in that they are alike in being shorter than the reference doll. On the other hand, seriation requires that each element be distinguished from the other, and ordination consists in the application of number to the successive elements in an ordered series. The child of the intuitive phase applies the number series to the series of items, but he fails to keep clear the issue of whether the reference doll belongs within the class "shorter than" or not. He suffers a confusion of which elements will be considered equivalent for numbering purposes and which will be viewed in terms of their asymmetrical relations as nonequivalent. Thus, the numbering operation requires the coordination of cardination and ordination. This coordination is apparently based upon the generalization of the qualitative operation and the differentiation between these qualitative operations and numerical operations.

Consequences of the concrete operations or "groupements." In the evidence synopsized, corresponding stages of development have been found for what Piaget (1942) considers the three fundamental "functional operations," classes, relations, and numbers. This evidence shows in the development of "intuitions" (II-A) and intuitive "regulations" (II-B). These "intuitions" and intuitive "regulations" culminate in "concrete operations" (III-A) with the conservation of the quantity. Conservation of quantity holds for a wide variety of materials, and it has associated with it the conservation of cardinal number, the ability to serialize with trial-and-error, and the number system in which cardinal and ordinal numbers are coordinated. In each of these, the transition from intuition to operational thought is marked within the child's activity, first by a subjective impression of certainty or logical necessity, and, second, by justifying with the logico-arithmetical properties such as (*a*) the fact that the apparent increase or decrease deriving from the change of shape (A to B) can be corrected by a reverse (B to A) change (simple reversibility), (*b*) "the increased height makes up for the width lost" (combinativity, reversibility), (*c*) "nothing has been added or removed" (identity, reversibility). Piaget (1947) sees such operational thought coming into being when the various intuitive relations are "grouped" into a whole (*structure d'ensemble*). The "mobile equilibrium" of his "structure d'ensemble" is achieved when all the following functional transformations, each with its logical properties, are simultaneously effected: "(1) two successive actions can be combined into one [transitive combinativity]; (2) the action-schema already at work in intuitive thought becomes reversible [reversibility]; (3) the point can be reached by two different paths without being altered [associativity]; (4) a return to the starting point finds the starting point unchanged [identity], and (5) when the same action is repeated, it either adds nothing to itself [tautology], or else is a new action with cumulative effect [numerical iteration]" (Piaget, 1947, pp. 141–42).

From a psychological standpoint, Piaget (1947) sees these changes as a consequence of what he calls "decentring" of thought in which thought becomes independent of perception and action. From a neuropsychological standpoint, in line with the theorizing of Hebb (1949) one may see these functional changes as a consequence of "increasing autonomy of central neural processes," i.e., central processes becoming relatively more independent of receptor inputs and motor outlets.

Games with rules and cooperation in social relations. In view of the fact that these structures of thought with logical properties are conceived to be based upon such fundamental psychological and neurological foundations, Piaget (1947) finds nothing surprising about the fact that their formation accompanies observable developments in social relationships.

In the area of social interaction, the mobile combinativity and reversibility of central processes make it possible for the child to appreciate the point of view taken by another individual. No longer is he bound within his own individual imagery and preconcepts. The observed developments, which will not be illustrated, are two.

In the area of social play, as already noted, Piaget (1945) has found games with rules making their appearance at age seven or eight, which is precisely the same age at which the children of Geneva typically manifest in their more explicitly intellectual behavior other evidences indicating the presence of concrete operations.

In social relationships, moreover, genuine cooperation becomes possible. It is again at the age of seven or eight that Piaget (1947) has observed children manifesting for the first time the capacity to share with another person a common goal and the capacity to recognize and to accept complementary responsibilities as a means of achieving that goal.

Egocentricity and concrete operations. In the area of social communication, finally, Piaget (1923) found long ago that it is at this age of seven or eight that children's communications cease to be "egocentric." Piaget used the term *egocentric* to refer to the tendency of children to announce their actions and wishes to each other, make claims and denials, and indulge in either monologues, in which the child's language follows the pattern of his own individual overt activities, or collective monologues, in which the language of each of the children in the group follows his own activity with little in the way of shared topics and mutual give and take. These criteria for egocentric speech were not clear to the American investigators who tried to use them, and most of them found considerably less egocentricity in the speech of preschool children in America than Piaget (1923) had found in the children of the Maison des Petits in Geneva (see McCarthy, 1930, 1954, pp. 562 ff.). It was commonly agreed, however, that some kind of transformation was taking place in the social behavior of children at about age seven. The nature of the transformation was not clear from either Piaget's early work or from the work of American investigators, but the nature of that transformation has been clarified to a considerable degree by this later work of Piaget and his collaborators reviewed here. With the development of the concrete operations, probably as a consequence of increasing autonomy of central processes, thought acquires a markedly increased degree of mobility that shows in the child's new ability to shift back and forth between part-part and part-whole relationships for classes and subclasses, and thought acquires a new independence of the child's own individual focus that shows in his seeing the conservation of quantity, numerical correspondence, etc. as a logical necessity. The increased mobility of thought permits the child to shift rapidly between the views of others and himself. The new independence of thought from perceptual and egocentric focus permits the child to sustain a topic. Together these capacities permit him to share a topic and also to share the obligation to keep the meanings of words used constant and the obligation not to contradict himself. Only thus can a communicative interchange take place in which there is progressive unfolding of a topic, the chief thing missing in egocentric speech.

The role of communication in the development of concrete operations. On the other hand, insofar as the concrete operations derive from the child's interactive encounters with his environment, concrete operations must, at least in the last stages of their development, grow out of social interaction and communication. This is less of a paradox than it may seem at first blush, for it is during the intuitive phase, after a substantial degree of imagery and capacity to use language has already been acquired during the preconceptual phase, that these concrete operations go through the last stages of their development. By this time, the child has shown a capacity for appreciating conceptual contradiction and incongruity that permits disconfirmation to provoke accommodative modifications. This appreciation of contradiction shows, for example, in phase II-B, where children manifest the signs of conflict over whether changes in shape imply changes in quantity. As the child's anticipatory, intuitive schemata meet with disconfirmation, they change. As they are repeatedly corrected, there is an increase in the proportion of encounters in which the child's anticipatory schemata are in agreement with both reality and communications from other people. All the while the autonomy and mobility of central processes are presumably increasing. When the effects of this increased autonomy and mobility are combined with an increased proportion of encounters in which anticipations are confirmed, one would get something approximating that which Piaget (1947) conceives as the mobile equilibrium comprising the concrete operations.

The construction of space. Although it is impossible to give here anything like the comprehensive account of the construction of space that has been discovered in the pretty experiments of Piaget & Inhelder (1948), it is possible to indicate their nature and the nature of the stages in the construction of spatial concepts during the intuitive phase.

Evidence from manual manipulation without vision. It has already been seen, in connection with the preconceptual phase, that children under four can seldom recognize through manual manipulation without vision anything but such highly familiar objects as a comb, a key, or a spoon. Their failure to recognize appears to be largely a function of their passive and unsystematic manner of manipulating the objects. They merely hold the object as it happened to get into their hands and show little in the way of active manipulative search.

Beginning roughly at the age of four, or at phase II-A, children become somewhat more active in their manipulation. Their examination may still be largely global. They pass the object from hand to hand as if it were a fairly heavy solid, but they begin to distinguish curved shapes from those with straight-lined edges and angles. During II-B children begin to manipulate the fingers actively, although still not systematically with repetition of puzzling parts. In consequence, they readily recognize such figures as the circle, the square, the triangle, and the ellipse, and occasionally even such figures as crosses and stars. At about seven, when the concrete operations appear in connection with classes, relations, and numbers (phase III-A), children manipulate the figures not only actively but systematically. What they feel is never left to chance; they feel their way around the edges of the figures and explore repeatedly those portions which prove puzzling. They show thereby in their behavior the reversibility which is characteristic of the concrete operations. As a consequence, they can recognize even such complex figures as the swastika and the half swastika. They may not recognize these figures by name, but if the manipulated figures are presented along with others, and the children are given a choice, they can pick out the appropriate figure with a high degree of accuracy.[10]

Evidence from copying geometric figures. From the method of having children copy geometric figures, Piaget & Inhelder (1948) also bring out the fact that it is during the intuitive phase that children gradually acquire the capacity to differentiate between squares and triangles on the one hand, and circles on the other. They are distinguished in the child's drawings according to their angles and even their dimensions. Moreover, during the seventh or eighth year, all the problems involved in copying geometric figures are solved, even that of copying a circle over a triangle in such a fashion that the corners extend beyond the boundary of the circle.

During the intuitive phase, children also begin to show some success in copying the linear order in which various colors of beads are put upon a string or garments are hung on a line. Such problems are, indeed, analogous to the serializing already described. During the eighth year, as the concrete operations typically develop, children no longer become confused when the model presented them is circular or when they are asked to reverse the order of the model. Thus, here again is evidence of the reversibility of operational thought.

These studies of space by Piaget & Inhelder (1948) bring out repeatedly the lag between conceptual space and perceptual space. The infant of six months can distinguish circles from squares perceptually; he can also distinguish curved lines from straight lines. On the other hand, he lacks a functional conception of a line. Children of the intuitive phase are unable to line up a series of matches stuck in plasticine bases to make a straight line between two points on a table unless he can follow the straight edge of a square table. Only at the sub-stage III-A, when the "groupements" are formed, do children come to line up the matches by sighting along them to form a straight line. Thus the conceptual construction of projective space itself appears to be associated with the forming of the concrete operations.

Evidence from attempts to draw objects from other's perspectives. From having children draw objects from the perspectives of others comes evidence of a similar development. Piaget's daughter, Jacqueline, at a year and a half of age, was able when on a walk with her father to keep memorial track of the fact that home was in one direction while grandfather had yesterday gone off in another direction and that the goal of the walk was in still another direction. Yet chil-

[10] For confirmatory observations concerning the progressive increase in manipulation and the progressive increase in the systematic nature of the manipulation, see Page (1959) and Peel (1960).

dren of the intuitive phase, some four years older, are still quite incapable of an independent representation of space. In the situation for testing this point, a child is presented with the three mountains depicted in Figure 6–4. A doll is placed variously in chairs at the other three sides of a table on which the mountains are placed. The child is asked what the doll sees. He can indicate this either by constructing the doll's perspective with cardboard cut-outs, by selecting which of several drawings represents what the doll would see, or by

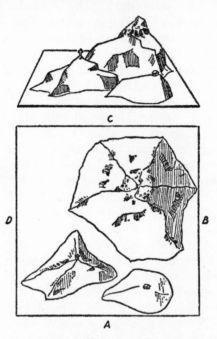

Fig. 6–4. The three mountains used to study the coordination of perspectives. From Piaget & Inhelder (1948, p. 211).

drawing what the doll sees. Children of the intuitive phase are incapable of such representative coordination of perspectives. Only at seven or eight years of age, when the elementary concrete operations are formed, do children begin to show an appreciation of the problem. When they are asked to arrange the cardboard cut-outs to show what the doll sees, they make a number of the transformations correctly, but they remain confused about others. Not until children achieve the later sub-stage of the phase of concrete operations (III-B), which Piaget and Inhelder have found to come typically when children are nine or 10 years old, do they achieve complete relativity of perspectives.

Evidence from drawing levels of liquid in tilted bottles. From having children draw the position of liquid in tilted bottles comes evidence that the Euclidean conception of three-dimensional space is not the elementary concept that it has long been considered to be. Rather, the work of Piaget & Inhelder (1948) indicates that in the developing child this is a late concept which follows the construction of topological relations and such concepts of perspective as straight lines, parallels, distances, and angles. In order to study the development of the horizontal axes, Piaget & Inhelder presented children with two narrow-necked bottles, one with straight, parallel sides and the other with rounded sides. Each was one-fourth filled with colored water, and the children were asked to guess the position the water would assume if the bottle were tilted. The younger children were presented with empty bottles, shaped like the models, and they were asked to show with their fingers the level of the water as these bottles were made to assume various degrees of tilt. Children of over five were provided with outlined drawings of the bottles tilted at various angles and asked to draw the position of the water corresponding to each position of the bottle. In the experiment, as soon as a child has made this drawing, the bottles containing the liquid are tilted while he observes them, and he is then asked to make a new drawing which corrects any errors he may have made.

Figure 6–5 illustrates the sort of drawings which children of the intuitive phase make. Here the horizontal and vertical axes remain still undiscovered. When the bottle is tilted, the child imagines the movement of the water without any regard to an external reference system. During the latter portion of the intuitive phase, a transition begins, as is shown by the fact that the child no longer draws the water as parallel with the base of the vessel, but he fails to coordinate his predictions with any such fixed reference system outside the jar as the table or the stand. Even after the level of concrete operations has been achieved (sub-stage III-A), the child is able to predict the level of the liquid only when the rectangular jar is lying on one side. Only in the later sub-stage of concrete operations (III-B), when the children are approximately nine or ten years old, can they make immediate predictions of both the horizontal and vertical as part of an over-all system of coordinates. The slow development of these concepts of space Piaget & Inhelder (1948) attribute to the fact that these systems of reference are logical multiplications between the elementary topological relations of order in two or three dimensions, and such concepts of perspective as straight lines, distances, measurements, parallels, and angles. These must be fused into a single operational whole.

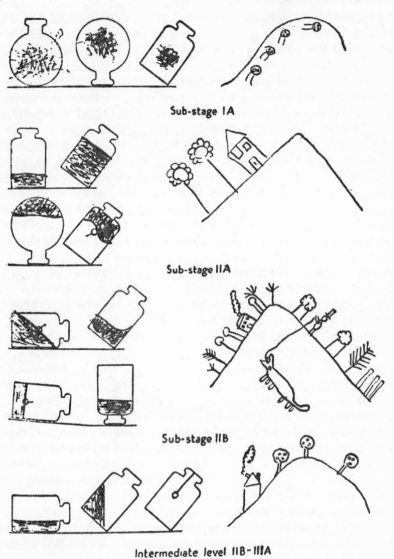

Sub-stage IA

Sub-stage IIA

Sub-stage IIB

Intermediate level IIB-IIIA

Fig. 6–5. Stages in the development of horizontal and vertical axes. From Piaget & Inhelder (1948, p. 383).

The construction of time. The elaboration of the concept of time is no simple function of perceptual data; rather, Piaget *et al.* (1946, and Piaget, 1955) point out that it involves a progressive structuring of perceptual data which is accomplished through a sequence of logical operations. As a logical concept, time has two aspects: the ordering of a succession of events (before, simultaneously, and after), and the duration of intervals separating successive events. Contrary to the view which has been commonly accepted by epistemologists, that time as a continuous flow is given in experience, the child's judgments of simultaneity and successiveness in time appear to depend upon the equality or inequality of the speed of objects moving along a path. So long as two objects, A and B, start together at the same place and arrive together at another place, having followed the same path and moved at the same speed, even three- and four-year-olds of the preconceptual phase recognize the simultaneity of both arrival and departure. On the other hand, should A, moving more rapidly than B, cover more distance between a simultaneous start and a simultaneous stop, even children of from four to six years of age of the later sub-stage of the intuitive phase, although they recognize the simultaneity of the start, refuse to believe that the objects stopped simultaneously, i.e., "together." One such child may think that A stopped "before" B because A is "ahead" of B in space. Another may judge that B stopped "first," i.e., before A stopped, because B is spatially closer to the starting point. In either case, the child at this stage cannot understand that both objects stopped moving "at the same time" because his conception of the "same time" is in no sense differentiated from the speeds of bodies or the distance over which the object moves. Time does not exist for the child as a homogeneous constant flow until the "concrete groupements" are formed.

This confusion works in the opposite fashion as well. When two objects (A and B) start at the same point and move at the same speeds, but A stops before B so that A moves through less distance than B, children of the intuitive phase show great difficulty in dissociating the temporal from the spatial. Commonly they report that B stopped first, i.e., before A, because B is ahead of A.

Duration presents special difficulties. When an object (A) leaves from position (1), moves along a straight line to position (2), and then continues to position (3), even three-year-olds of the preconceptual phase have no difficulty understanding that the distance (1) to (3) takes "more time" than the distance (1) to (2). In fact, the young child appreciates duration in terms of spatial distance. On the other hand, as soon as he is asked to make comparisons between two separate movements, difficulties related to speed again arise. Children of stage II-B, 6.5 years to 7.5 years, think that when two objects (A and B) "started at the same time" and "stopped moving at the same time" while A, the faster moving object, went further than did B, A therefore "took more time" than B. Again, duration has not been differentiated from the distance traversed.

Piaget (1955) and his collaborators (1946) find that about one-half of children master the operations of temporal succession before they grasp the operations of duration. One or the other is typically mastered at the seven-to-eight-year level. The logical bases of these two operations differ. Successive events constitute series (A before B, and B before C: therefore, A before C, etc.). On the other hand, duration involves seriation and a system of inclusions comparable to the nestings of logical classes (interval AB is less than interval AC is less than interval AD). Once one of these two systems of operation has been mastered, it must be coordinated with the other. Lack of coordination shows as follows. A child is asked if he has a friend who is older than he. Answering *yes,* the child may add that his friend is older "because he is bigger," as if age were a matter of height. When the child is then asked whether his older friend was born *before* him or *after* him, unless he has coordinated temporal succession with duration, he answers "I don't know, I've never asked him," or some approximate equivalent. Age and birth-date go uncoordinated in 75 per cent of the children of Geneva studied by Piaget and his collaborators until the concrete operations come when they are seven or eight.

Once the qualitative operations of sequential succession and duration are coordinated, the child is in a position to construct a system of time measurement. This, however, presupposes a concept of speed. At the intuitive phase, however, speed is represented only concretely as "passing" over "overtaking." When objects disappear at the same time and reappear at the same time, children of the intuitive phase judge that they have moved at the same speed even though they may previously have noted that the tunnel through which one of the objects disappeared was substantially longer than the tunnel through which the other disappeared. On the other hand, when the tunnel is removed, and the child sees that the object moving over the longer route either "catches up" or "passes" the one traversing the shorter route, he readily recognizes the difference in speed. Children of the intuitive phase, however, do not appreciate constancy of speed. Piaget (1955) shows this by asking children to draw the successive trials of a toy automobile that is made to move through a succession of steps, each of the same duration and speed. Up to the age of about seven, children draw distances which are unequal. Conservation of speed is achieved only at the level of concrete operations.

Only when the child has got the concepts of time and of speed solidly established can he understand that duration is not simply a function of distance traversed ($t = d$). Only then can he differentiate the reversible proportions required to grasp the systematic conception that distance (d) is a direct product of both time (t) and speed (v) (i.e., $d = tv$) and that time and speed are inversely proportional (i.e., $t = d/v$, and $v = d/t$). This is typically accomplished at about the age of nine or ten years when such Euclidean concepts of space as frames of reference and projective systems are also accomplished. From the psychological standpoint, both time and Euclidean space call for the coordination of differentiated concrete operations. Where space calls for the coordination of movements, irrespective of the attribute of speed, time calls for the coordination of speeds, irrespective of the attribute of distance moved. It is thus that these concepts of time and Euclidean space come later and that they constitute a second order of concrete operations in which these two differentiated concrete operations are in turn coordinated (sub-stage III-B).

SUMMARY. Although many unanswered questions remain, Piaget and his collaborators appear to have discovered a major transition in the development of intellectual capacity with what they call the "concrete operations" or the "concrete groupements." With the appearance of these structures, as central processes become increasingly autonomous and thought becomes loosened somewhat from its ties in perceiving and acting that Piaget calls "centrations," thought comes to show the logical properties of reversibility, transitivity, associativity, identity, and tautology. These logical properties account for what appears to be the relatively sudden and simultaneous appearance of a new level of intellectual capacity that is manifest in a very wide variety of situations. With the appearance of these concrete operations, children come to conserve quantities and numbers, get the capacities to serialize and to shift readily from part-part relationships to part-whole relationships, and construct the conceptions of space and time typical of adults. The conception of duration, however, demands a coordination of concrete operations which comes as a second sub-stage of the phase of concrete operations.

FROM CONCRETE OPERATIONS TO FORMAL OPERATIONS

Even though these concrete operations appear to influence the intellectual performance of children profoundly in a wide variety of situations, it is important to note that children at this stage still fall far short of the formal operations which are characteristic of the reasoning of human adults. For instance, children whose operations reveal transitive combinativity, reversibility, associativity, identity, and tautology or iteration when they are manipulating concrete objects cannot give performances that reveal these properties when they are asked to reason with verbal propositions. Thus, eight-year-olds and even ten-year-olds who perform with confidence and accuracy in the problem with the beads, cannot choose the proper alternative in the following example of Cyril Burt's (1919, 1940) tests of verbal reasoning: "Some of the flowers in my bunch are yellow," says a boy to his sisters. The first replies, "Then all the flowers are yellow." The second replies, "Some of your flowers are yellow," and the third replies, "None of your flowers is yellow." Who is right?

Similarly, eight-year-olds and even ten-year-olds, who have no trouble at all arranging a series of dolls or sticks according to height and who can readily pick out the stick that belongs to a given doll even when the order of the two series is reversed, can almost never manifest such transitive combinativity in dealing with such a verbal problem as the following (again from Burt's tests): "Edith is fairer than Susan; Edith is darker than Lilly; who is the darkest of the three?" Piaget (1947) reports that the eight-year-old may fail even to understand how to go about this problem. Children at nine or ten typically give such arguments as the following: "Edith and Susan are fair, Edith and Lilly are dark; therefore Lilly is darkest, Susan is fairest, and Edith is in between." Even the child of ten, therefore, appears to combine such propositions in about the fashion that the five-year-old orders sticks or dolls according to their height. It is not until about 11 or 12 years of age that children acquire a capacity to deal with such verbal expressions of logical relationships. These propositional relations require "formal operations" as distinct from the "concrete operations" just described. In fact, the latter are termed *concrete* because the child must have objects to manipulate in order to manifest performances showing the logico-arithmetical properties.

CONSERVATION OF QUANTITY, WEIGHT, AND VOLUME. It is also true that the concrete operations are not formed all at once. Although the formation of concrete operations results in conservation of quantities of substances, of classes, and of numbers and also shows profoundly in the conceptual constructions of space and time, this does not mean that all kinds of quantities are conserved. Children who conserve the quantity of substances need not conserve either the weight or the volume of those same substances. In fact, Inhelder (1944) has apparently found a natural ordinal scale of conceptualization and intelligence which she has demonstrated with the balls of plasticine or modeling clay depicted in Figure 6–6.

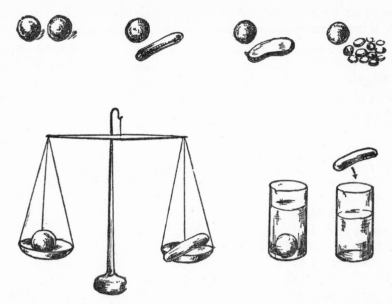

Fig. 6–6. Plasticine balls, balance, and beakers used in one method of investigating the conservation of quantity, weight, and volume. Conservation of quantity appears at the first sub-stage of the phase of concrete operations when, according to Piaget's observations, children are typically seven or eight years old. Conservation of weight appears only at the later sub-stage of the phase of concrete operations when children are typically nine or ten. Conservation of volume appears only at the earlier phase of the period of formal operations when children are typically 11 or 12. After Inhelder (1953, p. 77).

Materials and procedure. At the beginning of an experiment with a child, the two plasticine balls are weighed to show that they are equivalent in weight, and then they are shown to raise the level of water in a graduated beaker in the same amount, thereby showing by means of displacement that they have the same volume. Such materials are useful in the diagnosis of structures characteristic of children aged all the way from 4 to 12. With children four and five years of age, of the second, or intuitive, phase of the second period during childhood, the balls are made to represent cake dough. After one of the balls is rolled into a sausage, the child is asked whether he and the examiner both have the same amount of dough ("Which is bigger?").

Results: stages and ages.

Phase II-A. Children at the early sub-stage of the intuitive phase regularly see the change of shape as a change of quantity. In so doing, they behave just as they do with quantities of liquid or numbers of beads being poured into containers of differing shape.

Phase II-B: conflict. At the later sub-stage of the intuitive phase, children of 5.5 to 7 years may see as unchanged a sausage in which the length is as much as three times the width. But if the sausage is further elongated, or, if the sausage is divided into smaller sausages, they see the quantity changed. Their comments, however, show the signs of the sort of conflict already described for the conservation of liquid.

Phase III-A: quantity. In children with concrete operations, quantity is conserved no matter how much the shape of the ball is changed and no matter how many pieces it is divided into. Moreover, such children see this conservation of quantity as a logical necessity, and they support their judgments with the typical arguments already noted: (1) nothing has been added or taken away (operation of identity and reversibility); (2) even though the ball has been lengthened, what it has gained in length it has lost in thickness (combination of relations with reversibility); (3) the ball has only been lengthened and it would be easy to roll it back into a ball (simple reversibility).

Phase III-B: weight. On the other hand, these same children of from seven to nine, who consider conservation of substance a logical necessity, deny the conservation of weight. To justify their denial, they point out that the ball is longer, or thinner, etc. Later, they show the same conflict, but at between nine and ten years of age, children appreciate the conservation of weight, and consider it to be a logical necessity for the same three reasons given in the preceding paragraph.

Phase IV-A: volume. Yet these same children of nine or ten deny the conservation of volume and for the very same reasons that they earlier denied the conservation of substance and weight. It is not until they are 11 or 12 years old (IV-A) that children assume the conservation of volume, and again the same three basic arguments.[11]

Similar results with other methods. Piaget & Inhelder (1940) have found similar results with the assessing of conservation of quantity, weight, and volume by other means. For instance, while children of seven or eight can order objects serially according to their length or

[11] These stages in the development of the conservation of substance and weight have been confirmed, not only in the study of the feebleminded by Inhelder (1944), but by at least two investigations for other laboratories than Piaget's, e.g., Smedslund (1959), but with earlier ages for the landmarks of transition, and Lovell & Ogilvie (1960).

gross size, not until they are nine or ten years of age can they order these same objects by weight serially, and not until they are 11 or 12 years old can they order them by volume serially. When children come to the conservation of volume, they have also acquired the capacity to reason formally with verbal propositions.

A natural ordinal scale of intelligence. Inhelder (1944) has tested numerous feebleminded individuals by the method of the two plasticine balls. She reports (also Piaget & Inhelder, 1947) the fact that every individual who manifests conservation of volume also manifests conservation of weight and quantity, and every individual who conserves weight also conserves quantity. In other words, there appears to be a natural scale with the properties Guttman (1941, 1944) has ascribed to ordinal scales for measurement. Inhelder (1953) claims for the scaling of intelligence by this means a far greater degree of generalization than is possible with the Binet-type scales, which proceed by the summation of successes and failures on the basis of a model in which any item can compensate for any other (see Coombs, 1950, 1952) and the ordering derives from the average age at which the item is passed. If others also find that this order of conservation is invariant, this method does indeed provide a promising tool for the assessment of intelligence as a dependent variable and for the relation of its assessment to independent experiential antecedent-variables.[12]

Conservation of volume and the proportionality schema. The fact that quantity, weight, and volume come to be conserved in this order leads Piaget and his collaborators to look at the underlying logical operations required. Where compensation of quantity can readily be justified by simultaneously taking into account two variables (additive compensation), compensation of volume requires for its justification taking simultaneously into account three variables. This requires the logic of multiplicative compensation which implies the proportionality schema. When volume is conserved by multiplicative compensation of dimensions, Inhelder & Piaget (1955, pp. 326 ff.) point out that it is because when one of the sides is doubled, the product of the other two must be halved [i.e., $a : a' :: (b' \times c') :$

---

[12] Since this was written, the writer has found a paper by Peel (1959) that describes a study in which Guttman's (1944) method of scaling qualitative data has been employed to test the notion of stages in the development of children's drawing of geometric figures. It is interesting that the coefficient of reproducibility was higher (83.5%) with the final level achieved by each child than with the age of the child (71.7%). Such a finding indicates that Piaget's sequence of stages is better established than his age placements, and it lends support to the notion of a natural ordinal scale, at least within the range of children and background experience sampled.

(b x c)]¹³ Thus, conservation of volume depends upon the operation of proportionality. Inhelder (1953) remarks that "proportions are themselves operations applied to operations, or operations to the power two" (p. 85). Thus, with proportions come conservation of volume, an intuitive understanding of chance and probability which also depends upon logical multiplication, the capacity to reason with propositions, and a new approach even to concrete problems. This is the level of formal operations in which the concrete operations are conceived to be grouped and restructured at a higher level into a new whole (*structure d'ensemble*).

FORMAL OPERATIONS: THEORY: Another major transformation in thought processes is evident when formal operations come into being, typically when the child is becoming adolescent at about 11 or 12 years of age. This transformation shows in several ways. Where the child with only concrete operations can only classify, seriate, and count the various objects and events he perceives, the child or adolescent with formal operations can "operate with operations" by means of propositions. Where the child with only concrete operations cannot comprehend a law and must limit his concerns to how things go together in classes, orders, and numbers, the child or adolescent with formal operations can consider a general law because the hypothetically possible as well as the real come within his ken. Where the child's concrete thought operations occur in response to real situations, as in the case of the adolescent verifying a law, his thought about the hypothetically possible directs his perceiving and acting.

This transformation is presumed to take place as the child, becoming adolescent, takes further steps toward what Piaget (1947) calls the "decentring" and "reversibility" of thought. In other words, they take place as central processes become more autonomous and thereby acquire an increased dominance over the peripheral processes of perception and action. In consequence, the adolescent need no longer confine his attention to the real. He can consider hypotheses which may or may not be true, and consider what would follow if they were true. He can follow the form of an argument while dis-

---

¹³ In some fashion which the writer has been unable to clarify for himself, conservation of weight presumably also depends upon multiplicative compensation, but in a more elementary fashion, for conservation of weight appears at about nine or ten years of age while conservation of volume appears only at age 11 or 12 when the child begins to reason formally with propositions. Similarly, the notions of time, of speed, and of Euclidean space must depend upon the combining of operations just as intuitions combine preconcepts. These combinations, which Piaget (1947) terms *horizontal* separations, come into being at about the same time as the latter stage of the phase of concrete operations.

regarding its concrete content. It is from this last characteristic that *formal operations* get their name.

The development of formal operations opens to the adolescent the hypothetico-deductive methods of science. They also open to him the role of social reformer. With the new-found dominance of his thought processes, the adolescent can see that the way the world is run is only one out of a great variety of possible ways that the world might be run. He takes delight in conceiving of alternative ways to run the world that might be better.

Just as the onset of concrete operations brought a variety of new capacities, so again in connection with the onset of formal operations, a wide variety of new ways of thinking become available to the adolescent at about the same time. Piaget (1947) believes that this occurs because a wide variety of thought skills are based upon a relatively few basic operational structures. He characterizes this transition from concrete operations to formal operations as a "vertical separation" because into these new structures are presumably grouped the concrete operations of later childhood. Formal operations permit their possessor to operate on concrete operations. In this sense, they are operations of the second order, or, as "groupements" of the "concrete groupements," they are also "groupements" of the second order.

The abstract character of these few basic formal operational structures shows in the approach to general lawful relationships in a number of ways. When combinations are involved, a person with formal operations at his disposal takes into account all possible combinations. When comparison is involved, the comparison is made selectively by varying one factor while "all other things are equal." The chief concern of Piaget the logician (1949, 1953b) and a major concern of Inhelder & Piaget (1955) is to describe the few basic structures of thought in terms of their logico-mathematical properties.

The sixteen binary operations of two-valued propositional logic. One of these formal operational structures involves a combinatorial analysis of operations, as distinct from a combining of classes, which corresponds to the structure that mathematicians call "lattices" and logicians call, following Boole (1854), the "calculus of propositions." Suppose the propositions concern classes, and animals are divided two ways, into *vertebrates* (V) and *invertebrates* (I) and into those which live on land and are therefore *terrestrial* (T) and those which live in water and are therefore *aquatic* (A). Faced with the problem of describing the population of animals on a newly discovered planet, the child with only concrete operations could merely do the empirical task of searching for animals and assigning them to the four possible classes based on the two-way classification: (1) vertebrates terrestrial (VT), (2) vertebrates aquatic (VA), (3) invertebrates terrestrial (IT), and (4) invertebrates aquatic (IA). On the other hand, if an adolescent with formal operations were faced with such a task, he would be capable of considering all the various classes of animals that are conceivable, and he might set up a table of these possibilities before he began his exploration. The result would be a tabulation of the following 16 possibilities:

(1) No animals at all	(8) (VT) and (IA), but no (VA) or (IT)
(2) Only (VT)	(9) (VA) and (IT), but no (VT) or (IA)
(3) Only (VA)	(10) (VA) and (IA), but no (VT) or (IT)
(4) Only (IT)	(11) (IT) and (IA), but no (VA) or (VT)
(5) Only (IA)	(12) (VT), (VA), and (IT), but no (IA)
(6) (VT) and (VA), but no (IT) or (IA)	(13) (VT), (VA), and (IA), but no (IT)
(7) (VT) and (IT), but no (VA) or (IA)	(14) (VT), (IT), and (IA), but no (VA)
	(15) (VA), (IT), and (IA), but no (VT)
	(16) All four classes

It can readily be seen here how the adolescent's formal operations constitute operations on the concrete classificatory operations of the child. Moreover, as Piaget (1953b) and others have pointed out, each one of these 16 combinations of classes corresponds to one of the 16 relations between two propositions recognized by modern logic. Thus, the class-term vertebrate (V) is the equivalent of saying "*This animal has a backbone*," and the class-term *invertebrate* (I) is the equivalent of saying "*This animal has no backbone*." Similarly, the class-term *terrestrial* (T) is the equivalent of "*This animal lives on land*," and the term *aquatic* (A) is the equivalent of the proposition "*This animal lives in the water*." Combining these propositions leads to four if-then statements like the following: "*If an animal is a vertebrate, then it must live on land*." Since each such combined proposition may be either *true* or *false*, the permutations and combination of propositions in Boole's (1854) "calculus of propositions" also runs to 16 possible arrangements. Without any knowledge of these 16 combinatorial arrangements *per se*, the transformations that take place in the thought of the adolescent mean that nevertheless he has an implicit use of them. This shows in what is meant by the fact that the adolescent can be guided by the form of an argument while ignoring its content. For instance, when the child with only concrete operations hears one of Ballard's nonsense-sentences (*e.g.*, "I am very glad I do not eat onions, for if I liked them I would always be eating them, and I hate eating unpleasant things"), he criticizes the data themselves (*e.g.*, "Onions are not unpleasant"; "It is wrong not to like them," etc.). Adolescents with formal operations accept the data as such and devote themselves to bringing out the contradiction between "if I like them" and "onions are unpleasant" (see Piaget, 1953b, p. 18).

The INRC group. Another major acquisition of the adolescent is the system of operations known to logicians as the INRC group in which each operation has two distinct opposites. Thus, whereas a class (*e.g.*, all mammals) has the sort of opposite called an *inverse* (*e.g.*, all non-mammals) and a relation (A is twice as long as B) has the sort of opposite called *reciprocal* (B is twice as long as A), such a formal operation as "p implies q" has both an inverse ("p does not imply q") and a reciprocal ("q implies p"). The letters *I, N, R,* and *C* in the name for this group have the following referents:

(1) Identity operator (I) is an operation which, when performed on any proposition, leaves it unchanged.

(2) Negation or inverse (N) refers to the relationship between the operators in symbolic logic. Thus, *disjunction* is the inverse of *conjoint negation,* and *conjunction* is the inverse of *incompatibility.*

(3) Reciprocal (R) refers to the relationship between the operators *disjunction* and *incompatibility* on the one hand, and between the operators *conjunction* and *conjoint negation* on the other.

(4) Correlate (C) refers to the relationship between *disjunction* and *conjunction* on the one hand, and to the relationship between *incompatibility* and *conjoint negation* on the other (see Piaget, 1949, 1953b).

This INRC group is necessary for dealing with *proportionality* which, in turn, underlies the "eduction of correlates" that Spearman (1923) considered one of the distinguishing characteristics of intelligent acts (*e.g.*, Paris is to France as London is to Great Britain; feathers are to birds as hair is to dogs.) This INRC group, as will be seen, also underlies the understanding of the concept of equilibrium.

Perhaps the meaning of these second-order formal operations (or groupements of concrete operations) can best be grasped from a comparison of the attempts made by children and by adolescents to discover various elementary laws of physics. These comparisons derive from Inhelder's ingenious experiments.

THE GROWTH OF LOGICAL THOUGHT: EXPERIMENTS AND RESULTS. In order to investigate the development of logical thinking about causal relationships and to explore more thoroughly the transition from the concrete thought of the child to the formal thought of the adolescent, Inhelder and her collaborators have presented children of various ages with elementary problems of physics and chemistry, and asked their subjects, first, to do various concrete operations with the materials, and then, second, to formulate a law describing their operation. Piaget has then examined the protocols of these experiments for evidence of the implicit presence of the structures of thought which Boole (1854) captured in his "calculus of propositions." The result is a collaborative description of the growth of logical thinking (Inhelder & Piaget, 1955).

Archimedes' law of floating bodies. In the case of Archimedes' law of floating bodies, for example, the subject is presented with several buckets of water and a variety of objects. The subject is asked to classify these objects according to whether or not they float on water. After he has made his classification, based on his own experiments, he is asked to summarize his observations, and it is suggested that he look for a law.

Phase II-A. Four-year-olds of the early intuitive phase cannot make such a classification because they do not conserve the properties of objects over time, they attribute various properties to identical objects, and they give to analogous objects quite different properties. In consequence, children of this stage accept without any concern the most contradictory of reasons why an object will or will not float.

Phase II-B. At the later sub-stage of the intuitive phase children still fail to achieve a coherent classification. They give a variety of reasons why an object will not float ("because it is heavy," because it is big," "because it is long," "because it is small") and a similar variety of reasons for why objects will float. Thus, no experiment can "set the child right" because he attempts to rationalize why the body is observed to sink or to float in terms of the particular characteristics of those objects observed to sink or to float. For him logical imcompatibility among the explanations does not exist.

Phase III-A. At the early sub-stage of phase III, when the concrete operations develop with the conservation of quantity and number, children typically make a three-way classification: (1) objects that float (pieces of wood, matches, corks), (2) objects that sink (a key, some stones, metal disc, a needle, metal clamps, a heavy wooden ball), and (3) objects that either float or sink depending upon conditions (e.g., a metal cover, a hollow metal cylinder). When asked why the objects float, children of this level are likely to say that "they are light." Also, they sink because "they are heavy." On the other hand, they note also that a large piece of wood is considerably heavier than a needle, and they make an effort to resolve the contradiction. In consequence, children with concrete operations are likely to be led to a double-entry classification: small light objects, small heavy objects, large light objects, and large heavy objects. These four sub-classes of objects, obtained by logical multiplication, acknowledge the presence of the contradiction and show some signs of approaching the concepts of *density*, which concerns weight in proportion to volume, and of *specific gravity*, which concerns the proportional relation between the density of an object and the density of water. Inasmuch as children at this stage lack both the concept of weight and the concept of volume, however, this is as far as they can go.

Phase III-B. Children of nine or 10 years, who conserve the weight of objects regardless of their shape, make clean-cut classifications. They also make more sophisticated attempts at explanation, apart from the contradiction between the obvious notions that *light things float* while *heavy things sink*. At nine years, for instance, Ray approaches the concept of *specific gravity* by explaining that "the wood isn't the same as iron. It's lighter: there are holes in between." When asked about steel, Ray answers: "It stays under because there aren't any holes in between." Even at this later stage of the phase of concrete operations, however, children are continually pondering the puzzles provoked by their observations that a given object does or does not float while another object of superficially similar characteristics does just the opposite. Their quandaries derive directly from observations of the concrete.

Phase IV-A. Adolescents with formal operations, on the other hand, show these formal operations in quite a different approach to explanation. This difference shows, first, in the way they reject hypotheses, second, in the way they arrive at hypotheses that they take seriously, and, third, in how they go about verifying the hypotheses that they construct. First, they commonly discard hypotheses without direct reference to observation, whereas observation is the only basis used by the child with only concrete operations. Consider the following performance of 12-year-old Fran and especially his mode of rejecting hypotheses:

Fran (12:1) does not manage to discover the law, but neither does he accept any of the earlier hypotheses. He classifies correctly the objects presented but hesitates before the aluminum wire. "Why are you hesitating?—*Because of the lightness, but no, that has no effect.*—Why?—*The lightness has no effect. It depends upon the sort of matter; for example the wood can be heavy and it floats.* And for the cover: *I thought of the surface.*—The surface plays a role?—*Maybe, the surface that covers the water, but that doesn't mean anything* . . . Thus he discards all of his hypotheses without finding a solution." (Inhelder & Piaget, 1955, p.37).

Although Fran fails to find the law, his mode of rejecting his own hypotheses, which is based on propositional "implications and non-implications," shows one of the major characteristics of formal thinking. He eliminates absolute weight as a factor, for instance by saying: "Wood can be heavy and it floats." The role of the surface touching the water is rejected because "that doesn't mean anything." The innovation here at adolescence is the fact that, as Inhelder & Piaget (1955) put it, "the subject views the problem in terms of all possible combinations in such a way as to draw out their implications or non-implications instead of noting the empirical facts in order to draw tables of correspondence and classifications from them" (p. 39). Or, put in another way, all that is necessary to reject the assertion that *bodies will float* because *they are light* is to have lightness associated in memory with bodies which do not float, or to find that its opposite, *heaviness*, is associated with either floating or non-floating. This is what is meant by *proceeding* in terms of "implications or non-implications."

The approach of adolescents with formal operations to explanation shows, secondly, in the way they formulate hypotheses. Like children with only concrete operations, they typically start with comparing the *sinking* objects with the *floating* objects in terms of *heavier* and *lighter*, but shortly they relate the weight of these bodies to the weight of an equal quantity of water. Consider Ala's performance in arriving at the correct hypothesis:

Ala (11:9): "Why do you think this key will sink?—*Because it is heavier than water.*—This little key is heavier than water? (The bucket is pointed out.)—*I mean the same capacity of water would be less heavy than the key.*—What do you mean?—*You would put them* (metal or water) *in containers which contain the same amount and weigh them*" (Inhelder & Piaget, 1955, p. 38).

When Ala rejects the hypothesis that weight *per se* is the explanation, what remains for him to do is to relate the weight of the sinking body to that of an equal quantity of water. Inasmuch as the volume of water equal to the volume of the immersed key has no visible contours, it has to be abstracted, and this means calling up a previous conceptualization of relative weight or specific gravity. Moreover, this reasoning process is an advance, at least implicitly, over that of concrete operations in that it "consists of considering the variation of a single factor 'all other things being equal'" (Inhelder & Piaget, 1955, p. 41).

The formal characteristic of the adolescent's approach to explanation shows, third, in his approach to verification. Children at the preconceptual levels feel no need for proof and are incapable of any proof. Children at the level of concrete operations hardly feel spontaneously a need for proof, but when asked for proof, they can furnish it even though the only method of verification of which they can conceive is to accumulate facts. Proof for the adolescent, on the other hand, comprises a logical demonstration of the truth or falsehood of a particular or a general assertion. Moreover, proof for the adolescent takes into account the totality of possible combinations. Inhelder & Piaget (1955) see this grouping of combinations into a totality to be the same thing as selecting those cases where a single factor varies with all others held constant so as to isolate the universal relationships from simple contingent associations. It is in this fashion that formal operations of the adolescent's approach to verification are to be contrasted with the simple additive and multiplicative class inclusions characteristic of concrete operations.

Phase IV-B. Even so, it is not until the adolescents of Geneva reach 13 to 15 years of age that they typically use authentically and explicitly the schema of "all other things being equal" or what has also been called "the rule of one variable." It is apparently brought out implicitly in this particular situation because the two factors, weight and volume, are not independent. Their lack of independence forces an accommodation on the part of the subject to try to determine the relation between them and to link them into a new concept, *i.e., density.* Moreover, in comparing an object to the water on which it floats, it is easier to vary weight and leave volume constant than it is to hold the several independent factors constant.

The increased generality of this schema of "all other things equal" at phase IV-B over its implicit and specific use at phase IV-A is evident in the following protocol from WUR.

WUR (14:4): *"I take a wooden cube and a plastic cube which I fill with water.* (The cubes are the same size.) *I weigh them, and the difference can be seen on the scale according to whether an object is heavier or lighter than water"* (Inhelder & Piaget, 1955, p. 44).

In these experiments, the objects used include a cube of wood, a cube of iron, and an empty plastic cube (density about 1), and all three of the same volume. In the light of the schema "all other things being equal," Inhelder & Piaget (1955) found it striking to see that it was not until stage IV-B that subjects spontaneously turned to such objects for proof. Thus adolescents with formal operations (1) reject hypotheses without recourse to observation, and verification consists of "(2) separating out variables according to the combinations not given by direct observation, and (3) composition of these relationships according to operations of conjunction and implications such as those propositions" (p. 45).

Other experimental situations. In their studies of the development of logical thinking, Inhelder & Piaget (1955) use a variety of situations. In one of these, the ingenious apparatus consists of a game resembling billiards in which balls are launched from a tubular spring-plunger that can be pivoted and aimed against a projection wall. Here the task of the subjects is to discover the law that the angle of incidence equals the angle of reflection. While children with concrete operations succeed in isolating all the elements needed to discover the law of the equality of these angles, they can neither construct the law in implicit fashion nor formulate it verbally. They manage to order serially both the angles of incline and the angles of reflection, but they fail to note their equality and they do not generalize the reciprocity. For the adolescent, on the other hand, the concrete correspondences between the plunger's angles of inclination and the angles of reflection in the path of the ball after it strikes the buffer appear to lead automatically to the idea of necessary reciprocity, i.e., each incline implies the other and vice versa. One 16-year-old put it this way: "You have to move the lever according to the target and vice versa" (reciprocity) (Inhelder & Piaget, 1955, p. 14). The step from reciprocity to equality is facilitated by noting that if the plunger is pointed perpendicularly to the buffer (null incline) the ball returns to its starting point. A 15-year-old put it this way: "If the lever is straight, the ball returns exactly" (Inhelder & Piaget, 1955, p. 13). This discovery leads to the law of equality which the same 15-year-old put in this way: "You have to have two angles: the inclination of the lever equals the angle of the trajectory the ball makes" (from buffer to target) (Inhelder & Piaget, 1955, p. 13). Here again, formal thought processes direct the empirical observation, whereas with concrete operations, observations direct thought processes.[14]

Similar differences between the thought of children and the thought of adolescents show in the case of an experiment concerning the flexibility of rods, and dependence of that flexibility upon the material from which it is made, its length, its thickness, and the form of its cross-sections. These same differences show again in connection with the reactions of the child and the adolescent in problems con-

---

[14] Lovell (1961) has repeated 10 of the 15 experiments done by Inhelder & Piaget (1955) with very similar results, but Lovell contends that they have tended to force the protocols into the theoretical framework that Piaget has developed from his studies of logic.

cerning the factors controlling the frequency of oscillations of a pendulum. Here the subject's task is to determine which, among such factors as the length of the string, the weight of the object fastened to the string, the height of the dropping point, and the force of the push given by the subject, determines the amplitude of the oscillation. Here differences in the thinking of the child and the adolescent also show in attempts to isolate the factors controlling and to explain the rate that bodies fall on an inclined plane.

A roulette-like game and the 16 binary propositional operations. Especially interesting are the varying reactions of children of various ages to a roulette-like game in which the problem is to determine why a metal bar attached to a non-metallic rotating disc stops with the metal bar pointing to one pair of boxes instead of to any of the other pairs of boxes around the disc (see Figure 6–7).

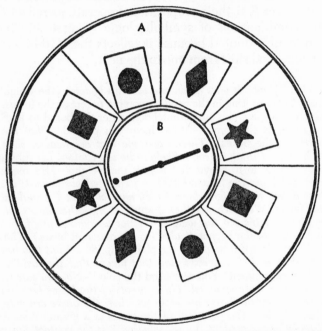

Fig. 6–7. Apparatus used to study propositional disjunctions and exclusions. "One pair of boxes (the starred ones) contains concealed magnets, whereas the other pairs contain only wax. The large board (A) is divided into sectors of different colors and equal surfaces, with opposite sectors matching in color. A metal bar is attached to a non-metallic rotating disc (B); the disc always stops with the bar pointing to one pair of boxes. The boxes (which are matched pairs as to color and design) can be moved to different sectors, but they are always placed with one of a pair opposite the other. The boxes are unequal in weight, and this provides another variable." From Inhelder & Piaget (1955, p. 94).

Phases III-A and III-B. Children typically begin with concrete disjunctions and exclusions. For the first few times, they may assume that "you can't tell in advance" which pair of boxes the metal bar will point toward when the disc stops rotating. Then they generalize that the needle always stops on the same color. When the experimenter puts the boxes containing the magnets, which are covered with a star design, on opposite sectors of another color, they change the hypotheses to the boxes, and commonly to the weight of the boxes. It is this process of guess-and-empirical-check (trial-and-error) that characterizes the performance of the children with only concrete operations.

Phases IV-A and IV-B. Adolescents, on the other hand, start immediately with propositional disjunctions and exclusions, and what is especially important for Piaget's contention that "logic reflects thought" is the fact that their propositional operations reflect the set of 16 binary combinations of symbolic logic (Piaget, 1953b). The following protocol is quoted because it reflects these 16 binary combinations in continual shift from one to the next.

GOU (14:11): *"Maybe it goes down and here it's heavier* (the weight might lower the plane, thus resulting in the needle's coming to rest at the lowest point) *or maybe there's a magnet* (he puts a notebook under the board to level it and sees that the result is the same).—What have you proved?—*That there is a magnet* (he weighs the boxes). *There are some that are heavier than others* (more or less heavy). *I think it's more likely to be the content* (in substance).—What do you have to do to prove that it isn't the weight?—(He removes the diamond boxes which are the heaviest.) *Then I changed positions. If it stops at the same place again, the weight doesn't play any role. But I would rather remove the star boxes. We'll see whether it stops at the other boxes which are heavier* (experiment). *It's not the weight. It's not a rigorous proof, because it does not come to rest at the perpendicular* (to the diamond boxes). *The weight could only have an effect if it made it* (the plane) *tip. So I'll put two boxes, one on top of the other, and if it doesn't stop that means that the weight doesn't matter:* (negative experiment) *You see.*—And the color?—*No, you saw when the positions of the boxes were changed. The contents of the boxes have an effect, but it's especially when the boxes are close together; the boxes are only important when they are close* (he puts half of the boxes at a greater distance). *It's either the distance or the content. To see whether it is the content I'm going to do this.* (He moves the star boxes away and brings the other closer.) *It's more likely to be distance* (new trial). *It seems to be confirmed, but I'm not quite sure. Unless it's the cardinal points* (he takes off the stars). *No, it's not that. The stars do have an effect. It must be the content. If it isn't a magnet, I don't see what it could be. You have to put iron on the metal boxes. If the magnet is there* (disc), *it will come* (to) *these boxes. If it is in the boxes* (stars) *there is iron under the disc* (he removes the star boxes). *I'm sure that it's the boxes"* (Inhelder & Piaget, 1955, p. 102).

Correspondence between performance and theory. Inhelder & Piaget (1955) distinguish the following 16 binary propositional operations in GOU's protocol:

(1) Disjunction $(p \vee q) = (p.\bar{q}) \vee (\bar{p}.q) \vee (p.q)$: "it's either the distance or the content (or both);"

(2) Its inverse, conjunctive negation $(\bar{p}.\bar{q})$: changing the position of the boxes verifies the hypothesis that neither weight nor color is the determining factor;

(3) Conjunction $(p.q)$: both content and distance are effective;

(4) Its inverse, incompatibility $(p/q)^{15} = (p.\bar{q}) \vee (\bar{p}.q) \vee (\bar{p}.\bar{q})$: the effect of the magnet is incompatible with moving the boxes from the center for the needle may stop without the boxes being moved and vice versa, or neither occurs;

(5) Implication $(p \supset q) = (p.q) \vee (\bar{p}.q) \vee (\bar{p}.\bar{q})$: if a magnet is attached

(6) Its inverse $(p.\bar{q})$: when it does not stop, non-implication is shown; to the disc, it will stop in front of the boxes containing iron;

(7) Converse implication $(q \supset p) = (p.q) \vee (p.\bar{q}) = (\bar{p}.\bar{q})$: if there is a magnet in the box, it will stop the disc;

(8) Its inverse $(\bar{p}.q)$ operates in (1), (4), (10), etc.;

(9) Equivalence $(p = q) = (p.q) \vee (\bar{p}.\bar{q})$: to assert that weight has an effect is equivalent to asserting that the needle stops because of the inclination of the plane;

(10) Its inverse, reciprocal exclusion $(p \vee\vee q) = (p.\bar{q}) \vee (\bar{p}.q)$: the fact that the plane is horizontal excludes the weight factor, for either the plane is horizontal and weight has no effect or weight has an effect and the plane is not horizontal;

(11) Independence of p in relation to q—i.e., p $[q] = (p.q) \vee (p.\bar{q})$: the stopping point may coincide either with a color or with its absence; thus color is excluded as a variable;

(12) Its inverse (which is also its reciprocal) $\bar{p}$ $[q] = (\bar{p}.q) \vee (\bar{p}.\bar{q})$: failure to stop may also coincide with the color or its absence;

(13–14) Independence of q and $\bar{q}$ in relation to p—i.e., q $[p]$ and $\bar{q}$ $[\bar{p}]$; these operations are found in (15);

(15) Complete affirmation or tautology $(p^*q) = (p.q) \vee (p.\bar{q}) \vee (\bar{p}.q) \vee (\bar{p}.\bar{q})$: all possible combinations, thus absence of particular links, for example between the box which contains the magnet and the colored sector on which it has been placed;

(16) Its inverse, complete negation or contradiction (0): to deny that weight has an effect and to reassert it would be a contradiction (Inhelder & Piaget, 1955, pp. 103–4).

Inhelder & Piaget use this example to show that even in a problem as simple as this, the transition from concrete to formal operations is distinguished by the appearance of a complete combinatorial system

[15] The quotation is changed here, Inhelder & Piaget (1955) give this item as $(p.q)$ (p. 103). Since $(p.q)$ is the notation for conjunction, whereas its inverse, incompatibility, is the negation of $(p.q)$, the original version must be an error. Elsewhere, Piaget (1953b) uses the symbol '/ ' as the notation for incompatibility, and it is so used here in emending the original version of the translation.

whose various types of disjunction and exclusion are continuously linked to implications.[16]

These 16 binary combinations constitute the structures that mathematicians call "lattices" and that logicians call the "calculus of propositions." Each of the 16 combinations corresponds to one of the 16 relations between two propositions recognized by modern logic. It is the utilization of such logico-mathematical "lattices" that produces systematic knowledge. Moreover, it is interesting to note that one of the functions of the electronic calculator is to make quickly just such complex combinatorial analyses.

Chemical substances and color: n by n combinations. The meaning of the adolescent's capacity to deal with the possible in the case of combinatorial analyses is shown in another way in an experiment in which the subject is presented with four similar flasks containing colorless, odorless liquids which look alike. Inhelder & Piaget (1955, p. 109) number them as follows: "(1) diluted sulphuric acid, (2) water, (3) oxygenated water, (4) thiosulphate." To these they added a bottle (g) which contains potassium iodide, and a medicine dropper. Since oxygenated water iodizes potassium iodide in an acid medium, a mixture of dilute sulphuric acid (1) and oxygenated water (3) with potassium iodide (g) yields a yellow color. Water (2) will not change the color, but the thiosulphate (4) will bleach the mixture (1 + 3 + g). Given the task of producing the yellow color, commonly thought of by the children as "syrup," children at the earlier stage of concrete operations (III-A) proceed merely by combining the potassium iodide in g with the substances of each of the various bottles, 1, 2, 3, and 4. The idea of combining several of the factors simultaneously does not occur to them. When they are encouraged to combine several factors, they make a few empirical attempts but do not continue. Children of the later stage of concrete operations (III-B) also begin by combining the substances in each of the four bottles with the substance in g, but they spontaneously mix two or more of the substances and add the combination to g. They do not, however, proceed systematically with such combinations.

Two innovations occur with the advent of formal operations in adolescence. First, the adolescent does proceed systematically to arrange for all the *n*-by-*n* combinations, and second, he understands from the beginning the fact that the color is due to some combination as such. Like the younger children, adolescents start by combining the potassium iodide with each of the other substances, but they

[16] The meaning of this notation, which is unnecessary for understanding the major point here, can be got from Piaget's (1953a) little book entitled *Logic and Psychology.*

proceed immediately with the substances taken in pairs, then in threes, etc. Because such a systematic procedure can hardly be carried in one's head, the adolescent shortly makes a written record of each combination and leaves a place for recording what he is to observe beside it. Here again, the possibilities which exist only in thought direct the experimental observations.

A balance: the proportionality schema and the INRC group. The role of the proportional schema and the INRC group shows clearly in comparisons of the performances of children and adolescents attempting to discover the relationships among weight, distance, and height in a balance-type weighing instrument (see Figure 6–8). Here the subject's tasks are to make the cross-bar balance and to discover what it is that controls this balance.

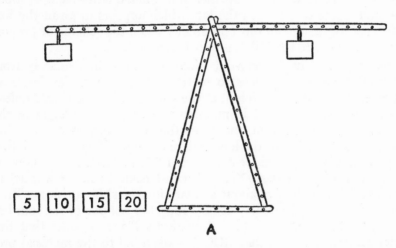

A

Fig. 6–8. Balance-type weighing instrument used in studying the child's discovery of the law of equilibrium. This is a conventional balance with varying weights which can be hung in holes at varying distances from the fulcrum along the crossbar. From Inhelder & Piaget (1955, p. 165).

Phase III-A. Children at the early sub-stage of the phase of concrete operations discover by trial-and-error that there is some kind of relationship between a smaller weight at greater distance than a greater weight at a smaller distance. For instance, even after discovering that a 5-gram weight at a distance of 10 holes balances a 10-gram weight at the distance of 5 holes, he cannot invert this weight-times-distance relationship on the opposite sides without another period of trial-and-error. Children at this stage get the idea that equal weights situated at equal distances from the fulcrum come into equilibrium by symmetry. They also recognize that equal weights at unequal distances do not balance and that unequal weights at equal distances do not balance. They can also substitute for one heavy object an equivalent set of lighter ones through additive operations. On the other hand, they cannot coordinate unequal weights and unequal distances.

Phase III-B. At the later stage of concrete operations, children of the order of 10 years old begin to formulate qualitative correspondences between unequal weights and unequal distances, e.g., "the heavier it is, the closer to the middle." Where the child of the early stage works mostly with substitutions (additions or subtractions) when two weights fail to come into equilibrium, children of this later stage tend to vary displacements on the notion that the same object will "weigh more when it is further out." Such qualitative operations are inadequate to establish the law which appears to await the formation of formal operations (phase IV) when the schema of proportions, analogous to the INRC group, is synthesized.

Phase IV-A. The 12-year-old adolescent turns immediately from qualitative correspondences to metrical proportions. For instance, after placing a 10-gram weight at the very tip of one arm (28 holes) ROG, aged 12 years and 11 months, puts a 20-gram weight at the middle of the other arm, measures the distance, and says: "That makes 14 holes. It's half the length. If the weight (20) is halved, that duplicates (10)" (Inhelder & Piaget, 1955, p. 173). Asked how he knows this, ROG replies: "The idea just came to me, I wanted to try." Asked if he knows about similar situations, he answers: "In a game of marbles, if five play against four, the last one of the four has the right to an extra marble." Inhelder & Piaget assume that this latter remark indicates that ROG has been led to the metrical proportion in the balance from qualitative notions of reciprocity and compensation got in the course of his experience in games of marbles. He does not recognize the second proportionality involving work.

Phase IV-B. Adolescents at the later stage of formal operations clearly recognize both sets of proportionality, involving work between weight (W) and height (H) ($W_1/W_2 = H_1/H_2$) as well as that between weight (W) and distance (D) from the fulcrum ($W_1/W_2 = D_1/D_2$). Consider the following protocol from SAM:

SAM (13:8) discovers immediately that the horizontal distance is inversely related to weight.—"How do you explain that?—*You need more force to raise weights placed at the extremes* (concept of work) *than when it's closer to the center . . . Because it has to cover a greater distance.*—How do you know?— *If one weight on the balance is three times the other, you put it a third of the way because the distance* (upward) *it goes is three times less.*—But once you referred to the distance (horizontal gesture) and once to the path covered (upward)?—*Oh, that depends on whether you have to calculate it or whether you really understand it. If you want to calculate, it's best to consider it horizontally; If you want to understand it, vertically is better. For the light one* (at the extremity) *the change is more* (vertically), *for the heavy one less"* (Inhelder & Piaget, 1955, pp. 174–75).

Correspondence between performance and theory. From such reports, Inhelder & Piaget (1955) infer that the adolescent at the later stage of formal operations understands transformations by inversions (N) and reciprocity (R) and can group them into a single system corresponding to the $INRC$ group. In examining the reasoning of such subjects on the changes of weight and horizontal distance, they let p represent the statement of a fixed increase in weight and q represent a fixed increase in distance; they let $\bar{p}$ represent a statement of corresponding dimunition of weight and $\bar{q}$ a corresponding dimunition of distance on the same arm of the balance. Statements p' and q' correspond to p and q on the opposite arm; likewise do $\bar{p}'$ and $\bar{q}'$ correspond to $\bar{p}$ and $\bar{q}$. By choosing $p.q$ (i.e., p and q) as the Identical operation I, the subject's understanding of the relations of inversion and reciprocity is shown by the following:

I $(p.q)$ $=$ to increase simultaneously the weight and the distance on one of the arms;

N $(\bar{p} \vee \bar{q})$ $=$ $(p.\bar{q})$ $\vee$ $(\bar{p}.q)$ $\vee$ $(\bar{p}.\bar{q})$ $=$ to reduce the distance while increasing the weight or diminish the weight while increasing the distance or diminish both [proposition 1];

R $(p'.\ q')$ compensates I by increasing both weight and distance on the other arm of the balance;

C $(\bar{p}'.\bar{q}')$ $=$ $(p'.\bar{q}')$ $\vee$ $(\bar{p}'.q')$ $\vee$ $(\bar{p}'.\bar{q}')$ $=$ cancels R in the same way that N cancels I. (Proposition: 1)

But since R $(p'.q')$ is equivalent to compensating action I $(p.q)$ with a reaction (symmetry) on the other arm of the balance, we find that it can be written $\bar{p}.\bar{q}$; and since $(\bar{p}' \vee \bar{q}')$ is also equivalent to compensating the action N by symmetry, we can write it $(p \vee q)$. Therefore proposition [1] above can be formulated as follows:

I $(p.q)$
N $(\bar{p} \vee \bar{q})$
R $(\bar{p}.q)$
C $(p \vee q)$. [Proposition: 1a]

The system of these transformations, which states only the equilibrium of weights and distances, is in itself equivalent to the proportionality:

$$\frac{p.q}{\bar{p}.\bar{q}} = \frac{p \vee q}{\bar{p} \vee \bar{q}} \text{ thus } \frac{Ix}{Rx} = \frac{Cx}{Nx} \text{ (where } x = p.q).$$

In other words, an understanding of the system of inversions and reciprocities [in statements 1 and 1a] follows directly from an understanding of this proportional relation: an increase of weight and distance on one arm of the balance is to the symmetrical increase on the other arm as an increase of weight or distance on one arm is to a reciprocal operation on the other (Inhelder & Piaget, 1955, pp. 178–79).

Inhelder & Piaget see this as the qualitative schema of logical proportions corresponding to the intuitional proportionality with which the younger adolescent subject begins, and they see the transition to numerical proportions as an easy accommodation to the weight and balance situation. Moreover, since all the subjects at the later stage of formal operations also understand that an increase in distance (q) (weight constant) implies a determinate increase in height (r) of the opposite arm, i.e., $q \supseteq_{\mathrm{C}} r$, it follows that the same system of relations of inversion and reciprocity outlined in the quotation above applies also with respect to the proportionalities between the distance of a weight from the fulcrum of the balance and the height-displacement of the cross-bar from the horizontal. Finally, such subjects also express in non-technical ways the notion that transfer of a weight to a higher point on the balance constitutes work, e.g., SAM says "more force to raise the weight." Inasmuch as the expressions of the adolescent subjects were not completely spontaneous on this point concerning work, however, Inhelder & Piaget (1955) go on to supplement this experiment with one on the hauling of a weight on an inclined plane. But those examples already given are sufficient to illustrate how they use the performance of children and adolescents in such experiments to achieve a demonstration of the "vertical" transformations of thought between concrete operations and formal operations, and of the fashion in which logic is reflected in these structures of thought.

SUMMARY

The work of Piaget and his collaborators over the past 30 years comprises a monument of research in the grand manner. In the light of this work, fixed intelligence looks like a misplaced generalization of the schema that gives permanence to objects and the schema that conserves the quantity, weight, and volume of static objects. Where the assumptions of both fixed intelligence and predetermined development appear to have presumed a kind of static fixity to the human personality and to intelligence, Piaget's observations and experiments indicate that the behavioral and thought structures comprising intelligence are continually changing as a consequence of the accommodation and assimilation involved in a person's encounters with his environment. Although a variety of implications can be pointed to and a variety of questions can be raised (see Chapter 7), it is relatively clear that experience, defined as the organism's encounters with his environment, is continually building into the developing human organism a hierarchy of operations for processing information and for coping with circumstances. Moreover, the complexity of these operations is still much greater than those which Newell, Shaw, and Simon (1958) have built into their "logic theorist." In returning to the point at which this attempt to synopsize the work of Piaget and his collaborators began, it is worth noting again that those who program computers to solve problems build into their machines a hierarchy of operations for processing information, that neurologists and neuropsychologists are finding both anatomical and functional signs of approximate counterparts for such a hierarchial system of operations within complex mammalian brains, and that Piaget finds experience building into human beings just such a hierarchially organized system of operations. The lines of evidence concerning what is involved in intelligent behavior are apparently coalescing.

CHAPTER 7

Some Implications of
Piaget's Work
and Other Evidence

In his book on the theories of learning, Hilgard (1948) suggested that it would be highly desirable for someone to take a notebook and follow a child around in order to discover the circumstances under which he learns, what performances provide for recall, for problem-solving, etc. (p. 352). Among psychoanalysts, Kardiner & Spiegel (1947) have made a similar suggestion. In a very real sense, this is what Piaget (1936, 1937, 1945) has done with his own three children in his observational studies of the development of sensorimotor intelligence and imagery. Moreover, these observational studies are almost as informative as Hilgard hoped they would be. The later studies of the development of intuition, concrete operations, and formal operations which use performance in problem-situations coupled with interrogation are equally informative about changes in the child's thought processes as his interaction with the environment builds into him central processes of increasing autonomy with increasing dominance over perception and action. Synoptic accounts of Piaget's work, even his own (1947, 1953b), have failed to supply the observational basis for his fresh and interesting theoretical formulations. The synopsis in the two preceding chapters has attempted to present enough of the observational and experimental detail to provide an understanding of what Piaget and his collaborators have seen in the behavior of children that induces the theoretical formulations. It remains, first, to note various implications of his observations, and, second, to examine the validity of certain of his formulations in the light of evidence available from other sources.

Five main themes dominate Piaget's theoretical formulations. One concerns the continual and progressive change in, or the epigenesis of, the structures of behavior and thought in the child. A second concerns the fixed nature of the order in which the successive structures make their appearance. A third concerns the invariant functions of accommodation and assimilation, or the adaptation to outer circumstances and the progress of inner organization, that operate in the child's continuous interaction with his environment. A fourth concerns the relation of thought processes to action in the course of development, their origin through a gradual internalization of action, their "decentring," and their growing dominance over perception and action, all of which may be seen to be the function of a growing autonomy and dominance of central neural processes. A fifth concerns the logical properties of the thought processes that develop. Several of these themes imply the need for change in commonly held beliefs about both epistemological and psychological problems. Several of them also contain principles or hypotheses which call for verification by way of evidence other than that available from Piaget's own approach.

IMPLICATIONS OF THE EPIGENESIS OF BEHAVIORAL AND THOUGHT STRUCTURES

The notion that behavior and thought change with age is certainly not new. It has presumably always been implicitly recognized by parents and teachers in the changing pattern of their reactions to children as the children develop. It was explicitly recognized by Plato in his educational program for his utopian Republic, but Plato was interested only in the talking child. Behavioral epigenesis got clear recognition in the recapitulation theory of G. Stanley Hall. Moreover, Arnold Gesell's descriptive studies of child development have been concerned primarily with this change. On the other hand, when Plato formulated his epistemology, he assumed that it is ideas which are immutable and that man's knowing task consists in laying hold of these perfect conceptual structures. Such preformationism has been predominant in classical epistemology ever since Plato. Examples of preformation also lurk in the conceptions of modern psychology.

IMPLICATIONS FOR CONCEPTIONS OF SPACE. It will be remembered that Inhelder (1953) has characterized Piaget as a zoologist by original training, an epistemologist by vocation, and a logician by method. Piaget the epistemologist has taken great pains to point out the implications of the epigenesis he finds in the child's construction of space, time, and causality. Preformation resides even in modern epistemological formulations. Poincaré (1906), for instance, ana- lyzed geometric space into changes in the external world that can be corrected by body movements which lead a perception back to its initial state. He distinguished such changes of position from genuine changes of state which cannot be eliminated by body movements because the difference in perception remains. It is from this analysis that Piaget gets his notion of *reversibility* and his mathematical con- cept of the "group" as any set of operations which can be nullified by a corresponding set of inverse operations. Poincaré considered the distinction between changes of position and changes of state to be elementary or to be given in the very nature of man. Piaget (1937, pp. 102 ff.) points out that Poincaré apparently reconstructed the development of spatial concepts more logically than psychologically, and he makes three objections to the latter's formulations. First, a change of position may be distinguished from a change of state only if the subject is able to conceive of the external world as composed of permanent objects. Since objects lack permanence for the human infant throughout the first year of his life, the act of finding a dis- placed image would be confused with "the act of recreating it." Sec- ond, if a change of position is to be distinguished from a change of state, the external universe must be distinguished from personal ac- tivity, and the human child is more than a year old before such a distinction is consistently evident in his behavior. Thirdly, to con- ceive of a change of position is equivalent to locating one-self in a spatial field conceived as external to the body and independent of action. Such a field emerges only gradually with the development of an interest in objects and their relationships, and it is not firmly es- tablished till the child is more than a year old. Its establishment depends upon the intercoordination of the schemata of sucking, look- ing, listening, and prehension, upon the differentiation of these in- tercoordinated schemata, upon an interest in object relationships, and finally upon the development of autonomous central processes which can represent these relationships. As has been seen in Chapter 6, the central processes which represent the Euclidean frames of reference in space are not developed until the child is about 10 years old. In other words, the spatial field is constructed gradually through the infant's and then the child's interaction with the environment as a coordinated function of accommodation and assimilation. The spatial field is, thus, a construct with its own epigenesis.

IMPLICATIONS FOR CONCEPTIONS OF CAUSALITY. In similar fashion, Piaget contrasts the developmental construction of causal schemata and conceptions with the five famous hypotheses concerning the origin of the conception of causality. Consider his synopsis of these hypotheses in his own words:

In the first place, associational empiricism inspired Hume [1739; 1748] to an interpretation of causality which retains all its interest; the foregoing facts permit a discussion of it in the same field chosen by the philosopher: that of the origin of habits. In the second place, the equally famous interpretation of Maine de Biran [1803] must be described as vitalistic. According to this, causality results from the awareness of voluntary activity conceived as a primary datum. It is in this doctrine of the self and of personal causality that Maine de Biran's vitalism deviates most definitely from ordinary rationalism. In the third place, the a priori interpretation of causality [Kant, 1791] implies a psychological hypothesis according to which the concept of cause constitutes a necessary structure inherent in every intellectual act and present, consequently, from the very first contacts of the mind with reality. In the fourth place, in the pragmatic theory of trial-and-error, causal relations constitute so many constructions destined to insure the provision of phenomena and the adaptation of personal action to the external world [Peirce, 1878; James, 1907], but these constructions are based neither on the nature of things nor on any necessary structure of the mind. Finally, in relativity, causality is the totality of the relationship elaborated by sensorimotor intelligence and later by thought in order to understand things, and its growing deductive success shows that these relationships correspond to a real interaction between subject and object (Piaget, 1937, p. 309).

Piaget then notes that Hume's interpretation, while quite outmoded with regards to the higher forms of causality, is applicable to the first three stages wherein, for instance, the baby turns his head in the direction of a sound to find the corresponding visual image and of the third stage when the child pulls a string to shake the dolls on his bassinet hood. At these stages, the association is purely phenomenalistic. Moreover, Piaget considers Hume correct in the notion that the baby discovers little by little that his desires govern the movements of his hands or legs. On the other hand, Piaget denies that causal connection therefore stems from the force of habit, because habits, considered as conditioned reflexes or associative transfers, are explained by an assimilation of certain symbols to the reflexive schemata or the combinations of them. Piaget, therefore, traces causal relationships back to reproductive assimilation where, having fortuitously set an interesting phenomenon in motion, the child attempts to prolong it or to reproduce it. It is this active effort, which may yield a habit, that constitutes the most elementary form of causal relationships. Relationships in this fashion are, of course, not rational. Rather, they are a mixture of phenomenalism and the feeling of efficacy. But the schemata constituting such causality are capable of "progressive structuring in the direction of reversibility and geometric connection and thus presage from the beginning the possibility of a later rationalism" (1937, p. 311).

While Piaget's emphasis on the schema and upon felt efficacy may seem to favor Maine de Biran's hypothesis, the elaboration of the central processes depends less upon contrasting the object and the subject or upon their mutual relationships arising through the child's coping with things. Against the Kantian *a priori* interpretation, according to which causality inheres in every intellectual act and must (as Piaget infers, but perhaps unnecessarily), therefore, be present from the first, is all the evidence for the epigenesis of the conception of causation. Against the pragmatic interpretation of Peirce and James—namely, that the construction of practical adaptations have only provisional value and derive neither from internal necessity nor from the nature of the external world—is the fact that the evolution of causality leads to the construction of schemata and later to logical conceptions which, as in the case of the adolescent's versus the child's conception of the basis for the equilibrium of a balance (see Chapter 6), show an increasingly close approximation between empirical experience on the one hand and deduction on the other. It is for this last reason that Piaget insists that

. . . causality consists in an organization of the universe caused by the totality of relations established by action and then by representation between objects as well as between object and subject. Hence causality presupposes at all levels an interaction between the self and things, but if the radical egocentrism of the beginnings first leads the subject to attribute all external events to personal activity, the formation of the permanent universe subsequently enables the self to be located among things and to understand the totality of the sequences which it sees or in which it is engaged as cause or effect. Such an elaboration pre-supposes an invariant functioning, as we have just seen, but a structuring which is progressive and not *a priori* . . . the progress of such a structuring stems from that of intelligence, and . . . causality must definitely be conceived as intelligence itself to the extent that the latter is applied to temporal relations and organizes a lasting universe" (1937, p. 315).

IMPLICATIONS FOR PSYCHOLOGICAL THEORY.

Means and ends. Preformationism, as has been said, still lurks in some unexpected aspects of psychological theory. One of these is the assumption that means, seen as instrumental actions, are from the beginning separate from ends, seen as deriving from organic needs or intense stimulation. While the early functionalism of James (1890), Dewey (1896), and Angell (1907) clearly opposed the analysis of acts into such elementary units as reflex arcs, and while this early functionalism, or a parallel development of theory, appears to be a forerunner of Piaget's theorizing through Flournoy and Claparède (see footnote on p. 112) even to the point of Angell's supplying the concept of accommodation, Dewey's (1910) use of the concept of "felt need" as the basis for thinking and learning and in his "pedagogical creed" helped lay the ground for a conception of ends and means as inherently separate from the beginning. Woodworth (1918), a student of James, introduced the concept and term *drive* as a basis for motivation into American psychology and helped further to separate motive from action and cognitive processes. Carr (1925), a student of Angell, incorporated Woodworth's motivational ideas into Chicago functionalism; Dashiell (1928) elaborated them further, and such latter-day descendants of the early functionalists as McGeoch (1942) and Melton (1941) have accepted the conception of ends (motivation) and means (instrumental activity) as inherently separate. Similarly, Freud (1915) conceived of the aim (end) of action and thought as the reduction of their source in a *Trieb* (drive) that is separate from action and thought. Finally, modern behavior theorists like Miller & Dollard (1941), Hull (1943), and Sears (1944) have generally accepted this same inherent separation. In these theories, motivation derives ultimately from either aversive stimulation or homeostatic need which are extrinsic to the perceptual and cognitive processing of information, but there has been a growing appreciation of the fact that motivation may also inhere in the processing of information itself (see Hunt, 1960).

Piaget's observations tend to corroborate this view that in a major share of behavior motivation inheres in the perceiving and acting and to indicate that in such cases ends and means become differentiated gradually in the course of behavioral epigenesis. The newborn infant reacts first in terms of his ready-made reflexive schemata. During the second stage these reflexive schemata become coordinated into habits and redundant patterns of stimulation come to be recognized. As the infant becomes less and less dependent upon external stimulation for action, various phenomena come to call forth activity designed to repeat them or to prolong them. Finally, in about the ninth month, any one of the child's schemata may become an end while various others are subordinated to it as means. Thus, the child may strike or push in order to grasp something, locomote and stretch in order to see something, etc. But, except as a conceptual distinction, means and ends do not become differentiated in the activity of a child until he is approaching the end of his first year of interacting with his environment.

Curiosity. Curiosity has recently received a great deal of attention (see Berlyne, 1960). It has been generally presumed that curiosity is an immutable motive reflecting a need for stimulation (Harlow, 1953) or an innate drive (Berlyne, 1960). Piaget's (1936) observations, on the contrary, indicate that curiosity derives from an interest in novelty, and further, that an interest in novelty derives from the child's attempts to perpetuate and repeat interesting experiences when, early in his second year, he begins actively to experiment with new means to achieve his ends.

Gestalt theory and preformationism. Gestalt theory has always fostered a kind of preformationism. The notion that the perceptual field is structured physically within the nervous system in a fashion not unlike the patterning of iron filings within the fields of a set of magnets (Köhler, 1940) by the intensive and qualitative variety within the field implies that the "laws of organization" (Köhler, 1929) are as immutable as Plato's "eternal ideas." Thus, perceptual constancies of shape, size, and color have been held not to be acquired but to be completely formed at all ages. Piaget & Lambercier (1943a, 1943b), on the other hand, have shown that some of this constancy is illusory in that it derives from the "error of the standard" coupled with estimations of distance. Constancy of size is underestimated by five-to-seven-year-old children while adults tend typically towards a "superconstancy." Moreover, Beryl (1926) and Brunswik & Cruikshank (1937) have also reported increasing perceptual constancies with age. Piaget (1947) rejects the notion of "permanent physical Gestalten" on these and other grounds, but he points out that this rejection need not force a reversion to the notion that perception is a synthesis of elementary sensations, for perception may also be conceived as a system of relations with each relation itself being a whole. From such an assumption Piaget derives the notion that complex perceptual structures are the product of progressive construction arising from "adaptive differentiations and combinative assimilations." Perceptual constancies arise as central processes, derived from the aspects of objects that provide the most redundant patterns of input, become sufficiently autonomous to be evoked as a whole when the imput concerned involves only small portions of the total pattern.

Perceptual transpositions of such patterns as melodies have been used by Köhler (1929) and others as a crucial argument against the notion of perception as a synthesis of elements and for the notion that the transposed melody is "the simple reappearance of the same form of equilibrium between new elements whose relations have been retained." Piaget (1947) proposes, on the other hand, that the transposed melody be considered as the "product of an assimilatory activity which integrates comparable elements into the same schema." In favor of this hypothesis, he cites what he calls a *fact* of improvement with age in the ability to transpose melodies. The act of transposing a melody, however, is quite different from the perceiving of a transposed melody, and the relevance of the fact may be questioned, but the issue is drawn.

In the case of the Gestalt theory of intelligence, Piaget (1927) emphasizes the fundamental contradiction between the rigidity of perceived patterns and the reversible mobility of the "operations" of thought. He finds quite inadequate the notion of "sudden restructurings" (see Wertheimer, 1920; Köhler, 1929) as an example of intelligence. Although placing a stick parallel with an ape's arm may suggest that the stick be perceived as an extension of the hand, this is a long way from shifting freely back and forth between superordinate and subordinate categories. Wertheimer's (1920) explanation of syllogistic reasoning as "re-anchoring" is similarly suspect. In the trite example, according to this re-anchoring principle Socrates is "uprooted from the class of men in order to be anchored in that of mortals" (Piaget, 1947, p. 60). Rather, what makes it possible to pass Socrates from the subordinate class of men to the superordinate class of mortals is the process of combination which, as noted in the reasoning of adolescents in Chapter 6, is but one of the complex of mobile operations characteristic of formal logical thought. In fact, Piaget (1947, p. 65) sees the essential structure of adult thought to be these "groupements" of mobile operations which he calls "formal operations." It is the complex of operations which have the character of a Gestalt or "structure d'ensemble." It is the logical characteristics mirrored in such operational thought that gives intelligence its flexibility and scope. But such operations do not come preformed. They are the product of a long course of development in which each level of achievement is incorporated hierarchically into the next. Such is the origin of the Gestalt-like structures whose epigenesis Piaget has made it his special task to discover and describe.

IMPLICATIONS OF THE FIXED ORDER IN THE APPEARANCE OF THE STRUCTURES OF BEHAVIOR AND THOUGHT

If the claimed immutability of the order in which the structures of behavior and thought appear in the successive stages be true, it has implications for the measurement of intellectual development and intelligence. Unlike Shirley (1933), Piaget assumes that this fixed order of appearance implies nothing concerning the experiential or hereditary basis for the order. The age of the stages can vary (Inhelder, 1953) with the nature of both the individual's experience and his hereditary potential. The order is assumed to be a fixed feature of the organism-environment interaction, to be both organismic and experiential. Piaget and his collaborators have not, however, examined this order of development in individuals from widely differing cultures. While even such cultural relativists as Margaret Mead (1953) have opined that the order in which the structures appear (i.e., the stages) would probably be constant across any cultures known to them, since Dennis (1960) has found that the commonly observed order of creeping, standing, and walking becomes scooting, standing, and walking (with creeping omitted) in the case of children left almost continuously on their backs during the early months, the claim that this order is universal must be verified.

Inhelder (1944), as already noted, has already checked the order in which conservation of quantity, weight, and volume appear with a large sampling of the feeble-minded. Perhaps the proper strategy is to look for exceptions where one is most likely to find them. One source of exception might derive from individuals with developmental experiences markedly different from what is typical. Orphanages like those Dennis (1960) has discovered in the Near East apparently provided developmental experiences further from the typical than can be found anywhere across cultures where children are reared in families. The order in which the structures of behavior and thought appear in the inmates of such orphanages should provide one severe test of the assertion that the order is fixed. Schizophrenic patients may provide another place where exceptions are most likely. It is a question whether conservation of volume will always mean conservation of both weight and quantity in the performance of schizophrenics.

The order for the earlier structures has not been widely tested. In fact, its empirical basis resided only in Piaget's observations of his own three children. This order too needs to be verified.

If the order or the appearance of the structures is fixed, and if the presence of a later one always implies the presence of those which have appeared earlier, the result is a natural scale of intellectual development and intelligence with the properties Guttman (1941, 1944) has described for ordinal scales. Inhelder (1953) has contended that diagnosis of the structures provides much greater power of prediction than can a score derived from passing tests which participate in the score on a compensatory basis (see Coombs, 1950) and are but statistically associated with age. Certainly the reports of Piaget and his collaborators make it appear that broad constellations of behavioral and thought performances arrive at the same time. These constellations cut across, for example, classifying, serializing, numbering, and conceptualizing space and time. The data from Piaget's laboratory are, however, cross-sectional, and the evidence is finding these various kinds of performance in different persons at about the same age. Whether given individuals will regularly manifest these constellations of capacity at a given age remains to be shown. If they do, it will pose problems. For of what do the individual differences in adult intelligence consist when formal operations are part of the equipment of all but the feeble-minded? Of what do the individual differences in the intelligence of children from seven to nine consist if they all share the basic concrete operational structures? Why have these structures, seemingly so basic and important, failed to appear in the factor-analytic studies of intelligence? Is it because these factor-analytic studies of intelligence have almost never been made across age groups? Have Thurstone's (1938) primary mental abilities failed to include evidence of formal operational structures because, being based upon college students, all subjects shared these basic structures? Such may be the answer, for Spearman (1927) has reported data suggesting that abilities are more specialized among older people, with the result that his g-factor played a lesser role than among children, and these data have been confirmed by various factor-analytic investigations (see Garrett, 1946). Tyler (1953) has reported that the scores of fourth-grade children on Thurstone's primary mental abilities can be predicted as well from total scores as from scores for the separate factor scores derived from tests the children had taken three years earlier. Yet a good many studies have also appeared to yield data inconsistent with this notion that intelligence becomes differentiated with age.[1] The issue awaits clarification.

If Piaget's successive structures prove to have a fixed order, a very useful ordinal scale of intelligence would result. The times between successive landmarks of transition could then provide an inverse index of the capacity of various kinds of child-environment interaction to foster intellectual development. Comparing average times between various pairs of successive landmarks for groups of children being reared under differing conditions should gradually yield new understanding of the factors in child-environment interaction, both socio-familial and physical, that hamper and foster intellectual development. With the improvement in such understanding, it should become feasible more nearly to maximize the intellectual potential of children.

[1] These studies include Balinsky (1941), Chen & Chow (1948), Curtis (1949), and Doppelt (1950); see Anastasi (1958, chap. xi).

CONTINUOUS ORGANISM-ENVIRONMENT INTERACTION: EVIDENCE FROM OTHER SOURCES

It is Piaget's third theme that the epigenesis of behavioral and thought structures derive from the invariant functions of accommodation and assimilation that operate in the child's continuous interaction with his environment that makes Piaget's picture of development so different from that of G. Stanley Hall or that of Gesell and the other investigators who have assumed that the intelligence of a person is fixed, like the weight or volume of a static object, and that his rate and level of development are predetermined. Such theorists and investigators have been satisfied merely to describe what behavior is typical, or normal in the sense of typical, at successive chronological ages. So long as behavior is assumed to be predetermined such normative description can pass as the equivalent of explanation, and G. Stanley Hall's famous parable of the tadpole's tail may be conceived to apply (see Chapter 4). Piaget, on the other hand, has been continually mindful of the cooperation of accommodation and assimilation in the environment-organism interaction to produce the changes in structures.

Piaget's conception of organism-environment interaction through assimilation and accommodation is neither hereditarian nor is it environmentalistic; it is both. The role of genetic influence is never denied, but it falls far short of being the whole story. In any given situation, the first response of the child is one of those behavioral structures (schemata) already present from past assimilation. What variations in the environment do is to force the child to cope with this variation, and, in the coping, to modify the structures. This latter is accommodation, and the modifications are then assimilated through repetition in practice play.

A series of separately formulated principles can be found within Piaget's theme of organism-environment interaction. One states that appropriate stimulation and opportunity to exercise schemata are required for the survival of both reflexive and acquired schemata. Unused reflexive schemata wane. Stimuli that evoke reflexive and habitual schemata and demand accommodative modifications are "aliments" of the schemata concerned if not also of the morphological structures which function in their occurrence. A second states that new accommodative modifications and new assimilative combinations of schemata are sources of function pleasure which promotes their rehearsal in practice play. This principle makes at least one kind of reinforcement an intrinsic and inherent part of perceiving and acting. A third principle states that the rate of development is in substantial part, but certainly not wholly, a function of environmental circumstances. Change in circumstances is required to force the accommodative modifications of schemata that constitute development. Thus, the greater the variety of situations to which the child must accommodate his behavioral structures, the more differentiated and mobile they become. Thus, the more new things a child has seen and the more he has heard, the more things he is interested in seeing and in hearing. Moreover, the more variation in reality with which he has coped, the greater is his capacity for coping. A fourth principle, hinted at but not quite formulated by Piaget, concerns the role of the still poorly understood factor of the match between the schemata within the organism and the circumstances of the situation in determining whether accommodative modification will occur in any given encounter with the environment. A fifth principle, on the border of the theme of organism-environment interaction, concerns the internalization of actions, i.e., of actions into central processes, of imitations into images, of images into intuitions, the grouping of intuitions and images into concrete operations, and of concrete operations into formal operations. According to this principle, intelligence becomes capable of extension into time and space as it becomes more and more independent of perception and action. This appears to be equivalent to saying that intelligence increases as central processes become at once more and more autonomous and more and more finely differentiated so that combinations can occur in a wider and wider variety of ways.

In inducing these principles or hypotheses, Piaget has probably clarified better than anyone else the nature of the child-environment interaction during development. Yet inducing such a series of hypotheses does not verify them. Since Piaget's observations during the sensorimotor period and his experimental interrogations during the later periods fail to separate antecedents from consequences, they permit no test of the hypotheses they suggest. One must look elsewhere for relevant evidence.

EXERCISE AND SCHEMA-SURVIVAL. Evidence that stimulation and exercise are necessary for the survival of either reflexive or of habitual schemata comes from several sources already reviewed in Chapter 4. Cruze's (1935) studies showed, for instance, that when chicks are allowed very little opportunity for pecking, the accuracy of their pecking fails to improve. When Padilla (1935) kept newly hatched chicks from pecking for eight consecutive days and longer, the chicks lost the inclination or capacity to peck. Such chicks would die of hunger beside a pile of grain. Again, any dairy farmer knows that if a young calf is taken from the cow and pail-fed for several days (how many days depends somewhat upon the breed and upon the individual calf), it is then perfectly safe to allow that calf among fresh cows. It will no longer attempt to suckle. Duration of the period without exercise is a critical factor here, and thus far systematic information about duration in relation to breeds, etc., does not exist. There is also such contrary evidence as that from Carmichael's (1926) studies of chloretoned amblystoma, but this can be explained (see Chapter 8).

In her wonderfully acute observations of the neuromuscular development of human infants, McGraw (1943) noted the waxing and waning of various reflexive activities. The waxing she attributed, as was the theoretical fashion, to an automatic unfolding in maturation. To explain the waning she used two neurological notions then prevalent. One of these held that the connection between the afferent and the efferent portions of reflexive activities occurs below the cortical level. Another held that the cerebral cortex has the function of inhibiting the functioning of lower centers. Thus, combining these two ideas led McGraw to explain the waning as a function of the maturation of the cortex. She observed, however, evidences of disorganization in reflexive behaviors during the waning phase. In the light of current neuropsychology, it is hard to see the basis for such functional disorganization in mere maturation of the cortex. Rather, it should probably be attributed to interference from central processes which are gradually being organized through the infant's other kinds of experiences and becoming dominant over the unused reflexive processes.

Piaget's notion that appropriate stimulation is an "aliment" for the schema concerned appears to be more than a metaphor in view of Riesen's (1947, 1958) discovery that the optic apparatus failed to develop properly in chimpanzees reared in darkness. Moreover, this finding, coupled with corresponding findings on such other species as the rabbit (see Chapter 4), suggest that the development of schemata may involve processes more fundamental than cortical firing systems. They may mean that even somatic growth and differentiation is in part a function of stimulation and exercise.

INTRINSIC REINFORCEMENT: FUNCTION PLEASURE. The principle concerning intrinsic reinforcement, which Piaget does not emphasize because he is concerned primarily with intellectual development rather than motivational development, is a radical and still poorly understood departure from what has for about 40 years been the dominant view that reinforcement is always extrinsic in the sense that it is a matter of changing the drive level in conjunction with instrumental acts. Yet a good many other observers have noted the behavioral phenomena that have led Piaget to remark on the intrinsic reinforcement of "function pleasure." It was apparently Bühler (1928) for whom the manifestations of pleasure associated with children's activities stood out so prominently that he drew the conclusion that pleasure need not be derived from the gratification of homeostatic needs and that it may be intrinsic to action itself, and he therefore recalled the concept of "function pleasure" which is as old as Aristotle. More recently, Hendrik (1943) has seen in children's playful repetition of various activities an "instinct to master" with properties similar to other instincts. Mittelmann (1954) has noted particularly the tendency of children to repeat motor actions, and he has seen in the tendency evidence of a "motor urge" no less compulsive than hunger and sex. White (1959), in a highly competent review of the relevant investigations, has proposed the naming of this tendency to repeat actions for their telic consequences as "competence." [2]

Piaget's observations lend some support to Hebb's (1949) hypothesis that a major share of motivation and of the reinforcement of patterns of response in learning is intrinsic to the storing and processing of the receptor inputs and motor outlets of daily experience. In this connection, it should be noted that Piaget has observed, first, that it is schemata which are in the process of organization that children tend to repeat playfully and with apparent pleasure, and, second, that once such schemata have become organized the signs of pleasure associated with their repetition disappears and they cease to be repeated except as they are combined into some new schema or serve as means to some end. These observations lend confirmation to Hebb's (1949) claims that "interest is likely to be preoccupied by whatever is new in the combination of familiar events" (p. 230) and that insofar as the repetitions of a schema "contribute to the current development in the cerebrum," they could be called pleasant. Hebb's emphasis in these claims concerns chiefly receptor inputs, so Piaget's observations may constitute something of an extension of them unless one assumes that it is the receptor inputs feeding back from the playful activity that yields the pleasure. How necessary or important the signs (including reports) of pleasure may be in such intrinsic reinforcement, however, is not yet clear. It should be noted

2 Perhaps the well-known tendency to return to uncompleted tasks (Ovsiankina, 1928) and the tendency to recall uncompleted tasks better than completed ones (Zeigarnik, 1927) are related phenomena. But, as Rosenzweig (1933) has shown, young children tend to return to those activities which they have completed rather than those they have failed to complete, and this may mean that these tendencies have a more restricted motivational basis than that of children for playful repetition of newly organized skills.

that Freud (1922) saw in essentially the same behavioral phenomena evidence for something "beyond the pleasure principle" which he termed the "repetition compulsion." At any rate Hebb's neuropsychological hypotheses about the nature of intrinsic motivation and reinforcement serve as a corrective for reward-behavior theory and are more likely to lead to fresh knowledge than are attempts at explanation by way of circular assumptions of instincts, or by way of the apparent telic consequences of the infant's tendency to repeat activities.

Although the issues of intrinsic reinforcement and "function pleasure" are still incompletely resolved by Piaget's observations, it is interesting to note that the exercise of an activity commonly associated with homeostatic need can apparently cause it to survive even though that homeostatic need is never gratified in association with the exercise of that activity. The evidence for this comes from the famous study by Sears & Wise (1950) of the babies who were cup-fed from birth. Some of these babies continued to suck their thumbs even though they had never got food from the breast or through a nipple. Such a finding can hardly be explained without assuming that mere repetition of an act or a receptor input, when appropriately timed, may bring its own inherent reinforcement that permits the survival of the schema. Presumably if calves had such handy things as thumbs to suck, they might not so readily lose the sucking reflex.

VARIATION IN CIRCUMSTANCES AND RATE OF INFANTILE DEVELOPMENT. Perhaps the most clarifying hypothesis deriving from Piaget's observations is that concerning the role of variation in circumstances for rate of infantile development. As Piaget (1936, pp. 274-79) has formulated this hypothesis, which because of his unconcern with motivation gets little emphasis, it states that the more new things an infant has seen and the more new things he has heard, the more new things he is interested in seeing and hearing; and the more variation in reality he has coped with, the greater is his capacity for coping. Such relationships derive from the conception that change in circumstances is required during the early sensorimotor stages to force the accommodative modifications in schemata and the assimilation of these modifications that, in combination, constitute development.

It is worth repeating that it is precisely here that Piaget's theorizing departs most widely from that of G. Stanley Hall, who emphasized recapitulation as the chief explanation of intellectual as well as morphological development, and from that of Hall's student, Arnold Gesell, who has emphasized the predetermined nature of development. Because he assumes development to be predetermined, a careful normative description of the behavior characteristic of each age constitutes for Gesell an explanation as well as a description. For Piaget, on the other hand, the relationship between a behavioral landmark and the age it appears is simply a convenient device; the explanation of development comes rather in the child-environment interaction. At first in this interaction, the human infant responds almost solely to changes in his stimulating circumstances. He initiates nothing. Moreover, his sensorimotor schemata resist change, and changes in circumstances are required to force the accommodative modifications in the ready-made schemata that, as they are assimilated, constitute development. As the infant's schemata have been accommodated to a wider and wider range of circumstances, variations in a wider and wider variety of circumstances acquire the capacity, through the discrepancy principle, to evoke his interest. As a wider variety of circumstances acquire the capacity to evoke his interest, he becomes curious about more things. With curiosity he develops what is commonly called initiative.

This hypothesis provides a pretty explanation for the effects of early experience on later capacity. It is an explanation quite consonant with, but perhaps more explicit than, that formulated by Hebb (1949, chap. xi). The various studies already reported (see Chapter 4) which were derived from Hebb's theorizing are both relevant and supportive of Piaget's formulation. Supportive is the fact, for instance, that pet-reared rats, which have been submitted to a wide range of circumstances, are capable of coping with a wider range of situations in the Hebb-Williams (1946) test of animal intelligence than are cage-reared rats which have experienced only the limited variety of circumstances within their laboratory cages. Especially interesting and supportive, moreover, is the work of Thompson & Heron (1954). In their study, one of the fortunate aspects is the fact that the "orientation test" which they used duplicates almost exactly the procedure employed by Piaget (1936) to test for the degree of permanence of the object-construct. Pet-reared dogs easily find food which has been placed behind a screen within their view, even though the placement is changed from trial to trial, whereas cage-reared fail to follow a series of changing placements and return almost regularly to the first place where they have found the food. The pet-reared dogs immediately followed the shift of placement, just as did Piaget's (1937) children at sensorimotor stage 5 when they were 13 to 15 months old. The dogs reared in isolation, in failing to follow the sequence of placements, behaved like Piaget's children at stage 4 when they were seven or eight months of age. Thus, in terms of developmental quotient, this constitutes a difference due to the manner of rearing for the first eight months of the order of 30 points. The difference in rearing experience is large, but in view of the smaller A/S ratio in dogs than in human beings perhaps 30 points of DQ represents a greater proportion of potential for development in a dog than it would in a human being. While such studies have disadvantages from being based on a species other than man, they also have the advantage of being uncomplicated by unknown variations in heredity, for the pet-reared dogs were litter-mates of the cage-reared dogs. The support such results lend to the hypothesis is strong.

At the human level, observations on the development of infants reared in orphanages also lend support to this hypothesis deriving from Piaget's observations. Because orphanages chronically have had to get along with a minimum number of persons to care for the infant inmates, the orphanage environment has seldom supplied anywhere near the degree of environmental variation that is available even in the poorer of foster homes. As a consequence of this difference in antecedent experience, two behavioral characteristics of orphanage inmates, as compared with children in general, have been observed with monotonous repetition. First, the rate of development in orphanage inmates lags behind the typical rate. Although the observations of Skeels, Updegraff & Wellman (1938) and those of Spitz (1945, 1946) have been criticized and doubted, the degree of retardation in locomotor functions claimed by these investigators is relatively small compared with that reported by Dennis (1960) for the inmates of an orphanage in Teheran where only 42 per cent of infants sit alone during the second year of life, and where only 40 per cent walk even while holding onto things during the third year of life and only 8 per cent walk alone before the end of the third year. Secondly, orphanage children show apathy, or low degree of interest in things in general, and marked fear of new things. As Gesell & Amatruda (1941) once put it, unfortunately without making any theoretical capital of the observation, orphanage children show "an exaggerated resistance to new situations." [3] So long as intelligence was assumed to be fixed, and development was assumed to be predetermined, every effort was made to show that differential heredity alone could account for the retardation and apathy. In the light of the newer developments in both conceptualization and evidence,

[3] These observations of retardation, apathy, and fearfulness are at least as old as the turn of the century (Chamberlain, 1900). Various pediatricians noted these characteristics of institutional children and wondered whether they were due to the institutional environment or to the genetic constitution of the children who get into such institutions (see Bakwin, 1941, for review).

heredity, while it may still be an important factor, can no longer be assumed to have major responsibility for these differences.

PERMANENCE OF THE EFFECTS OF SITUATIONAL VARIATION. Even though rate of development is seen to be a function of variation in the child's stimulation, this need not say that variations in their situation alter the ultimate level of their intelligence. T. E. Newland[4] has argued that rate and ultimate level are quite separate. He points out, moreover, that in the case of the Mongolian feebleminded, special educational procedures will increase the rate at which these individuals develop, but their final level of intelligence is unaltered. The Mongolians merely achieve their potential more quickly with such procedures. The question of whether the effects of early experience, as controlled by environmental circumstances, are permanent is not unequivocally answered. On the one hand, when Gauron & Becker (1959) repeated Wolf's (1943) study of the effects of selectively closing either the eyes or the ears of rat pups for 10 days during infancy on their later capacity to use visual and auditory cues in a competitive situation to get food, they found that those pups deprived of vision in infancy were at a disadvantage with visual cues and that those deprived of hearing in infancy were at a disadvantage with auditory cues. On the other hand, the differences between the groups tended to "wash out" rather rapidly as the animals continued to compete in this situation on consecutive days. On the other hand, in the study already noted by Thompson & Heron (1954) the superiority of the pet-reared dogs over those reared in isolation was fully evident at more than a year and a half after the experience was terminated. Apparently these effects were permanent.

In McGraw's (1939) follow-up of the twins used in her well-known study (1935) of the effects of training in infancy (see p. 270), the trained twin, Johnny, whose training concerned primarily such motor skills as swimming and roller-skating during the first two years of life, showed better motor coordination, less fear in strange situations, and a richer degree of phantasy than the untrained twin, Jimmy, at seven years of age and some five years after the training had stopped. This appeared even though Jimmy, starting at 22 months of age, got training in the same activities in which Johnny had been trained. The richer phantasy showed both in stories about pictures and in the Rorschach test. This evidence suggests that infantile motor experience may have long enduring effects in central as well as motor functions, but the evidence is only suggestive because Johnny and Jimmy, it was finally decided, were not identical twins.

[4] Personal communication.

The fact that Skeels & Dye (1939) found substantial upward changes in the IQ's of retarded infants who were moved from an orphanage, where they presumably got little variation in stimulation, to a ward in a school for the feebleminded populated by moron women, who gave the children a great deal of stimulation, suggests that the effects of homogeneity of stimulation during Piaget's sensori-motor period may be reversible to a considerable degree if they do not last too long and if the corrective opportunity for varied stimulation is increased sufficiently. On the other hand, when institutionalization lasts for a period of three years, the studies of Goldfarb[5] indicate that the effects endure in substantial degree at least to adolescence.

Goldfarb's studies are based on three samples of 15 matched pairs of children. In each pair, one of the children, following separation from the mother at between four and six months of age, was reared in an orphanage to an age of about 3.5 years when he was placed in a foster home; the other child was placed immediately in a foster home. An attempt was made to match these pairs for age, sex, educational level of known biological parents, and social-class level of foster parents. One of the samples of 15 pairs was tested when they were between 10 and 14 years of age, or at from about 7 to 10 years after what was presumably a different kind of early experience had terminated. At this time the IQ's of the institutional group averaged only 72.4 while those of the foster-home group averaged 95.4, a difference of 23 points, which was highly significant from a statistical standpoint and socially important if all the factors other than the early experience were properly controlled in the matching. Similarly, the social-maturity scores from the Vineland Scale averaged 79 for the institutional group and 98.8 for the foster-home group (Goldfarb, 1943a). In a comparison of the incidence of problem behavior in the two groups, Goldfarb (1943b) found some three times as many instances of problem behavior among the institutional children as among the foster-home children. When Goldfarb (1943c) gave Brown's frustration test, which is scored in terms of the subject's tendency to resume an interrupted task, an effect of institutional apathy was apparently brought out, since the institutional adolescents resumed the uncompleted tasks following interruptions less frequently than did those reared from the first in foster-homes. When Goldfarb (1944) had his 15 matched pairs of adolescents draw what they saw in the Rorschach ink-blots, the drawings of the institutional children were judged to show both less influence of imagination and poorer correspondence between drawn-interpretation

[5] See Goldfarb (1943a, 1943b, 1943c, 1945, 1947, 1949).

and blot-form than were those of the foster-home children. Goldfarb interpreted these results to mean that children who have spent their first three years in orphanages, with presumably an appreciably lesser opportunity for varied experience, were in "poorer contact with both physical and social reality" than those children who had spent their whole lives in foster homes.

A number of manipulable factors probably participate in controlling the degree and permanence of the effects of such variations in infantile experience. One of the crucial factors appears to be the duration of the infantile experience. Another appears to be the opportunity available for experience nicely calculated to be a corrective for the early deficiency. Or, on the other hand, when the early experience has been rich, it becomes important that the subsequent experience not fail to supply the opportunity for continuous growth. Another factor is probably what Hebb (1949) has called the A/S ratio within the brain of the subject species. The lower this ratio, the less the degree and the less the permanence of effects. It is likely that Newland's Mongolian imbecile youngsters are like animals with low A/S ratios in the sense they have markedly limited potential. It may well be that achieving the ultimate limit quickly in such individuals has no bearing on the permanence of effects in normal children whose potential limits for intellectual development are probably almost never achieved. This issue, however, is crying for investigation. It is important socially for educational and child-rearing practices. In the light of the evidence now available, it is not unreasonable to entertain the hypothesis that, with a sound scientific educational psychology of early experience, it might become feasible to raise the average level of intelligence as now measured by a substantial degree. In order to be explicit, it is conceivable that this "substantial degree" might be of the order of 30 points of IQ. In a technological culture which is requiring more and more people with a high level of intelligence, this is an important challenge. At this stage of investigation, however, it is still a challenge for investigation rather than one for application in social change.

ACCOMMODATIVE MODIFICATION AND GROWTH AS A FUNCTION OF THE MATCH BETWEEN ENVIRONMENTAL CIRCUMSTANCES AND EXISTING SCHEMATA

Although Piaget often remarks on the importance of basing educational practice on the natural phases of the child's interaction with the environment, and in a sense the work of his group is concerned with the problem, Piaget only hints at the principle that environmental circumstances force accommodative modifications in schemata only when there is an appropriate match between the circumstances that a child encounters and the schemata that he has already assimilated into his repertoire. He fails to formulate the principle directly or to clarify it. In a sense, this principle is only another statement of the educator's adage that "teaching must start where the learner is," but it is poorly understood.

Even though it be poorly understood, this principle appears to be of tremendous import for both theory and practice. On the side of theory, it is related to the discrepancy theory of positive interest and fearful avoidance proposed by both Hebb (1949) and McClelland & Clark (1953), to Festinger's (1957) notion of cognitive dissonance, and to the concept of "critical periods" in development suggested by Fuller and Scott.[6] It has significance for both motivational and intellectual development. On the side of practice, this notion of a proper match between circumstance and schema is what every teacher must grasp, perhaps only intuitively, if he is to be effective. It was such a match that "Teacher" extraordinary Anne Sullivan sought and found when she pumped water on Helen Keller's (1903) hand as she spelled the word into her hand and "got across" the learning set that "things have names." Since the arts of both teaching and communication depend upon controlling appropriately the match between what environmental circumstance (object, model, Socratic question, or explanation) the student or communicatee encounters and the schemata or concepts he has already assimilated, this matter needs to be better understood. What follows is only a modest attempt to bring the matter into focus.

MATCH AND THE "DISCREPANCY" HYPOTHESIS. It was pointed out in Chapter 6 that it is useless to ask a four-year-old child at the preconceptual phase of Piaget to arrange the three mountains as a doll seated on one of the other three sides of a square table would see them. Similarly, asking a child at this stage of development to formulate a law about the relationship between the angle of inclination and the angle of incidence is to go completely beyond his ken. No common ground exists between such circumstances and what the child has already assimilated. As Hebb (1946) has noted in connection with his studies of fear in chimpanzees, what is completely unfamiliar and beyond the ken of the chimpanzee leaves him unaffected. It is the "familiar in an unfamiliar guise" that evokes fear. But expectations based upon familiarity with perceptual inputs is not the

[6] See Scott (1945), Scott, Fredericson, & Fuller (1951), Scott & Fuller (1951), Williams & Scott (1953), and Fuller & Scott (1954).

whole story. It is the merit of Piaget's (1947) review of the studies of thought to show that expectations may be based on central operational processes with logical properties. It is apparently these which get modified by the discrepancy motivation that Festinger (1957) calls cognitive dissonance. Certainly the central processes involved are not limited to the Helsonian (1959) adaptation levels for various receptor inputs used by McClelland & Clark (1953) in their version of the "discrepancy principle." All these agree, however, that discrepancies which are too large constitute a source of distress and negative motivation. On the other hand, discrepancies of a lesser order are a source of positive interest (Hebb, 1949) and of curiosity (Berlyne, 1960). It would appear that when there is some common ground between them, any discrepancy between central processes and circumstance beyond the limits of an organism's capacity for accommodation evokes distress and avoidance, while any discrepancy within the limits of an organism's capacity for accommodation is a source of pleasurable interest or curiosity. Furthermore, when circumstance and central process match perfectly, the result is stultifying boredom in which development fails. Unfortunately such statements have only intentional meaning, for neither what-is-discrepant-from-what nor capacity for accommodation have definite enough operational meaning to permit verification.

MATCH AND THE HYPOTHESIS OF CRITICAL PERIODS. Conversely, the conception of critical periods is so grossly empirical that it provides relatively little in the way of theoretical synthesis. The basis for the hypothesis of critical periods derives from an observation made some years ago by Scott (1945). He isolated several lambs from their mothers and raised them for the first 10 days in association with only human beings. When these lambs were returned to the flock, they had obviously changed, for they did not follow the flock and never became strongly associated with it even after several years. Later a puppy was kept from other dogs for a period of about nine weeks, and Scott expected even more drastic effects than he had observed in the lambs. After a brief period with dogs, however, this pup could not be distinguished from its littermates. Superficially, it might appear from these results that infantile experience has great effect on the later behavior of the sheep, while it has little or no effect on the later behavior of dogs. The Thompson & Heron (1954) study makes the latter statement obviously false.

It was this pair of observations that motivated Scott, Fuller, and their collaborators to undertake systematic studies of the development of behavior in several species of mammals. Scott, Fredericson, &

Fuller (1951) have found fairly distinct natural periods, for instance, in the development of the dog. These periods are, like the stages of Piaget, marked by characteristics of the dog's behavior. In the first, neonatal period, the principal activities of the puppy are nursing, defecation and urination in response to licking by the mother, crawling, and whining. In the second, transitional period, which begins when the pup is between ten days and two weeks of age and continues until he is three weeks old, the behavioral criteria are the opening of the eyes and ears and changes in motor capacities so that the puppy can walk, take solid food, and defecate and urinate by himself outside the nest. Even so, the puppy remains difficult to condition during this period and is presumed to be largely insulated from environmental changes. In the third period, one of socialization, the puppy becomes readily conditionable and comes normally into contact for the first time with other individuals, either human or canine, outside the nest. This period lasts from age three weeks to about ten weeks, and if the pup fails to make contact with human beings during this period, it is difficult later to make a proper pet of him for the pup remains shy and uncertain of his relationships with human beings throughout life. In the fourth, juvenile period, the pup grows, acquires increasing physical skill and independence. This period ends, and the fifth, adult period begins when the mating patterns emerge.

What is important in the hypothesis of critical periods is the fact that various kinds of circumstances have effects when they occur at one period but not when they occur at another period. Whether or not circumstances have an effect appears to be a function of whether or not the organism has already developed within its repertoire any schemata which are relevant to those circumstances and which can be accommodatively modified by them. If one sees this matter of match in conjunction with continuous organism-environment interaction, it would appear that every period along the line of development must be critical for experience with certain types of circumstances. From this point of view, the notion of critical periods must refer to stages in the process of developing autonomous central processes which are characterized by the predominance of certain recognizable sensorimotor structures or schemata.

ILLUSTRATIONS OF MATCH IN McGRAW'S STUDY. Myrtle McGraw's (1935) famous study of Johnny and Jimmy contains some instructive illustrations of appropriate and inappropriate matches between environmental circumstances and already assimilated schemata. McGraw's method, it will be recalled, consisted in giving Johnny, the trained twin, exercise in various motor activities in which he had shown some capabilities and inclination. Here, evidences of capability and inclination were the clues that the appropriate schemata were present. This practice began when Johnny and Jimmy, the control twin, were 21 days old. It lasted until they were 22 months of age. Because of the then widely held belief that the human infant is unresponsive to practice and should never be over-stimulated, the aim of McGraw's study was to determine when the human individual begins to profit by experience, here defined as repetition of performance. The answer was: immediately, if the practice concerns a schema or response system which is present and which can be modified to accommodate the circumstances arranged. The study produced some spectacular results: Johnny swimming at less than a year; Johnny roller-skating with skill by the time he was 16 months old. The swimming "lessons" began when Johnny was about four months of age and when he accepted the circumstance of deep water and showed an inclination to make swimming movements. The roller-skating "lessons" started when Johnny was beginning to learn to walk at 11 months of age. These are instances of "good match" as is evidenced by the learning to swim and skate. On the other hand, an attempt to train Johnny to use the tricycle when he was 11 months of age produced no improvement until, at about 19 months of age, he became active in the practice. He then acquired an easy performance in about two months.

An additional portion of McGraw's (1935) method consisted in giving training to Jimmy, the untrained twin, in the same activities in which Johnny had received "lessons" but beginning when Jimmy was 22 months of age. In terms of the concept of match, it is especially interesting that tricycling, in which Johnny had failed for nearly a year, was acquired by Jimmy beginning at 22 months of age in even less time than the two months required by Johnny after he had begun at 19 months of age to practice actively. McGraw's finding for tricycling corresponds to those findings obtained in the studies by Gesell & Thompson (1929) of the effects of early practice with stair-climbing, tower-building, etc., and to those findings obtained by Josephine Hilgard (1932, 1933) with similar skills, including buttoning and cutting with scissors. Quite the opposite sort of results were obtained, on the other hand, in the case of roller-skating. Beginning at 22 months of age, Jimmy failed to acquire any facility whatever with two and a half months of practice. McGraw argued that Johnny's advantage in roller-skating may have derived from his relatively wide base and short legs at 11 months. These made falls less devastating. Moreover, at 11 months, Johnny was less distractible than Jimmy at 22 months. Such factors may have well been operative, but an alternate interpretation is suggested by the concept of match. When a child is developing the walking schema, the addition of roller-skates is only a relatively slight variation from the environmental situation he faces in getting up on his own two feet, and it is one with which he can cope. The modified walking-schema is thereby readily assimilated as the roller-skating skill. In the case of Jimmy, at 22 months, on the other hand, when skates were added to an already established walking-schema, the discrepancy of the feed-back inputs from roller-skating had become markedly different from the expected feed-back impulses from the walking-schema. Jimmy had, thus, not only to remake the already well-established central processes that mediate walking, he had also to overcome the emotional disturbance aroused by the strange receptor inputs from feed-back inputs from the skating.

Although this task of matching environmental circumstances to already assimilated schemata is of the utmost importance in teaching and in assessing environment for its capacity to promote development, what is involved in the matching is still vague. At this stage of knowledge about behavior and development, the matching process is essentially a matter of empirical trial and error. Anyone who attempts to modify a child's development by manipulating his encounters with environmental circumstances must artfully "cut-and-try" until he finds those situations which will call forth accommodative modifications. Moreover, inasmuch as experience and maturation are continually changing the schemata of the child, maximizing the richness of an environment calls for continual concern with the appropriateness of the match. This means that all too often the process of artful trial and error becomes exhaustive to anyone who attempts to manage a child's encounters to maximize accommodative growth.

Such a matching of circumstance and schema resembles to a considerable degree the art of applying reinforcement for the purpose of shaping behavior to some desired form (see Skinner, 1959). Because one can see whether a given bit of behavior approximates better or worse the desired form but cannot see the effect that an encounter with a circumstance is having on the central processes that mediate schemata, the art of applying reinforcement is of a lower order than the art of matching circumstances with schemata. Moreover, if Skinner's teaching machines are ever to be used to present materials or to ask questions so as to lead subjects to develop concepts, this problem of matching the presentations or the questions with what the subject already "knows" demands more knowledge than now exists about the process of matching.[7]

IMPLICATIONS OF PIAGET'S STAGES FOR MATCHING CIRCUMSTANCES AND SCHEMATA. The pertinent information about the matching process appears to be of two kinds. One kind concerns the nature of the organism's or child's existing central processes, i.e., his existing sensorimotor schemata, his level of logical operation, or his knowledge. This kind of information must come either from clues gleaned from observing samples of his behavior in circumstances like those to be matched to his existing schemata, from hearing him talk about relevant matters, or from knowledge of the given organism's or child's past experience. The second kind concerns the size of the steps in discrepancy between circumstance and central process, i.e., between circumstance and level of developed capacity, or between circumstance to be accommodated and those circumstances which have already been assimilated, which the individual organism or child can accommodate. The size of the steps which can be accommodated would appear to be a kind of measure of potential for intellectual development. Such information comes from observing the readiness of an individual to "catch onto" innovations, i.e., to accommodate new circumstances. Although such a variable has hardly been conceived in the theory of intelligence, one gets the impression that skillful teachers intuitively take such a variable into account. In teaching mathematics by the discovery method, for instance, when some of a group of children lag behind, the skillful teacher appears to "step back" and ask a series of questions or present a series of illustrations to the laggards which fall more nearly within their scope of capacity and interest. The questions asked appear from what is still crude impression to comprise smaller steps of discrepancy between "where the group was" a few minutes before the laggards "got left" and the new point or accommodation required by the questions that pulled the leaders on. Seen in this light, the problem of the match is only beginning to be appreciated, but the descriptions of the stages of intellectual development provided by Piaget are extremely helpful in the matching process as it is seen in a grosser sense. The periods between the various behavioral landmarks that mark Piaget's transitions or stages are, in a sense, "critical periods" for various types of environmental encounters.

---

[7] Since this was written, Smedslund (1961) has made a similar point. Moreover, he has reviewed several recent studies (Goustard, 1959; Greco, 1959b; and Matalon, 1959) stemming from Piaget's theorizing that demonstrate that a child's ability to profit from a given kind of experience depends upon whether there is sufficient match between the experience and the schemata that the child has already developed.

During the first 4.5 or 5 months of a child's life, what appears to be critical is variation in stimulation for the various receptor modalities. Such variation provides for a wider range of recognitive assimilations, and it is through such variation in stimulation that the infant gets an opportunity to coordinate his reflexive schemata. The variations afford him opportunity for repeated experiences of looking for things heard, of reaching for and grasping things seen, of sucking things grasped, etc. It is through such experiences that the various reflexive schemata are coordinated in primary circular reactions. Moreover, the wider the range of recognitive assimilations, the more likely the child is to find something in which to be positively interested later. A motivational dynamic is thereby fostered which, in turn, leads to more finely differentiated central processes that underlie intelligence.

During the second 4.5 or 5 months, or sensorimotor stage 3, it would appear to be critical for the child to have available a variety of relatively familiar situations which he can recognize, in which he has developed an interest, and on which he can act in a fashion that either prolongs or reproduces the phenomena that would interest him. It is interesting to note in this connection that the importance which Ribble (1944) and Spitz (1945, 1946) give to a one-to-one personal relationship between mother and child may be more a function of the cathexis or emotional attachment that derives from what Piaget calls recognitory assimilation than it is from feeding and handling. The recognition that comes to redundant patterns of stimulation appears to bring pleasure, as evidenced by the smiles and laughter associated with such recognition, and this pleasure may well be a reinforcement inherent in information processing to produce the emotional attachment. Only when such recognitive assimilation involves a single person, then, need the anxiety of separation be severe. From this standpoint, multiple mothering may have the advantages of inoculating a child against separation anxiety and building into him a more finely differentiated set of perceptual schemata, thereby widening his range of curious interest in human behaviors. The fact that children of India, who grow up in extended families, are said seldom to show separation anxiety when the mother leaves for a period of time lends some confirmation to this point. Whether such children also develop a more finely differentiated capacity for human relations is an unanswered question.

During the period when the child is from nine to 18 months of age, as means become separated from ends and as the child begins to explore various means to achieve his ends, it is probably critical for the child to have an opportunity to try out his new-found motor skills and to observe the effects of his variations in effort. This means, for instance, an opportunity to throw things and watch their trajectory, an opportunity for manipulative practice play with a wide variety of materials, and an opportunity to climb and walk freely. It is through such manipulations and motor activities that the child apparently develops the beginnings of his conceptions of space, time, and causality. If the differentiation of central processes depends in part upon such opportunity, as is suggested by the fact that McGraw's (1939) trained twin showed a richer degree of phantasy than the untrained twin in follow-up some five years after the training ended, it may well be that the curtailment, dictated by families living in quarters amid things which parents value highly, which is commonly imposed on children's activity at this stage may hamper their rate of development and even lower the final level of intelligence they can achieve.

In the preconceptual phase of the second period, when the child is diverting a major share of his time to playful imitation, having a variety of models to imitate which supply the basis for later intellectual skills would appear to be important. Evidence independent of Piaget's observations for this point is hard to come by, but a study, perhaps too poorly controlled to call evidence beyond the "hint level," lends some degree of confirmation and illustrates the nature of the experiments that need to be made.

The headmistress of a small private coeducational school in Providence, Rhode Island, was fond of saying that "the basis for arithmetic should be taught in the nursery school and kindergarten." She considered it unfortunate that children are often introduced to drill in addition, subtraction, multiplication, and division before they have had sufficient opportunity to discover at the concrete level what these operations mean. In consequence of her opinion, teachers of children of three, four, and five years of age in the nursery school and kindergarten were to encourage their young pupils to play games containing concrete "number experience." The method of encouragement consisted of the teacher playing "the games" and talking about them with enthusiasm, while the children watched and listened. One of these games consisted of arranging blocks in rows and columns to form rectangles, another of arranging blocks into three-dimensional volumes or "buildings." During these games, the teachers talked enthusiastically about the rows and columns of blocks in the "areas," and of the numbers of stories in the "buildings." Such talk was aimed not only at communicating enthusiasm but also at helping the children make useful discriminations. Moreover, for the children aged four and five, the teacher would often count the blocks. The children began to play such games spontaneously, and their play was apparently instigated by the opportunity to observe and imitate the teacher playing the games with enthusiasm. Time was regularly given for such "games" in the curriculum, and the children were encouraged by reinforcing approval to arrange the blocks into "areas," and to stack them into "building" or "volumes." While the children were playing such games, the teacher would ask them questions about how many rows and how many cloumns there were in the child's "area," or how many tiers, rows, and columns there were in the child's "volume." By kindergarten age, the children with such a background of experiences could typically give "action definitions" of *area* and *volume*. They would say, for instance, "Area is when you put four blocks this way and five blocks that way, and fill them all in, and count them." Or: "Volume (or building) is when you put blocks this way and blocks that way and then put more blocks on top and more blocks on top of them." Such "action definitions" are like those which children of this age typically give for objects, as is well known from the definitions given for the words in the vocabulary test of the Stanford-Binet. For instance: "A chair is to sit on." "A table is to eat on." "A hat is to wear on your head."

In the kindergarten and the first grade, the children of this school were also given repeated opportunity to play store. Play-money provided practice with concrete material in subtraction (take-away) and addition (this much and that much) in the course of making change. Toward the end of the first grade, at a point when about a third of the children had begun to ask the teacher how she could make change so fast, drill in addition and subtraction was introduced. Similarly, late in the second grade when the children had begun to ask how the teacher could know, for example, how many blocks there were in the volume so quickly, drill in multiplication and division began. In either case, drill began only after a number of children could see that adults made change or multiplied so quickly that they must have special tricks that permitted them to get the answer faster than one could by "counting on fingers," or working with an abacus. After this point, drill was emphasized and was socialized in competitive games.

The pay-off in competence from such testing was not immediately evident. As a member of the board of directors of this school, in charge of examining the educational records, the writer directed an analysis of the scores made by the children in each grade on the Metropolitan Achievement Test of arithmetic. Originally this analysis was made without any particular interest in assessing the effects of this teaching method. It was merely a project of the parent-teacher organization, done simply to see how well the children of this school were achieving as compared to other private-school children. The mothers of the children did the tabulating. The first analysis consisted merely of a tabulation of the percentile ranks achieved by the various students among private-school students across the country for each of the five grade-groups as they existed that year. It was disturbing at first to discover that nearly all members of the first grade were in the bottom tenth, all members of the second grade in the bottom quarter, and that nearly all members of the third grade were in the bottom half of the population of private-school children tested with the Metropolitan Achievement Test. Such findings were disturbing to the parents of children in the lower grades even though the fourth graders ranged over the upper two-thirds, and all the fifth graders who had attended the school continuously from nursery school were in the upper third of fifth grade children tested on the Metropolitan Achievement Test.

It was only after a second analysis of the percentile ranks obtained by the then current fifth graders during their previous grades that the implications for this mode of teaching began to be evident. The percentile ranks that these fifth graders had obtained when they were in fourth, third, second, and first grades showed the same trend as did that of the various current grade-groups. Thus, it appeared that while such teaching might look ineffective at the lower grades by the criterion of performance on the Metropolitan Achievement Test, from the standpoint of final outcome at the fifth grade, it looked highly effective. Obviously, it is here impossible to separate the effects of the nursery-school experience from the techniques of teaching used in the grades, but the fact that those children who had not attended this school continually from nursery school did less well than those who had attended the school continuously indicates that the early experience was probably a factor.

Perhaps the hints from this study suggest that the opportunities children now have to watch television may be supplying them with models which they can copy in their play, and which may be promoting intellectual development in a large portion of the population at a faster rate than it occurred before the advent of television. This does not say, of course, that the models supplied in the television shows the children watch provide ideal models. Many of them are phony, but even so, it may be that seeing them may be forcing accommodative modifications in the central processes of children that will hasten the development of those logical operations and the systems of information processing that appear to underlie intelligence. It may be that, in spite of their defects, the imitative opportunities supplied by television are promoting early differentiations of central processes that may show later as increased intelligence as now measured. Nothing can be said with confidence, and it is important to investigate the effects of the opportunities children have to imitate various activities during the preconceptual phase from 18 months to four years of age.

In all likelihood the relationship between later efficiency and earlier opportunities for experiences that force accommodative modifications in central processes contains some obscuring complications. The notion of a continuous organism-environment interaction need not imply that an increased rate of development during one period will necessarily be sustained if the circumstances of the later period fail to supply a proper match for the schemata which the child has already assimilated during the earlier period. For instance, since nursery schools for three-year-olds and four-year-olds have become common, many parents have observed that the kindergarten year is boring. This may well be due to the fact that the kindergarten is "too much of the same thing" for children who have already had two years of nursery school. Virginia Simmons (1960), a teacher with many years of experience, has observed that five-year-olds who have been to nursery school are "ready" to start reading and arithmetic. If such genuine school-experiences are not supplied, she finds that the five-year-olds are bored. Conversely, when they are supplied with learning experiences which to them represent "real school," Simmons (1960) and others report that five-year-olds not only learn the school skills readily, but they enjoy it. This is apparently what Inhelder (1953) means when she notes that the environment can supply or not supply the opportunity to learn. Moreover, here, hypothetically, lies the germ of a principle, namely, that at each age and level the environmental circumstances must supply encounters for the child which permit him to use the repertoire of schemata that he has already developed and which force him to accommodate them if the rate of development and motivational interest are to be maintained. Sustaining increases in rate based on experiences of short duration probably depends crucially on such continuity of opportunity just as deprivations of experience appear to be reversible unless they have endured beyond some still unknown limit.

It is worth emphasizing the factor of the children's enjoyment. The notion of predetermined development has led a great many mental hygienists and educators to look with disfavor on what they call attempts to "push children." This disfavor was once an important corrective, for when psychological preformationism held conceptual sway, and children were seen as little adults whose failure to learn

was merely a matter of their innate perversity which had to be overcome by punishment, it was important to get a change. Pestalozzi
(see Green, 1913) and Froebel (1892) introduced play into the
school curriculum for younger children as an antidote for the punish-
ing cruelty that had been necessary to motivate the learning of
school skills that were made widely available to children during the
Reformation. Then it was deemed important for them to be able to
read the Bible for their salvation, and the notion of "original sin"
readily justified the lack of motivation for such learning. Probably the
chief basis for the lack of interest in learning among young children
in these schools lay in the poor match between the material presented and the background of the children. The language of the
Bible and of the sages was well beyond the ken of youngsters of six,
seven, or eight years.

Now, to our discomfort, the shoe appears to be on the other foot.
The continuation of play in the kindergarten, after two years of similar play in nursery school, is boring and constitutes also an error of
match, but in reverse. What is needed is a curriculum which programs the child's progression of encounters with circumstances to
maximize his potential for intellectual development. Once it is recognized that positive motivation and pleasure inhere in the learning
process when there is a proper match between the situation encountered and the child's already assimilated schemata, it becomes unnecessary to worry about pushing children. Moreover, motivational
withdrawal from the school situation may derive as much from the
boredom that comes from "too much of the same" as from the distress
of the child being faced with things beyond his ken or from punish-
ing teachers.

In the intuitive phase of the second period, when the child is between four and seven years of age and is continually in the process
of bringing his intuitions in correspondence with reality, having
ample opportunity for corrective discussions would appear to be
crucial. If this be true, children reared in families where parents take
the pains to understand the child's questions, to explain to him the
reasons for actions, and to discuss with him the nature of things
should show more rapid rate of intellectual development than children whose parents ask for unquestionable obedience and for children to be only seen and not heard. This expectation gets support
from the results of a study by Baldwin, Kalhorn, & Breese (1945).

These investigators had the parents who cooperated in a longitudinal research program of the Fels Research Institute rated on a
battery of 30 scales descriptive of parental behavior that Champney
(1941) developed. These scales were then grouped into syndromes of

related variables, and the families in the study were classified into the following categories: actively hostile, passively neglectful, possessive, democratic, and warm democratic. Part of this investigation consisted in relating changes in the IQ's of the children of these families to the categories of atmosphere that were judged to prevail in them. Over a three-year period, small decreases in IQ were found in both the children of those families in which the actively hostile and the passively neglectful atmospheres prevailed. On the other hand, increases in IQ averaging approximately eight points were found over the three-year period for the children from families in which the democratic atmosphere prevailed. The democratic atmosphere was characterized as one in which parents take the pains to justify policy, let children participate in making many decisions, concern themselves with understanding a child's questions and with making appropriate explanations, and show concern with excellence of performance. Since the democratic atmosphere was associated with gains almost as large as was warm democracy, these findings are nicely consonant with the expectation stated above. The factor of warmth consists of child-centeredness, approval, acceptance, affection, and rapport. While these may be important for the development of various qualities, they add only an insignificant couple of extra points to the increase in IQ. It appears, as expected, that what is important for intellectual growth is the opportunity for variety of experiences combined with parental concern for the child's questions, and parental readiness to try to explain matters. In Baldwin's (1955) language: "Maturation is stimulated when the child meets challenges that are not too severe." This is another way of saying that accommodative modifications in central structures take place when the child encounters circumstances which so match his already assimilated schemata that he is motivated by them but can cope with them.[8]

[8] Since this was written, Smedslund (1961) has posed the issue of whether the child learns (a) by extrinsic reinforcement of response patterns already within his repertoire or (b) by the fact that being confronted with problems "forces him to organize his thinking." In one study (Smedslund, 1959) showed that both (a) direct observations of weighings which show that changes of shape do not alter the weight of plasticine balls (assumed to be direct and extrinsic reinforcement) and (b) a mixture of such experiences with practice on the operations of addition and subtraction (whose combination is assumed to underlie the concept of conservation) resulted in more rapid acquisition of the concept of conservation of weight. The fact that the former resulted in somewhat more transfer than the latter was interpreted to favor the hypothesis of learning through extrinsic reinforcement, but it should be noted that the weighings also face the child with dissonance (Festinger, 1957) if he expects change in weight and the scales do not show it.

In this same connection, an interesting study by Greco (1959a) has shown that the amount of transfer from training to testing for an understanding of spatial rotations

During the phase of the concrete operations in the elementary school years, opportunities to cope with a variety of objects, gadgets, and materials would appear to be important for intellectual development. While the child has reversible thought operations in his new-found capacities for classifying, serializing, and numbering, his thought operations require concrete materials for their instigation and direction. The child is capable at this phase of only situation-directed thought, as has been found by others (e.g., Serra, 1953a, 1953b) as well as Piaget.

Although no investigations relevant to the issue of whether increasing the opportunity for experience with a variety of concrete objects and materials during the early portion of this phase alters either the age at which the formal operations appear or IQ, it is likely that traditional school curricula have given too small a place to concrete laboratory experience of physical, chemical, and social causality. Obviously it is necessary to teach the traditional skills of reading, writing, and arithmetic in schools. Yet, in view of the fact that fewer and fewer have the opportunities of those children who once helped their parents with the concrete work of the household, the farm, and the construction trades, it is probably unfortunate that such experiences are left to chance in the case of today's children as they are typically reared in cities, suburbs, and exurbs. The interest which children tyically show in construction toys, chemistry sets, nature study in summer camps, etc., indicates that interest in such concrete experience is well-established, and it might be used if opportunities properly arranged could be made in school curricula. These opportunities could probably be arranged to provide experiences that would lead to ready grasp of the more abstract conception of causality to be found in the sciences. Even such defenders as Ausubel (1960) of verbal learning against the new-found emphasis of educators on "discovery" learning as distinguished from rote learning[9] have recognized that experience with materials and gadgets is im-

---

was much greater for a group that learned which color would appear when single rotations were mixed with double rotations than for a group that learned separately which color would appear with one rotation and which with two rotations. Similarly, Wohlwill (1959) found greater transfer from training to transfer for the conservation of number for a group trained on addition and subtraction than for a group given direct reinforcement on conservation over deformations. From such evidence, Smedslund (1961) has concluded that "situations which permit immediate and simple response learning with empirical control are unlikely to lead to any profound cognitive reorganization," whereas "situations stressing empirical control which do not permit simple response learning. . . . [and] direct exercise of the relevant operations are likely to induce cognitive change to the extent that . . . the child already has available schemata [that are properly matched with these situations]" (p. 9).

[9] See Brownell & Hendrickson (1950), Brownell & Simms (1946), and Easley (1958, 1959).

portant in establishing an underlying foundation for the understanding of scientific concepts of causality. It is the unexpected in concrete
phenomena which can most readily arouse the curiosity that motivates inquiry. It is probably the opportunity to manipulate objects,
gadgets, and systems that serves to internalize the thought processes
which become concepts of causality.

The aim of the child's manipulation of objects and systems is to
discover how they go together and how they work. This discovery
process demands strategies of inquiry or of the processing of information that are like learning sets. Moreover, their learning can be facilitated by providing proper experiences during at least the latter stage
of the phase of concrete operations. Evidence for this statement
comes from Suchman's (1960a, 1960b) program of research on
"inquiry training."

Suchman bases his method of training on the stages of the thinking
or problem-solving process. Ever since the studies of the Würzburg
school divided thought processes into stages for methodological purposes (see Titchener, 1909), it has been customary to see stages in
the problem-solving process. In view of the fact that many of the
later investigators[10] of inquiry or problem-solving have apparently
found stages which are roughly equivalent, these have nearly acquired the status of natural stages. The first stage is that which
Dewey (1910) termed the "felt difficulty." It is analogous to Festinger's (1957) cognitive dissonance, and it consists of the stage in
which the problem is posed and is the motivational source of accommodative modifications. In the phase of concrete operations, problems are probably best posed in terms of concrete situations which
present information that is to a proper degree dissonant with the
child's systematic expectations. This "felt difficulty" or dissonance is
a function of both the central structures which the child has already
assimilated and the circumstances he encounters, as was pointed out
in Chapter 6. The second phase of inquiry or problem-solving has
commonly been seen as "the analysis of the difficulty." This analysis
merges into a stage of "production" in which various solutions for
the problem are generated. The stage of production overlaps with
that of "verification," which, in turn, overlaps with the final stage
of "reapplication."[11] Each of these stages has in it generalized habits
resembling "learning sets." These get elaborated into a strategy of
search. It was Duncker (1945) who first elaborated the concepts of

[10] See Dewey (1910), Selz (1922), Duncker (1945), Polya (1948), Johnson (1955),
Ray (1955), and Guilford, Merrifield, Christensen, & Frick (1960).
[11] The terminology used here comes from Guilford, Merrifield, Christensen, & Frick
(1960).

"set," "determining tendency," and "anticipatory schema" from the Würzburg school into the more generalized concept of the "search model." This "search model" is akin to what Bruner, Goodnow, & Austin (1956) have characterized as "strategies," and what Guilford, Merrifield, Christensen, & Frick (1960) have found from their factor-analytic study to be a key factor in determining efficiency of creative activity.

Suchman (1960a) motivates inquiry in children by presenting in a short silent motion picture demonstrations of concrete "problem episodes." These "problem episodes" are from the drawing-room physics entertainments of the seventeenth and eighteenth centuries. They are selected, first, to perplex the child who does not already have the causal conceptions, and, second, to illustrate key physical principles. In one of these episodes, a varnish can containing a small amount of water is heated over a flame, corked, and observed to collapse as it cools. Why does it collapse? In the episode of the "Cartesian diver," an inverted bottle, partly filled with air, floats at the top of a tall cylinder full of water and having an elastic covering. Pressing the covering compresses the air inside the bottle so that it admits more water through its inverted opening and sinks; lifting the cover allows the air in the bottle to expand and drive out some of the water so that the bottle rises again. All this is presented in the motion picture, and again the child is presented with the question "Why?" Suchman uses 35 such problem episodes, and their understanding calls for a grasp of 28 principles or causal conceptions of physics. For each of the 35, one or more concepts are basic, while several others are of secondary importance. These problem episodes succeed well in arousing Dewey's (1910) "felt difficulty" or Festinger's (1957) cognitive dissonance. These are as successful at motivating an entertaining inquiry in children of ten years as they were during the seventeenth and eighteenth centuries in motivating entertaining conversation in cultivated adults.

Suchman (1960b) teaches in two phases which he terms "episode analysis" and "determination of relevance," what Duncker (1926) has called the "search model," what Bruner, Goodnow, & Austin (1956) have called "strategy of inquiry," and what Guilford *et al.* (1960) have termed the "preparation phase" and the "analysis phase." After seeing the film, the children themselves begin the inquiry by asking questions. The teacher demands that these analytic questions about what happened and what factors in the situation were relevant be phrased in such a fashion that he can answer them by "yes" or "no." At this later stage of the phase of concrete operations (10 years of age), children have the verbal skills to ask such questions. They may have the necessary skills even a couple of years earlier. Demanding that they ask them in a fashion which can be answered by "yes" or "no" puts the responsibility for the inquiry on them and forces them to cope in their verbalizations with what they have seen in the motion picture. In the episode analysis, the children are pushed by their own search for explanation in such a structure to sharpen the accuracy of their observation of objects, systems, conditions, and events (changes in condition) and to subordinate their observational operations to the end of explanation. In determining relevance, the children actually perform little experiments, but in verbal form, which serve to determine if the absence or the presence in some specifiable degree of the various objects, systems, and conditions make a difference in the occurrence of the phenonenon to be explained.

In both the episode analysis and the determination of relevance, the situation predominates in the direction of the child's thinking. The teacher helps in this by forcing the responsibility for selecting the kind of concrete information to be supplied directly on the shoulders of the children.

A second pair of phases Suchman calls the "induction of relational constructs" and "validation of constructs." These differ significantly from the former pair. Whereas in the former pair the child's observation directs his thought processes, in the latter the child's thought processes direct his observations.

The induction of relational constructs consists in formulating hypotheses about the causes of the phenomena observed. The validation consists in testing the constructs by making predictions and testing their accuracy. In practice the two phases are intertwined. Again the children must formulate their questions in a fashion that can be answered by "yes" or "no." Moreover, if they should ask whether a given object, system, or condition is the cause and answering this question could result in a loss of responsibility for the inquiry on the part of the child, the teacher answers by asking: "How would you find out?" The child must then think of a plan which could direct his observation. If, for instance, a child suspects that the cork in the varnish can was a necessary condition for the collapse of the can, he might ask, "Does putting in the cork make the can collapse?" Should the teacher say "yes," the child's responsibility for the direction of the inquiry would be diminished. But, when the teacher asks, "How would you find out?" the child may ask, in turn, "If the cork had not been placed in the mouth of the can when the can was hot, would the can have collapsed?" By such means, Suchman (1960b) gets the children to formulate the plan of little experiments. For such a question, the teacher's "no" supports the hypotheses that the corking of the can is necessary and also the implicit hypotheses that the can must be air-tight before it is cooled. The relationship is thereby formulated in the imaginal construction of the verifying procedures.

Each "practice session," in which only ten children participate, lasts about half an hour. At the end of each such session comes the "period of critique." In these periods the strategy and tactics of the group are reviewed and evaluated by the teacher, by nonparticipating members of the class, and by members of the participating group. The weaknesses in the group's strategy of inquiry are pointed out. Lecture-like presentations of what good strategy would be are made to help the group understand. These lectures provide the child also with generalized concepts of inquiry strategy, and sometimes special recordings of model inquiry sessions are played. Such critique has been found to be indispensable. When it is eliminated, the morale of the group deteriorates and inquiry progressively loses its effectiveness. On the other hand, with such critique, the skills of the class rapidly improve.

The protocols show that the children ask more questions as they get more of such experience. They grow more accurate in describing what they saw in the movie. They grow sharper in their ability to bring out the properties and conditions of the objects and systems depicted in the episode. They grow more skilled in indicating the changes of condition and parameters which are not directly observable but which may yet be factors in the causation of a phenomenon. They grow more adept in asking questions concerning which of the various conditions and parameters are relative to the event whose explanation they are seeking. They grow more productive in formulating relationships among objects, systems, and events. They even come to see their explanatory objective in terms of statements of rules that express a relationship between factors.

Suchman and his collaborators are also constructing a test to measure the results of such training in the children's understanding of the 28 physical concepts employed in the 35 problem episodes. The test employs three criteria of understanding: prediction, conditions required for occurrence of the depicted phenomenon, and the rule that governs the set of conditions required. The test depicts a phenomenon in picture, and in typical multiple-choice form the child is presented (1) with several alternative predictions, (2) with several sets of conditions, and (3) with several statements of rules from which to choose. The results of the training have not yet been assessed in the terms of this test of concept understanding.

It is possible that such training has even more fundamental re-

sults. The fact that 10-year-old children learn to formulate generalized rule-propositions within the eight weeks of training suggests
that these weeks may be the equivalent of a year to a year and a half
of ordinary experience in the development of formal operations. It
will be important to determine whether such training hastens, for
instance, the conservation of volume in the Piaget-Inhelder (1947)
test with the two plasticine balls. The fact that children find such
inquiry training fascinating, as the writer has found from knowing
youngsters who have experienced it, may indicate that the skills in
inquiry get practiced elsewhere and generalize to other kinds of situations. At the Iowa Child Welfare Research Station, Ojemann and
Muus, moreover, have found evidence suggesting that training children to think in analytic and causal fashion may be a way of fostering
mental health.[12] For instance, children who have a strong causal orientation show more tolerance of ambiguous stimuli and less tendency
for premature closure on a test of tolerance for ambiguity than do
children low on causal orientation. Finally, if strategies of inquiry are
of as much general significance as current neuropsychology and Piaget's observations would indicate, such training may generalize widely
and perhaps even affect some maturational processes within the
nervous system. Only future investigation can tell, but such suggestive evidence as exists and the importance of the problem in our
technological culture, with its demand for many more people with
high intelligence, make urgent business of such investigation.

   *After the formation of the second order groupements or formal
operations,* verbally presented abstract arguments and conceptions
become the important kind of learning experience. At this stage the
child has both language and the capacity to appreciate the form of
an argument. He also has operations with the logical properties of
lattices, the 16 binary operations, and the INRC groups (see Chapter
6 or Piaget, 1953b). Although much remains to be learned about the
import of the transition from concrete to formal operations, the fact
that Inhelder & Piaget (1955) find that observation directs thought
before, and that thought directs observations after, the arrival of the
formal operations suggests that both substantive information and
skill in logico-mathematical thought can perhaps best be acquired
at this stage via verbal communications and exercises. In the controversy between those who contend that concepts and generalizations
are best learned, even at the adult level, by the "discovery method"

[12] This program, which was initiated by Ojemann, has resulted in a stream of publications. See Ojemann & Wilkinson (1939), Morgan & Ojemann (1942), Ojemann,
Levitt, Lyle, & Whiteside (1955), and Ojemann & Clark (1956); and see also Muus
(1959, 1960a, 1960b, and 1960c).

with concrete materials (see Brownell & Simms, 1946; Brownell & Hendrickson, 1950) and those who have defended verbal learning for adults (see Ausubel, 1960a), the implications of what Inhelder & Piaget (1955) have found to be characteristic of adolescent and adult thought favor the defenders of verbal learning. Furthermore, the fact that thought directs observation and action and the notion that information is stored hierarchically in lattice-like arrangements suggests that after the formation of formal operations it is important to provide the learner with general principles and categories into which he can organize lesser categories and details of information.

Such a theory has been advocated by Ausubel, Robbins, & Blake (1957) and by Ausubel (1961). Moreover, Ausubel (1960b) has found experimentally that supplying college students verbally with background concepts of a high level of generality, abstractness, and inclusiveness facilitates the readiness with which detailed and unfamiliar information is incorporated and increases its retention as indicated by later ability to make appropriate choices among alternatives in a multiple choice test.

To what degree verbally presented information can make up for lack of concrete experience with a range of materials and systems is undetermined. Just what may be the nature of the effects of the early experience, whether of the infantile period or of the period of elementary school, remains to be determined. But it appears to be clear, as an implication of Piaget's discovery of formal operations, and from everyday experience, and from such studies as those of Ausubel, that verbally acquired information can substitute to a substantial degree for lack of earlier concrete experience.

Thus, in summary, Piaget's description of the successive stages of intellectual development removes the necessity for some of the trial and error in determining an appropriate match between environmental circumstances and the nature of the central processes already developed for sustaining a positive interest in the environment and promoting accommodative growth of those central processes that underlie intelligence. Even so, the stages are gross divisions and many questions remain unanswered. What is the nature of the accommodative modifications in those central processes at the various stages? To what extent can experiences in later stages alter the rate and course of intellectual development that has been established in earlier stages? To what degree, for instance, can the retardation that appears to result from unvaried stimulation in the early months be removed by corrective experiences in later months? How long can the retardation remain and yet be corrected? Conversely, to what degree can the acceleration that appears to result from varied stimulation in the early months be lost by experiences in later months and years where the child encounters circumstances that fail to supply a challenging match with his already developed central processes? Also, how does one go about refining the match to maximize intellectual growth in individuals?

THOUGHT AS INTERNALIZED ACTION WITH THE NEUROPSYCHOLOGICAL IMPLICATIONS

Piaget's developmental observations have led him to see intelligence increasing as actions become internalized to become thought and as thought becomes "decentred" and dominant over the child's perceptions and activities. He sees this development starting with the sensorimotor units he calls reflexive schemata. These become coordinated into more complex schemata, and these more complex schemata become recoordinated and then recoordinated again into mobile action-systems and imitations as the child's independence from immediate stimulation increases. These complex sensorimotor schemata and imitations become internalized as images, and these in turn become coordinated as intuitions. The intuitions are gradually "decentred" and grouped into reversible and associative operations with concrete objects and materials. Then the concrete "groupements" are, in turn, regrouped into formal operations as the adolescent becomes independent of actual objects and situations and becomes able to think of the possible and to direct observation and action with his thought.

This process may be seen as one in which the central neural processes that mediate or constitute thought become more and more autonomous and more and more dominant over receptor inputs and motor outputs. Although Piaget has not, for the most part, been directly concerned with the neurological basis of thought, this description of the development of intelligence has neurological implications, and, as already noted, Piaget has at least once (1949a) concerned himself with the problem. It is interesting to consider these implications in the light of various kinds of theory and evidence.

The concept of the sensorimotor schema as the fundamental unit has itself implications. While there are many parallels between the thinking of Piaget and Hebb which have already been pointed out, here is a major difference. Hebb's (1949) theory of primary learning has made it a matter of building cell assemblies and phase sequences with redundant receptor inputs. These cell assemblies and phase sequences are presumably built within the association areas of the brain which, in higher organisms, separate those portions of the cortex immediately involved with receptor inputs and motor outputs. It is these autonomous central circuits that gradually provide for stimulus control of action in Hebb's theory. In Piaget's theory, on the other hand, receptor inputs always have some control over those motor outputs that constitute the schemata ready-made at birth. Development consists then of the coordination of the looking-schema with the schemata of limb and body movements, of these schemata with the listening-schema, etc. Hebb's theory would appear to state that primary learning takes place without motor involvements. On the other hand, Piaget's would appear to state that motor involvements are always present and that primary learning is a matter of coordinating and recoordinating the sensorimotor units into larger organizations which become mobile in the sense that they can be combined into one system for one purpose, then differentiated and then recombined into a different kind of system for some other purpose. Pribram's (1960) recent reviews of the theorizing about cerebral neuropsychology indirectly lend some support to Piaget's view. It has been traditional to conceive of neural organization going on across the cortex, but Pribram points out that firing systems appear to be organized from the center of the neural tube outward toward the cortex and back; thus, more than receptor inputs from the distance and peripheral receptors appear to be involved in these systems. Such a difference may be minor, however, for the main concern with intelligence. For this concern it is enough that the central processes which mediate thought become established within those regions of the brain not immediately involved with receptor inputs and motor outputs, or to use Pribram's (1958) terminology, within the *intrinsic* regions of the brain.

Both Hebb and Piaget have assumed that characteristics of the structure of the brain must serve to set limits on intelligence, perhaps by limiting the number of central systems which can be differentiated for combination and recombination into various temporary systems. The fact that Hebb (1942) has found that damage to the cerebrum early in life leads to a feeble-minded pattern of behavior in which the concrete operations of performance tests excel verbal performance while brain injury late in life produces the opposite pattern suggests that Hebb's A/S ratio[13] may provide at least one of the limiting factors. Such a ratio has definite meaning as the brains of animals up and down the phylogenetic scale are compared. It

[13] The writer finds himself tempted to alter the term for this concept to the I/E ratio, i.e., the ratio of the size of the intrinsic regions of the brain to the size of the extrinsic regions, but the concept of such regions needs to be better established before it dominates terminology.

may, when natural opportunities afford, also be profitable to compare with this concept in view the brains of the feeble-minded with brains of persons who have shown high intellectual achievement.

Piaget's concept of thought developing as the internalization of action corresponds to the short-circuiting process remarked upon by all observers of learning. In implying a close relationship between thought and action, it resembles the Watsonian (1914) view of thought as implicit motor responses and the motor theory of consciousness presented by Holt (1931) and Langfeld (1931). On the other hand, Piaget's idea that thought becomes "decentred" as the reversible and associative operations especially characteristic of intelligence develop suggests that thought should ultimately acquire independence of peripheral motor contractions.

The motor theory of consciousness got some support from the work of Edmund Jacobson (1932). When he taught his subjects to relax so completely that electromyographic evidence of tension was eliminated from skeletal musculature, for instance, the subjects reported that their "minds were a blank." On the other hand, evidence also exists to indicate that the peripheral musculature need not be involved in thinking. Lashley (1958) has reported, for instance, that he

. . . once invented a thought-reading machine; a system of levers which magnified and recorded movements of the tongue. I first had my subjects speak a word, then think it silently. Movements of the tongue were minute but otherwise identical with those of speech. However, it was soon evident that when the subject thought for a few moments without speech, the tongue dropped to the back of the mouth and showed no movements, not even when the subjects were doing mental arithmetic: squaring three-place numbers and giving correct answers . . . A study of movements of the closed eyes during thinking of directions in space or of simple geometrical figures gave similar though less consistent results . . . Such observations provide evidence that the neural activities in thought are identical with those of action, save for the lack of facilitation of the final motor path (p. 540).

The fact that Piaget has observed the development of the higher levels of intelligence to be associated with the "decentring" and with the increasing dominance of thought processes over perception and action suggests further that there might be a correlation between tested intelligence and education on the one hand, and the degree to which thought processes are independent of tension in the peripheral musculature on the other hand. Evidence tending to confirm this implication comes from the studies of Max (1934, 1935, 1937).[14] In his investigations of muscular tension in thinking, Max (1937) hit

[14] I am indebted to Mr. James Moore for calling to my attention the connection between Max's work and this implication from Piaget's observations.

upon the ingenious innovation of recording from the arm muscles of deaf mutes that control the action of the fingers. Inasmuch as deaf mutes use their fingers in communication, these readily accessible muscles might be expected to be active in thought. They were. When the deaf mutes who served as subjects either talked, thought of talking, or dreamed of talking, electromyographic signs of tension appeared in those muscles that move the fingers. Within given individuals, the amount of tension appeared to be a function of the difficulty or the familiarity of the thought-task. Easy addition or multiplication, for example, evoked few or no action currents in the muscles whereas difficult arithmetic problems evoked many. Lashley (1958) made similar observations. Action currents became highly prominent whenever a deaf subject came to fear that his computations were going wrong. But the most interesting item of evidence in Max's (1937) findings for the implication that individual differences in the level of intelligence are a function of the autonomy and dominance of central neural processes is that of a significant and substantial degree of correlation between individual differences in amount of muscular tension as indexed electromyographically during thought tasks and the intelligence and education of the subjects. The higher the tested intelligence and the more the education, the less was the amount of muscular tension. Such investigations should be repeated.

Piaget's conception of the successive stages in the development of intelligence as processes whereby former schemata become incorporated into those which follow while at the same time differentiation is taking place appears to imply a hierarchical organization of these processes within the nervous system. Pribram's (1958, 1960) review of the deficits produced in behavior by damage to the anatomy subtending the posterior intrinsic systems indicates that their nature is consonant with the hypothesis of such a hierarchical organization. In a monkey, when the tracts connecting the parietal cortex with the pulvinar nucleus and other centers located medially in the cerebrum are cut, the monkey can still catch a gnat in mid-air with a hand. Such primitive eye-forelimb schemata remain intact. He can also react

. . . to variations of illumination by varying his rate of response in an operant situation . . . But when he is given alternative responses to make to differences in luminance, pattern, etc. (the alternative indicated by a peanut, for example), he fails to make any consistent choice. It is apparent that even with this complex relation between cues, alternatives for response and the indicators of these alternatives allows some invariant properties to be extracted. Otherwise, intact monkeys and people would not be able to respond consistently. Somehow, through repetition in time, these properties are identified; and, when the tracts of the posterior intrinsic systems are interfered with, identification goes awry. The situation becomes unintelligible to the organism, it cannot make the differential discrimination; it does not know what to do; it has an agnosia. The posterior intrinsic system must, in some way or other, make possible the separation of the invariant properties that characterize the situation in contrast with other, less regular variables. This could be accomplished if some coded representation of the invariance is established in the posterior intrinsic mechanism (Pribram, 1960, p. 17).

Presumably the invariances which derive from the redundant aspects of receptor inputs from objects viewed at various distances and at various angles provide the basis for both the perceptual permanence of objects and for the perceptual constancies of object-shape, object-size, and object-color. Presumably these invariances must also establish some coded representation within the posterior intrinsic mechanism.

Images, concrete operations, and formal propositional operations also appear from their development to be hierarchically arranged. But inasmuch as they derive from actions, they would be expected to involve the anterior intrinsic mechanism, composed in considerable part of the anterior dorsal nucleus of the thalamus and the frontal lobes, where Goldstein (1930) found structural damage caused a loss of his "abstract ability" and where Nichols & Hunt (1940) found that damage to the frontal poles in a patient seemed to cause a loss of ability to induce generalizations from concrete experience and a loss of ability to separate and to coordinate several lines of activity into one. Such active operations appear also to require the utility of the coded invariances stored in the posterior intrinsic mechanism, so they presumably involve both intrinsic mechanisms. What hierarchical organization means at the level of cerebral neural organization is not yet clear. One reason that it is not clear may be the fact that it has always been exceedingly difficult to describe the deficits in thought, which are paradoxically both so obvious and yet so vague in nature, that are associated both with psychoses and with lesions in the human brain (see Hunt & Cofer, 1944).

THE LOGICAL PROPERTIES OF THOUGHT PROCESSES

In recent years Piaget's major theme has concerned the explanation of thought in terms of its logical properties. In this theme, he has reversed the direction of explanation for those who have seen thought reflecting logical properties, for Piaget (1947) sees logic reflecting thought. Life being an open-ended process, he conceives it possible that future developments, as man accommodates his thought to the problems raised by complex electronic computers, atomic power, and interstellar travel, may result in thought with yet new logical properties.

Piaget is not alone in seeing a connection between the central neural activity of thought and logic, but his basis for the connection is different from that seen by others. McCulloch & Pitts (1943) thought they had found a connection between Boolean algebra and neural activity in the all-or-none law of neurone firing, but this all-or-none law has since been called into question for neurones of the cerebrum (Li, Cullen, & Jasper, 1956). Newell, Shaw, & Simon (1958) thought they saw an indirect connection by way of their programming electronic computers to solve logical problems. A useful upshot of their work has been the inference that brain-functions must be active processes akin to the programs built into computers for processing information in problem-solving. Piaget's basis for the connection derives directly from the similarities between the characteristics of logical operations and problem-solving behavior. It is in this sense that the algebra of logic supplies at once one kind of description of intelligent behavior and an explanation of it.

Piaget (1953b) conceives of the "structured wholes" comprising both concrete and formal operations in terms of a concept which is new and strange to most investigators of behavior. He rejects the hypothesis that either concrete or formal operations arise from late maturation of certain neural connections, but no evidence known rules out the possibility that something akin to "stimulus induced maturation" (Wheeler, 1940; Baldwin, 1955) occurs in connection with their development. The finding that the visual apparatus does not develop properly without light stimulation by Brattgård (1952) and by Riesen (1958) indicates that "stimulus induced maturation" is a genuine developmental process, and it is probable that it may be especially important during the early months when epigenesis is most rapid. Piaget rejects the hypothesis that these operations represent "*a priori* forms of the mind" because they have an epigenetic history. He also rejects the hypothesis that they are merely the cumulative products of past experience because the adolescent who uses them is quite unaware of them. Here Piaget apparently assumes that that which has been experienced is remembered, and he has on his side the fact that one can usually be articulate about his mathematical processes. It is Piaget's contention, rather, that these operations represent forms of mobile equilibrium attained by thought and presumably therefore autonomous central neural activities which mediate intentions and represent objects and events from past experience.

Piaget defines a mobile equilibrium as a state

. . . in which all the virtual transformations compatible with the relationships of the system compensate each other. From a psychological point of view, the logical structures correspond precisely to this model. On the one hand, these structures appear in the form of a set of virtual transformations, consisting of all the operations which it would be possible to carry out starting from a few actually performed operations. On the other, these structures are essentially reversible, that is to say, the virtual transformations which they permit are always self-compensatory as a consequence of inversions and reciprocities . . . In this way we can explain why the subject is affected by such structures, without being conscious of them. When starting from an actually performed propositional operation, or endeavoring to express the characters of a given situation by such an operation, he cannot proceed in any way he likes. He finds himself, as it were, in a field of force governed by the laws of equilibrium, carrying out transformations or operations determined not only by occurrences in the immediate past, but by the laws of the whole operational field of which these past occurrences form a part (1953b, p. 41).

This notion of mobile equilibrium is new and unfamiliar. Although it makes the central neural processes that mediate or constitute thought highly active, it still serves to give them a relatively stable structure. It is these stable structures of autonomous neural processes that are presumed to provide the ability to process information. In fact, the level of ability achieved by an individual is a function of these mobile equilibrii with their logico-mathematical properties.

It is not immediately easy to see how useful such an explanation of thought will be. It can be seen, however, that it is these structures of reversible operations that can account for the Gestalt-quality of thought. It can be seen also that the inter-subjectivity of reasoning, which Werkmeister (1940) has termed the "compellingness of thought" and Hull (1943) has referred to as "objective deduction," can derive from the fact that these concrete and formal propositional operations are governed by the laws of equilibrium which are isomorphic with logical operations.

Piaget's use of the algebra of logic to describe and to explain thought has already been highly useful in the developmental sphere. It has suggested modes of examining the thinking of children which have brought out hither-to unsuspected characteristics. It has helped to differentiate both experimentally and descriptively between the thought of adolescents and pre-adolescents, and between school-age children and pre-school children. The experimental work has brought out the fact that a wide band of apparently disparate abilities and conceptions emerge in the children of Geneva at about the age of seven, a lesser band at about the age of nine, and another wide band again at about the age of 12. Conceiving of these bands of apparently disparate abilities and concepts being dependent upon a few basic operational structures of thought serves to explain their essentially simultaneous appearance in the course of development.

Piaget's observations need to be repeated in other laboratories, and to be built upon by other investigators. It is particularly important, as already noted, to determine if the order of development in the landmarks of the successive transitions is quite fixed, because from this may be derived a natural ordinal scale of intelligence. It is important to determine how and to what degree the age at which these landmarks appear is a function of the child's encounters with the environment. Because Piaget's conceptions are unfamiliar and some, like that of a mobile equilibrium, are basically new to behavior theory, it will also be important to aviod confusions from misunderstandings. In the only instance of an investigation directed to Piaget's later experimental work on the thought of children found by the present author at this writing,[15] Braine (1959) has attempted to investigate inference based upon the grouping of asymmetrical relationships, (i.e., A>B, and B>C, therefore A>C) by non-verbal means. The rudiments of measurement are considered to be based upon such inferences. Braine made getting a piece of candy dependent upon accurate comparisons of the heights of pairs of objects that varied in shape and were too similar in height to discriminate with the naked eye. The comparison was made by showing the children who served as subjects that a stick supplied with an arm at a right-angle

---

[15] Since this was written, I am indebted to Mr. William J. DeMarco for bringing to my attention several such studies. I am also indebted to Professor A. L. Baldwin for bringing to my attention the interesting work of Jan Smedslund (1959, 1960, 1961), concerning the nature of the role of experience in the development of operational thought and the extensive but still unpublished efforts of the Canadian investigator, Father Adrien Pinard, to construct and to standardize an instrument for assessing intelligence based on the work of Piaget.

From America come the studies by Estes (1956) and Mogar (1960). Estes attempted to investigate the development of concrete operations as manifest in the conservation of number and in projective space as shown in lining up matchsticks diagonally across a cardboard, and she reports failure to confirm Piaget's findings, but her presentation indicates that she has probably misunderstood both Piaget's theory and his procedure.

Chiefly from Britain comes another group of studies. The general picture of the stages leading to conservation of substance and quantity and weight have been confirmed by Hyde (1959), Lovell & Ogilvie (1960), Peel (1959), Slater (1958), and Smedslund (1959). Moreover, the studies by Slater (1958) and Hyde (1959) suggest strongly that the rate at which concepts of conservation develop is influenced by experience, even though the order of development remains constant. Page (1959) has confirmed the observations of Piaget & Inhelder (1948) that topological space is conceptualized before Euclidean space, and Lovell (1959) has also confirmed part of these observations, but he finds that geometric figures bounded by curved lines are recognized as quickly as topological figures. Lovell (1961) has also confirmed in the main the observations of Inhelder & Piaget (1955) on the growth of logical thinking from childhood to adolescence.

could be twirled over one of the objects but not the other, and they were then to tell the experimenter where to look for the candy. For one group the candy was always to be found under the shorter object, and for the other, under the taller object. By this procedure, which resembles that used by Harlow (1949) in developing "learning sets," Braine found that such inferences could be got typically in children of five years, an age two years younger than the seven years at which children of Geneva become capable of systematic serializing, etc. In what appears to be an unfortunate partial misunderstanding of the meaning of Piaget's operations and stages, Braine concludes (1) that the age at which the inference based upon the transitivity of asymmetrical relations appears depends upon how the problem is posed, and (2) that gradual transitions in intellectual development exist which make the stages less definite than Piaget has claimed. In the case of the former, Braine is undoubtedly correct at one level, but the point is trival at this level. The force of Braine's conclusion lies in his thinking of this inference as a capacity, regardless of how the task is presented. The fact that the child gets the capacity for such an inference early as a kind of "learning set" in a specific situation has little bearing on Piaget's conception of this inference as an operation of thought readily available and serving the end of seeing how things work. In fact, the experience that Braine gave his subjects may have hastened in them the development of these operations of thought. In the case of the latter, Braine appears to have missed the fact that Piaget has repeatedly emphasized that the epigenesis of the structures of behavior and thought is both continuous and gradual. It is important to avoid pseudo-problems. On the other hand, the fact that Piaget's conceptions are so different from those traditional and familiar, and partially therefore so unclear, will probably make a spate of pseudo-problems inevitable.

Perhaps another contribution from Piaget's attempts to explain thought in terms of logical operations will come via attempts to simulate thought in electronic computers. Already the studies of automata (see Shannon & McCarthy, 1956) and of such efforts to program electronic computers to solve logical problems as those made by Newell, Shaw, & Simon (1958) have suggested looking for active systems for the processing of information in the cerebrums of higher mammals. These, in turn, have begun to alter experimental methodology and have already led to signs that crude counterparts of the kinds of strategies programmed in computers to process information for the solving of problems may exist within brains, as Pribram (1958, 1960) has noted. Progress in this area cannot be based entirely upon study of the man-made "thinker," however, for as von Neumann

(1958) has noted, the correspondences between the mathematics of computers and the implicit mathematics of brains in operation are too poor. Progress must depend in considerable part upon describing precisely how thought operates. Piaget's procedures for diagnosing logical operations in human problem-solving have contributed greatly to this much-needed descriptive precision.

Perhaps yet another of the contributions of Piaget's use of such logical structures as the INRC group and the proportionality schema may be to help to clarify the nature of various kinds of psychological deficit. Perhaps the distinction between "abstract thought" and "concrete thought" made by Goldstein (1939) is but a vaguer formulation of the same distinction that Piaget has made between formal and concrete operations. The writer has long observed difference in the deficit typically found in persons with such so-called functional psychoses as the schizophrenias and in persons with cerebral lesions (Hunt, 1935; Hunt & Cofer, 1944) but he has had relatively poor success in specifying the essential nature of this difference. Perhaps adapting Piaget's later objective procedures for this purpose would yield clarification, considerably greater clarification, in fact, than Cameron (1938a, 1938b, 1938c, 1939a, 1939b) was able to obtain by means of Piaget's earlier verbal procedures for this same purpose. The fact that logical operations clarify the variations in thought that occur with the development of thought suggests that they might help clarify the variations that occur with the dissolution of thought.

THE PROBLEMS RAISED BY FACTOR-ANALYTIC STUDIES. Piaget (1947) has confessed a lack of interest in the investigations of the manner in which abilities are correlated among individuals. Nevertheless, the evidence from the investigation of intra-individual differences in abilities and from the correlational approach to the organization of intelligence raises problems needing clarification for his conception of intelligence as mobile equilibrii of thought with logical properties.

One of these problems derives from what appears to be a contradiction between the implication of a homogeneous intelligence, and the fact of intra-individual differences. A second problem is raised by the fact that correlational or factor analyses of test performances have failed to uncover the concrete operations and formal operations which make their appearance at about age seven and at about age eleven respectively.

Homogeneous versus heterogeneous intelligence. Homogeneous intelligence appears to be an implication of Piaget's conception of the hierarchical nature of intelligence deriving from a progressive coordination and differentiation of schemata and central processes and also from his observation of a fixed order in the successive landmarks of transition in the development of the processes of thought. The implication of homogeneous intelligence gets further support from the observation by Piaget & Inhelder (1947) that conservation of volume always implies conservation of both weight and quantity, and that conservation of weight always implies conservation of quantity. Such considerations suggest that Piaget's progression of landmarks of transitions may comprise a natural ordinal scale of intelligence. The very notion of such an ordinal scale appears to imply a homogeneous level of intellectual functioning which belies the evidence of asymmetries or heterogeneity in talent that comes from other sources.

Evidence for these asymmetries comes from at least three sources (see Anastasi, 1958, pp. 318 ff). First, and most spectacular of this evidence, is the existence of what have been called *idiots savants*. Most of the earlier cases reported have been summarized by Tredgold (1915), and Rife & Snyder (1931) for instance, cite the case of a 27-year-old man with a mental age of three years who, when given a pencil and presented with arithmetic problems, could write the answer almost immediately. In describing the performance of this case, they write: "When the series [of squares] 2, 4, 16 was started, he immediately continued this [series], the sixth number being 4,294,967,296. Then 9—3 was written, in the attempt to indicate square root. Under this, several numbers such as 625, 729, and 900 were written. The square root of each was immediately and correctly written" (1931, p. 554). Such a discrepancy between arithmetic ability and other abilities appears hard to square with any notion of a homogeneous level of intellectual functioning, but since such instances are exceedingly rare, one might consider their very occasional existence of slight importance for general theory.

But second, whenever representative samples of normal older children or adults have taken a number of tests and all scores have been represented in such comparable units as standard scores, intraindividual differences among abilities in substantial degree have been found (see Hull, 1927; Pieron, 1940).

Third, and most important, is the abundant evidence coming from the correlational or factor analyses of test scores. Ever since Spearman (1904) intercorrelated the test-scores of children and published his two-factor theory of intelligence, these intra-individual differences in abilities have been under investigation.

Although intra-individual differences in abilities exist, agreement among the factor analysts about the nature of abilities has been far from perfect. Spearman (1927) working almost entirely with the test-performances of elementary-school children, attributed the intra-individual differences among their abilities to special factors in each test and to errors of measurement. It was the fact that the abilities of children also appeared to be regularly correlated positively that, in his view, would enable the tester of abilities to predict the variation in the performance of children across situations. In order to account for these regular positive correlations he postulated a *general* factor which he called *g*. He also recommended for the measurement of intelligence that a single test which is highly saturated with *g* should be substituted for the heterogeneous collection of items that had characterized such instruments as the Binet-Simon scales. Raven's (1938) "progressive matrices" constitutes an example of a test constructed on the basis of Spearman's theory. The test consists of a progressive series of abstract geometrical designs. From each of these a part has been removed. The subject's task is to pick out the missing part from a given set of alternatives. At the lower level, the tests require chiefly accuracy of visual perception. At the higher levels, they involve analogies and other logical relations which were chosen on the basis of Spearman's notion that intelligence depends basically on a capacity for the "education of relationships." Although Spearman emphasized *g*, specific factors (*s*), and error, he also recognized that when the scores for very similar activities are correlated, a degree of relationship may appear which is attributable to neither *g* nor *s* but to something intermediate.

American investigators, working chiefly with college students who are older than the school children of Spearman's studies and who comprise a sample in whom the range of intelligence is sharply curtailed by having at least its lower half eliminated, have found the variance in the scores on their tests better accounted for by factors intermediate between *g* and *s*. These have been characterized as *group* factors. On such grounds, Kelley (1928) argued that *g* is of relatively minor importance and can probably be attributed to the heterogeneity of the subjects (the full range of ability) and to the verbal nature of the tests employed (not true of Raven's matrices). It was on the basis of such evidence from a variety of performances by college students that Thurstone (1938) proposed his "primary mental abilities." The abilities, which have received repeated corroboration from the factor analyses of other investigators, include the following: V—*verbal comprehension;* W—*word fluency;* N—*number,* which consists chiefly of speed and accuracy of simple arithmetic computations; S—*spatial relations;* M—*associative memory;* P—*perceptual speed;* and I—*induction.* Since 1940, various investigators have intercorrelated and factored the scores of series of test of perceiving, of reasoning, and of verbal ability to find that within each of these limited categories of ability other group factors of a still narrower scope exist. In reviews of these studies, Guilford (1956) has identified some 40 intellectual factors and notes that gaps exist within his conceptual scheme where others are likely to be found, and French (1954) has identified 59 factors of ability which, in spite of the fact that they overlap, he believes should be regarded as distinct. Such an atomizing of abilities with emphasis on the intra-individual variations among them is sharply dissonant with the conception of a homogeneous intelligence that comes from Piaget.

Many factor analysts, moreover, have contended that the method uncovers genuine causal entities, genuine ability entities.[16] Such a view, especially when it is accompanied by the assumption that the ability entities are biologically based, predetermined by heredity, and fixed, constitutes almost the opposite picture from that which comes from the work of Piaget.

Such a view, however, is hardly dictated by the facts, and the picture from Piaget is less sharply dissonant with the facts than is this view from factor analysts who emphasize the independence of factors and who assume that the factors are predetermined and fixed by the genes.

First of all, Spearman's (1904) original discovery that abilities of all kinds are regularly correlated positively still stands. Moreover, when ability factor-scores are intercorrelated, they also show positive relationships, and when factored lead to second-order factors of greater generality. If such a procedure is followed for a sample of subjects where the range of ability is not curtailed, one is led back to the general factor (g) of Spearman, and on the way one finds group factors of varying degrees of breadth. The dominant view of the structure of abilities among British investigators is, in fact, hierarchical in nature. At the top, as Vernon (1950) describes the hierarchy, is Spearman's g. This general factor subdivides into a few major group factors. These include verbal-educational or intellectual ability and practical-mechanical aptitude, and to these may be added a major group-factor of speed in simple operations, and ultimately perhaps others may be found in musical ability, artistic ability, etc.[17] These group factors may be seen to factor into minor group factors.

---

[16] See Cattell (1952), Guilford (1940), Holzinger (1937), and Thurstone (1935).

[17] I am indebted to a lecture by, and conversation with, Professor Lloyd G. Humphreys for calling a number of these points to my attention. I am also indebted to Professor Humphreys for the opportunity to read and to use here ideas from an unpublished paper entitled "The problem of test hierarchies in factor analysis," by Humphreys and John Schmid, Jr.

Such appears to be the case for Thurstone's (1938) "primary mental abilities;" they may be seen as minor group factors of intellectual ability. The Differential Aptitude Tests constructed by Bennett, Seashore, & Wesman (1947) constitute another example of minor group factors within the intellectual sphere. Mechanical aptitude might readily be differentiated in similar fashion, and Rimoldi (1951) has shown that the speed factor subdivides into minor group factors. In turn, minute, splinter-like factors emerge with the factoring of test-scores from those tests used to measure each of the separate minor group-factors (French, 1954; Guilford, 1956).

It may be worth noting here that the usefulness of g and of these group factors of various degrees of breadth in predicting such criteria as performance in school, in mechanics training, in learning to fly, in clerical work, and in professional training of various kinds depends upon the age of the subjects and the range of ability being considered. Garrett (1946) and Preston (1947), for instance, have both found the intra-individual differences increasing with age. At the level of grade school, even the major group factors are of little use, and as Spearman (1927), whose work was based on the performance of such children contended, measures of g alone suffice for such predictive tasks as school placement. At the level of junior high school, the major group factors as well as g become useful in helping children to choose the directions in which they are most likely to be successful. At the level of high school, the minor group factors such as verbal versus quantitative ability, the "primary mental abilities" of Thurstone (1938) or the various factors on the Differential Aptitude Test (Bennett, Seashore, & Wesman, 1947) become helpful in predicting the directions in which a youth is likely to be successful in college, but in no situations are the minute, splinter-like factors of predictive significance. Their usefulness appears to reside in the information they provide to help the test-constructor in proper sampling of the narrower categories of aptitude.

Secondly, these group factors need not imply fixed entities of aptitude or ability. Although many factor analysts have contended that factors are genuine fixed causal entities of ability, other factor analysts have conceived of them only as *descriptive categories*.[18] As descriptive categories they need be neither predetermined nor fixed, and they may be conceived to have as their causes both the genetic constitution of the person and the circumstances of his life-history. Moreover, Anastasi (1936), Fleishman & Hempel (1954), and Woodrow (1938, 1939) and others have demonstrated that the factor structure of a given group of test measures changes as a conse-

18 See Burt (1940), Thomson (1939), Tryon (1935), and Vernon (1950).

quence of practice in certain of the skills represented in the group. Also, in a highly provocative logical analysis of the relationship of ability and learning, Ferguson (1954, 1956) has shown that a hierarchical factor structure of abilities that changes with practice is precisely what would be expected from assuming that abilities represent the transfer of the effects of learning in a variety of situations on tested performances.

Ferguson (1956) notes that the term *ability* has at least three different but consonant kinds of meaning. First, ability refers to measures of performance in any situation when these measures, subject to error, locate the individual performers on an underlying latent variable. Second, it refers in factor analysis to a derivative of the first meaning, namely, the weighted additive sum of measures of performance on separate tasks, and this also implies a latent factor variable. Third, it refers to some attribute of the organism or person which "may be identified vaguely with neurophysiological structure and process which is modified by environmental and genetic factors." Ferguson (1954) assumes also that the various ability factors which have achieved relative stability have done so through overlearning and are approaching a crude limit beyond which no systematic improvement is likely to occur with further practice. *Transfer,* the other main term, Ferguson (1956, 1959) defines after the mathematical concept of function. Transfer "implies change in performance on one task is a function of change resulting from practice on another." Transfer may be either positive or negative. The concept of a general ability factor and a considerable degree of positive correlation among psychological tests is explained by the process of positive transfer, and the distinctive major factors which emerge in the adult of any culture are those tending to facilitate rather than to inhibit each other.

Humphreys (1959) has gone further to suggest the manner in which the experimental manipulations which have traditionally been used to study the transfer of training could account for the obtained correlations among abilities. The traditional design of the experiment on the transfer of training goes as follows:

Group I: Pre-Test$_1$—Transfer Training—Post Test$_1$

Group II: Pre-Test$_1$—Inactivity—Post-Test$_1$

In Group I training is interpolated between the tests to promote transfer, while in Group II either inactivity or some meaningless activity like color-naming is interpolated between the tests. The amount of transfer is assessed by the difference between the mean scores for the past two post-tests, assuming the two pre-tests were comparable. Now, one may add a second test-variable, as follows:

Group I: Pre-Test₁—Transfer Training—Post-Test₁
Pre-Test₂—   ”   ”   —Post-Test₂

Group II: Pre-Test₁—   Inactivity   —Post-Test₁
Pre-Test₂—   ”   —Post-Test₂

Here the amount of transfer to Test 1 may be measured by computing the difference between the means of the scores on post-test₁ for Groups I and II, and the amount of transfer to Test 2 may be measured by the difference between the means of the scores on post-test₂ for Groups I and II. Previous to the special training, the variation in scores on Test 1 and Test 2 may be orthogonal, i.e., may vary quite independently, but if the special training should transfer to both Tests 1 and 2, the scores on these two tests for the two groups would become positively correlated. The amount of this correlation would be a function of the changes in the means of the scores on the post-tests produced by the special training. While this correlation might ordinarily be called spurious because it is produced by the change in the means and the "within groups correlation" would remain at zero, there would, nevertheless, be an over-all correlation between these tests following the special training where previously none existed. If one were to add Tests 3, 4 . . . *m*, and the same transfer effect were to continue to operate in varying degree for the various new tests, the degree of intercorrelations among these *m* post-tests would depend upon the amount of transfer arising from the special training. Humphreys (1959) adds:

Now, let us add to this picture by introducing *N* variations of the independent variable [of special training]. Again any correlations produced will be a function of the changes in the means. These variations of the independent variable do not have to be along a single continuum because with respect to plotting the correlation for the "group as a whole" we simply, in effect, use as the continuum the size of the difference produced by the various [kinds of special training].

"If [special training] *X* produces the largest amount of transfer for these variables consistently, then this group will in effect have its scores in the top of the score distribution. Let us now make one other assumption, namely, that in place of doing this in a laboratory, we assume that this takes place in life-in-the-home, in the school, or on the playground. In this instance I think we shall have generated the intercorrelations among [ability] tests that Professor Ferguson (1959) has talked about (1959, pp. 186–87).

It is thus that the abilities of man can be seen to be developed and to become differentiated through learning, or through organism-environment interaction.

Such a view is quite consonant with that of Piaget. The latent variable of intelligence implied by the successive landmarks of transition in development might be seen to correspond to g. Piaget and his collaborators have been unconcerned about intra-individual differences in ability, and, because they have worked largely with young children and only very recently with those of junior high school age, they have had little opportunity to note them because intelligence is quite homogeneous during early childhood even when factor analyzed. It would be only later that distinct major ability factors could be expected to become differentiated, and these could readily be seen to emerge in terms of Piaget's theory through the special accommodative modifications demanded by encounters with special varieties of circumstances. Moreover, it may also be noted that Piaget's invariant processes of accommodation and assimilation have counterparts in the theory of Ferguson. Accommodative modifications correspond to Ferguson's changes in performance that occur with practice, while the assimilation of those accommodative modifications corresponds to Ferguson's notion of transfer of training to performance in test situations. Thus the evidence from factor analysis proves less dissonant with the conceptions of Piaget after analysis than is at first apparent. Moreover, the interpretation of Ferguson and of Humphreys is highly consonant with that of Piaget.

The failure of concrete and formal operations to become manifest in factor-analytic studies. It might appear that factor-analytic studies of intelligence have revealed the roof, the walls, and the cupola of the intelligence barn but missed the basic structure of the barn itself. Several hypothetical reasons can be found for this. First, since only intra-individual variations in ability can show up in factor analyses, and since the factor studies have nearly all used as subjects either high school or college students all of whom share the formal operations, the factor method has been incapable of picking them out. Similarly, the attempts to factor-analyze the intelligence-test performances of children have typically confined themselves to children of a relatively narrow age range, so again the thought structures present would probably have been common to all. Second, even though a few factor studies have used as subjects children of various ages, they may well not have included an appropriate set of performances to bring out Piaget's thought structures.[19] Third, getting

[19] This statement appears to be wrong. Since this was written, Mr. William J. De Marco has brought to my attention Hofstaetter's (1954) factor analysis of the matrix of correlations among the scores from repeated testings of the children in the Berkeley Growth Study (Bayley, 1949). In that study, the children were tested repeatedly from ages two months to 18 years with standard tests of "intelligence." Hofstaetter subtitled his paper "a study in T-technique" after the terminology of Cattell's (1952) "Co-

psychological significance out of a set of factor loadings may rest so heavily upon the insight of the investigator that the nature of such thought structures would never occur to him unless the investigator knew what he was looking for. Fourth, the match between such variables as test-scores may be so poor with the observational operations by means of which the logico-mathematical properties of Piaget's thought structures are uncovered that factor analysis of test-scores can yield no evidence of these structures.

In the light of such considerations as those briefly indicated here, the two sorts of problems posed for Piaget's conception of intelligence may be seen as essentially superficial.

CONCLUSION

The evidence reviewed in this chapter appears to indicate that Piaget's work contributes in highly varied ways not only to the theory of intelligence and the theory of development, whence it derived, but to the general theory of behavior and, at least potentially, to neuropsychology. His observations of the epigenesis in the structures of behavior and thought bring out and help to correct the preforma-

---

variation chart" for factor analyses of repeated testings of the same sample of individuals. This matrix yielded three factors by Thurstone's centroid method and left only negligible residuals. Hofstaetter wrote, "In some 15 years of factorial work this writer has never seen a more beautiful set of factor loadings; i.e., one that shows as much regularity as the one presented here" (p. 159). Factor I shows loadings on age that start at +.45 at 2 months, rise to +.88 and remain above +.80 from 8 to 14 months, then drop (+.53 at 21 months, +.35 at 32 months, and +.03 at 40 months and thereafter). Because these first 40 months comprise the period when the "intelligence scales" consist of sensorimotor items, Hofstaetter called this Factor I "sensorimotor alertness." Factor II shows negative loadings (−.48 at 2 months, −.28 at 5 months, and −.13 at 8 months) during the first three-fourths of a year, then positive loadings that rise to +.65 at 32 months, then drops to loadings of approximately zero at and after 108 months. With reservations, Hofstaetter called Factor II "persistence" because it loads negatively on age during the first three-fourths of a year, and then positively. It is interesting to note that loadings begin to be positive at precisely the time that Piaget (1936) observed the beginnings of interest in external events for themselves. Factor III shows loadings of negligible size till the children are about 21 months old; then they increase to an asymptote approximating +.97 at age 108 months (9 years) and continue at this high level thereafter. The loadings rise rapidly from +.68 at 48 months to +.90 at six years. Hofstaetter speculates that Factor III can be identified with what Freud has called *"Probehandeln"* and that it may correspond to Spearman's *"g."* It is exceedingly interesting that it shows its most rapid rise precisely at the time that children are going through what Piaget (1947) calls the "intuitive stage" when images are in the process of becoming consolidated into the "groupements" or "concrete operations." It should be noted, however, that no new factors appear associated with ages 9–10 and 11–12. Whether this is due to the fact that the standard tests of intelligence used in the California Growth Study do not permit such factors to appear is unclear, and the question can only be answered when such longitudinal data become available from Piaget-type tests.

tionism that still lurks in both epistemology and psychological theory.

Many of the principles uncovered by Piaget get at least suggestive support from evidence deriving from quite diverse sources. The principle that the rate of development is a function of variety of stimulation during the early months of life gets support from those studies of the role of experience in the development that stem from Hebb's theorizing and from the studies of the retardation that follows homogeneous stimulation in some orphanages. While there is little doubt that great degrees of retardation can result from lack of variety in early stimulation, the degree to which such retardation is permanent or can be reversed remains an unsettled question. Similarly, the question of the degree to which the rate of development now characteristic of life in what is considered the best of home-rearing could be increased also remains open, but it is tenable to believe that with better knowledge of the process whereby schemata and central structures are modified by experience, the rate of development might be increased substantially, and with pleasure for the developing child.

Piaget's description of the consecutive stages of thought, each of which incorporates the processes of the preceding stage, appears to imply that intelligence is a function of autonomous central processes established as a consequence of varied functioning in the intrinsic systems of the brain. Such a principle gets at least suggestive support from the finding of Max that muscle action currents accompany the solving of mental problems less commonly in older deaf children than in younger deaf children and less commonly in those who show high intelligence than in those who show low intelligence on tests. The incorporating of the processes of each stage into the new processes of the succeeding stage suggests a hierarchical organization of central processes that corresponds fairly well with the manner in which electronic computers are programmed to process the information required to solve logical problems, and this has suggested to neuropsychologists that the central processes must also be organized in hierarchical fashion within the brain.

Finally, the principal theme of Piaget's most recent work, that of explaining thought in terms of logical operations, has lent precision to the description of variations among the thought processes of adolescents, elementary-school children, and pre-school children. These logical operations and Piaget's testing methods also promise to lend precision to the description of the psychological deficit that is associated with psychoses and with cerebral lesions; they may also aid in finding correspondences between human thought and the programs arranged for electronic computers. Although the various thought structures that Piaget has described appear at first to be dissonant with the facts that derive from the factor-analytic studies of intelligence, this dissonance proves upon analysis to be superficial.

CHAPTER **8**

Some Reinterpretations

Before recapitulation, it remains to look again at some of the old concepts and at some of the old facts which have been interpreted to support the assumptions of fixed intelligence and predetermined development. These old concepts and facts remain. Is their meaning altered by the conception of intelligence as central processes comprising strategies for processing information that develop in the course of the child's interacting with his environment? It remains also to re-examine the issue of the proportional contributions of heredity and environment to tested intelligence, to examine the predicted fall in the intelligence of future generations from the fact of differential fertility in the social-class structure, and to indicate the investigative, educational import of the theory and evidence reviewed here.

THE MEANING OF INTELLIGENCE-TEST SCORES

SEMANTICS AND LOGIC. Although the assumption of fixed intelligence has a basis in the history of thought, as reviewed in Chapter 2, it is worth noting that it may have yet another basis in semantics and in the unwarranted generalization of certain conceptual sets. On the semantic side, intelligence has commonly been termed a *dimension* and has been seen as a dimension of a person. The tests of intelligence have been termed *scales* as if they were measuring a fixed dimension of the person or the person's behavior. Such terminology derives from the physical sciences where objects are constant, at least relatively so for most purposes, and where the systems of relationships among them are closed. Objects are constant, for instance, with respect to such dimensions as height, circumference, weight, volume, and shape, and this constancy is one of the concepts mediated by the central processes that grow with experience. The systems of relationship among them are closed in the sense that, with the relevant conditions specified, certain events involving their relations always occur, as in the case of the law of falling bodies.

The application of such terms as *dimension* and *scale* may at once tend to carry their meaning in the physical world over to the world of organismic behavior and to imply that the concept of constancy of dimensions is being generalized from static objects to non-static persons and their behavior. On the conceptual side, moreover, since persons change relatively slowly, especially in adulthood, it is easy to see how such conceptual sets as object-constancy, quantity-conservation, and number-conservation would readily be generalized from the world of static things to the world of changing organisms and persons. Once change has come to be conceived to be a matter of mere appearances behind which exists a constant essence, it is no easy matter to distinguish essences which are in fact static from essences which are in fact changing. It is probable that unwarranted generalization of conceptual constancy-sets is one factor behind the persistence of the belief in fixed intelligence. Fixed intelligence is a conception like the preformationistic notion that the bodily structure of a species is to be found within the egg or the sperm. Both rest upon such an ancient conceptual constancy-set as "hair cannot come out of not-hair, nor flesh out of not-flesh" attributed to Anaxagoras of Clazomenae (Cornford, 1930) and which may be generalized as "no essence can be derived from something which does not include that essence." Once one has acquired such a conceptual constancy-set, the idea that an essence like intelligence can change tends to produce "cognitive dissonance." And one tends to build defenses against such emotional disturbance. In the light of such considerations, calling intelligence a *dimension* and speaking of tests as *scales* may be unfortunate. Insofar as they may serve to reduce the dissonance that would come with recognizing the full implications of the epigenesis in the development of intelligence, they may also obscure reality.

In the light of such considerations, moreover, the assumption of predetermined development looks like a withdrawal from the untenable position of preformationism to the next redoubt. Exaggerating the degree of *predetermination* in development may gain one a defensive preservation of his constancy-set; he may thereby avoid the dissonance that would come from recognizing that organisms not only change but that the process of change is itself open-ended. In the words of Dobzhansky (1956), the geneticist, "at any stage of development, the [phenotypic] outcome of the development depends on the genotype and on the succession of environments which the developing organism has encountered up to that stage." But more than cognitive dissonance may be involved here. One implication of this idea that the development of organisms and persons is an open-ended process puts a logical limitation on the predictive validity[1] of tests of intelligence or on measures of any personal characteristic. Recognizing such limitation would disturb anyone who aspired to predictions from tests which have the supposed support of logical necessity. Prediction in science, however, is always a matter of stating what will happen to given objects in a closed system for which the relevant conditions can be and are fully specified. It is this fact that makes scientific prediction an essential criterion for understanding and for the correctness of predictions as formulated. It may become possible to formulate laws which predict the characteristics that organisms with specified genetic constitutions will develop under specified programs of encounters with the environment. It would appear to be outside the realm of scientific possibility, however, to predict with precision the future characteristics or phenotypic fate of any organism from knowing merely its present characteristics, without being able to specify the future conditions under which it will live. Since it is impossible to specify what any person's future encounters with his environment will be, attempting to predict his future behavior from test performances alone is at best a matter of statistical empiricism. At worst it smacks of occult prophecy. Although these considerations eliminate the support of logical necessity from all predictions of future behavior made from tests, either intelligence tests or tests of other characteristics, it avails nothing to deny these considerations except possibly to avoid some of the insecurity felt by some of those professionally concerned with predicting the behavior of people from their performances on tests. The tests have neither more nor less empirical usefulness in practical affairs because they lack the support of logical necessity for the empirical predictions derived from them.

[1] By predictive validity is meant here the capacity of the test-scores of individuals from testing at one stage of development to predict either the test-scores or the criterion performances of those individuals at a later period of their lives. It should be noted that this is not always the definition given to predictive validity. Cronbach (1949), for instance, has used predictive validity in the sense that criterion validity is used here, namely, to refer to the capacity of the performance of persons on tests to predict such contemporary criteria as their school grades, their success in flight training, or the quality of their clerical work. For Cronbach's usage, the time between the two performances (test to test, or test to criterion) is not a matter of explicit consideration in the definition.

THE NATURE OF INTELLIGENCE AND OF INTELLIGENCE TESTS. The semantics of *dimension* and *scale* fit the procedures of testing less well than do the semantics of sampling behavior for evidence of the presence of such organizational structures as schemata, operations, and conceptions. Intelligence tests consist essentially of samplings of behavior. The vocabulary tests, for example, sample the subject's knowledge of the meaning of words; absurdities test sample recognitions of the logical relationships among various concepts, and most other tests sample the subject's grasp of various relationships or whether or not he does educe various relationships. In traditional tests, what is sampled is typically named in terms of such skill categories as verbal or arithmetic skill. The attempts by factor analysts, including Spearman's (1927) *g*, Thurstone's (1938) primary abilities, and Guilford's (1956, 1957) factor structures of intellect, to specify what is sampled yield what is probably best conceived as systems of coordinates which simplify the comparing of people in their test-performance and perhaps facilitate making predictions about the efficiency of people.[2] These systems of coordinates, regardless of the names given to them, may—yes, probably—have little or nothing to do with the natural structures, schemata, operations, and concepts organized within individuals that determine their problem-solving. It is the merit of Piaget to give attention to the natural structures of the central processes that mediate problem-solving. It is an intriguing paradox, moreover, that, if the temporal order of appearance of the landmarks diagnostic of the structures proves to be fixed, his work will have produced the first evidence to justify what might properly be called a natural scale of intelligence. That scale will be ordinal in nature, and it will be based upon sampling behavior to determine the presence or absence of the various hierarchically arranged structures with their logical characteristics (see Chapter 7).

RELIABILITY AND VALIDITY OF TESTS

The semantics of sampling behavior for signs of such structures as sensorimotor schemata, operations, and conceptions do no violence to the facts concerning the reliability and validity of intelligence tests. Intelligence-test scores are reliable chiefly in the sense that the individual's rank in a group as determined by a part of a test (split half) or by one test approximates his rank in that group or in another comparable group as determined in the same fashion. Insofar as the

---

[2] This is, of course, but one point of view, the one held also by Anastasi (1936, 1938), Burt (1940), Thomson (1941), Vernon (1938). Against this view are the arguments of Cattell (1952), Guilford (1940), Holzinger (1937), Kelley (1935), and Thurstone (1926) for the notion that the factors are genuine causal entities.

central structures mediating intelligent behavior change only gradually, their presence at one time should indicate their presence again at another time if the two times are not too widely separated and no encounters with circumstances have intervened that force radical changes in them.

Validity is a term with various meanings. Two of these meanings are especially relevant. First, *criterion validity:* Test-scores may be said to be valid in the sense that the rank of an individual in a group derived from his performance on an intelligence test approximates his rank in that group or a comparable one derived from such criteria as his performance in school or on a variety of jobs. Again the concept of the sampling of structures does no violence to the facts, for insofar as the structures of central processes that constitute or mediate intelligence generalize across situations, the persons who shows them in the test situation should also show them in school or workaday situations.

Second, *predictive validity:* Test-scores may also be said to be valid if the individual's rank in a group at one time as determined by his performance on tests approximates his rank in that group or a comparable one at a later time, as determined by his performance on tests. This is the kind of validity involved when an attempt is made to predict the final adult level of intelligence from tests given earlier in youth, childhood, or infancy (Bayley, 1954). The finding that the degree of correlation between the score at any testing and the score at age 18 drops off with the amount of time that separates the testing from the determination of the final level is not consonant with the assumptions of either fixed intelligence or predetermined development, but it is precisely what one would expect from the conception of intelligence as central structures developed in the course of child-environment interaction, with the role of heredity being that of setting limits.

CONSTANCY AND FLUCTUATIONS OF DQ AND IQ. The DQ and IQ are rates of development, at least for children, if not for adults. They do not, however, describe the absolute rate of change in intelligence structures per unit of time. Rather, they are rates relative to age which provide chiefly a scale for the comparison of individuals. In any absolute sense, the rate of change in schemata and intelligence structures is largest during the early months of life, and it drops off thereafter. In this slowing process, the development of behavioral structures follows a course resmbling that of the embryological development or morphological structures. The notion of fixed intelligence implies that individual differences in the relative rate should be constant. The curves of the IQ from successive testings of individual children in such longitudinal studies as the Berkeley Growth Study (see Chapter 2 or Jones, 1954) fail to show the constancy to be expected from the notion of fixed intelligence. While the develop-mental rate is high during the preschool years, great variability in scores from successive testings is not uncommon (see Chapter 2). An appreciable degree of constancy emerges only after about age five when the developmental rate has slowed greatly and when going to school brings a relatively common program of environmental en-counters into the lives of children.

While the fluctuations of DQ's and IQ's during the early years are highly embarrassing to the assumption of fixed intelligence, and also to that of predetermined development, unless one makes with Good-enough & Maurer (1942) the additional *ad hoc* assumption of pre-determined patterns in rate of development, they are entirely con-sonant with the notion of intelligence as central processes developing as a function of the child's interactions with the environment. More-over, in view of the fact that any pair of parents may have attitudes and child-rearing practices which foster very rapid rates of develop-ment at some stages and interfere with development at other stages, one might expect that a child would be quite advanced at one stage and retarded at another during these early months and years. Mur-phy (1944) has pointed out that there is a constant interaction be-tween the mother's personality and the characteristics of the young infant and child. She has written, for example, that

. . . in infancy, that protective mother may give the child a great deal of satisfaction [and we might add variety of stimulation] if she is the kind who is protective because she is fond of babies and gets a great deal of satisfaction from them. But at the age of expanding locomotion and exploration [when the child needs to throw things and to indulge in activities that might apparently be harmful both to himself and to valuable things], the over-protective mother be-comes an inhibitor and deprives the child of opportunities which he needs to use his new abilities . . . the excessively scientific mother [on the other hand] who deprives the child of emotional satisfaction at the infancy level, may by contrast, give the child more approval and emotional satisfaction at the loco-motor period, because she is pleased by the new signs of independence (p. 658).

Such considerations suggest the possibility of discovering important relationships between the age at which Piaget's behavioral land-marks appear, if they do constitute a genuine ordinal scale, and the manner in which parents manage their children at various stages of development. It is just possible, for instance, that the negative cor-relation that Bayley (1954) has found between DQ's and IQ's in children of less than a year in age and the educational level of par-ents may result from the misinformation about child-rearing that has been communicated to those who read and can act upon what they learn by reading. If this line of reasoning is correct, it may be possible, from a knowledge of the parental attitudes toward the various phases of infantile development, to make roughly accurate predictions of the phases at which children in given families will be advanced or retarded.

Viewing intelligence as a sampling of schemata makes it sensible to use tests in early development as a method of assessing some of the consequences of parental practices and attitudes. Parental behaviors are very probably much more important determinants of rates of development than are such traditional indices of intellectual environment as level of parental education, socio-economic level, number of books in the house, etc. In fact, these traditional indices of intellectual environment may be very poor indicators of the behaviors which are important determinants. Finally, inasmuch as developmental rates are most rapid, in absolute terms, during the early months and first couple of years, this is probably the period of most importance for maximizing intellectual potential. Such a verdict is completely contrary to what has been believed from assuming that intelligence is fixed and that development is predetermined and from assuming that experience, especially during the early years, is of no significance for future intellectual level.

The notion that intelligence tests are sampling schemata and intellectual structures helps to clarify the fact, pointed out by Anderson (1940), that the predictive invalidity of infant tests derives from the fact that they have few elements which are common to the successive age levels. This is no accident. It derives inevitably from the fact that the child at a year has absorbed almost all of the schemata observable at six months into a new set of structures, and the child at two years has absorbed those evident at a year into another new set. It derives inevitably and directly from the fact that the epigenesis of intellectual structures is very rapid in the preschool years.

On the other hand, it is quite incorrect to consider the infant tests invalid. Bayley (1940) has shown that the reliability of the infant tests is of the order of +.9 so long as only a week or two elapses between tests. In the sense that the infant tests fail to predict the ultimate level of intelligence, they do lack predictive validity, but predictive validity could be expected only by assuming fixed intelligence and predetermined development. Otherwise, as already noted, prediction would be impossible without understanding fully all the influential factors in the child-environment interaction and without being able to specify completely the program of encounters that the child will have with the environment throughout the period between testing and the determination of final level. Insofar as the infant tests indicate what the child can do at a given time, insofar as they indicate the structures which are present at a given time, they are entirely valid. Insofar as the DQ and IQ represent the appearance of genuine capacities relative to age, they are also valid. These structures should generalize from the testing situation to criterion situations, but unfortunately criterion situations have seldom been a consideration in the preschool years. The meaning of validity has been limited to predictive validity. If they are seen as having criterion validity, the infant tests may also be seen as potentially sensitive indicators of the effects of various kinds of environments. On the other hand, for such purposes, it may be wiser to use such natural landmarks in behavior as Piaget has uncovered.

REINTERPRETATIONS OF SOME OF THE EVIDENCE USED TO SUPPORT THE ASSUMPTION OF PREDETERMINED DEVELOPMENT

Some of the facts which have been seen to support the conception of predetermined development will also bear re-examination. The low A/S ratios of the organisms used in the investigations that have been most widely cited to support the assumption of predetermined development and the notion of unlearned behavior may well account for the results obtained in these investigations. These results need not hold for higher organisms with larger A/S ratios. Even at the embryonic phase of development, moreover, functional encounters with environmental conditions appear to have an important influence on development. The relatively brief duration of the infantile experiences used appears to be another important factor in the observed impermanence of their effects. Finally, the nature of the skills practiced may also help account for the short-lived effects of the early practice in some of the studies most widely quoted to show this evanescence of practice effects.

EFFECTS OF EARLY EXPERIENCE AS A FUNCTION OF THE COMPLEXITY OF SCHEMATA AND THE A/S RATIO OF SUBJECTS. The influence of the opportunity to exercise functions on later development probably decreases markedly as one goes down the phylogenetic scale. This is one of the points of Hebb's conception of the A/S ratio which indicates the portion of cerebral tissue uninvolved immediately with either receptor inputs or motor outputs, and also the portion of cerebral tissue in which central firing circuits must be established before either receptor inputs or autonomous central processes acquire control of motor outputs. With their small A/S ratios, those organisms low in the phylogenetic scale would be expected to require less in the way of experience to give receptor inputs cerebral control over muscular activity. Such a hypothesis gets empirical support, moreover, from the fact that the effects of increasing the variety of early experience appear to be quite appreciably greater in the dog (Thompson & Heron, 1954) than in the rat (Forgays & Forgays, 1952; Forgus, 1954, 1955a, 1955b).

Schemata differ, too, in the degree to which they require autonomous central processes. Some, like reflexes, appear to be almost direct sensorimotor connections. Some, like swimming and walking, appear to require the coordination of relatively more primitive elements but achieve a final form which does not then change. Others, like playing music from a score and all intelligent acts, appear to depend upon an array of autonomous central activities to process the receptor inputs and to give them control over the final common path to the musculature.

In the light of such considerations, the fact that Carmichael (1926, 1927, 1928) could detect no effects either of absence of practice in the first swimming movement of his chloretoned salamander and frog tadpoles or of increased stimulation in the age at which such tadpoles first exhibited swimming need not embarrass the principle that appropriate experience is required for the development in higher organisms of behavioral and intellectual schemata requiring the mediation of autonomous central processes. This fact need not embarrass the principle because the swimming schema requires little in the way of mediation through autonomous central processes, and also because probably no other vertebrates exist with a much lower A/S ratio than those of the salamander and the frog. Thus, the fact that a schema like swimming may appear without practice in an organism with such a low A/S ratio should not be generalized to more complex schemata in higher organisms.

Anatomical Maturation and Behavior. Probably no evidence has been more widely cited than the epochal work of Coghill to support that corollary of predetermined development which holds that behavior unfolds automatically with the anatomical maturation of the nervous system. It was because behavioral development followed the same sequential course from head to tail found for anatomical development and because of the results of his studies of neural mechanisms that Coghill (1929) concluded that behavior follows anatomical maturation. In consequence he rhapsodized over the adaptive consequences of a millionth of an inch of growth in axones or dendrites of central neurones that changed the tadpole from an inert creature to one which can withdraw from noxious stimulation and which can move about in seeking the wherewithal to gratify its needs. The empirical basis for that millionth of an inch of growth was hardly made clear. Moreover, the direction of the cause-effect relationship from anatomical maturation to behavior was only suggested and not proved. Nevertheless, Coghill's rhapsody was effective debating, and Coghill's observations and great authority were widely used to support the assumption, already strong for historical reasons, that the basic behavioral repertoire unfolds automatically in all organisms as the anatomical structures which mediate it mature. Kuo (1932d) has criticized many of Coghill's conclusions from the evidence he got by studying the behavioral development of embryo chicks.

The work of Z. Y. Kuo. Kuo's investigations of the development of behavior in the embryos of the domestic chicken are also epochal. They represent a program of research in the grand manner, and they deserve to be as well known as Coghill's work. Kuo's (1932a) first paper, for instance, describing distributions of the first manifestations of the various items in the chronology of the embryo chick's repertoire, represented observations of behavior during incubation in over 7,000 chicken eggs.

Kuo's method permitted him to make repeated behavioral observations throughout the course of incubation from its beginning to hatching in some 3,000 of these eggs. The eggs of fowl make fortunate subjects for the study of embryonic development. If the development of behavior in a mammalian embryo is to be examined, the mother of the embryo must undergo surgery (see Carmichael, 1951). Inasmuch as this mother is the environmental host for the parasitic embryo, it becomes impossible to determine how much any surgical damage to the mother influences physiologically the behavior of the embryo. Such considerations, moreover, render repeated observation of behavioral development in given embryos at widely separated developmental stages impossible (see Carmichael, 1954). It is feasible, of course, to watch the development of behavior in the embryos of amphibia (frogs and salamanders) and fishes. Both have unshelled eggs and the embryos develop in open water. But no such organism has a high A/S ratio. Although the neopallium or new brain of the birds, which contains the cerebral structures not immediately involved with either receptor inputs or motor outputs, differs from that of the mammals in the sense that the birds' neopallium evolved from the optic brain of its reptilian ancestors while that of the mammals evolved from the olfactory brain of its ancestors (Papez, 1929), the A/S ratio for many birds is approximately the equivalent to that in many mammals.

Kuo arranged to see the embryo in the chicken egg by cutting both the shell and the outer membrane away from the blunt end of the egg. He then applied melted vaseline to the intact inner membrane with a Chinese writing brush. The melted vaseline made the inner membrane sufficiently transparent to permit seeing and photographing the embryo. It also continued to protect the developing embryo and so permitted repeated observations of given embryos.

Kuo's (1932a) chronology of behavioral development in the chick is unimportant for the story told here, but his (1932b) description of the mechanical factors operating at the various stages of embryonic development is highly relevant. His observations lead to principles that correspond to many of those found in Piaget's observations of his children. Organism-environment interaction, for instance, can be seen even in embryonic development. The chick embryo's almost continual activity, once started, undergoes continual modifications as conditions of the chick's relation to its environment change. For example, among the first movements is the lifting and lowering of the head-end. As the head increases in size and the neck grows long but remains small, this lifting and falling is transformed to a lateral, sidewise turning. For another example, bending and extension and lateral twisting of the trunk disappear when the size of the embryo increases to a point where extension and lateral twisting cannot easily occur within the limited space offered by the eggshell. In the place of these movements come jerking and wiggling. Movements of the rudimentary limbs appear almost as soon as the limbs start to grow. Contrary to Coghill, furthermore, they appear to be quite independent of movements of the trunk. These limb buds first move in a vibrating fashion. By day five or six, as the limbs become longer and jointed, they move only headward and tailward along the longitudinal course of the body of the embryo. Thus, each phase of the chick's embryo development appears to be conditioned to a considerable degree by its environmental situation.

Corresponding to a second principle also found by Piaget, Kuo finds initiative for action shifting gradually from the environment and extra-embryonic structures to the embryo proper. The first movements of the embryo appeared to Kuo to derive entirely from the extra-embryonic structures. They appeared to be commuted mechanically to the embryo, but later he observed the embryo to initiate movement when these structures were quiescent. By the sixty-sixth hour, the embryo became almost continuously active and then the circumstances served chiefly to modify the form of activity.

Principles distinctive for the prenatal phase of development also derive from Kuo's work. In one, he (1932c) points out that all the various movements in the repertoire of the newly-hatched chick have been exercised strenuously for periods of considerable duration during embryonic life. The head-bobbing that constitutes part of the pecking response is, as already noted, one of the first embryonic movements to appear. The beak movements appear on the sixth and seventh days of incubation. These beak movements include not only the opening and closing of the bill but also bill-thrusting. Even swallowing may be observed to accompany the thrusting and the clapping, or closing, of the bill.

Kuo (1932d) notes also that the responses comprising the locomotor pattern have been well practiced before hatching. This practice starts with vibratory motions of the wing-buds and leg-buds. These motions are both headward-tailward and inward-outward. As the legs lengthen and the joints appear, the movements become flexion and extension. At about the eleventh day of incubation, the yolk sac characteristically moves over to the ventral side of the embryo. This means that the legs must fold on the breast and be held there by the yolk sac. From this point on, the legs cannot be fully extended. They are forced to remain in the folded position with only infrequent extensive thrusts against the yolk sac through the remainder of incubation.

This condition, Kuo argues, establishes a fixed resting posture for the legs. Thus, for one or two days after hatching, Kuo observed that the chick tends to sit on the floor most of the time with the legs folded in exactly that posture in which they were long held by the yolk sac during fetal development. This posture carries over even into adult life as the posture of the roosting bird at rest. Kuo also observed that even in standing and walking, the newly hatched chick walks on its shanks instead of its feet. This manner of standing and walking lasts for several hours, and it is with considerable difficulty, accompanied by repeated trial and failure, that the young chick learns to walk on its feet. Although lack of muscular strength may well be a factor, Kuo argues that if the infant chick did not have to break up the well-fixed pattern of folding the legs on the breast, the difficulty it has in acquiring the adult manner of standing and walking might be considerably decreased.

Kuo's (1932d) contention that the normal posture of the legs is fixed under mechanical pressure from the yolk sac would carry relatively little weight if the evidence consisted entirely of the observations he made during the course of embryonic development. It so happens, however, that Kuo also has as evidence for this contention the results of "an experiment of nature." In the 7,000 embryos observed, nearly 200 crippled chicks appeared. These crippled chicks could neither stand nor walk after hatching. Neither could they sit in the roosting position, for their legs were deformed. Over 80 per cent of these deformed leg-positions occurred in those instances where the yolk sac failed for some reason still unknown to move over to the ventral side of the embryo. Such evidence strongly supports Kuo's contention that the influence of environmental circumstances on movements of the embryo alter post-hatching behavior and constitute important factors in the development of behavior during the embryonic phase.

In the light of such considerations, Kuo (1932e) objected strenuously to the generalization of Coghill's (1929) conclusion that behavior can be explained solely in terms of the anatomical growth of the nervous system to such higher vertebrates as chicks and mammals. Against the assumption of unlearned behavior in animals of such a phylogenetic level as the chick, moreover, Kuo (1932e) brought both the observation that behavior is first commuted to the organism and becomes spontaneous only gradually and the observation that the embryo practices all of those movements which comprise the behavioral schemata of the chick at hatching. Kuo (1932d) warned that "those who have observed that the newly hatched chick can peck and swallow without learning and who have, therefore, concluded that these reactions are instinctively pure and simple must be reminded of the fact that these reactions have a long history of development in the egg which they have ignored entirely in their studies" (p. 115). Kuo suggested further that the case can hardly be different in mammalian embryos just because the latter cannot easily be observed. From such considerations, it would appear that the behavioral characteristics of a species may be conditioned by the organism-environment interaction during gestation, and that its consistency from member to member of the species derives not only from the genotype but also from a highly standardized environment during the embryonic phase when development is most rapid. Probably the fact that provision for a constant environment during the embryonic phase is lacking only in those organisms as low in the phylogenetic scale as frogs and amblystoma is evidence of the lesser importance of experience in the development of species-characteristic behavior in such organisms. Only in such organisms can the characteristic behavioral patterns come "unlearned," and automatically, as a function of anatomic maturation.

Kuo (1939a) also objected to the Gestalt conception of organized mass-actions from which something approximating individual reflexes is gradually differentiated, because numerous factors influence the spread of movement over the body of an embryo in response to stimulation. When the embryo is healthy, the spread of movement is wider than when the embryo is unwell for any reason. When the egg is so placed that the embryo chick rests on its back, there are more local movements than when the embryo rests on its ventral portion. When the chick is in an active phase, a stimulus evokes more local movements than are evoked when the chick is in an inactive phase. Thus, at the phylogenetic level of the chicken, organism-environment interaction appears to be as characteristic of embryonic behavioral development as it is of postnatal behavioral development, and with important consequences for the postnatal response repertoire. Both the argument from A/S ratios and the evidence indicate that Coghill's conclusions cannot properly be generalized to more complex organisms.

The factor of the duration of infantile experience. The importance of the factor of the duration that environmental circumstances prevail at any stage in the course of development has already been brought out, but it is worthwhile to bring it out again in connection with the reinterpretation of the evidence which has been used to support the idea of predetermined development. Two of the studies which are among those most widely quoted to support the corollary that subtracting the opportunity for experience has little or no effect on the development of behavior are those of Carmichael (1926, 1927, 1928) on salamanders (*Amblystoma*) and frogs and those of Cruze. (1935, 1938) on chicks. Carmichael, concerned as he was with a test of the conception of unlearned behavior, kept his experimental tadpoles immobilized with chloretone anesthesia only until the swimming movements had appeared, i.e., until the control tadpoles were exhibiting the typical swimming reaction, a period of eight days. The chloretoned tadpoles manifested the normal swimming pattern within half an hour. On the other hand, Carmichael's results do not demonstrate, and Carmichael himself never claimed that they did, that exercise of function can be omitted indefinitely without effects. When Matthews & Detwiler (1926) left salamander tadpoles immersed in a chloretone solution for 13 days or more, the swimming schema was permanently impaired when the tadpoles were returned to tap-water. Moreover, although Carmichael (1927) obtained the same results using the tadpoles of the frog as he got with the salamander, Fromme (1941) found that immobilizing the tadpoles of one species of frog (*Rana pipiens*) resulted in a quantitative deficit in the swimming ability of the tadpoles, as compared with that of a control group, which increased with the length of time that the tadpoles remained in chloretone.

Cruze (1935, 1938), it will be recalled, found that preventing newly hatched chicks from pecking by keeping them in darkness for

up to five days had no permanent effect on the accuracy of the pecking response. On the other hand, allowing only such practice as the
chicks got in the test situation for a period of 20 days kept the chicks
at a low level of accuracy. The pecking pattern failed to develop.
Moreover, when Padilla (1935) kept chicks in darkness for a period
of eight days or longer, they did not, thereafter, learn to peck at all.
They would starve in the midst of plenty. Inasmuch as Kuo has
shown that the various components of the pecking response get much
exercise while the chick is undergoing embryonic and fetal development within the egg shell, one can see the studies of Cruze and of
Padilla as examples of preventing the exercise of a schema for varying
durations. Preventing exercise for short duration has little effect, but
preventing exercise for periods beyond a certain critical duration appears to destroy the schema.

Duration of the early experience is probably also a factor in determining the permanence of effects of enrichments of early experience.
Those studies of the effects of practice which yielded but temporary
advantage to the practiced children provided the occasions for special practice for only a matter of six or eight weeks (see Gesell &
Thompson, 1929; Hilgard, 1932, 1933). On the other hand, Myrtle
McGraw's (1935) evidence of more permanent effects came from
"training" Johnny for about 11 months on roller-skating. These various studies indicate that statements about the relationship between
opportunities for exercise of a schema and their effects on later behavior must take into account the factor of duration..

Schema and the evanescence of the effects of early practice. The
effects of practice proved highly temporary in many of those early
studies of the matter for at least one other reason. In the case of those
most-often-quoted studies of the effects of practice on stair-climbing
and tower-building by Gesell & Thompson (1929) and of buttoning,
cutting paper with scissors, etc., by Hilgard (1932, 1933), the added
practice experience was not only brief but the effects of the practice
were measured on the very skills practiced. Those children who got
no practice in these skills until a later age mastered the skills with
greater ease than those who got the earlier practice. While there are
probably a number of tricky and poorly understood relationships
involved, at least one point missed in those studies was the idea that
the effects of practice with one schema or skill can make it easier to
learn other quite different skills. More is involved here than traditional conceptions of the transfer of training. The point at issue is
Hebb's conception of primary learning and of Piaget's notion that
the early coordinations achieved in the circular reactions prepare the

way for later acquisitions or accommodations.[3] From this standpoint, it is likely that whatever the control twins or groups were doing in these studies while the experimental twins or groups were practicing these tasks made almost as much of a contribution to the development of the central processes required for mastery of the skills involved as did the practice on them. The conclusion typically drawn from these studies that the response repertoire unfolds automatically without exercise does not follow.

McGraw's studies of the marked effectiveness of giving training in swimming and roller-skating serve as corrective for this conclusion, and indicate that something in the nature of the schema practiced is important. As already discussed in Chapter 7, that something probably has to do with the capacity of the schema practiced to effect changes in the neural processes developing with the intrinsic mechanisms of the brain, and it probably also has something to do with the match between the schema practiced and the structure of the neural processes already available, but exactly what that something is needs yet to be clarified.

HEREDITY VERSUS ENVIRONMENT

Ever since Francis Galton (1883) pioneered with the use of twins to compare the relative influence of heredity and environment in the causation of various traits, efforts have been directed chiefly toward assessing the proportional importance of each. Thorndike (1905) attempted to answer this question with respect to intelligence in his classical application of correlational methods to the study of the differences in the intellectual achievement of twins. In 1913, moreover, he indicated that, while in one sense, nothing in human nature is due either to heredity or to environment, "in another sense, the most fundamental question of human education asks precisely that we assign separate shares in the causation of human behavior to man's original nature on the one hand and his environment on the other." Some 20 years later, Shuttleworth (1935a) saw the problem of selecting methods of improving the health, intelligence, and general

[3] In a sense, this is the point that G. Stanley Hall was making in his parable of the tadpole's tail. The point is that later developments (e.g., the appearance of legs) depend upon earlier developments (e.g., the appearance and disappearance of the tail). In Hall's recapitulation theory, however, each of these patterns was predetermined. In the sense of Hebb and Piaget, on the other hand, it is the opportunity for coping with certain types of circumstances early in development that determines the child's readiness to cope with quite different types of circumstances later. One must see organism-environment interaction in conjunction with the epigenesis of behavioral structures to understand this point.

welfare of mankind to be dependent upon an answer to this proportion question. In 1941, Woodworth echoed the same view in the
introduction to his critical survey of the studies of twins and foster
children. Very recently, Cattell (1958; Cattell, Stice, & Kristy, 1957)
and his collaborators have expressed this view again. Without doubt-
ing that both the genes and the series of encounters with the environment during development influence individual differences in tested
intelligence, one can have grave doubts about both the method by
which answers have been sought to this proportion question, about
the answerability of the question, and about the strategy of asking
this particular question.

SAMPLINGS OF THE TRADITIONAL VIEW. In a competent review of
the studies which have attempted to answer this proportion question,
Jane Loevinger (1943) has credited Fisher (1918) with introducing
the statistical model and technique for answering the proportion
question. Using the correlations between relatives (identical twins,
siblings, foster-children, etc.), he assumed additive Mendelian factors as the hereditary causes of the physical traits in which he happened to be interested, and he assumed that the effects of the environment would be added to the effects of heredity. Fisher, moreover, used the ratio of variances, now familiar as F, to assess the
proportional contributions. The proportion of variance attributable
to heredity, for instance, is the ratio of the variance contributed by
indicators of the hereditary factor to the variance in the trait concerned; here the trait is some measure of intelligence. Since the F-
ratio of the variance of the differences between pairs (of identical
twins, foster-children, etc.) in test-score or IQ to the variance for the
whole sample of paired individuals is equal to twice the complement
of the coefficient of correlation between the pairs [$V_d/V_{sample} =
2 (1 - r)$, where d refers to the pair differences, and r refers to the
correlation between the pairs], correlations can be used directly in
such analyses. In some instances, moreover, the square of the coefficient of correlation, which states the variance common to the correlated variables, has been used to assess the variance attributed to
the special factor the two have in common.

In one approach, which has yielded two of the most widely quoted
answers to the proportion question, Burks (1928) and Leahy (1935)
compared the correlations obtained from foster-children and from
biological children with various indicators of the inter-familial differences in the intellectual value of their homes. Using father's IQ,
mother's IQ, material advantages of the home, cultural advantages
of the home, and income (i.e., of foster parents for foster children,
and of biological parents for their children), Burks got multiple cor-

relations of + .42 for the foster children and + .61 for the biological children. She wrote, " . . . the *square* of this [former] multiple (.17) represents the variance of children in ordinary communities that is due to home environment." Squaring the latter coefficient, she got .37 as the proportion of the variance which "represents the combined effect of home environment and parental mental level . . ." This latter proportion leaves 63 per cent of the variance not accounted for. Inasmuch as only one-half of the chromosomes of each parent are present in a child, however, Burks inferred that the correlation between the IQ's of children and their parents would underestimate the true correlation between intelligence and heredity. She therefore considered that the major share of this residual variance would be due to genetic constitution, and so concluded that "close to 75 or 80 per cent of the IQ variance is due to innate and heritable causes." Leahy did not use multiple correlation, and the corresponding co-efficients that she obtained were + .23 (foster children with foster parents and homes) and + .53. The same procedure yields estimates of 5 per cent of variance in IQ attributable to environment and over 90 per cent to heredity.

In a second approach, Wright (1921a, 1921b, 1923) devised the method of "path coefficients" for this same purpose. His approach assumed that the variance in an effect variable is equal to the weighted sum of the variances in a set of causal variables. From the correlations between the effect variable and measures of several related factors, he computed the weights that he called "path coefficients." The squares of these weights were then taken as the proportional contributions of the cause of the variance in the effect variable. After finding fault with Burks' (1928) analysis, Wright (1931) suggested as an alternative a procedure based on the fact that parents' intelligence is a variable correlated with the other variables in Burks' biological families but uncorrelated with heredity in the foster group. Using the two sets of correlations between child IQ and parent IQ to solve for the unknown correlations with the postulated "heredity factor," Wright developed "path coefficients" from which he concluded that home environment contributed approximately only 9 per cent of the variance in IQ, and he assumed that the residual 91 per cent should be attributed to error and to heredity, with error getting but a very minor share.

In a third widely quoted approach, Newman, Freeman, & Holzinger (1937) explicitly limited their answer to the proportion question to fraternal twins reared together. Because the gene patterns of identical twins are identical, they assumed that any differences between the pairs must be attributed to environment. In essence they developed from the formula relating variance to correlation a method of subtracting the variance of the differences attributable to environment, between pairs of identical twins, from the variance of the differences between fraternal twins, and then determining the proportion that the remaining variance of the differences between pairs of fraternal twins was of the total variance among their sample of fraternal twins. This was achieved in their formula for h^2 [$h^2 = (_ir - _fr) / (1 - _fr)$, where $_ir$ is the coefficient of correlation between identical twins, and where $_fr$ is the correlation between fraternal twins]. For their sample, the proportions of variance thus attributed to heredity in fraternal twins reared together ranged from .65 for Binet mental age to .80 for Otis IQ.

From such types of evidence come the commonly quoted statement that 80 per cent of the variance in tested intelligence can be attributed to heredity, only 20 per cent to the environment.

Recently efforts have been made to refine the analysis-of-variance model for answering the proportion question. Cattell (1953, 1958) designates four sources of individual differences: (1) between-family environmental differences, (2) between-family hereditary differences, (3) within-family environmental differences, and (4) within-family hereditary differences. He contends that it is these variances and their interactions that need to be taken into account in the predictions that the clinician and the educator must make.

EXISTING CONDITIONS VERSUS POTENTIAL CONDITIONS AND THE PROPORTION QUESTION. So long as the goal is obtaining a general answer to the proportion question, efforts to refine the statistical model are irrelevant to the contention that various classes of hereditary and environmental variance are what need to be taken into account by the clinician and the educator. There is no general answer to the proportion question, and any educational or welfare policies formed on the basis of any given answer purporting to be general are likely to have unhappy consequences.

Although such geneticists as Hogben (1933) and Haldane (1938) and such investigators of the genetic factor in human intelligence as Schwesinger (1933) and Newman, Freeman, & Holzinger (1937) have warned against seeking a general answer to the proportion question, the effort to find one seems never to die, and those answers available get implications attributed to them which they do not have. Although Woodworth (1941) made several still highly pertinent and useful suggestions for future research on the roles of heredity and environment, he, for instance, also included among the conclusions of his review of attempts to answer the proportion question from the studies of twins and foster children the statement that "not over a fifth, apparently, of the variance of intelligence in the general population can be attributed to differences in homes and neighborhoods acting as environmental factors" (p. 85). Following the assumptions underlying the sort of contentions about what needs to be taken into account by clinicians and educators attributed above to Cattell, this statement has been used to justify the estimate that no matter what might be done in the way of manipulating a child's encounters with the environment during the course of his development, one could not expect to modify his IQ appreciably, and certainly not by more than about 20 per cent of the variance in IQ to be found in the population. The available data provide no justification for such an estimate. Leaving aside the appropriateness of the analysis-of-variance model, so long as samplings are based on any given set of existing conditions, the answer to the proportion question obtained from them says nothing about what answer might be obtained from another set of conditions.

Inferring from existing answers to the proportion question to clinical or educational policy assumes that samples of the existing variation in the conditions of heredity and environment are statistically representative. They are probably not representative for heredity, and they definitely cannot be representative for the environment. The fact is that between-family and within-family variations in environment within the full range of the social classes in the culture of America constitute but a small part of the variation that has existed historically on the face of this earth. Moreover, if the assumptions that intelligence is largely fixed and that development is largely predetermined are discarded, and if behavior scientists devote themselves to the task of manipulating the encounters of children with their environments to maximize their potential for happy intellectual growth, who knows what the limits are? It is inconceivable that they are to be fixed by any given set of existing conditions.

In order to simplify this point, consider the potentialities for variance in Binet IQ attributable to environmental conditions in the case of identical twins, where heredity is held constant. From the work of Newman, Freeman, & Holzinger (1937), one finds the correlation between the IQ's of identical twins reared together to be +.88. According to the formula for relating variance ratio to correlation presented above, the proportion of variance attributable to environment would be 24 per cent [i.e., 2 (1 − .88)]. From the same study, when the IQ's of identical twins reared apart were correlated, the resulting coefficient was +.67, and the variance attributable to environment became, by the same logic, 66 per cent. Now, suppose that one obtains a sample of identical twins in which one of each pair is reared in a family while the other is reared in an orphanage like the one Dennis (1960) found in Teheran, what will the proportion attributable to environment become? Any answer would be pure conjecture, but it could be expected to drop further. If the interaction between heredity and environment, a factor assumed to be omitted by the analysis-of-variance model, is not great across such a contrast in environments, considerable correlation might continue to be evident, and the main evidence of effect might show in the difference between the pairs. But if the interaction is considerable, the correlation between the pairs would drop considerably. Now again, suppose that one obtains yet another sample of identical twins in which one is reared in such an orphanage while the other is given an enriched program of encounters with the environment such as McGraw (1935) arranged for her trained twin, Johnny. What will the correlation between the IQ's of these twins be?

It is obvious from such considerations that the answer to the proportion question depends upon the environmental conditions sampled, and that the potential range of variation in environmental conditions is limited only by the inventive genius of behavior scientists. Since such genius grows as it feeds upon the results of its efforts, the potential range is not specifiable. On these grounds alone, there is thus no general answer to the proportion question.

It is obvious also from such considerations that any policies concerning division of effort in the clinic or the classroom based on the commonly quoted answer of a 20/80 percentage split between environment and heredity would be quite wrong. Even if the figure has the meaning for the general population that Woodworth (1941) attributed to it, this does not mean that intellectual development is predetermined by the genes, but rather, given the existing culture of the subjects used in the studies of twins and foster children, children's encounters with the environment during their development is sufficiently similar in its growth-evoking capacity to yield this figure. On the side of reducing the variation of stimulation, it is clear from Dennis' (1960) observations of children in the orphanage in Teheran that the appearance of the walking schema can be delayed by at least from age two to age four, a DQ shift of 50 points. On the side of manipulating children's encounters with the environment from birth on to maximize intellectual growth, who knows what might be done? Various bits of evidence reviewed here indicate that substantial increases in intelligence as now measured may be possible. The important question for educational policy, the important question for the welfare of man now living in technological cultures that demand a higher and higher proportion of people with high capacity for the manipulation of symbols in problem-solving, is to determine what the potential for increasing intellectual capacity may be. Answers to the proportion question based on an analysis of the variance within any sampling from the status quo have no bearing on this potential.

CRITIQUE OF THE ANALYSIS-OF-VARIANCE MODEL. But answers to the proportion question based on the analysis of the variance in tested intelligence attributable to heredity and environment are suspect also on the grounds that the analysis-of-variance model fits the data from the heredity-environment relationship too poorly to permit a meaningful answer. As Fisher (1918) constructed it, and as Dunlap & Cureton (1930) have pointed out, this model is based on the principle that the variances from heredity and environment are additive and without interaction. As Loevinger (1943) has put it, "this principle states that *if* the score on the dependent variable is the sum of scores on a set of independent variables, then the variance on the dependent variable is the sum of variances on the set of independent variables." How well does this principle fit what is known from various other sources about the operation of heredity and environment? Loevinger (1943) has answered this question, and the present writer believes correctly, by saying "that (1) the additive assumption concerning the causation of intelligence is ambiguous in meaning, (2) is not supported by the known evidence, and (3) leads to no results capable of verification" (p. 746).[4]

The additive assumption is ambiguous in meaning, first, because neither heredity nor environment operates directly on behavior, and certainly not directly in the terms of the various scales by means of which they are assessed; and second, because it is unlikely that intelligence, heredity, or environment are properly regarded even as scales, not to say scales based upon family income, the vocabularies of father and mother, the Whittier scale, etc.

The genes must operate indirectly through a chain of mechanisms. Beadle (1945) has assembled evidence that appears to indicate that each of the various genes controls a biochemical step in metabolism. How many steps there may be in the chain of influence between biochemical steps in metabolism and mental age or the IQ no one knows. Even in the case of maximal directness, as in the case of

[4] It should be noted that this critique of the model does not condemn it for use as a method of testing the statistical significance of variance attributable to specific variations of either hereditary or environmental influences. Neither does it condemn its use as a way of estimating the relative proportions of the total variance in a given set of intelligence measures that can be attributed to specific variations of hereditary and environmental influences.

phenylpyruvenic feeblemindedness (Jervis, 1939) where the gene concerned blocks the conversion of phenylaline to tyrosine so that it accumulates and is excreted in the urine, the remaining steps in the chain of influence are only partially clarified. The maze-brightness of Tryon's (1940) selectively bred rats appears to be based on cue-preferences (Krechevsky, 1933) and on emotionality (Searle, 1949), but how many links may exist in the chains of influence between these behavioral bases and the metabolic actions of various genes is not even a topic for responsible speculation. The IQ may have a genetic basis in something akin to Hebb's concept of the A/S ratio and also in something like the ease with which cerebral systems are modified by experience, because certain low-grade feebleminded human beings do not acquire learning sets much more readily than rats (House & Zeaman, 1949). But each of these hypothetical factors might be expected to go through an indirect chain of causal links of unknown number. It is commonly assumed that the influence of the genes through these many links will randomize after the fashion of the normal curve of probability, but how this justifies the additive assumption in the analysis-of-variance model is unclear.

The environment also operates indirectly in forcing accommodations at the early stage of development in schemata which have little that is obviously in common with the performances tested. Considerable space was taken in Chapter 7 to discuss the problem of matching a child's schemata with the environment that he encounters at each stage to maximize the rate of the child's intellectual development. Until this problem is solved, it is impossible even to rank environments meaningfully in terms of their capacity to foster intellectual growth. Moreover, Fuller & Scott (1954) have shown that one class of environmental encounters, wherein a standard is enforced, serves to reduce variance among either individuals or strains. Another class wherein each individual moves to a new level as soon as he has acquired the old one, serves to expand individual differences. Just how two such disparate programs of environmental influence can be meaningfully put onto the same interval continuum is unclear. Furthermore, what relationship the effective encounters that children have with their environments may have to do with such matters as family income, father's vocabulary, mother's vocabulary, and scores on the Whittier scale for home grading it is impossible to specify.

In sum, to say that the additive assumption is ambiguous when applied to the influence of heredity and environment on the development of intelligence constitutes an understatement of large degree.

The absence of interaction between heredity and environment implied by the additive assumption is not supported by the available evidence. Absence of interaction would mean that any given heredity would have the same force in the production of the IQ regardless of the kind of environment, and vice versa. Ever since Johannsen (1903, 1909), whom geneticists rank with Mendel as a progenitor of the science of genetics, did the classic work that led to the distinction between the *genotype* (referring to the constellation of genes in the organism) and the *phenotype* (referring to the organism's observable characteristics at any given time), evidences of interaction between the genotype and the organism's encounters with the environment have been accumulating. Hogben (1939), for instance, cites the experiment of Krafka on the fruitfly (*Drosophila*) showing that the curve which expresses the dependence of the number of eye-facets on the temperature at which the larvae are raised varies with the genotype. Thus, while increasing the temperature tends to reduce the number of facets, the reduction that occurs over temperatures ranging from 16° to 25° C. is about five times as great in one genotype as in another. In another instance, Sinnot, Dunn, & Dobzhansky (1958) cite Rappoport's discovery that when the larvae of typical brown vinegar flies (*Drosophila melanogaster*) are fed food containing silver salts, they develop into yellow flies which cannot be distinguished from a yellow mutant found by Morgan in 1910. When Morgan's yellow mutants are raised on food containing silver salts, they also become yellow flies anyway.

Even such a fundamental characteristic as sex can be altered by the conditions under which development occurs. At the University of Illinois, William Horsfall (see Horsfall & Anderson, 1961) has got phenotypic female mosquitoes from genotypic male larvae by exposing them continually to a temperature of 29° C. This transformation occurs in *Aedes stimulans*, a snow-pool mosquito common to northern latitudes. In temperatures up to 24° C, the larvae of genotypic males develop antennae, palpi, mouth parts, external genitalia, accessory glands, seminal vesicles, vasa deferentia, and testes that are normal in appearance and function. When the larvae of genotypic males are reared in a temperature of 29° C, they become like females in all respects except for slight differences in palpi. Internally, these genotypic males that have developed into phenotypic females have ovaries, oviducts, and spermathecae, and they lack testes, vasa deferentia, seminal vesicles, and bilobed accessory glands. Their ovaries have globular egg chambers indistinguishable from those of young genotypic females. Moreover, the fact that eggs have been observed in the process of development suggests that these genotypic male but phenotypic female parts may be functionally as well as morphologically transformed. Abnormally high temperatures have no effect on the development of genotypic females, and the degree of effect upon genotypic males is a function of the duration of exposure. Neither do such temperatures affect the genotypic males of species of mosquitoes that ordinarily develop in higher temperatures. Clearly, interaction between genotype and environment has been demonstrated in the case of a variety of characteristics, and even including such a fundamental one as sex.

In the case of intelligence, several of those who have used the statistical procedures based on the additive assumption have also argued, and inconsistently, that the influence of the environment may vary with the individual's genetic endowment. In this inconsistency, the argument appears to be more correct than the choice of statistical procedure, for wherever children are given an opportunity to proceed at their own speed in learning such a subject as mathematics, where each step builds upon earlier acquisitions, individual differences in achievement increase. Such has been the experience in the project of the University of Illinois Committee on School Mathematics.[5] In such an environment, those who lag soon drop out with feelings of failure. Contrariwise, when teaching proceeds by lock step, the bright may get bored, lose out from lack of motivation, and then get the feeling that they do not like and cannot do mathematics. This is a matter of the match between environmental encounters and central structures discussed in Chapter 7. Inasmuch as such interaction between genotypes and environments in the production of phenotypes appears more likely to be the rule than absence of such interaction, it follows that there is an indefinite number of answers to the proportion question, and therefore, no answer.

Paradoxically, the way in which to maximize the role of heredity in the IQ would not be to standardize the environment; it would be to individualize the encounters that each child has with his environment in such a fashion as to maximize his potential for growth.

---

[5] This program is under the direction of Professor Max Beberman. Even though the students in the program have been selected for both high academic ability and high academic interest, some have soon so outdistanced others that it has been necessary to divide the classes. Failure to divide groups on the basis of achievement sufficiently early traumatizes some with the feeling that they cannot do mathematics, and they give up, while the program fails to maintain the challenge of the subject-matter for others. The ablest achieve rapidly. One group of seven students has got ready for a rigorous course in calculus by the end of their junior year. Since most of these students have already done the seventh and eighth grades in one year, they are still but 15 years old. Thus, as 16-year-old high school seniors they will be doing the level of mathematics that college students usually get to only when they are college juniors of 20.

The resulting variation in children's intelligence would then be completely a function of their genotypes. As already seen, it would tend to increase individual differences.

The verification of any proposition purporting to state generally the contribution of heredity or environment to the IQ demands, as Loevinger (1943) has pointed out, that it be possible to replicate the effective conditions of both heredity and environment. Replication, she notes, would mean that any two persons of a given age with heredity of, say, .7 standard deviations above the mean and environment of, say, 1.2 standard deviations above the mean would be alike not only in heredity but in environment and in interaction between the two. But since the indicators of heredity and environment now used say so little about what elsewhere are conceived to be the effective aspects of either heredity, the constellation of genes, or environment, the child's encounters with the circumstances of his life in the course of development, it becomes impossible to replicate the effective conditions.

In sum, in spite of the recent efforts to improve the analysis-of-variance model, using it to get a general answer to the question about the proportions of variance in intelligence caused by heredity and environment is about like using a bulldozer to study the details of the topography of an area. Or, when one considers the matter of making policy decisions concerning education, child-rearing, and clinical work from such general answers, perhaps it is worse. Perhaps using the model for a general answer is more like attempting to ascertain the ideal topography of an area by going over the existing details with a bulldozer while giving no thought to what those details might become.

MORE APPROPRIATE QUESTIONS. It appears that Thorndike's (1913) question about the proportionate shares of heredity and environment in the causation of intelligence is an unfortunate one. A more sensible strategy is to ask specific questions which are of significance either for programs of education, child-rearing, and human welfare in general, or for specific issues in the theory of human development and human nature.

To questions significant for educational planning and human welfare belongs the one about how much the intelligence of the feeble-minded children can be elevated by such special programs of environmental encounters as come in nursery-school experience. Kirk (1958) has asked this question and obtained one answer in a carefully conducted study. This one answer, of course, is a function of the particular nursery-school experiences supplied. Some 81 retarded children, aged between three and six and with IQ's between 45 and

80, were identified and studied over a period of years. A group of 28 attended a special nursery-school in the community and were followed up with tests and observations from three to five years after leaving school. A second group of 15 children, all of whom had been committed earlier to an institution for mental defectives, were enrolled in an institutional nursery-school, and these were followed up after discharge from the school either to the institutional primary school or to the community. A third group of 26 children, similar in age, IQ, and social status to those in the community group, remained in their community environments without attending nursery school. A fourth group of 12 children, already committed to a second institution for mental defectives, remained in their institutional environment without attending nursery-school. Both of these latter two groups were tested at the same intervals as were those children who got the special nursery schooling, and they were also followed up after they entered primary schools at the age of six. The evidence was processed both as case studies of the various experimental children and in terms of statistical comparisons of the two groups that got nursery schooling with the two contrast-groups that got none. The over-all effects of the nursery schooling on these retarded children were positive. Of the 43 retarded children who received the nursery-school experience 30 (70 per cent) showed an acceleration in rates of intellectual growth ranging from 10 to 30 points in IQ. The over-all average increase in IQ for the experimental groups was greater than that for the contrast groups ($p < .05$). Moreover, and this is an important item, the children retained the accelerated rates of growth established during the nursery-school experience during the follow-up period of from three to five years. Such findings indicate that society would not be wasting its time to supply nursery-school experience for retarded youngsters of the pre-school age. For instance, six of the 15 children in the institutional nursery-school gained enough to permit them to be placed in foster homes in the community with apparently good adjustments, whereas not one of the 12 contrast children could be placed. Inasmuch as the United States Public Health Service has estimated that committing a child to an institution for the retarded at an early age and keeping him there for life costs the state approximately $50,000, an institution could apparently save a state money simply by employing one nursery-school teacher for each five such children, even if only one instead of two out of five were placed after nursery-school experience of two or three years.[6]

[6] The matter of weighing ability against cost can be applied more broadly. Graffam (1949) has made an interesting study in which he has compared the mean scores of large random samples of 18-year-old Navy recruits from the Northeastern, Western,

But this experiment also has some theoretical significance. It adds, for instance, another item of evidence against the notion that rates of growth are irrevocably fixed by inheritance or by the conditions of the organism at the time of testing. On the other hand, 30 per cent of the children failed to gain from the nursery-school experience. Would other approaches in nursery-school affect them? How are they limited?

Especially important for both educational practice and theory of human development and nature are questions, as Anastasi (1958b) has pointed out, about *how* both the genotype and the environment operate to produce such phenotypical characteristics as intelligence. At the present stage of behavior science in this area, strategy still concerns what kinds of factors make a difference. Thus, on the environmental side, it is important that Pasamanick, Knobloch, & Lilienfeld (1956) have found that various deficiencies of maternal diet associated with socioeconomic level can produce complications of both pregnancy and parturition which result in intellectual retardation and behavioral disorders in offspring. It is important that Harrell, Woodyard, & Gates (1955) have found evidence that supplements for maternal nutrition in women whose diets were known to be deficient resulted in significantly higher IQ's in their offspring at ages three and four than were found in the offspring of control mothers not given the supplement. It is important that Milner (1951) has found reading readiness in the first grade to be a function of opportunities for verbalization at home. On the genetic side, it is important that Jervis (1939) has traced some of the mechanisms whereby the gene that controls the enzyme which disposes of phenylpyruvic acid in cerebral metabolism causes feeblemindedness. It is important to look for the kinds of genetic factors that indirectly, as Dobzhansky (1950) puts it, set the "norm" or, in the terminology of psychological statistics, the "range of variation" within which environmental circumstances determine the eventual outcome. Hebb's A/S ratio may be one of these factors. Another may reside in biochemical conditions which limit the readiness with which cerebral firing-systems can be established and modified.

Much of the evidence reviewed in this work is concerned with showing that experience, and especially early experience, is of importance. In spite of all the information psychologists have gathered about learning, much of the conceptualizing is unfruitful, and so

Middle Western, and Southern regions of the U. S. on the Navy's classification tests, with emphasis on tests of reading, arithmetic reasoning, and spelling. The mean performance for each region appears to be a function of educational opportunity as indicated by the amount of money spent per child for education.

much remains to be learned about how encounters with the environment influence the rate of development that one can say only that beginnings of essential knowledge are available.

In asking *how* experience influences development, moreover, knowledge of *how much* comes inevitably, because amounts of change in such variables as tested intelligence or the age at which landmarks of intellectual development appear become the criteria by which answers to the question of *how* are to be recognized. For instance, Dennis' (1960) finding that the conditions of development prevailing in a Teheran orphanage increase the age at which nearly all children learn to walk from a little less than two years to more than four years, a reduction in DQ of over 50 points, does not by itself say *how* the orphanage experience works, but a hint comes from the fact that Dennis & Dennis (1940) found no delay in the age at which the walking-schema appeared in Hopi children reared for the first year on cradle boards, even though the boards greatly hampered their use of their legs. It should be noted, in connection with the question *how*, that these Hopi children got a rich variety of visual and auditory experience while being carried about on the backs of their mothers. One may hypothesize, for the purpose of future testing, that it is relatively unimportant that the firing-systems established in those regions of the brain not immediately involved with either receptor inputs or motor outputs be based on use of legs. Hebb (1949) may be essentially correct in his emphasis on perceptual experience in primary learning. On the other hand, he may be missing the fact that both looking and listening involve motor outputs as well as receptor inputs, i.e., the fact that they are, as Piaget (1936) calls them, sensorimotor schemata. Perhaps it is true, nevertheless, that the visual and auditory schemata are of essential importance during the early months while the use of the limbs is not. Perhaps it is only later after these early cerebral firing-systems have been established and such schemata as walking are already established that motor activities become important for future development. But this is not the place to go into detail. The point to be made here concerns the fact that it is by determining *how much* rates of growth and the ages at which various behavioral landmarks appear are displaced by various programs of encounters with the environment that one learns *how* experience operates. Such questions, emerging from the view of development as continuous organism-environment interaction, are markedly different from the traditional proportion question, and they promise to be much more fruitful. The answers should supply the basis for an educational psychology of infancy which should bring the race to a new level of adaptability.

DIFFERENTIAL FERTILITY AND INTELLIGENCE

The problem of the effect of differential fertility on the future intelligence of the race also takes on new perspective when examined in the light of intelligence conceived as central oprations for the processing of information which are developed in the course of children's encounters with their environments. Ever since the seventeenth century, it has been evident that those of the lower socioeconomic classes have larger families than those of the upper classes and thereby contribute more than their share of the next generation (United Nations, 1953, 1955). Because the IQ's of day laborers average approximately 20 points below the IQ's of professional people (see Anastasi, 1958a, p. 515), it has been common to see this fact of differential fertility as evidence that humanity is drifting down hill intellectually. More recently, evidence of such a drift that has been interpreted to be absolutely direct has appeared in the repeated reports from various American and European countries of a negative correlation between the numbers of children in families and their tested intelligence.[7] Anastasi (1956) has reviewed these studies and noted that the correlations reported are typically of the order of −.3. When Cattell (1937) multiplied the number of people at each level by the reproduction rate at that level and computed the new mean as an estimate of the IQ of the next generation, a procedure which assumes perfect correlation between the IQ's of parents and children, he got an expected drop of a little over three points a generation, or about one point a decade. This he characterized as a "galloping plunge toward intellectual bankruptcy," and he issued a clarion call for corrective action to preserve the intelligence of the population of the United Kingdom.

With negative correlations of the order of only −.3 (9 per cent of variance common), one must assume both that intelligence is essentially fixed and predetermined and that the tests measure this predetermined trait in almost pure fashion in order to see such dire consequences. From an empirical standpoint, how accurate are these predictions in terms of the evidence that is available? From a theoretical standpoint, what other interpretations can be made of this negative correlation between number of siblings and IQ?

PREDICTION DISCONFIRMED BY THE RISING IQ. The available longitudinal studies of tested intelligence in various populations have

[7] See Burks & Jones (1935), Burt (1946), Carter (1953), Cattell (1937), Chapman & Wiggins (1925), Eydt (1938), Gille, Henry *et al.* (1954), Heinen (1938), Lentz (1927), Moshinsky (1939), O'Hanlon (1940), Papavassiliou (1954), Roberts (1941), Sutherland & Thompson (1926), Thomson *et al.* (1949, 1953), and Willoughby (1928).

typically found small but statistically significant increases in average IQ instead of the drops predicted from differential fertility and from the negative correlation between family size and intelligence.

Perhaps the most outstanding studies of this kind are the Scottish Surveys conducted by Thomson *et al.* (1933, 1949, 1953) of the Scottish Council for Research in Education. In 1932, nearly all 11-year-old children in Scotland got a group test of intelligence. Again in 1947, an attempt was made to reach all Scottish children who were then aged 11. The two samples numbered 87,498 and 70,805 children, respectively, and because of the national drop in birth rate, they represented 87 and 88 per cent of the estimated total number of 11-year-old children living in Scotland on the two separate occasions. These samples missed only those children whose sensory or motor handicaps were considered to preclude valid testing, those children who happened to be absent on the day of testing, and those few children attending private schools for whom the required background data were absent. The same group-test was administered on both occasions. The Stanford-Binet was also given individually to smaller random samples of these children, Terman's 1916 revision in 1932 and Form L of the 1937 revision in 1947. Contrary to the expected drop in intelligence over this 15-year period, the children in the 1947 sample showed a gain in mean IQ of 2.28 points, and from a statistical standpoint, this gain was highly significant.

Thirteen years following his prediction of "a galloping plunge toward intellectual bankruptcy," Cattell (1950) himself published a study comparing the 10-year-old children living in the city of Leicester in 1949 with the 10-year-olds living in that city in 1936. In place of the predicted drop by something slightly more than one point in mean IQ, Cattell actually found an increase of 1.28 points which, although small, was highly significant from a statistical standpoint. This upward shift occurred, moreover, with a non-verbal, supposedly culture-free test which was given to both samples by the same examiner.

Other investigators, using longitudinal samples from settings in which cultural and educational opportunities had presumably improved considerably have found gains in mean IQ of considerably larger magnitude. Smith (1942) compared the scores of children in the various schools of Honolulu in 1924 with the scores of children in those same schools of Honolulu in 1938. He made a serious effort to obtain scores for all the public-school children in the schools between the ages of 10 and 15. The scores from the various school-samples of 1938 averaged substantially higher than did those from the school-samples of 1924 in both verbal and non-verbal tests. Inasmuch as immigration to Hawaii from the Orient had been highly limited by law following 1924, it might have been expected that the bigger gain would occur for the Oriental groups in the verbal tests, but this was not the case. The largest gains were found in the non-verbal tests. In these, the mean mental age for the 10-year-olds of 1938 exceeded the mean mental age for the 12-year-olds of the 1924 sampling. This gain is roughly equivalent to 20 points of IQ instead of a loss of 1.5.

In this connection, the apparent effects of the changes in cultural and educational opportunities promoted by the Tennessee Valley Authority in the relatively isolated mountain regions of eastern Tennessee are especially interesting. When Wheeler (1942) compared the tested intelligence of a sample of children got before these developments with a sample 10 years later chosen to be closely comparable and coming from the same families, he found the median IQ of the later sample to be 10 points higher than that of the earlier. This is a gain of the order of 10 times as great as the decrease that Cattell (1937) predicted for a decade.

The ordinary increase in cultural and educational opportunities in America appear also to be associated with substantial increases, rather than decreases, in tested intelligence. Finch (1946) has compared the tested intelligence of all the students in a sample of high schools in the 1920's with the tested intelligence of all the students in those same high schools in the 1940's, and found average increases of the order of 10 to 15 points of IQ. Moreover, since a larger portion of the total population was attending high school at the end than at the beginning of this 20-year period, a decrease in mean score would be expected unless the total population had improved sufficiently to counteract such a drop.

Tuddenham (1948) has compared a representative sample of draftees from World War II with a sample of draftees from World War I on comparable revisions of the Army Alpha Group Test. The shift upward in score is substantial. The median for the sample of draftees from World War II falls at the 82nd percentile for the sample of draftees of World War I. This means that somewhat over half of the World War II population belongs in the upper fifth of the World War I population, if the samples are truly representative of the population at the two periods. Clearly these empirical results from longitudinal studies of tested intelligence in various populations fail to confirm the predicted "gallop to intellectual bankruptcy."

A GENETICIST'S VIEW. On the theoretical side, various geneticists have failed to see the dire consequences of differential fertility that psychometric psychologists, who have been especially prone to see intelligence as fixed, have tended to see. Penrose (1948, 1950a,

1950b), for instance, has questioned whether either differential fertility or the negative correlation between intelligence and num-ber of siblings means that the intellectual ability of Western man is drifting down hill. Inasmuch as mating is typically assortative with respect to intelligence, inasmuch as mental defectives seldom re-produce, and inasmuch as those of borderline intelligence tend to beget children of about average intelligence, he reasoned that the intellectual level of the population would remain about constant despite the existence of differential fertility.

EXPLANATIONS OF THE DISCONFIRMATION OF THE PREDICTED DROP. Those who predicted a decline in the tested intelligence of succes-sive generations because of differential fertility and the negative correlation between family size and intelligence have turned gen-erally to two explanations of the actual rises found. One of these ex-planations attributes the rise to an increase in test-taking sophistica-tion. This hypothesis assumes that the behavioral changes found are restricted to test-performance and do not generalize to criterion abilities, but the criterion validity of intelligence tests has shown no appreciable decline. The intelligence tests, and the aptitude tests derived from them, still correlate better with criterion abilities than do any others. Notwithstanding the complaints of collegiate educa-tors to the contrary, the academic and information-processing skills appear to be at a higher level in the population today than ever before. Moreover, when Thomson *et al.* (1953) examined the scores of the children in their Scottish Surveys, the scores of those with some test-taking experience were not higher than those without it.

Cattell (1950) has given a second explanation which extends the same argument to say that the predicted fall in innate intelligence has actually occurred, but that this fall has been masked by an ad-vance in education and test-taking sophistication sufficient to pro-duce the observed rise in the IQ of about twice the magnitude of the actual genetic fall. He cites Finch's (1946) finding of intergenera-tional increases in the IQ's of high-school students between the 1920's and the 1940's as evidence that such improvements can occur. Such an argument, however, confuses the concept of geno-type with that of phenotype. As Anastasi (1956) points out, it is "analogous to arguing that the 'true, innate' height of the population has declined as a result of a negative correlation between height and family size, and that the observed rise in mean height is illusory. Moreover, it could then be argued that we should devise a 'culture-free' meter-stick to measure innate height freed of environmental in-fluences" (p. 199). Such arguments, and Cattell is not the only one to make them, appear to derive from complete faith in the assumption of fixed intelligence and from acceptance of such definitions of intelligence as that of Burt *et al.* (1934) that "by intelligence, the psychologists understands inborn, all-round intellectual ability. It is inherited, or at least innate, not due to teaching and training . . ." When the definition of the phenotype includes the genotype, the very confusion that Johannsen (1909) attempted to obviate with the distinction between *genotype* and *phenotype* that he made half a century ago becomes inevitable. The aim of testing *innate intelligence,* moreover, confuses the inherent impossibility of getting high predictive validity for tests over long intervals of time because environmental encounters cannot be specified in advance, with a supposed lack of criterion validity which may be quite absent. Lack of the predictive validity does not imply lack of criterion validity.

THE ARGUMENT FOR REVERSING THE DIRECTION OF CAUSALITY. In the light of the conceptions of intelligence presented here, the direction of causality accounting for the negative correlation between number of siblings and tested intelligence may quite reasonably be reversed. Since time and energy are limited in the most nurturant of parents, the young infant in a family with several closely spaced siblings must inevitably get less parental contact and stimulation than the young infant in a family where it is the only child or one of two or three widely spaced children. If amount of adult contact and variety of stimulation are the factors that account for the slower rates of intellectual development found in orphanage children than in foster-home children, the same factors would be expected to operate to a lesser degree in families with large numbers of closely spaced children as operate in orphanages, and the lower tested intelligence found in large families would be expected from the experimental or environmental side rather than from the genetic side.

Several lines of evidence lend at least suggestive support to this hypothesis of a reversed direction of causation. First of all, it should be noted that this negative correlation between number of siblings and intelligence does not imply any correlation between the intelligence of parents and their children. In fact, various investigators have found that this negative correlation holds within all occupational groups of various levels except those at the very top economically where outside help in the care for the children can be afforded.[8] Moreover, when Willoughby & Coogan (1940) followed up 373 persons who had graduated from high school some 12 years earlier and for whom intelligence-test scores were available, they found no correlation between intelligence, as tested in high school,

[8] See Cattell (1937), Moshinsky (1939), Gille, Henry *et al.* (1954), Thomson *et al.* (1933).

and age at marriage, age at birth of first child, or number of children at the time of the survey. Again, Anastasi (1956) reports that West-off & Mishler, who have obtained data on the fertility of the 216 couples that E. Lowell Kelly studied during their engagement period in the 1930's, have found positive rather than negative correlations between the intelligence of these couples at the time they were engaged and the number of children they have had in the 20-odd interim years. Thus, the negative correlation between number of siblings and intelligence need not imply a negative correlation between parental intelligence and family size, and the existing evidence appears to indicate that no such correlation exists from the middle class up.

Second, if it is the lack of parental care associated with large families that accounts for that 9 per cent of the variance involved in the negative correlation of approximately +.3 between sib-number and intelligence, one would expect to find intelligence suffering in other categories of situation where individualized care and variety of stimulation might be expected to be at a reduced level. Having either twins or two children very close together would tend to limit the possibility of providing care and variety of stimulation during the early months just as effectively as having a large number of children well spaced. Just such appears to be the case. In the second Scottish Survey, Thomson et al. (1949) found that the tested intelligence in their 974 pairs of twins averaged about five points of IQ below that of the singletons in their large sample. In the comparable French survey, Gille, Henry et al. (1954) also found that the intelligence of their 750 pairs of twins averaged lower than that of singletons. When they carried the analysis further, they found that the twins suffered most in comparison with single children, and that the difference washes out in families with four or more children. Tabah & Sutter (1954) have compared the tested intelligence of children in families with only two widely separated in age with that of children in families with only two close together in age. Dividing these families at the median of the separation in age, they found the intelligence of the more widely separated pairs significantly higher than that of the less widely separated pairs. Moreover, the average intelligence of those less than a year and a half apart in age did not differ from the average intelligence of twins. Here the force of the reversal is especially strong, for from the point of view taken, these data may be seen to suggest further that environmental conditions during the early months of life, when maturation is most rapid, are especially important for future intellectual development. They even suggest further that the early deficit in experience is not readily made up by adolescence.

Third, Nisbet (1953) of Scotland has also offered the hypothesis that the negative correlation of intelligence with family size is a product of the relative lack of parental contact during the early months with children in large families, and he has analyzed three types of data from several thousand school children in Aberdeen. He found that the correlation between family size and verbal intelligence was reduced to —.04 when the correlation between verbal intelligence and language scores was partialled out. When number of siblings and language scores were correlated, with intelligence as measured by Raven's Progressive Matrices (a non-verbal test which is relatively independent of culture) partialled out, the resulting partial correlation was —.11, which for the larger sample used was significantly higher than the former correlation of —.04. Moreover, scores on verbal tests showed higher correlations with numbers of siblings than did scores from such non-verbal tests as Raven's Progressive Matrices. Finally, Nisbet found the correlation between tested intelligence and number of siblings rising with age in both cross-sectional samplings and in the longitudinal samplings of a small number of families. Such a finding might be taken to argue against attributing the fact that widely spaced doubletons show higher intelligence than closely spaced doubletons or twins to lack of stimulation during the early months. Yet it is hard to see how it would be particularly easier for parents to give more individualized attention to children widely spaced than narrowly spaced once they get older, unless it comes as a matter of habit in relationships established during the early months. It is quite as reasonable to assume that the comparative disadvantage established through lack of stimulation in infancy increases with age unless special corrective measures happen to occur or are arranged.

Although no final decision can be made between these two hypothetical directions of causality, a preponderant portion of the evidence appears to favor the hypothesis that the negative correlation between number of siblings and intelligence derives from the fact that children in larger families, especially those in which children are closely spaced, tend to get less adult care and varied stimulation during the early months than is got by children in smaller families, and especially those in which children are widely spaced. Again the conception of intelligence that has been developed from the various sources of evidence supplies the basis for a reinterpretation of another problem concerning intelligence.

SUMMARY AND CONCLUSION

The meaning of the old concepts and facts that have been interpreted to support the assumptions of fixed intelligence and predetermined development change in the light of the new conceptions of intelligence and the new evidence with respect to its development.

With respect to the assumption of fixed intelligence, it has been seen that the semantics of *dimension* and *scale* in the assessment of intelligence tend to lead to an over-generalization of the conceptual habit of seeing dimensions and scaled characteristics as fixed attributes of static objects so that dimensionalized intelligence and scaled traits tend also to be seen as fixed characteristics of persons and organisms. Because persons and organisms are open systems in which change will occur as a function of unspecifiable future conditions, such transfer is unwarranted, and it probably constitutes one of the spurious semantic supports for the assumption of fixed intelligence. The alternative semantics of *sampling behavior for evidences of such organizational structures as schemata, operations, and concepts* have been seen to fit the actual procedures even of traditional intelligence-testing better than do the semantics of *dimension* and *scale*. Moreover, it has been argued that the semantics of sampling for evidences of such organizational structures also fit the facts of the predictive and the criterion validity of intelligence-test scores and also the facts of the inconstancy of the IQ early in life, when epigenesis is rapid, and the relative constancy of the IQ after epigenesis slows down and after schooling tends to introduce a relatively standard program of encounters with the environment.

With respect to the assumption of predetermined development, the finding that development of the swimming schema is independent of practice in swimming in the tadpoles of salamanders and frogs need not apply to the development of the central processes that mediate intelligent behavior in higher organisms. This lack of application results both from the fact that the swimming schema is one which requires little in the way of autonomous central processes and from the fact that the A/S ratio for the brains of salamanders and frogs is about minimal. Against the conclusion from Coghill's work that behavior unfolds automatically with anatomic maturation are not only these theoretical considerations but also the observations of Kuo on the development of behavior in the embryos of chickens. Kuo's work shows quite clearly that organism-environment interaction in the control of development extends back into the early embryonic phase of development. Against the early evidence that infantile deprivations and enrichments of experience have only very evanescent effects is the fact that when the duration of such experiences has been increased, the effects show considerable permanence. Also against the conclusion from the evanescent effects of infantile practice in the early studies is the consideration that the practice and their effects concerned the same performance. The investigators missed what is now a basic consideration in "primary learning," namely, that the everyday experiences of their nonpracticed subjects may have had as much influence on the development of the central processes mediating the skills measured as did practice on those skills.

The question concerning the variance in IQ attributable to heredity and environment has been seen to have no general answer. First, there is no general answer because each answer obtained by way of analysis of the variance in the IQ for any given sample of individuals involves only an existing range of hereditary and environmental conditions. No such sample can be considered representative of all conditions so long as anyone is capable of inventing a new program of environmental encounters for children during their development. Second, there is no general answer because genotype and environment interact. Third, the answers available from the analysis-of-variance model are meaningless because this model fails to fit what is known about the interactive operation of heredity and environment in the course of development. Since no general answer can be got, and since the model upon which the commonly quoted answers are based is inappropriate, educational and child-rearing policies decided on the basis of the obtained answers are almost certain to be wrong. Differential fertility across the social-class structure has been reinterpreted to appear less dire in its consequences, at least for intelligence, than has been contended. In fact, the negative correlation between family size and intelligence, which has commonly been interpreted to be the most direct evidence of "the galloping plunge toward intellectual bankruptcy," is probably more reasonably interpreted to be an environmental consequence based on the fact that infants in large and closely spaced families cannot get the same variety of stimulation that comes from individualized attention from adults as can infants in a small, widely spaced family unless there is the wealth with which to pay for nursemaids.

In view of the technological developments in Western culture during the past half century, which demand that a higher and higher proportion of the population have a high level of ability to manipulate symbols in the solution of problems, probably the most unfortunate consequences of the assumptions of fixed intelligence and genetically predetermined development lie, first, in the encouragement they have given to the policy of leaving infants essentially alone during their early months so that they can grow undisturbed by excessive stimulation, and second, in the discouragement they have given to the investigation of the effects of various programs of child-environment interaction during the full course of development from birth to maturity.

It is fairly clear from the evidence surveyed in these chapters that impoverishments of experience during the early months can slow up the development of intelligence. In terms of the traditional measurement of intelligence, this means reducing the IQ. Various bits of the evidence have strongly suggested that such slowed development is permanent, that it may result not only in a permanently reduced IQ but in a failure of the basic criterion capacities of individuals to develop to the degree that they might have developed under other, more varied programs of encounters with the environment which were appropriately matched to the intellectual structures developing within the child. But much remains to be learned about the degree of permanence in such failures to develop and about the conditions under which these failures to develop become permanent.

But there is also a positive side to the picture. It is highly unlikely than any society has developed a system of child-rearing and education that maximizes the potential of the individuals which compose it. Probably no individual has ever lived whose full potential for happy intellectual interest and growth has been achieved. Various bits of the evidence reviewed hint that if the manner in which encounters with the environment foster the development of intellectual interest and capacity were more fully understood, it might be possible to increase the average level of intelligence within the population substantially. In view of the interaction between genotype and environment, it would be probable that individual differences would be increased, and that the biggest gains would occur in those genotypes with the highest hypothetical potential. There would be, of course, a long step between learning how to effect changes in child-rearing and getting them adopted by the culture, but learning how is the first step. The hope of increasing the average level of intelligence by proper manipulation of children's developmental encounters with their environments, a hope which becomes reasonable with the evidences surveyed here and with relinquishing the assumptions of fixed intelligence and predetermined development, provides a challenge of the first order. It has great implications for human welfare as the growth of technology in Western cultures demands a higher and higher percentage of people who can manipulate symbols and solve complex problems. In this challenge the theory of man's nature and the fate of his welfare are obviously intertwined.

CHAPTER 9

Recapitulation and Conclusion

Intelligence has been a topic of central concern for those seeking to understand human nature. Even though tests of intelligence and of the aptitudes derived therefrom have been of more practical help than tests of any other kind in selecting people for quality of performance in various situations, discussions of intelligence have typically been marked by polemics. These polemics have usually concerned two of the beliefs or assumptions about intelligence that have dominated thought on the topic from the turn of the twentieth century through World War II. According to these two dominant assumptions intelligence is fixed and immutable, and the development of the individual's basic repertoire of responses and capacities is predetermined by his heredity.

The implications of these two assumptions spilled over in various directions. Intelligence came to be defined as "inherited capacity," and it was looked upon as a basic dimension of an individual person. The hope of improving man's lot was shifted from the euthenic strategy of improving his upbringing and education to the eugenic strategy of finding some way to select only the more intelligent for the propagation of the race. Differential fertility came to be viewed with alarm. Investigative effort concerning child nature and child development was directed toward the normative mode of measuring individual characteristics and relating the measures to age. Individual characteristics were quantified and discussed in the language of *dimensions* and *scales* without ascertaining their developmental and neuropsychological characteristics. Investigations of the effects of various kinds of experience at various ages on the development of intellectual capacity were discouraged. Practical educational efforts to cultivate intellectual capacity, particularly in the very young, were discouraged. With behavioral development conceived to be a process in which anatomic maturation automatically brought with it the response repertoire, experts warned parents not to overstimulate their infants but rather to leave them alone to grow. Finally, the assumptions of fixed intelligence and predetermined development may well have had something to do with what has probably been an overemphasis on personnel selection and an underemphasis on problems of both training and arranging the social climate of institutions to foster personal interest and growth.

FIXED INTELLIGENCE

The assumption of fixed intelligence has historical roots in Darwin's theory that evolution occurs by way of the survival of those inherited chance variations which show their fitness by growing up and propagating. It was his cousin, Francis Galton, who launched the study of individual differences, developed some of the first anthropometric tests, and founded the eugenics movement. Although Binet, who with Simon developed the method of intelligence testing that survived, conceived of intelligence as a fundamental and complex faculty, he did not regard it as immutable. But it was Cattell, a student of Galton, who introduced the interest in measuring individual differences to America. Moreover, it was the students of G. Stanley Hall, the evolutionist who saw in the notion that "ontogeny recapitulates phylogeny" an explanation of both individual differences and individual development, who translated Binet's tests into English and cultivated their use in America. In both instances, the testing movement came to America via people who believed in fixed intelligence, and at least partially for this reason the belief has tended to dominate the testing movement.

Evidence consonant with the notion of fixed intelligence came with the finding, artifactual though it was, that the mean IQ obtained from groups of differing ages is constant. Moreover, the scores for individual children showed considerable constancy for the years of later childhood and adolescence; and scores from various tests showed considerable correlation both with each other and with measures of such criterion performances as those in school and those on various types of jobs. Finally, direct evidence of hereditary influence came from the fact that the correlations among the test-scores of people closely related are higher than are those among the test-scores of people not closely related.

Evidence dissonant with the assumption of fixed intelligence came from the fact that the correlation between the IQ's of identical twins reared apart is lower than that for the IQ's of identical twins reared together. More of such evidence came from the fact that the IQ's of infants, obtained at successive ages, show considerable variation, and also from the fact that the IQ's of infants show little correlation with their IQ's as adults. But the import of such facts was largely explained away by assuming that the infant tests lacked validity, without, however, distinguishing between what has here been termed criterion validity and predictive validity. Still more such evidence came from the fact that orphanage-reared children score lower on tests than do children reared in foster homes, but this fact was explained away by assuming that the children who got into orphanages are so selected as to be innately inferior to the children who got placed in foster homes. Finally, the finding of improvement in IQ with nursery-school experience was explained away in terms of defects in the designs of the investigations in which they appeared, and also in terms of validity for the changes in tested intelligence. Some of the urgency of the effort to explain away these bits of dissonant evidence may well have derived not only from the historical sources but from generalizing the conceptual set of seeing the dimensions of objects as immutable to seeing the characteristics of organisms and persons as also immutable.

PREDETERMINED DEVELOPMENT

Historically, the belief in predetermined development replaced the belief in preformationism when, in the latter half of the eighteenth century, C. F. Wolff marshaled effectively both the evidence and the arguments for an epigenesis of body structures in the embryological development of the chicken egg. This belief got further support from Darwin's theory of natural selection and from the notion that "ontogeny recapitulates phylogeny." G. Stanley Hall communicated both of these beliefs to his students and to the child-study associations emerging in America. They tended, therefore, to become accepted as "common sense" beliefs. Indirect conceptual support came historically from a complex development in comparative psychology. Darwin and Romanes attempted to show that the faculties of mind, such as emotion, for instance, and intelligence, were continuous between animals and man. The loose analogical reasoning about mental faculties in these studies led Lloyd Morgan to extirpate them with Ockham's razor of parsimony and to substitute the concept of "trial and error." Jacques Loeb's utilization and development of the concept of forced movements or tropisms as the fundamental units of behavior set the stage for the emphasis on peripheral factors in the place of central factors in behavior. Thorndike's law of effect made response survival, like variation or mutation survival, a matter of the fitness of the response, and the stage was set for what has been called the "empty organism." From this standpoint, development consisted of two essentially distinct processes, maturation and learning. The basic response units were conceived to come automatically with the maturation of the anatomical structures upon which they were presumed to depend. These response units were then conceived to be hooked up into various combinations by means of stimulus-response bonds. Such a conceptual schema got a good deal of support from the conception of the brain as a kind of static switchboard. Although this conceptual schema was probably somewhat dissonant with the notion of intelligence as a dimension, little was made of this because the investigators concerned with this picture of behavioral development composed a group which had little communication with the group concerned with measuring individual differences, and especially individual differences in intelligence. Moreover, the general notion that behavioral development is an automatic aspect of anatomic maturation could also lend indirect support to the assumption of fixed intelligence. Although the Gestalt psychologists composed yet another group, and one opposed to the notion of elementary units of behavior being hooked up into various more complex systems, the physical *Gestalten* of the brain were also conceived to come automatically with anatomic maturation. Thus, their emphasis on "insight" in problem solving as restructuring of these physical *Gestalten* offered no corrective for the notion of predetermined development.

Evidence apparently consonant with the notion of predetermined development came from several sources. Coghill found the head-to-tail and center-outward orders of anatomical maturation to hold for the development of the swimming reaction in the tadpoles of salamanders (*Amblystoma*). Carmichael found that the tadpoles of frogs and salamanders that had developed without any opportunity for behavior while anesthetized with chloretone swam as well as others that had developed normally in unadulterated water, and he took this to be a demonstration of the existence of "unlearned behavior." When Mary Shirley found not only the head-tailward order of behavioral development in human children but also a marked degree of consistency in the order in which various responses appear in children, her findings were conceived to indicate that principles induced from observing the behavioral development of the lowly salamander generalize to man, and she herself argued that the consistency in order favored the notion of predetermined maturation. The early experiments in which various kinds of experience were either subtracted or added seemed to have little permanent effect on behavior. Chicks reared in darkness for a few days actually learned to peck accurately with a greater rate of improvement than did chicks that had had every opportunity to practice pecking. Children who were given special practice in such skills as tower-building, stair-climbing, cutting with scissors, etc., showed improvement, but children who were not given such special practice appeared to achieve the same degree of mastery of these skills with much less practice at a later age. Dennis found that the Hopi Indian children who were reared on cradle-boards, which prevented their using their legs, learned to walk at the same average age as Hopi children who were reared with full use of their legs.

Bits of evidence clearly dissonant with the conception that development is entirely predetermined also appeared. Altering developmental experience was found to interfere with the development of instinctive patterns. For instance, Birch found that the maternal behavior of female rats reared with collars to prevent them licking their own genitalia ate their young at parturition instead of retrieving them and licking them. Moreover, Riess found that rats reared in cages devoid of nesting materials failed to build nests at parturition even though proper materials were available. Apropos the Gestalt principles of perception and thinking, it was observed that when people deprived of visual experiences from birth by congenital cataracts were operated on to restore their vision, they might immediately distinguish between figure and ground and be able to say whether two impressions were the same or different, but they could not recognize objects without months of visual experience. Moreover, various investigators found that insightful responses tended to appear only in those monkeys and chimpanzees who had been observed to play with the tools to be used insightfully.

A NEW EMPHASIS ON CENTRAL PROCESSES

Very shortly after Morgan had extirpated the mental faculties with Ockham's razor of parsimony and Loeb, Thorndike, and Watson had attempted to explain all complex behavior in terms of stimulus-response chaining, Lashley destroyed the explanatory value of such chaining for complex behavior by pointing out that time would not permit such a sequence of central-peripheral synoptic connections in the case, for example, of a pianist playing a rapid candenza on the piano. Then stimulus-response method, as distinguished from stimulus-response theory, began producing evidence that motivated re-furnishing the empty organism with conceptualized processes inter-vening between stimulus and response. There resulted the symbolic processes of Hunter, the intervening variables of Tolman, the "pure stimulus acts" of Hull, the response-produced drives and cues of Dollard and Miller, and the mediational responses of Osgood. In the case of each of these, however, an attempt was made to tie the inter-vening variable to both its roots in past experience and to its mani-festations in overt behavior.

Recently, however, emphasis on central processes has been greatly increased by developments in several areas with important implica-tions for the theory of intelligence. In neuropsychology, Hebb, prompted by noting that behavior is to a considerable degree inde-pendent of receptor inputs and failing to find intellectual deficits on standard tests of intelligence following removal of upwards of 20 per cent of the mass of the cerebrum in adults while noting that cere-bral lesions in infancy produce feeble-mindedness, led off with his attempts to conceptualize the semi-autonomous central processes that intervene between receptor inputs and motor outputs. His notions of cell-assemblies and phase-sequences, established within the associative regions of the cerebral cortex by primary learning, which he conceived to be largely perceptual in nature, set a new trend. His concept of the A/S ratio, i.e., ratio of association areas to areas concerned directly with either receptor inputs or motor out-puts, appears to have considerable explanatory power.

INTELLIGENCE AS CENTRAL PROCESSES AND AS STRATEGIES FOR THE PROCESSING OF INFORMATION

Hebb's conceptions led to a substantial revision in the conception of intelligence. His notion of the important role of autonomous cen-tral processes in behavior suggested that intelligence would prob-ably be a function of the variegation and mobility of the cell as-semblies established through primary learning within those regions of the brain not immediately concerned with receptor inputs or motor outputs. This conception suggested further that adult intelli-gence should vary with opportunities for perceptual and perhaps even motor experience in which a variety of inputs with appropriate degrees of redundancy are available. It also stimulated a number of studies of the effects of infantile experience on later learning and problem-solving. These studies have shown that rats reared with ample opportunities for a variety of perceptual experience do learn mazes more readily than rats reared with minimal opportunities for a variety of such experience. Pet-reared rats with a background of highly varied experience have been found to perform with more facility on the Hebb-Williams test of intelligence than do cage-reared rats with a background of little variation in experience. Similarly, Thompson & Heron have shown that in a wide variety of situations pet-reared dogs behave in a fashion much more intelligent than their litter-mates who were cage-reared for the first eight months of their lives. The fact that the effects of such differences in early experience on adult intelligence appear to be considerably greater in dogs than in rats is consonant with the expectation that the importance of infantile experience for later intelligence is a function of the size of the A/S ratio in the species concerned. In yet another example of the effects of infantile experience, this time on perception, Riesen has found that chimpanzees kept in darkness for the first months of their lives lack object-recognition and the various responses which depend upon such recognition. Moreover, even the anatomic development of the visual apparatus appears to be hampered by lack of visual stimulation.

Combined with Hebb's theorizing and the work stimulated by it in this new emphasis on central processes and their dependence upon experience are other developments. The people who program electronic computers for the solving of problems have begun to systematize the conception of the requirements of problem-solving in terms of strategies for the processing of information. These strategies resemble the logical operations of the logical calculus as described by Boole. The strategies are arranged hierarchically for access and application. From studies of animal problem-solving, Harlow has shown that by repeatedly learning the solution to any given type of problem, monkeys develop learning sets which give them the capacity to solve that type of problem almost immediately with the information derived from perception of the situation. These "learning sets" look fairly analogous to the strategies for the processing of information that programmers wire into their electronic computers. The thought that the computer and the brain have similarities of operation has prompted a re-examination of the theory of brain function. Although von Neumann has warned that the mathematics of the brain in operation fail to correspond to mathematics as now conceived, such neuropsychologists as Pribram have pointed to approximate counterparts of the hierarchies of strategies for processing information and executing action within the brain. Pribram conceives these to be stored in those regions of the brain that receive no receptor inputs and have no direct access to musculature. These include the anterior and posterior nuclei of the thalamus with their tract-connections, respectively, with the frontal lobe and with the parietal and temporal lobes. These are termed intrinsic mechanisms and are conceived to have a function similar to Hebb's association areas. Hierarchical systems of memories for the redundant aspects of past perceptions are conceived to be stored in the posterior intrinsic mechanism, while the anterior mechanism is conceived to contain the hierarchical arrangement of intentions which are based on an organization of the homeostatic mechanisms localized in the reticular core around the midline ventricles. Damage to the tracts under the cortex of the parietal and temporal lobes may not interfere with such reflexive acts as catching a fly on the wing, but it does interfere with perceptual recognition. Damage to the tracts under the frontal lobe may not interfere with perceptual recognition, but it does interfere with the execution of sequential systems of action. The unit of response is conceived to be one of "test-operate-test-exist (TOTE)." Intelligence, from the standpoint of such a conceptual scheme, would appear to be a matter of the number of strategies for processing information that have been differentiated and have achieved the mobility which permits them to be available in a variety of situations.

PIAGET'S OBSERVATIONS OF THE DEVELOPMENT OF INTELLIGENCE

The conception of intelligence deriving from Piaget's observations of the development of adaptive ability in children resembles so much that which derives from considering the computer and the brain and from the work of Hebb and Harlow that his observations may be considered to lend further empirical support to this new conception of intelligence. A basis for the hierarchical arrangement of the central processes that mediate intelligence appears in Piaget's description of behavioral development wherein the sensorimotor organizations of each stage become incorporated, in the course of the child's assimilations of both food and the modifications in his sensorimotor schemata deriving from his psychological interactions with the environment, into the more complex sensorimotor organizations of the next stage. Things heard become things to look at; things seen become things to grasp; things grasped become things to suck, etc. In the course of such coordinations, inputs from the distance receptors, and especially the eyes, acquire control over motor activities. Intentions emerge, means are distinguished from ends, interest in activities and in objects develops, and behavior becomes more and more variable and adaptive. All this happens presumably as central processes become both coordinated and redifferentiated. The sensorimotor period ends when the child is about 18 months old and the sensorimotor schemata and imitations begin to become internalized as images. During this same sensorimotor period of 18 months, objects acquire permanence, while causality, space, and time become objective.

During the preconceptual phase from about 18 months to four years of a second major period (from 18 months to 12 years) images accumulate to form intuitions. Intuitions are grouped at about seven years to form the first of the mobile equilibrii. These are the concrete operations with the logical properties of reversibility, associativity, transitivity, identity, and tautology. They arrive as the child begins to think generally with concrete objects and as he acquires the capacity to conserve quantity and number and the capacity to order objects serially by such properties as length. These concrete operations are further elaborated at about age nine or ten when the child acquires the capacity to conserve weight and to order objects serially by the property of weight. At age 11 or 12, he acquires the still higher level of capacity to conserve volume and to order objects serially by the property of volume. Inhelder & Piaget have also reported that conservation of volume always includes the capacities to conserve weight and quantity, and that the conservation of weight always includes the capacity to conserve quantity and number. Such findings suggest that Piaget's landmarks of transition in the development of intelligence and thought represent a natural ordinal scale of intelligence. During these successive elaborations of the concrete operations, parallel transformations are occurring in the child's conceptions of causality, space, and time.

Finally, during a third major period beginning at about age 11 or 12, the concrete operations are regrouped into formal operations as the young pre-adolescent acquires the proportionality schema that permits him to conserve volume. At this landmark of transition, he also acquires the capacity to deal with propositions as he has hitherto been able to deal only with concrete objects. It is thus that he achieves the level of formal reasoning. At this transition, instead of observation directing thought as it has in the period of concrete operations, the adolescent's thought directs his observing. He thereby acquires the essential intellectual capacity for the scientific method. Moreover, inasmuch as the observed conditions of society can now be seen in comparison with imagined ideal conditions of society, the adolescent also acquires the capacity required for social reform. These formal operations of the adolescent Piaget describes in terms of their logico-mathematical properties which include the proportionality schema, the INRC group structure, and the 16 binary operations of the Boolean logical calculus. In fact, Inhelder & Piaget find that it is these logico-mathematical schemata operating implicitly in the thought of adolescents that direct their observing in science-like problem-solving.

PIAGET'S THEORY: IMPLICATIONS AND VALIDITY

Five main themes dominate Piaget's theoretical formulations. The first concerns the continual and progressive change, or epigenesis, in the structures of behavior and thought in the developing child. This theme serves as a corrective for the preformationism that still lurks in both epistemology and psychology. The second theme concerns the fixed nature of the order in which the successive structures make their appearance. If this order is corroborated by other investigators, in view of the hierarchical organization indicated, it may indeed supply the basis for a natural ordinal scale of intelligence. Furthermore, the existence of such a natural ordinal scale would suggest the investigative method of measuring the effects of various kinds of experience on the rate of development in terms of the time elapsing between the successive landmarks of transition.

Piaget's third theme concerns the invariant functions of accommodation (adaptive change to outer circumstances) and of assimilation (incorporation of the external into the inner organization with transfer or generalization to new circumstances) that operate in the child's continuous interaction with the environment. The nature of accommodation suggests that the rate of development is to a considerable degree a function of the child's encounters with the environment. Piaget formulates a principle to account for such a relationship between intelligence and experience in essentially motivational terms: the more an infant has seen and heard, the more he later wants to see and hear. This principle gets empirical support from the studies of the dependence of intelligence upon early experience in animals, which studies were generated by Hebb's theorizing. The principle also gets support from the retarding effects of the relatively unchanging stimulation in various orphanages. As recently reported by Dennis, in some instances this retardation, even of such functions as sitting alone and walking alone, can be great. While such evidence clearly supports the principle that the rate of development depends upon the nature of the child's encounters with the environment, it does not say how irreversible such retardation may be, and neither does it indicate the degree to which the adult level of intelligence is ultimately reduced. On the other hand, the fact that Thompson & Heron have found that dogs pet-reared for the first eight months of their lives do show a substantially higher level of intelligence at 18 months of age than do dogs cage-reared for their first eight months suggests considerable permanence for these effects of early experience.

Within the domain of Piaget's third theme, the nature of accommodation implies great importance for the match between the kind of external circumstances encountered and the kind of internal organization already present in determining the nature and degree of effect of any given encounter. This match is still poorly understood, but it is the appropriateness of the match between the circumstances that the child encounters as he develops and the nature of his own intellectual organizations at the time of the encounters that appears to determine in very large part his rate of intellectual development. Put another way, the richness of an environment for intellectual growth is a function of the appropriateness of this match between inner organizations and external circumstances in a child's succession of encounters with his environment. While it is highly unlikely that even the "best" of contemporary child-rearing and education comes near maximizing the potential of children, any attempt to facilitate intellectual development with improvements in child-rearing and education demands a markedly increased understanding of this matter of the match. Piaget's description of the stages in the development of intelligence in children, which receives empirical support from the study of behavioral development in animals by such investigators as Fuller and Scott, helps to take some of the guess-work out of such matching.

Within this third theme of Piaget's, one also finds a number of parallels with the theorizing of Hebb which are relevant to this problem of the match. Both Piaget and Hebb see behavior and intelligence determined by central processes. Both see these central processes changing with experience. Both see early experience as of probably crucial importance in determining both the rate and the final level of ability. Some of the parallels concern motivation, but Piaget makes little of his observations and pronouncements about motivation while Hebb has motivation near the center of his concern. Both see a basis for pleasure in discrepancies between the existing central processes that mediate anticipations and the receptor inputs from environmental circumstances. Pleasure occurs if this discrepancy is of a proper degree. Both also see a basis for fear and distress in such discrepancies when they are too great to be accommodated. While this line of theorizing is still vague in its implications for experimental operations, it has the happy implication that with proper control of the match between the internal structure of a child's central processes and the circumstances that he encounters, maximizing his rate of intellectual growth should also be a source of exciting interest and pleasure.

Piaget's fourth theme concerns the relation of thought processes to action. Thought processes are conceived to originate through a process of internalizing actions, which is essentially like the short-circuiting principle offered by Hebb, Osgood, and many others. Piaget also conceives that intelligence increases as thought processes are loosened from their bases in perception and action and thereby become reversible, transitive, associative, etc. This conception, in turn, implies that intelligence develops as central neural processes become increasingly autonomous. The fact that Max has found a negative correlation between tested intelligence and amount of education, on the one hand, and, on the other, the frequency of muscular action potentials in deaf-mutes asked to solve problems mentally, tends to lend empirical support to such a conception of the relation between intelligence and the autonomy of central neural processes and action. In this theme, Piaget's theory makes a considerably greater place for action than does Hebb's, but since looking and listening are conceived by Piaget to be reflexive schemata with both sensory and motor aspects, whereas Hebb conceives of them largely as receptors, the difference may be more apparent and verbal than operational.

Piaget's fifth theme concerns the logical properties of thought processes. He sees these properties to be products of a mobile equilibrium in which all the virtual transformations compatible with the relationships of the system compensate each other. The reversibility of thought operations account for the Gestalt-like quality of thought. The laws of the mobile equilibrium account for the intersubjectivity of reasoning.

Factor-analytic studies of intelligence pose some problems for the conception of intelligence that derives from this fifth theme of Piaget's theory. The grouping of images and intuitions into concrete operations at about seven or eight and the regrouping of concrete operations into formal operations at about 11 or 12, with each having such apparently far-reaching consequences in intellectual functioning, imply a homogeneity of intelligence that appears to be dissonant with the heterogeneity of intelligence found in the factor-analytic studies of intelligence. The notion that the successive landmarks of transition in the development of intelligent behavior and thought may constitute a natural ordinal scale of intelligence also implies a homogeneity of intelligence that is dissonant with the heterogeneity found in the factor studies. This dissonance is diminished, however, by considering that heterogeneity of abilities is relatively slight in childhood, which constitutes the period when most of Piaget's observations have been made. This dissonance is further diminished by considering that a hierarchical factor structure, with Spearman's g at the apex as the English factor analysts have tended to conceive of intelligence, is precisely what would be expected from considering abilities as the accumulative effects of the transfer of training or learning in varied situations. It has been the merit of G. A. Ferguson to make these points in a pair of highly provocative theoretical papers. The dissonance between the implications of Piaget's conceptions and the results of factor-analytic studies is essentially eradicated by considering that Piaget's conception of accommodation corresponds to the change in function that occurs with training or learning and that Piaget's conception of assimilation corresponds to the notion of transfer of training.

A factor analyst might also raise the question as to why, if the concrete operations and the formal operations are intellectual structures of such importance, the factor-analytic investigations of intelligence have not uncovered them. Several reasons can be found. Perhaps most important is the fact that most factor studies have been cross-sectional in nature. They have used subjects varying little in age. In consequence, all of the subjects used in each such investigation share these basic intellectual operations, and they can therefore appear in the factor studies only as the basis for the fact that abilities are regularly positively correlated in any sample of individuals. In fact, these intellectual structures of Piaget might be seen as an explanation of Spearman's g. Moreover, support for such a view comes from Hofstaetter's factorization of the repeated longitudinal testings of children in the Berkeley Growth Study, for the finding of a large factor of "intellection" on which the loadings on age increase especially rapidly between the ages of four and eight is almost exactly what one would be led to expect.

Although Piaget's work has led him to a concern with both the strategies for information processing utilized in programming computers and with the neural basis of operational thought, the fact that a major share of his observations antedate these later developments and are yet consonant with them is very interesting.

SOME REINTERPRETATIONS

In the light of this newer conception of intelligence, which puts its neural basis in autonomous central neural processes located largely in the intrinsic regions of the brain and which explicitly gives its roots in the child's encounters with his environment, the old evidence once considered disturbing is what would be expected. Moreover, the old evidence once conceived to support the assumptions of fixed intelligence and predetermined development can readily be reinterpreted to be consonant with the newer conception.

The semantics of *dimension* and *scale* for tests of intelligence actually fit the procedures of testing less well than would a semantics of sampling behavior for evidence of the presence of such organizational structures as schemata, operations, and conceptions. The validity of tests can be divided into at least two kinds, *predictive validity*, or the capacity of a score from a testing at one time to predict the score from a testing at a later time in the individual's life, and *criterion validity*, or the capacity performance on tests to predict performances at the same stage of development in various types of life situation. The fact that the scores from repeated testing in infancy, when the rate of change in the intellectual structures is greatest, fluctuate radically and the fact that such scores show poor predictive validity are precisely what would be expected if intellectual capacity depends to a considerable degree upon the child's encounters with his environment, but such fluctuations are highly embarrassing to the assumptions of fixed intelligence and predetermined development. Lack of predictive validity, so long as the child's encounters with his environment are not controlled, would be expected, but lack of predictive validity need not imply that the infant tests lack criterion validity.

In view of the low A/S ratio in the brains of frogs and salamanders, and since the effects of experience appear to increase with the size of the A/S ratio, Coghill's finding that behavioral development follows the head-tailward and proximo-distal orders found for anatomical development need not imply that the behavioral development of organisms with higher A/S ratios is largely a function of anatomical maturation. In fact, the work of Kuo indicates that the embryo chick's interaction with its environment in the egg has much to do with its behavioral development and later abilities. Similarly, the fact that Carmichael found swimming movements coming without opportunity for practice in the chloretoned frog and salamander tadpoles, with their low A/S ratios, need not imply that encounters with the environment are unimportant for behavioral development in higher organisms. The apparent evanescence of the effects of either subtracting or adding experience in the development of various organisms was apparently to some degree a function of the short duration of the subtraction or the addition. When frogs were kept in chloretoned water longer than Carmichael kept them there, they failed to learn to swim properly. When chicks were kept in the dark longer than Cruze kept them there, they lost the pecking response. Although the advantage got from a few weeks of special early practice in tower-building, stair-climbing, buttoning, and scissoring quickly disappeared when the controls, who started later, got to practicing these same skills, when Myrtle McGraw gave her trained twin, Johnny, nearly a year's experience at roller-skating, the untrained twin, Jimmy, was not able to catch up quickly. In fact, where Johnny had had little trouble learning to roller-skate at 11 months of age, Jimmy could not learn the skill at all at 22 months of age.

In view of the Hebbian distinction between primary learning and later learning, moreover, it is hardly surprising that the special practice on such activities as tower-building, stair-climbing, buttoning, scissoring, etc., produced but evanescent superiority in these skills because, presumably, the incidental activities of the control children in these experiments might have been expected to have produced as much development in the central processes mediating these activities as would the direct practice on them, and perhaps even more.

Although the fact that change in the intellectual structures is most rapid during the early months and years suggests that the effects of environmental encounters during the early period should perhaps be most potent, it remains to be determined in crucial fashion how great and how permanent such effects can be.

Probably the question concerning the relative proportion of the variance in intelligence attributable to heredity and to environment, which is the one most frequently asked, has been unfortunate. No general answer to this question is possible. This impossibility has long been recognized by geneticists, for only the phenotype can be measured, and how much any genotype can be altered by experience can be ascertained only by submitting that genotype to all possible life programs of encounters with the environment. Much more pertinent are specific questions relevant to either problems of educational and welfare practice or to the theory of human intelligence and its development. Inasmuch as Dennis has very recently found that in orphanage environments where the variety of stimulation is minimal, only 42 per cent of the children sit alone at two years of age, and only 15 per cent walk alone at four years of age, it appears to be quite clear that the rate of development is not predetermined by the genes. On the other hand, although it is unlikely that any person has ever achieved his full potential for intellectual development, it is not known how much various procedures for improving the match between circumstances and level of behavioral development to foster the accommodative modification of central structures might increase the rate and the final level of intellectual capacity over the rate and level common under existing circumstances. No general answer can be made to questions of this sort, but a variety of such investigations might be expected to lead to generalizations about the nature of environments rich or poor in their capacity to promote intellectual development.

Many investigators have been concerned about the supposed loss of intelligence associated with differential fertility. They point to the negative correlation between number of siblings and tested intelligence as perhaps the most direct evidence for this loss. Inasmuch as about the same degree of inferiority appears for twins and for doubles born close together as appears for those in large families, and inasmuch as this negative correlation disappears among the well-to-do who can afford to have help in the care of their infants during the early months, it is quite as logical to see this negative correlation as evidence of intelligence failing to develop from lack of the stimulation that comes from young infants having ample adult contact as it is to see it as evidence that those genetically inferior are supplying more than their share of the next generation.

CONCLUSION AND THE CHALLENGE

In view of the conceptual developments and the evidence coming from animals learning to learn, from neuropsychology, from the programming of electronic computers to solve problems, and from the development of intelligence in children, it would appear that intelligence should be conceived as intellectual capacities based on central processes hierarchically arranged within the intrinsic portions of the cerebrum. These central processes are approximately analogous to the strategies for information processing and action with which electronic computers are programmed. With such a conception of intelligence, the assumptions that intelligence is fixed and that its development is predetermined by the genes are no longer tenable.

In the light of these considerations, it appears that the counsel from experts on child-rearing during the third and much of the fourth decades of the twentieth century to let children be while they grow and to avoid excessive stimulation was highly unfortunate. It was suggested in the text above that perhaps the negative correlations found between intelligence test scores for the first two years and the late adolescent level of intelligence may possibly be attributable to such counsel, inasmuch as it would be those educated people at the higher levels of tested intelligence who read and can act in terms of what they read who would have been most likely to follow this advice. The problem for the management of child development is to find out how to govern the encounters that children have with their environments to foster both an optimally rapid rate of intellectual development and a satisfying life.

Further in the light of these theoretical considerations and the evidence concerning the effects of early experience on adult problem-solving in animals, it is no longer unreasonable to consider that it might be feasible to discover ways to govern the encounters that children have with their environments, especially during the early years of their development, to achieve a substantially faster rate of intellectual development and a substantially higher adult level of intellectual capacity. Moreover, inasmuch as the optimum rate of intellectual development would mean also self-directing interest and curiosity and genuine pleasure in intellectual activity, promoting intellectual development properly need imply nothing like the grim urgency which has been associated with "pushing" children. Furthermore, these procedures, insofar as they tended to maximize each child's potential for intellectual development, would not decrease individual differences in intellectual capacity as assessed by tests but would increase them. The discovery of the ways to govern the encounters children have with their environments for this purpose would require a great deal of expensive and difficult investigation of the effects of various kinds of early experience on later intellectual capacity. Even after the discovery of the ways, if they can be found, the task of effecting the necessary changes within the culture in child-rearing practices and in educational procedures would be Herculean. Nevertheless, ours is a technological culture of increasing complexity. Its development continually demands an ever larger proportion of the population with intellectual capacity at the higher levels. It calls also for intellectual giants to solve the problems that become increasingly complex. The fact that it is reasonable to hope to find ways of raising the level of intellectual capacity in a majority of the population makes it a challenge to do the necessary research. It is one of the major challenges of our times. It is a challenge, moreover, where the chances are fairly good that the behavioral sciences can make a contribution of great social, as well as theoretical, significance.

Author Index and Bibliography

The dates following the names of the authors are those by which the citations are identified in the text. They are, to the best of the writer's knowledge, the original dates of publication. When a second date appears at the end of a reference, this is the one to which the writer has had access, and any pages given for quotations in the text refer to the publication of the second date. Numbers in brackets at the end of entries refer to pages in this text.

This index includes names for which no references are given, and also a few references that the writer has never seen. In case of the latter, the source is cited with the reference.

ALBERTINI, BARBARA VON. *See* Piaget & Albertini, 1950.

ALLEN, L. See Honzik, Macfarlane, & Allen, 1948.

AMATRUDA, CATHERINE S. *See* Gessell & Amatruda, 1941.

ANASTASI, ANNE. 1936. The influence of specific experience upon mental organization. *Genet. Psychol. Monogr.*, 18, 245–355 [301, 311].

ANASTASI, ANNE. 1938. Faculties *versus* factors: a reply to Professor Thurstone. *Psychol. Bull.*, 35, 391–395 [311].

ANASTASI, ANNE. 1948. The nature of psychological "traits." *Psychol. Rev.*, 55, 127–138 [311].

ANASTASI, ANNE. 1956. Intelligence and family size. *Psychol. Bull.*, 53, 187–209 [337, 340–342].

ANASTASI, ANNE. 1958a. *Differential psychology*. (3rd Ed.) New York: Macmillan [18, 257, 298, 337].

ANASTASI, ANNE. 1958b. Heredity, environment, and the question "How?" *Psychol. Rev.*, 65, 197–208 [335, 337].

ANAXAGORAS. [36, 309].

ANDERSON, J. E. 1940. The prediction of terminal intelligence from infant and preschool tests. *Yearb. Nat. Soc. Stud. Educ.*, 39, (I), 385–403 [23, 314].

ANDERSON, J. E. 1956. Child development: an historical perspective. *Child Develpm.*, 27, 181–196 [4].

ANDERSON, J. F. *See* Horsfall & Anderson, 1961.

ANDERSON, L. D. 1939. The predictive value of infancy tests in relation to intelligence at five years. *Child Develpm.*, 10, 203–212 [21–23].

ANGELL, J. R. 1907. The province of functional psychology. *Psychol. Rev.*, 14, 61–91 [133, 252–253].

ARISTOTLE. [37].

ARNETT, V. *See* Echlin, Arnett, & Zoll, 1952.

AUSTIN, G. A. *See* Bruner, Goodnow, & Austin, 1956.

AUSUBEL, D. P. 1960a. In defense of verbal learning. *Educ. Theory*, 11, 15–25, 1961 [287].

AUSUBEL, D. P. 1960b. The use of advance organizers in the learning and retention of meaningful verbal material. *J. educ. Psychol.*, 51, 267–272 [287].

AUSUBEL, D. P. 1961. A subsumption theory of meaningful verbal material and retention. *J. gen. Psychol.*, in press [287].

AUSUBEL, D. P., ROBBINS, LILLIAN C., & BLAKE, E., JR. 1957. Retroactive inhibition and facilitation in the learning of school materials. *J. educ. Psychol.*, 48, 334–343 [287].

BAKWIN, H. 1941. Emotional deprivation in infants. *J. Pediat.*, 35, 512–521 [264].

BALDWIN, A. L. 1955. *Behavior and development in childhood.* New York: Holt, Rinehart & Winston [280, 293–295].

BALDWIN, A. L., KALHORN, J., & BREESE, F. H. 1945. Patterns of parent behavior. *Psychol. Monogr.,* **58** (Whole No. 268) [279].

BALDWIN, J. M. 1906. *Genetic logic: thought and things.* Vol. 1. New York: Macmillan [119].

BALINSKY, B. 1941. An analysis of the mental factors of various age groups from nine to sixty. *Genet. Psychol. Monogr.,* **23,** 191–234 [257].

BALLARD, P. B. [232].

BARRETT, H. E., & KOCH, HELEN L. 1930. The effect of nursery-school training upon the mental test performance of a group of orphanage children. *J. genet. Psychol.,* **37,** 102–122 [27].

BAYLEY, NANCY. 1940. Mental growth in young children. *Yearb. Nat. Soc. Stud. Educ.,* **39** (II), 11–47 [21–22, 314].

BAYLEY, NANCY. 1949. Consistency and variability in the growth from birth to 18 years. *J. genet. Psychol.,* **75,** 165–196 [22].

BAYLEY, NANCY. 1954. Some increasing parent-child similarities during the growth of children. *J. educ. Psychol.,* **45,** 1–21 [312–313].

BEACH, F. A. 1942. Central nervous mechanisms involved in the reproductive behavior of vertebrates. *Psychol. Bull.,* **39,** 200–206 [84].

BEADLE, G. W. 1945. Biochemical genetics. *Chem. Rev.,* **37,** 15–96 [41, 329].

BEBERMAN, MAX [332].

BECKER, W. C. *See* Gauron & Becker, 1959.

BENNETT, G. K., SEASHORE, H. G., & WESMAN, A. G. 1947. *Differential Aptitude Tests, Manual.* New York: Psychological Corp. [301].

BERLYNE, D. E. 1957. Recent developments in Piaget's work. *Brit. J. educ. Psychol.,* **27,** 1–12 [111–113].

BERLYNE, D. E. 1960. *Conflict, arousal, and curiosity.* New York: McGraw-Hill [148, 254, 269].

BERNARD, L. L. 1924. *Instinct: a study in social psychology.* New York: Holt, Rinehart & Winston [65].

BERYL, R. 1926. Über die Grossenauffassung bei Kindern. *Z. Psychol.,* **100,** 344–371 [254].

BEURLE, R. L. 1956. Properties of a mass of cells capable of regenerating pulses. *Phil. Trans. Roy. Soc. London, Ser. B.,* 240, 55–94 [91].

BEXTON, W. H., HERON, W., & SCOTT, T. H. 1954. Effects of decreased variation in the sensory environment. *Canad. J. Psychol.,* **8,** 70–76 [263].

BINET, A. 1909. *Les idées modernes sur les enfants.* Paris: Ernest Flamarion. (Cited from Stoddard, 1939.) [13, 16, 44, 348].

BINET, A., & HENRI, V. 1895. La psychologie individuelle. *Année psychol.,* **2,** 411–463 [12].

BINET, A., & SIMON, T. 1905. Méthodes nouvelles pour le diagnostic du niveau intellectuel des anormaux. *Année psychol.,* **11,** 191–244 [12, 15–17].

BINET, A., & SIMON, T. 1908. Le développement de l'intelligence chez les enfants. *Année psychol.,* **14,** 1–94 [15–16].

BINET, A., & SIMON, T. 1911. La measure du développement de l'intelligence chez les jeunes enfants. *Bulletin de la Société libre pour l'Étude psychologique de l'Enfant,* Paris [15–16].

BINET, A., & SIMON, T. 1916. *The development of intelligence in children.* Trans. by Elizabeth S. Kite. Baltimore: Williams & Wilkins [12–13].

BINGHAM, H. C. 1928. Sexual development in apes. *Comp. Psychol. Monogr.,* **5** (23), 1–165 [52, 63].

BINGHAM, H. C. 1929. Chimpanzee translocation by means of boxes. *Comp. Psychol. Monogr.,* **5,** 1–91 [62, 77].

BIRCH, H. G. 1945. The relation of previous experience to insightful problem-solving. *J. comp. Psychol.,* **38,** 367–383 [63, 77, 351].

BIRCH, H. G. 1956. Sources of order in maternal behavior of animals. *Amer. J. Orthopsychiat.,* **26,** 279–284 [59, 351].

BIRD, C. 1925. The relative importance of maturation and habit in the development of an instinct. *Ped. Sem.* (*J. genet. Psychol.*), **32,** 68–91 [54]

BIRD, C. 1926. The effect of maturation

upon the pecking instinct of chicks. *Ped. Sem.* (*J. genet. Psychol.*), 33, 212–233 [54].

BIRD, C. 1933. Maturation and practice: Their effects upon the feeding reaction of chicks. *J. comp. Psychol.*, 16, 343–366 [54].

BLAKE, E., JR. See Ausubel, Robbins, & Blake, 1957.

BOLTON, T. L. 1891. The growth of memory in school children. *Amer. J. Psychol.*, 4, 362–380 [12].

BOOLE, G. 1854. *An investigation of the laws of thought.* New York: Dover, 1953 [231–234, 353].

BORING, E. G. 1929. *A history of experimental psychology.* New York: Appleton-Century-Crofts [43].

BORING, E. G. 1950. The influence of evolutionary theory upon American psychological thought. In P. Stow (Ed.), *Evolutionary thought in America.* Chap. VII. New Haven: Yale Univer. Press [12, 14].

BOYNTON, P. 1933. *Intelligence: its manifestations and measurement.* New York: Appleton-Century-Crofts [10].

BRAINE, M. D. S. 1959. The ontogeny of certain logical operations: Piaget's formulation examined by nonverbal methods. *Psychol. Monogr.*, 73, No. 5 (Whole No. 475), 1–43 [196, 295–296].

BRASH, H. See Yates & Brash, 1941.

BRATTGÅRD, S. O. 1952. The importance of adequate stimulation for the chemical composition of retinal ganglion cells during early postnatal development. *Acta Radiol.*, Stockholm. Suppl. 96 [94, 293].

BRAZIER, MARY A. 1959. A historical development of neurophysiology. In H. W. Magoun (Ed.), *Neurophysiology.* Vol. 1, Sec. 1, 1. Washington, D. C.: American Physiological Soc.; Baltimore: Williams & Wilkins.

BREED, F. S. 1911. The development of certain instincts and habits in chicks. *Behav. Monogr.* 1, No. 1 [53].

BREED, F. S. See Shepard & Breed, 1913.

BREESE, F. H. See Baldwin, Kalhorn, & Breese, 1945.

BROWNELL, W. A., & HENDRICKSON, G. 1950. How children learn information,

concepts and generalizations. In *Yearb. Nat. Soc. Stud. Educ.*, 49, (I), 92–128 [281, 287].

BROWNELL, W. A., & SIMMS, V. M. 1946. The nature of understanding. In The measurement of understanding. *Yearb. Nat. Soc. Stud. Educ.*, 45, (I) [281, 287].

BRUNER, J. S. 1957. On perceptual readiness. *Psychol. Rev.*, 64, 123–152 [89].

BRUNER, J. S., GOODNOW, JACQUELINE J., & AUSTIN, G. A. 1956. *A study of thinking.* New York: Wiley [283].

BRUNSWIK, E. See Tolman & Brunswik, 1935.

BRUNSWIK, E., & CRUIKSHANK, RUTH M. 1937. Perceptual size constancy in early infancy. *Psychol. Bull.*, 34, 713 [254].

BÜHLER, CHARLOTTE. 1930. The first year of life. Trans. by P. Greenberg & Rowena Ripin. New York: John Day [122].

BÜHLER, CHARLOTTE. 1933. The social behavior of children. In C. Murchison (Ed.), *A handbook of child psychology.* (Rev. Ed.) Worcester, Mass.: Clark Univer. Press [122].

BÜHLER, CHARLOTTE, & HETZER, HILDEGARD. 1927. Inventar der Verhaltungsweisen des ersten Lebensjahres. *Quel. Stud. Jugkd.*, 5, 125–250 [122].

BÜHLER, CHARLOTTE, & HETZER, HILDEGARD. 1929. Individual differences among children in the first year of life. *Child Stud.*, 1, 11–13 [122].

BÜHLER, K. 1928. Displeasure and pleasure in relation to activity. In M. L. Reymert (Ed.), *Feelings and emotions: The Wittenberg symposium.* Chap. 14. Worcester, Mass.: Clark Univer. Press [119, 141, 178, 261].

BULBROOK, MARY ELIZABETH. 1932. An experimental study into the existence and nature of "insight." *Amer. J. Psychol.*, 44, 409–503.

BURKE, C. J. See Estes & Burke, 1953.

BURKS, BARBARA S. 1928. The relative influence of nature and nurture upon mental development: A comparative study of foster parent-foster child resemblance and true parent-true child resemblance. *Yearb. Nat. Soc. Stud. Educ.*, 27 (I), 219–316 [19, 324, 325].

BURKS, BARBARA S. 1939. Review of "Chil-

BURKS, BARBARA S. 1939. (Cont.) dren in foster homes; a study of mental development" by Marie Skodak. J. educ. Psychol., 30, 548–555 [19].

BURKS, BARBARA S. 1942. A study of identical twins reared apart under differing types of family relationships. In Q. McNemar & Maud A. Merrill (Eds.), Studies in personality. New York: McGraw-Hill [20].

BURKS, BARBARA S., & JONES, H. E. 1935. A study of differential fertility in two California cities. Human Biol., 7, 539–554 [337].

BURNS, B. D. 1958. The mammalian cerebral cortex. London: Arnold [88].

BURT, C. 1946. Intelligence and fertility. London: Hamilton [337].

BURT, C. 1947. Family size, intelligence, and social class. Popul. Stud., 1, 177–186 [337].

BURT, C., JONES, E., MILLER, E., & MOODIE, W. 1934. How the mind works. New York: Appleton-Century-Crofts [10, 341].

BURT, C. L. 1919. The development of reasoning in school children. J. exp. Pedag. 5, 68–77 [226].

BURT, C. L. 1940. The factors of the mind. London: Univer. London Press; New York: Macmillan, 1941 [226, 301, 311].

CAMERON, N. 1938a. Individual and social factors in the development of graphic symbolization. J. Psychol., 5, 165–184 [297].

CAMERON, N. 1938b. Reasoning, regression, and communication in schizophrenics. Psychol. Monogr., 50, 1–34 [297].

CAMERON, N. 1938c. A study of thinking in senile deterioration and schizophrenic disorganization. Amer. J. Psychol., 51, 650–665 [297].

CAMERON, N. 1939a. Schizophrenic thinking in a problem-solving situation. J. ment. Sci., 85, 1–24 [297].

CAMERON, N. 1939b. Deterioration and regression in schizophrenic thinking. J. abnorm. soc. Psychol., 34, 265–270 [297].

CARMICHAEL, L. 1926. The development of behavior in vertebrates experimentally removed from influence of external

stimulation. Psychol. Rev., 33, 51–58 [52, 260, 316, 321, 349, 360].

CARMICHAEL, L. 1927. A further study of the development of behavior in vertebrates experimentally removed from the influence of external stimulation. Psychol. Rev., 34, 34–47 [53, 316, 321, 349, 360].

CARMICHAEL, L. 1928. A further study of the development of behavior. Psychol. Rev., 35, 253–260 [53, 316, 321, 349, 360].

CARMICHAEL, L. 1951. Ontogenetic development. In S. S. Stevens (Ed.), Handbook of experimental psychology. Chap. 8. New York: Wiley [317].

CARMICHAEL, L. 1954. The onset and early development of behavior. In L. Carmichael (Ed.), Manual of child psychology. Chap. 2. New York: Wiley [51, 317].

CARNAP, R. 1942. Introduction to semantics. Cambridge: Harvard Univer. Press [175].

CARR, H. A. 1925. Psychology, a study of mental activity. New York: Longmans, Green [253].

CARTER, C. O. 1953. Differential fertility in 1951. Eugen. Rev., 45, 101–103 [337].

CARTER, C. O. 1954. Differential fertility and intelligence. Bull. World Fed. ment. Hlth., 6 (2), 101–103 [337].

CATTELL, J. McK. 1890. Mental tests and measurements. Mind, 15, 373–381 [13, 348].

CATTELL, J. McK. 1893. The progress of psychology. Pop. Sci. Mon., 43, 779–785 [13].

CATTELL, R. B. 1937. The fight for our national intelligence. London: King [337, 339, 341].

CATTELL, R. B. 1940. Effects of human fertility trends upon the distribution of intelligence and culture. Yearb. Nat. Soc. Stud. Educ., 39 (I), 221–233 [337, 341].

CATTELL, R. B. 1950. The fate of national intelligence: test of a thirteen-year prediction. Eugen. Rev., 42, 136–148 [18, 338–340].

CATTELL, R. B. 1952. Factor analysis: an introduction and manual for psycholo-

gist and social scientist. New York: Harper [300, 311].

CATTELL, R. B. 1953. Research designs in psychological genetics with special reference to multiple variance. *Amer. J. hum. Genet.*, **5**, 76–91 [326].

CATTELL, R. B. 1958. Variance analysis equations and solutions for nature-nurture research. *Psychol. Rev.*, **67**, 353–372, 1960 [324, 326].

CATTELL, R. B., STICE, G. F., & KRISTY, N. F. 1957. A first approximation to nature-nurture ratios for eleven primary personality factors in objective tests. *J. abnorm. soc. Psychol.* **54**, 143–159 [324].

CHAMBERLAIN, A. F. 1900. *The child: a study in the evolution of man.* New York: Scribner's; London: Scott [264].

CHAMPNEY, H. 1941. The measurement of parent behavior. *Child Develpm.*, **12**, 131–166 [279].

CHAPMAN, J. C., & WIGGINS, D. M. 1925. Relation to family size to intelligence of offspring and socio-economic status of family. *J. genet. Psychol.*, **32**, 414–421 [337].

CHARLES, MARGARET S. *See* Scott & Charles, 1954.

CHEN, T. L., & CHOW, H. 1948. A factor study of a test battery at different educational levels. *J. genet. Psychol.*, **73**, 187–199 [257].

CHILD, C. M. 1921. *The origin and development of the nervous system from a physiological viewpoint.* Chicago: Univer. Chicago Press [49–51].

CHOW, K. L. 1954. Behavioral effects following destruction of some thalamic association nuclei in monkey. *A.M.A. Arch. Neurol. Psychiat.*, **71**, 762–771 [89].

CHOW, K. L. *See* Riesen *et al.*, 1951.

CHOW, K. L., & NISSEN, H. W. 1955. Interocular transfer of learning in visually naive and experienced infant chimpanzees. *J. comp. physiol. Psychol.*, **48**, 229–237 [96].

CHOW, K. L., RIESEN, A. H., & NEWELL, F. W. 1957. Degeneration of retinal ganglion cells in infant chimpanzees reared in darkness. *J. comp. Neurol.*, **107**, 27–42 [94, 293].

CHRISTENSEN, P. R. *See* Guilford, Merrifield, Christensen, & Frick, 1960.

CLAPARÈDE, E. 1910. *Experimental pedagogy and the psychology of the infant.* Trans. by Mary Louch & Henry Holman. New York: Longmans, Green, 1911 [176].

CLAPARÈDE, E. 1933. La genèse de l'hypothèse. *Arch. Psychol. (Genève)*, **24**, 1–155 [112].

CLARK, J. W. *See* Ojemann & Clark, 1956.

CLARK, R. W. *See* McClelland, Atkinson, Clark, & Lowell, 1953.

COFER, C. N. *See* Hunt & Cofer, 1944.

COGHILL, G. E. 1929. *Anatomy and the problem of behavior.* Cambridge: Cambridge Univer. Press; New York: Macmillan [49–51, 316–337, 320, 344, 350, 360].

COLE, F. J. 1930. *Early theories of sexual generation.* Oxford: Oxford Univer. Press.

COMBE, A. 1871. *Management of infancy, physiological and moral.* New York: Appleton [44].

CONANT, J. B. 1947. *On understanding science.* New Haven: Yale Univer. Press. Also Mentor Books, M68, 1951 [39].

CONANT, J. B. 1951. *Science and common sense.* New Haven: Yale Univer. Press [149].

CONRAD, H. S., & JONES, H. E. 1932. A field study of the differential birth rate. *J. Amer. Statist. Ass.*, **27**, 153–159 [18].

CONRAD, H. S., & JONES, H. E. 1940. A second study of familial resemblance in intelligence: environmental and genetic implications of parent-child and sibling correlations in the total sample. *Yearb. Nat. Soc. Stud. Educ.*, **39** (II) [18].

COOGAN, MARGUERITE. *See* Willoughby & Coogan, 1940.

COOMBS, C. H. 1950. Psychological scaling without a unit of measurement. *Psychol. Rev.* **57**, 145–158 [229, 256].

COOMBS, C. H. 1952. A theory of psychological scaling. *Univer. Michigan Engng. Res. Inst. Bull.*, No. 34. Ann Arbor: Univer. Michigan Press [229].

CORNFORD, F. M. 1930. Embryology and the homeomereity of Anaxagoras. *Classical Quart.*, **24**, 14–24 [36, 309].

Cox, Catherine M. 1926. The early mental traits of three hundred geniuses. *Genetics studies of genius.* Vol. II. Stanford, Calif.: Stanford Univer. Press [17].

Crawford, M. P. 1937. The cooperative solving of problems by young chimpanzees. *Comp. Psychol. Monogr.*, 14 (68) [175].

Crissey, O. L. 1937. Mental development as related to institutional residence and educational achievement. *Univer. Iowa Stud. Child. Welf.*, 11 (1) [31].

Cronbach, L. J. 1949. *Essentials of psychological testing.* New York: Harper [310].

Cruikshank, Ruth M. *See* Brunswik & Cruikshank, 1937.

Cruze, W. W. 1935. Maturation and learning in chicks. *J. comp. Psychol.*, 19, 371–409 [54–56, 60, 259, 321].

Cruze, W. W. 1938. Maturation and learning ability. *Psychol. Monogr.*, 50, No. 5 [54, 321].

Cullen, C. *See* Li, Cullen & Jasper, 1956.

Cureton, E. E. *See* Dunlap & Cureton, 1930.

Curti, Margaret W. 1938. *Child psychology.* (2nd Ed.) New York: Longmans, Green [110].

Curtis, H. A. 1949. A study of the relative effects of age and of test difficulty upon factor patterns. *Genet. Psychol. Monogr.*, 40, 99–148 [257].

Da Cuna, A. B., Dobzhansky, T., Pavlovsky, O., & Spassky, B. 1958. Genetics of natural populations. XXVIII. Supplementary data on the chromosomal polymorphism in *Drosophila Willistoni* in its relation to the environment. *Evolution*, 13, 389–404 [335].

Daniel, R. S., & Smith, K. U. 1947. The migration of newly-hatched loggerhead turtles toward the sea. *Science*, 106, 398–399 [46].

Darwin, C. 1859. *Origin of the species.* London: Murray [11, 42].

Darwin, C. 1872. *The expressions of the emotions in man and animals.* New York: Appleton-Century-Crofts, 1873 [36, 45, 47, 62, 348–349].

Dashiell, J. F. 1928. *Fundamentals of general psychology.* Boston: Houghton Mifflin, 1937 [10, 253].

De Aromati, Joseph [37].

De Condolle, 1832 [45].

de Groot, A. D. 1948. The effects of war upon the intelligence of youth. *J. abnorm. soc. Psychol.*, 43, 311–317 [27].

de Groot, A. D. 1951. War and the intelligence of youth. *J. abnorm. soc. Psychol.*, 46, 596–597 [27].

De Marco, W. J. [295, 304].

Denenberg, V. H. 1960. Critical periods for the effects of infantile experience on adult learning. *Science*, 131 (3395), 227–228 [269–270].

Dennis, W. 1941. Spalding's experiment on the flight of birds repeated with another species. *J. comp. Psychol.*, 31, 337–348 [147].

Dennis, W. 1960. Causes of retardation among institutional children. *J. genet. Psychol.*, in press [6, 51, 61, 83, 149, 256, 264, 328, 336, 356, 361].

Dennis, W., & Dennis, Marsena G. 1935. The effect of restricted practice upon the reaching, sitting and standing of two infants. *J. genet. Psychol.*, 47, 21–29 [57].

Dennis, W., & Dennis, Marsena G. 1937. Behavioral development during the first year as shown by 40 biographies. *Psychol. Rec.*, 1, 349–360 [58].

Dennis, W., & Dennis, Marsena G. 1938. Infant development under conditions of restricted practice and minimum social stimulation: a preliminary report. *J. genet. Psychol.*, 53, 151–156 [57].

Dennis, W., & Dennis, Marsena G. 1940. The effect of cradling practice upon the onset of walking in Hopi children. *J. genet. Psychol.*, 56, 77–86 [57, 60, 336, 351].

Dennis, W., & Dennis, Marsena G. 1941. Infant development under conditions of restricted practice and minimum social stimulation. *Genet. Psychol. Monogr.*, 23, 149–155. Also as: Development under controlled environmental conditions in W. Dennis (Ed.), *Readings in child psychology.* New York: Prentice-Hall, 1951 [57, 123].

Dennis, W., & Najarian, Pergrouhi. 1957. Infant development under environmental handicap. *Psychol. Monogr.*, 71, No. 7 (Whole No. 436) [60–61].

DETWILER, S. R. *See* Matthews & Detwiler, 1926.

DEWEY, J. 1896. The reflex arc concept in psychology. *Psychol. Rev.*, 3, 357–370 [48, 112, 133, 252].

DEWEY, J. 1910. *How we think.* (New Ed.) Boston: Heath, 1933 [253, 282].

DEWEY, J. 1938. *Logic: the nature of inquiry.* New York: Holt, Rinehart & Winston.

DOBELL, C. 1932. *Antony van Leeuwenhoek and his "Little Animals."* London: Bale & Danielsson.

DOBZHANSKY, T. 1950. Heredity, environment and evolution. *Science,* 111, 161–166 [335].

DOBZHANSKY, T. 1956. *The biological basis of human freedom.* New York: Columbia Univer. Press [42, 310].

DOBZHANSKY, T. *See* Sinnott, Dunn, & Dobzhansky, 1958.

DOLLARD, J. *See* Miller & Dollard, 1941.

DOLLARD, J., & MILLER, N. E. 1950. *Personality and psychotherapy: an analysis in terms of learning, thinking, and culture.* New York: McGraw-Hill [68, 351].

DOPPELET, J. E. 1950. The organization of mental abilities in the age range 13 to 17. *Teach. Coll. Contr. Educ.*, No. 962 [257].

DUNCKER, K. 1926. A qualitative (experimental and theoretical) study of productive thinking (solving of comprehensible problems). *Ped. Sem. (J. genet. Psychol.)*, 33, 642–708 [200, 282].

DUNCKER, K. 1945. On problem solving. Trans. by L. S. Lees. *Psychol. Monogr.*, 58, (Whole No. 270) [200, 282].

DUNLAP, J. W., & CURETON, E. E. 1930. On the analysis of causation. *J. educ. Psychol.*, 21, 657–680 [329].

DUNLAP, K. 1919. Are there any instincts? *J. abnorm. soc. Psychol.*, 14, 307–311 [65].

DUNN, L. C. *See* Sinnott, Dunn, & Dobzhansky, 1958.

DYE, H. B. *See* Skeels & Dye, 1939.

EASLEY, J. A., JR. 1958. Is the teaching of scientific method a significant educa-tional objective? In I. Scheffler (Ed.), *Philosophy and education.* Boston: Allyn & Bacon [281].

EASLEY, J. A., JR. 1959. The Physical Science Study Committee and educational theory. *Harvard educ. Rev.*, 29, 4–11 [281].

EBERT, E., & SIMMONS, K. 1943. The Brush Foundation Study of child growth and development: I. Psychometric tests. *Monogr. Soc. Res. Child Devel.*, 8, No. 2, 113 [21].

ECHLIN, F. A., ARNETT, V., & ZOLL, J. 1952. Paroxysmal high voltage discharge from isolated and partially isolated human and animal cortex. *EEG clin. Neurophysiol.*, 4, 147–164 [88].

ELDERTON, E. M. 1923. A summary of the present position with regard to the inheritance of intelligence. *Biometrika,* 14, 378–408 [18].

ELLINGER, T. U. H. 1952. *Hippocrates on intercourse and pregnancy.* New York: Schuman [36].

ELLIOTT, ROGERS [195].

ESTES, BETSY W. 1956. Some mathematical and logical concepts in children. *J. genet. Psychol.*, 88, 219–222 [210, 295].

ESTES, W. K. 1950. Toward a statistical theory of learning. *Psychol. Rev.*, 57, 94–107 [67].

ESTES, W. K., & BURKE, C. J. 1953. A theory of stimulus variability in learning. *Psychol. Rev.*, 60, 276–286 [67].

EYDT, A. 1938. Auslese und Ausmerze in der Volksschule. *Volk u. Rasse.*, 13, 344–351 [337].

FERGUSON, G. A. 1954. On learning and human ability. *Canad. J. Psychol.*, 8, 95–112 [302].

FERGUSON, G. A. 1956. On transfer and the abilities of man. *Canad. J. Psychol.*, 10, 121–131 [302].

FERGUSON, G. A. 1959. Learning and human ability: A theoretical approach. In P. H. DuBois, W. H. Manning, & C. J. Spies (Eds.), *Factor analysis and related techniques in the study of learning.* A report of a conference held at Washington University in St. Louis, Mo., February, 1959. Technical Report No. 7, Office of Naval Research Con-

FERGUSON, G. A. 1959. (*Cont.*) tract No. Nonr 816 (02). Pp. 174–182 [302–303, 359].

FESTINGER, L. 1957. *A theory of cognitive dissonance.* Evanston, Ill.: Row, Peterson [14, 199, 205, 268–269, 280–282].

FINCH, F. H. 1946. Enrollment increases and changes in the mental level. *Appl. Psychol. Monogr.*, No. 10, 75 [339–340].

FISHER, R. A. 1918. The correlation between relatives on the supposition of Mendelian inheritance. *Trans. Roy. Soc. Edinburgh*, 52, 399–433 [324, 329]

FISHER, S. C. 1925. The psychological and educational work of Granville Stanley Hall. *Amer. J. Psychol.*, 36, 1–52 [43].

FLEISHMAN, E. A., & HEMPEL, W. E., JR. 1954. Changes in factor structure of a complex psychomotor test as a function of practice. *Psychometrika*, 19, 239–252 [301].

FLEISHMAN, E. A., & HEMPEL, W. E., JR. 1955. The relation between abilities and improvement with practice in a visual discrimination reaction task. *J. exp. Psychol.*, 49, 301–312 [301].

FLOURNOY, T. [112, 253].

FORGAYS, D. G., & FORGAYS, JANET W. 1952. The nature of the effect of free environmental experience in the rat. *J. comp. physiol. Psychol.*, 45, 322–328 [100, 316].

FORGUS, R. H. 1954. The effect of early perceptual learning on the behavioral organization of adult rats. *J. comp. physiol. Psychol.*, 47, 331–336 [100, 316].

FORGUS, R. H. 1955a. Influence of early experience on maze-learning with and without visual cues. *Canad. J. Psychol.*, 9, 207–214 [100–101, 316].

FORGUS, R. H. 1955b. Early visual and motor experience as determiners of complex maze-learning ability under rich and reduced stimulation. *J. comp. physiol. Psychol.*, 48, 215–220 [100–102, 316].

FORGUS, R. H. 1958a. The effect of different kinds of form pre-exposure on form discrimination learning. *J. comp. physiol. Psychol.*, 51, 75–78 [102].

FORGUS, R. H. 1958b. The interaction between form pre-exposure and test requirements in determining form discrimination. *J. comp. physiol. Psychol.*, 51, 588–591 [102].

FORLANO, G. *See* Pintner & Forlano, 1942.

FREDERICSON, E. *See* Scott, Fredericson, & Fuller, 1951.

FREEMAN, F. N. *See* Newman, Freeman, & Holzinger, 1937.

FRENCH, J. W. 1951. The description of aptitude and achievement tests in terms of rotated factors. *Psychometr. Monogr.*, No. 5 [300].

FRENCH, J. W. 1954. *Manual for kit of selected tests for reference aptitude and achievement factors.* Princeton, N. J.: Educational Testing Service [300–301].

FREUD, S. 1915. Instincts and their vicissitudes. *Collected Papers*, 4, 60–83. London: Hogarth, 1927 [133, 253].

FREUD, S. 1922. *Beyond the pleasure principle.* Trans. from second German edition by C. J. M. Hubback. New York: Boni & Liveright [262].

FRICK, J. W. *See* Guilford, Merrifield, Christensen, & Frick, 1960.

FROEBEL, F. 1892. *The education of man.* Trans. by W. N. Hailman. New York: Appleman [5, 279].

FROMME, A. 1941. An experimental study of factors of maturation and practice in the behavioral development of the embryo of the frog *Rana pipiens. Genet. Psychol. Monogr.*, 24, 219–256 [321].

FRYER, D. 1922. Occupational intelligence standards. *Sch. & Soc.*, 16, 273–277 [17].

FULLER, J. L. 1956. Heredity and the selective canalization of behavior. Paper presented at a symposium on *Heredity and the development of behavior.* Meetings of the APA, September, 1956.

FULLER, J. L. 1960. Behavior genetics. *Ann. Rev. Psychol.*, 11, 41–70 [7].

FULLER, J. L. *See* Scott, Fredericson, & Fuller, 1951.

FULLER, J. L., & SCOTT, J. P. 1954. Heredity and learning ability in infrahuman mammals. *Eugen. Quart.*, 1, 28–43 [6, 268, 330, 357].

FULLER, J. L., & THOMPSON, W. R. 1960. *Behavior genetics.* New York: Wiley [6].

FURFEY, P. H., & MUEHLENBEIN, J. 1932.

The validity of infant intelligence tests. *J. genet. Psychol.,* **40,** 219–223 [21–23].

GALANTER, E. H. *See* Miller, Galanter, & Pribram, 1960.

GALTON, F. 1869. *Hereditary genius: an inquiry into its laws and consequences.* London: Macmillan [11].

GALTON, F. 1883. *Inquiries into human faculty and its development.* London: Macmillan [11, 323].

GALTON, F. 1886. Regression towards mediocrity in heredity stature. *J. Anthrop. Inst.,* **15,** 246–263 [12].

GALTON, F. [13, 348].

GARRETT, H. E. 1946. A developmental theory of intelligence. *Amer. Psychologist,* **1,** 372–378 [257, 301].

GATES, A. I. *See* Harrell, Woodyard, & Gates, 1955.

GATES, A. I., & TAYLOR, G. A. 1925. An experimental study of the nature of improvement resulting from practice in a mental function. *J. educ. Psychol.,* **16,** 583–593 [55–56].

GAURON, E. F., & BECKER, W. C. 1959. The effects of early sensory deprivation on adult rat behavior under competition stress: an attempt at replication of a study by Alexander Wolf. *J. comp. physiol. Psychol.,* **52,** 689–693 [97, 265].

GERARD, R. W., & YOUNG, J. Z. 1937. Electrical activity of the central nervous system of the frog. *Proc. Roy. Soc.* (London), **122,** 343–352 [88].

GESELL, A. 1945. *The embryology of behavior: the beginnings of the human mind.* New York: Harper [35, 249, 258, 263].

GESELL, A. 1954. The ontogenesis of infant behavior. In L. Carmichael (Ed.), *Manual of child psychology.* Chap. 6. New York: Wiley [264].

GESELL, A. [43, 249, 258, 263].

GESELL, A., et al. 1940. *The first five years of life.* New York: Harper [35].

GESELL, A., & AMATRUDA, CATHERINE S. 1941. *Developmental diagnosis: normal and abnormal child development, clinical methods and practical applications.* New York: Harper [168, 264].

GESELL, A., & THOMPSON, HELEN. 1929. Learning and growth in identical twin infants. *Genet. Psychol. Monogr.,* **6,** 1–124 [57, 94, 161, 271, 322].

GIBSON, E. J., & WALK, R. D. 1956. The effect of prolonged exposure to visually presented patterns on learning to discriminate between them. *J. comp. physiol. Psychol.,* **49,** 239–242 [102].

GIBSON, E. J., WALK, R. D., PICK, H. L., JR., & TIGHE, T. J. 1958. The effect of prolonged exposure to visual patterns on learning to discriminate similar and different patterns. *J. comp. physiol. Psychol.,* **51,** 584–587 [102].

GIBSON, J. J. 1941. A critical review of the concept of set in contemporary experimental psychology. *Psychol. Bull.,* **38,** 781–817 [84].

GIBSON, J. J. 1950. *The perception of the visual world.* Boston: Houghton Mifflin [62].

GILLE, R., HENRY, L., TABAH, L., SUTTER, J., BERGUES, H., GIRARD, A., & BASTIDE, H. 1954. Le niveau intellectuel des enfants de 'age scolaire: la détermination des aptitudes; l'influence des facteurs constitutionnels, familiaux, et sociaux. *Inst. nat. d'études démographique: travaux et documents,* Cahier **23,** 294 [337, 341–342].

GODDARD, H. H. 1912. *The Kallikak family: a study in the heredity of feeblemindedness.* New York: Macmillan [14, 43].

GODDARD, H. H. [43].

GOLDFARB, W. 1943a. Effects of early institutional care on adolescent personality. *J. exp. Educ.,* **12,** 106–129 [266].

GOLDFARB, W. 1943b. Infant rearing and problem behavior. *Amer. J. Orthopsychiat.,* **13,** 249–266 [266].

GOLDFARB, W. 1943c. The effects of early institutional care on adolescent personality. *Child Developm.,* **14,** 213–223 [266].

GOLDFARB, W. 1944. Effects of early institutional care on adolescent personality: Rorschach data. *Amer. J. Orthopsychiat.,* **14,** 441–447 [266].

GOLDFARB, W. 1945. Psychological privation in infancy and subsequent adjustment. *Amer. J. Orthopsychiat.,* **15,** 247–255 [266].

GOLDFARB, W. 1947. Variations in ado-

GOLDFARB, W. 1947. (*Cont.*) lescent adjustment of institutionally-reared children. *Amer. J. Orthopsychiat.*, **17**, 449–457 [266].

GOLDFARB, W. 1949. Rorschach test differences between family-reared, institution-reared and schizophrenic children. *Amer. J. Orthopsychiat.*, **19**, 624–633 [266].

GOLDSTEIN, K. 1939. *The organism: a holistic approach to biology derived from pathological data in man.* Trans. by H. L. Ansbacher. New York: American Book [48, 297].

GOODENOUGH, FLORENCE L. 1928. A preliminary report on the effect of nursery school training upon the intelligence test scores of young children. *Yearb. Nat. Soc. Stud. Educ.*, **27** (I), 361–369 [27].

GOODENOUGH, FLORENCE L. 1939. A critique of experiments on raising the IQ. *Educ. Meth.*, **19**, 73–79. Reprinted in W. Dennis (Ed.), *Readings in child psychology.* New York: Prentice-Hall, 1951 [23, 26, 28, 31].

GOODENOUGH, FLORENCE L. 1940. New evidence on environmental influence on intelligence. *Yearb. Nat. Soc. Stud. Educ.*, **39** (I), 307–365 [26].

GOODENOUGH, FLORENCE L., & MAURER, KATHERINE M. 1942. *The mental growth of children from two to fourteen years; a study of the predictive value of the Minnesota Preschool Scales.* Minneapolis: Univer. Minnesota Press [23–24, 313].

GOODNOW, JACQUELINE J. *See* Bruner, Goodnow, & Austin, 1956.

GOUSTARD, M. 1959. Étude psychogénétique de la résolution d'un problème (Labyrinthe en T) *Études d'Épistémol. génét.*, **10**, 83–112 [200, 273].

GRAFFAM, D. T. 1949. *A comparative study of educational achievement in four groups of states, based on the Navy tests of reading, arithmetical reasoning, and spelling.* Unpublished doctor's dissertation Univer. Southern California [334].

GRANIT, R. 1955. *Receptors and sensory perception.* New Haven: Yale Univer. Press [88–89].

GRECO, P. 1959a. L'apprentissage dans une situation à structure opératoire con-

crète: les inversions successives de l'ordre linéaire par des rotations de 180°. *Études d'Épistémol. génét.*, **7**, 68–182. (From Smedslund, 1961) [280].

GRECO, P. 1959b. Induction, déduction et apprentissage. *Études d'Épistémol. génét.*, **10**, 3–59 [200, 273].

GREEN, J. A. 1913. *The life and work of Pestalozzi.* London: Univer. Tutorial Press [279].

GROOS, K. 1896. *The play of man.* Trans. by Elizabeth L. Baldwin. New York: Appleton-Century-Crofts, 1905 [176, 183].

GROOS, K. 1898. *The play of animals.* Trans. by Elizabeth L. Baldwin. New York: Appleton-Century-Crofts, 1902 [176, 183].

GROOT, A. D. DE. *See* de Groot.

GUILFORD, J. P. 1940. Human abilities. *Psychol. Rev.*, **47**, 367–394 [300, 311].

GUILFORD, J. P. 1956. The structure of intellect. *Psychol. Bull.*, **53**, 267–293 [300–301, 311].

GUILFORD, J. P. 1957. A revised structure of intellect. *Rep. psychol. Lab.*, No. 19. Los Angeles: Univer. Southern California [311].

GUILFORD, J. P., MERRIFIELD, P. R., CHRISTENSEN, P. R., & FRICK, J. W. 1960. A factor-analytic study of problem-solving abilities. *Rep. psychol. Lab.*, No. 22. Los Angeles: Univer. Southern California [282–283].

GUTHRIE, E. R. 1935. *The psychology of learning.* New York: Harper [47, 67].

GUTTMAN, L. 1941. The quantification of a class of attributes: a theory and method of scale construction. In P. Horst (Ed.), *The prediction of personal adjustment.* Pp. 319–248. New York: Bull. No. 48, Social Science Research Council [169, 229, 256].

GUTTMAN, L. 1944. A basis for scaling qualitative data. *Amer. sociol. Rev.*, **9**, 139–150 [169, 229, 256].

HAKE, H. W. 1957. *Contributions of psychology to the study of pattern vision.* WADC Technical Report 57–621; Astia Document No. AD 142035. Air Research and Development Command, U. S. Air Force, Wright-Patterson Air

Force Base, O [89].

HALDANE, J. B. S. 1938. *Heredity and politics.* New York: Norton [326].

HALL, G. STANLEY [35, 42, 43, 44, 63, 183, 249, 258, 262, 323, 348, 349].

HALL, M. 1837. On the spinal marrow, and on the excito-motor system of nerves. Lectures given before the Royal Society, privately printed. (From Brazier, 1959) [47].

HALLER, A. VON. *See* von Haller.

HAM, J. *See* van Leeuwenhoek & Ham, 1677.

HARLOW, H. F. 1949. The formation of learning sets. *Psychol. Rev.*, 56, 51–65 [8, 65, 77–82, 107, 115, 125, 137, 157, 188, 296, 354].

HARLOW, H. F. 1951a. Primate learning. In C. P. Stone (Ed.), *Comparative psychology.* Chap. 7. New York: Prentice-Hall [81–83].

HARLOW, H. F. 1951b. Thinking. In H. Helson (Ed.), *Theoretical foundations of psychology.* Chap. 10. Princeton, N. J.: Van Nostrand [81–83].

HARLOW, H. F. 1953. Motivation as a factor in the acquisition of new responses. In *Current theory and research in motivation.* Pp. 24–49. Lincoln: Univer. Nebraska Press [180, 254].

HARLOW, H. F., MEYER, D. R., & SETTLAGE, P. H. 1951. Effect of large cortical lesions on the solution of oddity problems. *J. comp. physiol. Psychol.*, 18, 44–50 [81].

HARLOW, H. F., & WARREN, J. M. 1952. Formation and transfer of discrimination learning sets. *J. comp. physiol. Psychol.*, 45, 482–489 [77–82].

HARNLEY, M. H. 1940. The temperature responses of flies with the deficiency vestigial-depilate in Drosophila melanogaster. *Genet.*, 25, 521–533 [41].

HARRELL, RUTH F., WOODYARD, ELLA, & GATES, A. I. 1955. The effect of mothers' diets on the intelligence of the offspring. New York: Bur. Publ. Teach. Coll., Columbia Univer. [335].

HARTSOEKER, N. 1694. *Essay de Dioptrique.* Paris (From Needham, 1959) [38–39].

HARVEY, W. [37–38].

HEBB, D. O. 1937a. The innate organization of visual activity: I. Perception of figures by rats reared in total darkness. *J. genet. Psychol.*, 51, 101–126 [92].

HEBB, D. O. 1937b. The innate organization of visual activity: II. Transfer of response in the discrimination of brightness and size by rats reared in total darkness. *J. comp. Psychol.*, 24, 277–299 [92].

HEBB, D. O. 1939. Intelligence in man after large removals of cerebral tissue: report of four left frontal lobe cases. *J. genet. Psychol.*, 21, 73–87 [84].

HEBB, D. O. 1942. The effect of early and late brain injury upon test scores, and the nature of normal adult intelligence. *Proc. Amer. Phil. Soc.*, 85, 275–292 [84, 289].

HEBB, D. O. 1945. Man's frontal lobes: a critical review. *Arch. Neurol. Psychiat.*, 54, 1–24 [85].

HEBB, D. O. 1946. On the nature of fear. *Psychol. Rev.*, 53, 259–276 [148, 268].

HEBB, D. O. 1947. The effects of early experience on problem-solving at maturity. *Amer. Psychologist*, 2, 306–307 [83].

HEBB, D. O. 1949. *The organization of behavior.* New York: Wiley [8, 62, 65, 83–99, 107–108, 125, 151, 158, 179, 199, 216, 261–269, 288–289, 315, 330, 351–358].

HEBB, D. O. 1959. A neuropsychological theory. In S. Koch (Ed.), *Psychology: a study of a science.* Vol. 1, 622–643. *Sensory, perceptual, and physiological formulations.* New York: McGraw-Hill [86].

HEBB, D. O., & RIESEN, A. H. 1943. The genesis of irrational fears. *Bull. Canad. psychol. Assoc.*, 3, 49–50 [148, 268].

HEBB, D. O., & THOMPSON, W. R. 1954. The social significance of animal studies. In G. Lindzey (Ed.), *Handbook of social psychology.* Chap. 15. Reading, Mass.: Addison-Wesley [175].

HEBB, D. O., & WILLIAMS, K. 1946. A method of rating animal intelligence. *J. genet. Psychol.*, 34, 59–65 [98–99, 100, 106, 263, 353].

HEGEL, G. W. F. [43].

HEINEN, A. 1938. Schulleistungen, väterlicher Beruf, und Kinderzahl. *A. mensch. Vererb. Konst. Lehre*, 21, 599–608 [337].

HELSON, H. 1959. Adaptation level theory.

HELSON, H. 1959. (*Cont.*)
In S. Koch (Ed.), *Psychology: a study of a science*. Vol. 1, 565–621. *Sensory, perceptual, and physiological formulations*. New York: McGraw-Hill [202, 269].

HEMPEL, W. E., JR. See Fleishman & Hempel, 1954.

HENDRICKSON, G. See Brownell & Hendrickson, 1950.

HENDRIK, I. 1943. The discussion of the "instinct to master." *Psychoanal. Quart.*, 12, 561–565 [179, 261].

HENRY, C. E., & SCOVILLE, W. B. 1952. Suppression-burst activity from isolated cerebral cortex in man. *EEG clin. Neurophysiol.*, 4, 1–22 [88].

HENRY, G. W. 1941. Organic mental diseases. In G. Zilboorg (Ed.), *A history of medical psychology*. Chap. 13. New York: Norton [49].

HERON, W. See Thompson & Heron, 1954.

HESS, E. H. 1959. The relationship between imprinting and motivation. In M. R. Jones (Ed.), *Nebraska symposium on motivation*. Pp. 44–77. Lincoln: Univer. Nebraska Press [65].

HETZER, HILDEGARD, & WOLF, KATHE. 1928. Eine Testserie für das erste Lebensjahr. Z. *Psychol.*, 107, 62–104 [33–34].

HILDRETH, GERTRUDE H. 1925. The resemblance of siblings in intelligence and achievement. *Teach. Coll. Contr. Educ.*, No. 186 [18].

HILDRETH, GERTRUDE H. 1928. The effect of school environment upon Stanford-Binet tests of young children. *Yearb. Nat. Soc. Stud. Educ.*, 27 (I), 355–359 [27].

HILGARD, E. R. 1948. *Theories of learning.* New York: Appleton-Century-Crofts [66, 248].

HILGARD, E. R. 1956. *Theories of learning.* (2nd ed.) New York: Appleton-Century-Crofts [161].

HILGARD, E. R., & MARQUIS, D. G. 1940. *Conditioning and learning*. New York: Appleton-Century-Crofts [84, 191].

HILGARD, JOSEPHINE R. 1932. Learning and maturation in preschool children. *J. genet. Psychol.*, 41, 36–56 [56, 161, 271, 322].

HILGARD, JOSEPHINE R. 1933. The effect of early and delayed practice on memory and motor performances studied by the method of co-twin control. *Genet. Psychol. Monogr.*, 14, 493–567 [57, 161, 271, 322].

HINGSTON, R. W. G. 1929. *Problems of instinct and intelligence*. New York: Macmillan [65].

HIPPOCRATES. See Ellinger, 1952.

HOBBS, G. E. 1941. Mental disorder in one of a pair of identical twins. *Amer. J. Psychiat.*, 98, 447–450 [20].

HOFSTAETTER, P. R. 1954. The changing composition of "intelligence": a study in T-technique. *J. genet. Psychol.*, 85, 159–164 [304, 359].

HOGBEN, L. 1933. *Nature and nurture.* London: Allen & Unwin.

HOGBEN, L. 1939. *Nature and nurture.* (2nd ed.) London: Allen & Unwin [326, 331].

HOLLINGWORTH, LETA S. 1942. *Children above 180 IQ*. Yonkers, N. Y.: World Book [17].

HOLT, E. B. 1931. *Animal drive and the learning process.* New York: Holt [290].

HOLZINGER, K. J. 1937. *Student manual of factor analysis*. Chicago: Dept. Education, Univer. Chicago [300, 311].

HOLZINGER, K. J. See Newman, Freeman, & Holzinger, 1937.

HONZIG, MARJORIE P., MACFARLANE, JEAN W., & ALLEN, L. 1948. The stability of mental test performance between two and 18 years. *J. exp. Educ.*, 4, 309–324 [21–24, 31].

HORSFALL, W. R., & ANDERSON, J. F. 1961. Suppression of male characteristics of mosquitoes by thermal means. *Science*, 133 (3467), 1830 [331].

HOUSE, BETTY J., & ZEAMAN, D. 1959. Position discrimination and reversals in low-grade retardates. *J. comp. physiol. Psychol.*, 52, 564–565 [83, 330].

HUANG, I. 1943. Children's conception of physical causality: a critical summary. *J. genet. Psychol.*, 63, 1–121 [110].

HULL, C. L. 1927. Variability in amount of different traits possessed by the individual. *J. educ. Psychol.*, 18, 97–104 [298].

HULL, C. L. 1930. Knowledge and purpose

as habit mechanisms. *Psychol. Rev.*, 37, 511–525 [68–69, 107].

HULL, C. L. 1943. *Principles of behavior.* New York: Appleton-Century-Crofts [68, 72, 112, 133, 209, 253, 294, 351].

HULL, C. L. 1952. *A behavior system.* New Haven: Yale Univer. Press [68].

HUME, D. 1739. *Treatise on human nature.* New York: Oxford Univer. Press, 1928 [251].

HUME, D. 1748. *An enquiry concerning human understanding.* (Harvard Classics) New York: Collier & Sons, 1910 [251].

HUMPHREYS, L. G. 1959. Discussion of Dr. Ferguson's paper. In P. H. DuBois, W. H. Manning, & C. J. Spies (Eds.), *Factor analysis and related techniques in the study of learning.* A report of a conference held at Washington University, St. Louis, Mo., February, 1959. Technical Report No. 7, Office of Naval Research Contract No. Nonr 816 (02). Pp. 183–187 [302–304].

HUNT, J. McV. 1935. Psychological loss in paretics and schizophrenics. *Amer. J. Psychol.*, 48, 64–81 [297].

HUNT, J. McV. 1960. Experience and the development of motivation: some reinterpretations. *Child Develpm.*, 31, 489–504 [253].

HUNT, J. McV. *See* Nichols & Hunt, 1940.

HUNT, J. McV., & COFER, C. N. 1944. Psychological deficit. In J. McV. Hunt (Ed.), *Personality and the behavior disorders.* Chap. 32. New York: Ronald [292, 296].

HUNTER, W. S. 1912. The delayed reaction in animals and children. *Behav. Monogr.*, 2 (1), 1–85 [67, 106].

HUNTER, W. S. 1918. The temporal maze and kinaesthetic sensory processes in the white rat. *Psychobiol.*, 2, 339–351 [67, 106].

HUNTER, W. S. 1924. The symbolic process. *Psychol. Rev.*, 31, 478–497 [67–68, 175].

HYDE, D. M. 1959. *An investigation of Piaget's theories of the development of the concept of number.* Unpublished doctor's dissertation, London University (From Smedslund, 1961) [295].

HYMOVITCH, B. 1952. The effects of experimental variations in early experience on problem solving in the rat. *J. comp. physiol. Psychol.*, 45, 313–321 [99].

INHELDER, BÄRBEL. 1936. Observations sur le principe de conservation dans la physique de l'infant. *Cahiers Péd. Exp. Psychol. de l'Enfant*, 9 [113].

INHELDER, BÄRBEL. 1944. *Le diagnostic du raisonnement chez les débiles mentaux.* Neuchâtel: Delachaux et Niestlé [226–229, 256].

INHELDER, BÄRBEL. 1953. Criteria of the stages of mental development. In J. M. Tanner & Bärbel Inhelder (Eds.), *Discussions on child development.* Pp. 75–85. New York: Int. Univer. Press [113].

INHELDER, BÄRBEL. 1954. Les attitudes experimentales de l'enfant et de l'adolescent. *Bull. Psychol.*, 7, 272–282.

INHELDER, BÄRBEL. *See* Piaget & Inhelder, 1948.

INHELDER, BÄRBEL, & PIAGET, J. 1955. *The growth of logical thinking from childhood to adolescence: an essay on the construction of formal operational structures.* Trans. by Anne Parsons & S. Milgram. New York: Basic Books, 1958 [115, 229–246, 287, 295].

ISAACS, SUSAN S. 1930. *Intellectual growth in young children.* New York: Harcourt, Brace & World [110].

JACKSON, T. A. 1942. Use of the stick as a tool by young chimpanzees. *J. comp. Psychol.*, 34, 223–235 [63, 77, 152].

JACOBSEN, C. F. & NISSEN, H. W. 1937. Studies of cerebral function in primates: IV. The effects of frontal lobe lesions on the delayed alternation habit in monkeys. *J. comp. Psychol.*, 23, 101–112 [89].

JACOBSEN, E. 1932. The electrophysiology of mental activities. *Amer. J. Psychol.*, 44, 677–694 [290].

JAMES, W. 1890. *Principles of psychology.* New York: Holt, Rinehart & Winston, 1910 [43].

JAMES, W. 1907. *Pragmatism.* New York: Longmans, Green [43, 46, 251–253].

JASPER, H. H. *See* Li, Cullen, & Jasper, 1956.

JENNINGS, H. S. 1906. *The behavior of lower organisms.* New York: Columbia Univer. Press [46].

JENNINGS, H. S. 1930. *The biological basis of human nature.* New York: Norton [41].

JERVIS, G. A. 1939. A contribution to the study of the influence of heredity on mental deficiency. The genetics of phenylpyruvic oligophrenia. *Proc. Amer. Assoc. Stud. ment. Def.,* 44, 13–24 [330, 335].

JOHANNSEN, W. 1903. *Über Erblichkeit in populationen und in reinen Linien.* Jena: Gustav Fisher [7, 41, 331].

JOHANNSEN, W. 1909. *Elemente der exakten Erblichkeitslehre.* Jena: Gustav Fisher [7, 41, 331, 341].

JOHNSON, D. M. 1955. *The psychology of thought and judgment.* New York: Harper [282].

JONES, H. E. 1954. The environment and mental development. In L. Carmichael (Ed.), *Handbook of child psychology.* Chap. 10. New York: Wiley [16, 18, 22–25, 28, 313].

JONES, H. E. *See* Conrad & Jones, 1940.

JONES, H. E., & JORGENSEN, A. P. 1940. Mental growth as related to nursery-school attendance. *Yearb. Nat. Soc. Stud. Educ.,* 39 (II), 207–222 [30].

KALHORN, J. *See* Baldwin, Kalhorn, & Breese, 1945.

KANT, I. 1791. *Critique of pure reason.* New York: Macmillan, 1929 [251–252].

KARDINER, A., & SPIEGEL, H. 1947. *War stress and neurotic illness.* New York: Hoeber [248].

KARN, M. N. *See* Stocks & Karn, 1933.

KAUFMAN, M. E. 1956. The formation of learning sets with mentally retarded children. *Dissertation Abstr.,* 16, 156 [83].

KELLER, HELEN A. 1903. *The story of my life.* New York: Grosset & Dunlap, 1911 [187, 268].

KELLEY, T. L. 1926. *The influence of nurture upon native differences.* New York: Macmillan.

KELLEY, T. L. 1928. *Crossroads in the minds of man: a study of differentiable mental abilities.* Stanford, Calif.: Stanford Univer. Press [17, 299].

KELLEY, T. L. 1935. *Essential traits of mental life.* Cambridge: Harvard Univer. Press [311].

KELLY, E. L. [342].

KIRK, S. A. 1948. An evaluation of the study by Bernadine G. Schmidt entitled: Changes in personal, social and intellectual behavior of children originally classified as feebleminded. *Psychol. Bull.,* 45, 321–333.

KIRK, S. A. 1958. *Early education of the mentally retarded.* Urbana: Univer. Illinois Press [333].

KNOBLOCH, HILDA. *See* Pasamanick, Knobloch, & Lilienfeld, 1956.

KOCH, HELEN L. *See* Barrett & Koch, 1930.

KÖHLER, W. 1925. *The mentality of apes.* New York: Harcourt, Brace & World [48, 62–63, 77, 83, 107, 161, 175].

KÖHLER, W. 1929. *Gestalt psychology.* New York: Liveright, 1929 [48, 62, 107, 254–255].

KÖHLER, W. 1940. *Dynamics in psychology.* New York: Liveright [254].

KRECHEVSKY, I. 1932. "Hypotheses" versus "chance" in the pre-solution period in sensory discrimination-learning. *Univer. Calif. Publ. Psychol.,* 6, 27–44 [68].

KRECHEVSKY, I. 1933a. Hereditary nature of "hypotheses." *J. comp. Psychol.,* 16, 99–116 [68, 151, 330].

KRECHEVSKY, I. 1933b. The docile nature of "hyotheses." *J. comp. Psychol.,* 15, 439–444 [68, 151, 330].

KRISTY, N. F. *See* Cattell, Stice, & Kristy, 1957.

KÜHLMANN, F. 1922. *A handbook of mental tests.* Baltimore: Warwick & York [43].

KÜHLMANN, F. [43].

KÜHLMANN, F., & ANDERSON, ROSE G. 1940. *Kuhlmann-Anderson intelligence tests.* (5th ed.) Minneapolis, Minn.: Educational Test Bureau [31–32].

KÜLPE, O. [200].

KUO, Z. Y. 1921. Give up instincts in psychology. *J. Phil.,* 18, 645–664 [65, 360].

KUO, Z. Y. 1922. How are instincts acquired? *Psychol. Rev.,* 29, 334–365 [65, 360].

KUO, Z. Y. 1932a. Ontogeny of embryonic behavior in aves: I. The chronology and general nature of the behavior in the chick embryo. *J. exp. Zool.*, **61**, 395–430 [116, 317–318].

Kuo, Z. Y. 1932b. Ontogeny of embryonic behavior in aves: II. The mechanical factors in the various stages leading to hatching. *J. exp. Zool.*, **62**, 453–487 [50, 318].

Kuo, Z. Y. 1932c. Ontogeny of embryonic behavior in aves: III. The structural and environmental factors in embryonic behavior. *J. comp. Psychol.*, **13**, 245–271 [318].

Kuo, Z. Y. 1932d. Ontogeny of embryonic behavior in aves: IV. The influence of embryonic movements upon the behavior after hatching. *J. comp. Psychol.*, **14**, 109–122 [65, 317–320].

Kuo. Z. Y. 1932e. Ontogeny of embryonic behavior in aves: V. The reflex concept in the light of embryonic behavior in birds. *Psychol. Rev.*, **39**, 499–515 [116, 320].

Kuo, Z. Y. 1939. Development of acetylcholine in the chick embryo. *J. Neurophysiol.*, **2**, 488–493 [320].

Kurke, M. I. *See* Riesen, Kurke, & Mellinger, 1953.

Lambercier, M. *See* Piaget & Lambercier, 1943a, 1943b, 1944, 1946, 1953.

Langfeld, H. S. 1931. A response interpretation of consciousness. *Psychol. Rev.*, **38**, 87–108 [290].

Lashley, K. S. 1917. The accuracy of movement in the absence of excitation from the moving organ. *Amer. J. Physiol.*, **43**, 169–194 [74, 107].

Lashley, K. S. 1929. *Brain mechanisms and intelligence: a quantitative study of injuries to the brain.* Chicago: Univer. Chicago Press [351].

Lashley, K. S. 1938. The mechanism of vision: XV. Preliminary studies of the rat's capacity for detail vision. *J. gen. Psychol.*, **18**, 123–193 [92].

Lashley, K. S. 1958. Cerebral organization and behavior. *Proc. Ass. Res. nerv. ment. Dis.*, **36**, 1–18. Reprinted in *The neuro-psychology of Lashley.* Paper 31. New York: McGraw-Hill, 1960 [290–291].

Lawrence, E. M. 1931. An investigation into the relation between intelligence and inheritance. *Brit. J. Psychol. Monogr. Suppl.*, **16**, 1–80 [18].

Leahy, Alice M. 1935. Nature-nurture and intelligence. *Genet. Psychol. Monogr.*, **17**, 235–308 [19, 324].

Leeuwenhoek, A. van. *See* van Leeuwenhoek & Ham.

Leham, H. C., & Witty, P. A. 1927. *The psychology of play activities.* New York: Ronald.

Lentz, T. F., Jr. 1927. Relation of IQ to size of family. *J. educ. Psychol.*, **18**, 486–496 [337].

Levine, J. 1945. Studies in the interrelations of central nervous system in binocular vision. II. The conditions under which interocular transfer of discriminative habits takes place in the pigeon. *J. genet. Psychol.*, **67**, 131–142 [96].

Levine, S. 1956. A further study of infantile handling and adult avoidance learning. *J. Pers.*, **25**, 70–80.

Levine, S. 1957. Infantile experience and consummatory behavior in adulthood. *J. comp. physiol. Psychol.*, **50**, 609-612.

Levine, S. 1958. Noxious stimulation in infant and adult rats and consummatory behavior. *J. comp. physiol. Psychol.*, **51**, 230–233.

Levine, S. 1959. The effects of differential infantile stimulation on emotionality at weaning. *Canad. J. Psychol.*, **13**, 243–247.

Levine, S., Chevalier, J. A., & Korchin, S. J. 1956. The effects of early shock and handling on later avoidance learning. *J. Pers.*, **24**, 475–493.

Levitt, E. E. *See* Ojemann, Levitt, Lyle, & Whiteside, 1955.

Li, C. L., Cullen, C., & Jasper, H. H. 1956. Laminar microelectrode analysis of cortical unspecific recruiting response and spontaneous rhythms. *J. Neurophysiol.*, **19**, 131–143 [91, 293].

Lilienfeld, A. M. *See* Pasamanick, Knobloch, & Lilienfeld, 1956.

Lilly, J. C. 1956. Mental effects of reduction of ordinary levels of physical stimuli on intact, healthy persons. *Psychiat. Res. Rep.*, **5**, 1–9.

Line, W., & Kaplan, E. 1933. Variation in IQ at the preschool level. *J. exp. Educ.*, **2**, 95–100.

LOEB, J. 1890. *Der Heliotropismus der Thiere und seine Überstimmung mit dem Heliotropismus der Pflanzen.* Würzburg: Hertz [45–46, 349, 351].

LOEB, J. 1918. *Tropisms, forced movements, and animal conduct.* Philadelphia: Lippincott [35, 349, 351].

LOEVINGER, JANE. 1943. On the proportional contributions of differences in nature and nurture to differences in intelligence. *Psychol. Bull.,* **40,** 725–756 [324, 329, 333].

LORENTE DE NÓ, R. 1938a. Synaptic stimulation of motoneurones as a local process. *J. Neurophysiol.* 1, 195–206 [85].

LORENTE DE NÓ, R. 1938b. Analysis of the activity of the chains of internuncial neurones. *J. Neurophysiol.,* 1, 207–244 [85].

LORENTE DE NÓ, R. 1943. Cerebral cortex: architecture. In J. F. Fulton, *Physiology of the nervous system.* (2nd ed.) Pp. 274–301. New York: Oxford Univer. Press.

LORENZ, K. Z. 1952. *King Solomon's ring.* New York: Crowell [65].

LORGE, I. 1945. Schooling makes a difference. *Teach. Coll. Rec.,* 46, 483–492 [26].

LORIMER, F., & OSBORN, F. 1934. *Dynamics of population.* New York: Macmillan.

LOVELL, K. 1959. A follow-up study of some aspects of the work of Piaget and Inhelder on the child's conception of space. *Brit. J. educ. Psychol.,* **29,** 104–117 [194, 295].

LOVELL, K. 1961. A follow-up study of Inhelder and Piaget's *The growth of logical thinking. Brit. J. Psychol.,* 52, 143–153 [238, 295].

LOVELL, K., & OGILVIE, E. 1960. A study of the conservation of substance in the junior school child. *Brit. J. educ. Psychol.,* 30, 109–118 [207, 228, 295].

LYLE, W. H. *See* Ojemann, Levitt, E. E., Lyle, W. H., & Whiteside, 1955.

McCARTHY, DOROTHEA. 1930. The language development of the preschool child. *Inst. Child Welf. Monogr. Ser.,* No. 4. Minneapolis: Univer. Minnesota Press [110, 217].

McCARTHY, DOROTHEA. 1954. Language development in children. In L. Car-

michael (Ed.), *Manual of child psychology* (2nd ed.). Chap. 9. New York: Wiley [110, 186].

McCARTHY, J. *See* Shannon & McCarthy, 1956.

McCLELLAND, D. C., ATKINSON, J. W., CLARK, R. W., & LOWELL, E. L. 1953. *The achievement motive.* New York: Appleton-Century-Crofts [199, 268–269].

McCULLOCH, W. A., & PITTS, W. 1943. A logical calculus of the ideas immanent in nervous activity. *Bull. math. Biophys.,* 5, 115–133 [293].

McDOUGALL, W. 1908. *An introduction to social psychology.* Boston: Luce [35, 65].

MACFARLANE, JEAN W. *See* Honzik, Macfarlane, & Allen, 1948.

MACFARLANE, JEAN W., ALLEN, L., & HONZIK, M. D. 1954. A developmental study of the behavior problems of normal children between 21 months and 14 years. *University of California Publications in Child Development.* Vol. 2. Berkeley: Univer. California Press [25].

McGEOCH, J. A. 1942. *The psychology of human learning.* New York: Longmans, Green [253].

McGRAW, MYRTLE B. 1935. *Growth: a study of Johnny and Jimmy.* New York: Appleton-Century-Crofts [265, 270–271, 322–323, 328].

McGRAW, MYRTLE B. 1939. Later development of children specially trained during infancy. *Child Develpr.l.,* 10, 1–19. Reprinted in W. Dennis (Ed.), *Readings in child psychology.* Pp. 199–223. Englewood Cliffs, N. J.: Prentice-Hall, 1951 [265, 275, 361].

McGRAW, MYRTLE B. 1943. *The neuromuscular maturation of the human infant.* New York: Columbia Univer. Press [260].

McHUGH, G. 1943. Changes in IQ at the public school kindergarten level. *Psychol. Monogr.,* 55, No. 2, 34 [30].

McHUGH, G. 1945. Changes in Goodenough IQ at the public school kindergarten level. *J. educ. Psychol.,* 36, 17–30 [30].

McNEMAR, Q. 1940. A critical examination of the University of Iowa studies of environmental influences upon the IQ. *Psychol. Bull.,* 37, 63–92 [26, 29].

McNemar, Q. 1945. Note on Wellman's re-analysis of IQ changes of orphanage preschool children. *J. genet. Psychol.,* 67, 215–219 [26].

Maine de Biran, P. 1798. *The influence of habit on the faculty of thinking.* Trans. by Margaret D. Boehm. Baltimore: Williams & Wilkins, 1929 [251–252].

Malphigi, M. 1672. *De Formatione Pulli in Ovo.* London (From Needham, 1959) [37–38].

Marquis, D. G. 1930. The criterion of innate behavior. *Psychol. Rev.,* 37, 334–349 [48].

Marquis, D.G. *See* Hilgard & Marquis, 1940.

Matalon, B. 1959. Apprentissages en situations aléatoires et systematiques. *Études d' Épistémol. génét.,* 10, 61–91 [200, 273].

Matthews, S. A., & Detwiler, S. R. 1926. The reaction of Amblystoma embryos following prolonged treatment with chloretone. *J. exp. Zool.,* 45, 279–292 [321].

Maurer, Katherine M. *See* Goodenough & Maurer, 1942.

Max, L. W. 1934. An experimental study of the motor theory of consciousness. I. Critique of earlier studies. *J. genet. Psychol.,* 11, 112–125 [290, 358].

Max, L.W. 1935. An experimental study of the motor theory of consciousness. III. Action-current responses in deafmutes during sleep. *J. comp. Psychol.,* 19, 469–486 [290].

Max, L. W. 1937. Experimental study of the motor theory of consciousness. IV. Action-current responses of the deaf during awakening, kinesthetic imagery, and abstract thinking. *J. comp. Psychol.,* 24, 301–344 [290–291].

Mead, Margaret. 1953. Comments. In J. M. Tanner & Bärbel Inhelder (Eds.), *Discussions on child development.* Pp. 92–93. New York: Int. Univer. Press [256].

Mellinger, Jeanne C. *See* Riesen, Kurke, & Mellinger, 1953.

Mellinger, Jeanne C. *See* Riesen & Mellinger, 1956.

Melton, A. W. 1941. Learning. In W. S. Monroe (Ed.), *Encyclopedia of educational research.* New York: Macmillan [253].

Melzack, R., & Scott, T. H. 1957. The effects of early experience on the response to pain. *J. comp. physiol. Psychol.,* 50, 155–161 [7].

Merrifield, P. R. *See* Guilford, Merrifield, Christensen, & Frick, 1960.

Messinger, Virginia M. 1940. *A longitudinal comparative study of nursery school and non-nursery school children.* Unpublished doctor's dissertation, Univer. Iowa [27].

Meyer, D. R. *See* Harlow, Meyer, & Settlage, 1951.

Meyer, E. 1935. La representation et relations spatiales chez l'enfant. *Cahiers Ped. exp. Psychol. de l'Enfant,* 8 [113].

Miles, Catherine C. 1954. Gifted children. In L. Carmichael, (Ed.), *Manual of child psychology.* Chap. 16. New York: Wiley.

Miller, G. A., Galanter, E. H., & Pribram, K. H. 1960. *Plan and the structure of behavior.* New York: Holt, Rinehart and Winston [8, 91, 119, 199].

Miller, N. E. 1948. Studies of fear as an acquirable drive. I. Fear as motivation and fear-reduction as reinforcement in the learning of new responses. *J. exp. Psychol.,* 38, 89–101 [71].

Miller, N. E. *See* Dollard & Miller, 1950.

Miller, N. E., & Dollard, J. 1941. *Social learning and imitation.* New Haven: Yale Univer. Press [68–69, 107, 191, 253].

Milner, B. 1958. Psychological defects produced by temporal lobe excision. *The brain and human behavior.* (*Res. Publ. Ass. nerv. ment. Dis.,* pp. 244–257.) Baltimore: Williams & Wilkins [90].

Milner, Esther A. 1951. A study of the relationships between reading readiness in grade one school children and patterns of parent-child interaction. *Child Develpm.,* 22, 95–112 [335].

Milner, P. M. 1957. The cell assembly: Mark II. *Psychol. Rev.,* 64, 242–252 [91].

MISHKIN, M., & PRIBRAM, K. H. 1956. Analysis of the effects of frontal lesions in monkeys: II. Variations of delayed response. *J. comp. physiol. Psychol.*, 49, 14–20 [89].

MITTELMANN, B. 1954. Motility in infants, children, and adults. *Psychoanal. Stud. Child* 9, 142–177 [261].

MOGAR, MARIANNA. 1960. Children's causal reasoning about natural phenomena. *Child Develpm.*, 31, 59–65.

MOORE, JAMES [290].

MORGAN, C. L. 1894. *An introduction to comparative psychology.* (2nd ed.) London: Scott, 1909 [45–47, 63, 65–66, 106, 349].

MORGAN, C. L. 1900. *Animal behavior.* London: Arnold [46].

MORGAN, C. T. 1943. *Physiological psychology.* New York: McGraw-Hill [84].

MORGAN, I. MILDRED, & OJEMANN, R. H. 1942. The effect of a learning program designed to assist youth in an understanding of behavior and its development. *Child Develpm.*, 13, 181–194 [286].

MOSELEY, D. 1925. The accuracy of the pecking response in chicks. *J. comp. Psychol.*, 5, 75–97 [54].

MOSHINSKY, PEARL. 1939. The correlation between fertility and intelligence within social classes. *Sociol. Rev.*, 31, 144–165 [337–341].

MOWRER, O. H. 1936. "Maturation" vs. "learning" in the development of vestibular and optokinetic nystagmus. *J. genet. Psychol.*, 48, 383–404 [92].

MUHLENBEIN, J. *See* Furfey & Muhlenbein, 1932.

MULLER, H. J. 1925. Mental traits and heredity. *J. Hered.*, 16, 433–448 [20].

MUNN, N. L. 1950. *Handbook of Psychological research on the rat.* Boston: Houghton Mifflin [52].

MUNN, N. L. 1955. *The evolution and growth of human behavior.* Boston: Houghton Mifflin [35].

MURPHY, LOIS B. 1944. Childhood experience in relation to personality. In J. McV. Hunt (Ed.), *Personality and the behavior disorders.* Chap. 21. New York: Ronald [313].

MUUS, R. E. 1959. A comparison of "high causally" and "low causally" oriented sixth grade children on personality variables indicative of mental health. *Proc. Iowa Acad. Sci.*, 66, 388–394 [286].

MUUS, R. E. 1960a. The relationship between "causal" orientation, anxiety, and insecurity in elementary school children. *J. educ. Psychol.*, 51, 122–129 [286].

MUUS, R. E. 1960b. The effects of a one- and two-year causal learning program. *J. Pers.*, 28, 479–491 [286].

MUUS, R. E. 1960c. A comparison of "high causally" and "low causally" oriented sixth grade children in respect to a perceptual "intolerance of ambiguity test." *Child Develpm.*, 31, 521–536 [286].

NAJARIAN, PERGROUHI. *See* Dennis & Najarian. 1957.

NEEDHAM, J. 1959. *A history of embryology.* New York: Abelard-Schuman [37–40].

NEWELL, A., SHAW, J. C., & SIMON, H. A. 1958. Elements of a theory of human problem solving. *Psychol. Rev.*, 65, 151–166 [8, 74–76, 83, 88, 91, 107, 111, 173, 247, 293, 296].

NEWELL, A., SHAW, J. C., & SIMON, H. A. 1959a. Report on a general problem-solving program. The RAND Corporation Paper, J–1584, February [88].

NEWELL, A., SHAW, J. C., & SIMON, H. A. 1959b. A variety of intelligent learning in a general problem solver. The RAND Corporation Paper, P–1742, July [88].

NEWELL, A., & SIMON, H. A. 1959. The simulation of human thought. The RAND Corporation Paper, P–1734, June [88].

NEWLAND, T. E. [265].

NEWMAN, H. H., FREEMAN, F. N. & HOLZINGER, K. J. 1937. *Twins: a study of heredity and environment.* Chicago: Univer. Chicago Press [18–20, 325–327].

NICHOLS, I., & HUNT, J. McV. 1940. A case of partial bilateral frontal lobectomy: a psychopathological study. *Amer. J. Psychiat.*, 96, 1063–1083 [90, 292].

NISBET, J. D. 1953. *Family environment: a direct effect of family size on intelligence.* London: Cassel [343].

NISSEN, H. W. *See* Chow & Nissen, 1955.

OCKHAM, WILLIAM OF [46, 349].

ODEN, MALITA H. See Terman & Oden, 1947.

OGILVIE, E. See Lovell & Ogilvie, 1960.

O'HANLON, G. S. A. 1940. An investigation into the relationship between fertility and intelligence. *Brit. J. educ. Psychol.,* 10, 196–211 [337].

OJEMANN, R. H., & CLARK, J. W. 1956. School-community programs. *Rev. educ. Res.,* 26, 479–501 [286].

OJEMANN, R. H., LEVITT, E. E., LYLE, W. H., & WHITESIDE, F. MAXINE. 1955. The effects of a "causal" teacher-training program and certain curricular changes in grade school children. *J. exp. Educ.,* 24, 95–114 [286].

OJEMANN, R. H., & WILKINSON, F. R. 1939. The effect on pupil growth of an increase in teacher's understanding of pupil behavior. *J. exp. Educ.,* 8, 143–147 [286].

OSGOOD, C. E. 1952. The nature and measurement of meaning. *Psychol. Rev.,* 49, 192–237 [127].

OSGOOD, C. E. 1953. *Method and theory in experimental psychology.* New York: Oxford Univer. Press [69–73, 76, 85, 99, 107, 128, 151, 351, 358].

OVSIANKINA, M. 1928. Die Wiederaufnahmen von unterbrochenen Handlungen. *Psychol. Forsch.,* 11, 302–389 [261].

OWEN, R. D. See Srb & Owen, 1957.

PADILLA, S. G. 1935. Further studies on the delayed pecking of chicks. *J. comp. Psychol.,* 20, 413–443 [259, 322].

PAGE, E. I. 1959. Haptic perception: a consideration of one of the investigations of Piaget and Inhelder. *Educ. Rev.,* 11, 115–124 [194, 219, 295].

PAPAVASSILIOU, I. T. 1954. Intelligence and family size. *Popul. Stud.,* 7, 222–226 [337].

PAPEZ, J. W. 1929. *Comparative neurology.* New York: Crowell [317].

PASAMANICK, B., KNOBLOCH, HILDA, & LILIENFELD, A. M. 1956. Socio-economic status and some precursors of neuropsychiatric disorder. *Amer. J. Orthopsychiat.,* 26, 594–601 [335].

PAVLOV, I. P. 1927. *Conditioned reflexes.* Trans. by G. V. Anrep. London: Oxford Univer. Press [67, 112].

PEEL, E. A. 1959. Experimental examination of some of Piaget's schemata concerning children's perception and thinking, and a discussion of their educational significance. *Brit. J. Educ. Psychol.,* 29, 89–103 [219, 229, 295].

PEIRCE, C. S. 1878. Pragmatism. In J. Buchler (Ed.), *The philosophical writings of Peirce.* New York: Dover, 1950 [251–252].

PENROSE, L. S. 1948. The supposed threat of declining intelligence. *Amer. J. ment. Defic.,* 53, 114–118 [339].

PENROSE, L. S. 1950a. Genetical influences on the intelligence level of the population. *Brit. J. Psychol.,* 40, 128–136 [339].

PENROSE, L. S. 1950b. Propagation of the unfit. *Lancet,* 259, 425–427 [340].

PESTALOZZI [5, 279].

PETERSON, J. 1925. *Early conceptions and tests of intelligence.* New York: Harcourt, Brace & World [14].

PETERSON, W. M. The development of learning sets in normal children. *Dissertation Abstr.,* 16, 165 [83].

PIAGET, J. 1923. *The language and thought of the child.* Trans. by Marjorie Worden. New York: Harcourt, Brace & World, 1926 [216–217].

PIAGET, J. 1924. *Judgment and reasoning in the child.* Trans. by Marjorie Worden. New York: Harcourt, Brace & World, 1928 [110].

PIAGET, J. 1926. *The child's conception of the world.* Trans. by Joan and Andrew Tomlinson. New York: Harcourt, Brace & World, 1929 [185].

PIAGET, J. 1927. *The child's conception of physical causality.* Trans. by Marjorie Worden Gabian. New York: Harcourt, Brace & World, 1930 [110, 255].

PIAGET, J. 1932. *The moral judgment of the child.* Trans. by Marjorie Worden Gabian. New York: Harcourt, Brace & World, 1932 [110].

PIAGET, J. 1936. *The origins of intelligence in children.* Trans. by Margaret Cook. New York: Int. Univer. Press, 1952 [94, 99, 110–138, 147–161, 167, 174–179, 190, 248, 254, 262–263, 336].

PIAGET, J. 1937. *The construction of reality in the child.* Trans. by Margaret Cook. New York: Basic Books, 1954 [110–116, 123, 129, 130–131, 140–141, 155, 158, 162–167, 248–252, 263].

PIAGET, J. 1941. Le mechanism du développement mental et les lois du "groupement" des opérations. *Arch. Psychol.* (*Genève*), 28, 215–285 [113, 115].

PIAGET, J. 1942a. *Classes, relations et nombres. Essai sur les "groupements" de la logistique et la réversibilité de la pensée.* Paris: Vrin [113, 115].

PIAGET, J. 1942b. Les trois structures fondamentales de la vie psychique: rythme, régulation, et groupement. *Schweiz. Z. Psychol. Anwend.*, 1, 9–21 [199, 215].

PIAGET, J. 1943. Une expérience sur le développement de la notion de temps. *Schweiz. Z. Psychol. Anwend.*, 1, 179–185 [224].

PIAGET, J. 1945. *Play, dreams, and imitation in childhood.* Trans. of *La formation du symbole chez l'enfant*, by C. Gattegno & F. M. Hodgson. New York: Norton, 1951 [113–115, 132, 141–145, 153–154, 159–160, 166–167, 170–199, 216, 248].

PIAGET, J. 1946. *Les notions de mouvement et de vitesse chez l'enfant.* Paris: Presses Universitaires de France [113].

PIAGET, J. 1947. *The psychology of intelligence.* Trans. by M. Piercy & D. E. Berlyne. London: Routledge & Kegan Paul [111–115, 170–175, 199–202, 215–218, 226, 230–231, 248, 254–255, 269, 291–293, 297, 304–306].

PIAGET, J. 1949a. Le problème neurologique de l'intériorisation des actions en opérations réversibles. *Arch. Psychol.* (*Genève*), 32, 241–258 [113, 160, 288–289].

PIAGET, J. 1949b. Les illusions relatives aux angles et à la longuer de leurs cotés. *Arch. Psychol.* (*Genève*), 32, 281–307 [113, 199, 205, 231].

PIAGET, J. 1949c. *Traité de logique.* Paris: Colin [199, 205, 231].

PIAGET, J. 1950a. Perception et intelligence. *Bull. Gr. Étude Psychol.*, 4, 25–34 [113].

PIAGET, J. 1950b. Une experience sur la psychologie du hasard chez l'enfant le tirage au sort des couples. *Acta Psychol.*, 7, 323–336 [113].

PIAGET, J. 1952. *Essai sur les transformations des opérations logiques: Les 256 opérations ternaires de la logique bivalente.* Paris: Presses Universitaires de France [113].

PIAGET, J. 1953a. *Logic and psychology.* Trans. by W. Mays & T. Whitehead. Manchester: Manchester Univer. Press; New York: Basic Books [110, 115, 201].

PIAGET, J. 1953b. Structures opérationelles et cybernétique. *Année Psychol.*, 53, 379–388 [111, 171, 231–232, 240–242, 248, 293–294].

PIAGET, J. 1953c. Remarks about himself. In J. M. Tanner, & Bärbel Inhelder (Eds.), *Discussions on child development.* Pp. 31–33. (Proceedings of the First Meeting of the World Health Organization Study Group on the Psychological Development of the Child.) New York: Int. Univer. Press [115, 201].

PIAGET, J. 1954a. Ce qui subsiste de la théorie de la Gestalt dans la psychologie contemporaine de l'intelligence et la perception. *Schweiz. Z. Psychol. Anwend.*, 24, 72–83 [113].

PIAGET, J. 1954b. Le language et la pensée du point de vue génétique. *Acta psychol.*, 10, 51–60 [113].

PIAGET, J. 1955a. The development of time concepts in the child. In P. H. Hoch & J. Zubin (Eds.), *Psychopathology of childhood.* New York: Grune & Stratton [113, 222, 224].

PIAGET, J. 1955b. Essai d'une nouvelle interprétation probabiliste des effets de centration de la loi de Weber et celles des centrations relatives. *Arch. Psychol.* (*Genève*), 35, 1–24 [113, 222, 224].

PIAGET, J. 1957. The child and modern physics. *Sci. Amer.*, 196 (3), 46–51 [139].

PIAGET, J. *See* Inhelder & Piaget, 1955.

PIAGET, J., & ALBERTINI, BARBARA VON. 1950. L'illusion de Müller-Lyer. *Arch. Psychol.* (*Genève*), 33 (129), 1–48 [113].

PIAGET, J., ALBERTINI, BARBARA VON, & ROSSI, M. 1944. Essai d'interprétation probabiliste de la loi de Weber et celles des centrations relatives. *Arch. Psychol.* (*Genève*), 30, 95–138 [113].

PIAGET, J., BUSSMANN, ESTHER, MEYER, EDITH, RICHLI, VRONI, & VAN REMOORTEL, MYRIAM. 1946. *Le développement de la mode de temps chez l'enfant.* Paris: Presses Universitaires de France [222, 224].

PIAGET, J., & INHELDER, BÄRBEL. 1940. *Le développement des quantités chez l'enfant. Conservation et atomisme.* Neuchatel: Delachaux et Niestlé [228].

PIAGET, J., & INHELDER, BÄRBEL. 1947. Diagnosis of mental operations and theory of intelligence. *Amer. J. ment. Def.*, 51 (3), 401–406 [229, 286, 298].

PIAGET, J., & INHELDER, BÄRBEL. 1948. *The child's conception of space.* Trans. by F. J. Langdon & J. L. Lunzer. London: Routlege & Kegan Paul, 1956 [115, 192–198, 218–222, 295].

PIAGET, J., INHELDER, BÄRBEL. 1951. *La genèse de l'idée du hasard chez l'enfant.* Paris: Presses Univer. de France [113].

PIAGET, J., INHELDER, BÄRBEL, & SZEMINSKA, ALINA. 1948. *The child's conception of geometry.* Trans. of *La géométrie spontanée de l'enfant,* by E. A. Lunzer. New York: Basic Books, 1960 [113].

PIAGET, J., & LAMBERCIER, M. 1943a. La comparison visuelle des hauteurs à distances variables dans le plan frontoparallèle. *Arch. Psychol. (Genève)*, 29, 175–253 [254].

PIAGET, J., & LAMBERCIER, M. 1943b. Le problème de comparaison visuelle en profondeur constancy de la grandeur et l'erreur systématique de l'étaton. *Arch. Psychol. (Genève)*, 29, 255–308 [254].

PIAGET, J., & LAMBERCIER, M. 1944. Essai sur un effet d'(Einstellung) survenant au cours de perception visuelle successive (effet Usnadze). *Arch. Psychol. (Genève)*, 30, 140–196 [110].

PIAGET, J., & LAMBERCIER, M. 1946. Transpositions perceptives et transitivité opératoire dans les comparaisons en profondeur. *Arch. Psychol. (Genève)*, 31, 325–368 [113].

PIAGET, J., & LAMBERCIER, M. 1953. La comparaison des différences de hauteur dans le plan fronto-parallèle. *Arch. Psychol. (Genève)*, 34, 73–107 [113].

PIAGET, J. LAMBERCIER, M., BOESCH, E., & ALBERTINI, BARBARA VON. 1942. Introduction a l'étude des perceptions chez l'enfant et analyse d'une illusion relative a la perception visuelle des cercles concentriques (Delboeuf). *Arch. Psychol. (Genève)*, 29 (113), 1–107 [113].

PIAGET, J., & SZEMINSKA, ALINA. 1939. Quelques experiences sur la conservation des quantités continués chez l'enfants. *J. Psychol. norm. Path.*, 36, 36–65.

PIAGET, J., & SZEMINSKA, ALINA. 1941. *The child's conception of number.* Trans. by C. Gattegno & F. M. Hodgson. New York: Humanities Press, 1952 [113, 199, 203–213].

PIÉRON, H. 1940. L'hétérogénéité normale des aptitudes. *Année psychol.*, 41, 1–13 [298].

PINNEAU, S. R. 1955. The infantile disorders of hospitalism and anaclitic depression. *Psychol. Bull.*, 52, 429–459 [34].

PINTNER, R., & FORLANO, G. 1942. Season of birth and intelligence. *J. genet. Psychol.*, 61, 81–86 [124].

PINTER, R., & FORLANO, G. 1943. Season of birth and mental differences. *Psychol. Bull.*, 40, 25–35 [124].

PITTS, W. See McCulloch & Pitts, 1943.

PLATO [249].

POINCARÉ, H. 1906. *The value of science.* In *The foundations of science.* Pp. 201–354. Trans. by G. B. Halstead. New York: Science Press, 1929 [115, 123, 163, 250].

POLYA, G. 1948. *How to solve it.* Princeton: Princeton Univer. Press [282].

PORTEUS, S. D. 1937. *Primitive intelligence and environment.* New York: Macmillan [61, 192].

POSTMAN, L. 1947. The history and present status of the law of effect. *Psychol. Bull.*, 44, 439–453 [47].

PRATT, K. C. 1954. The neonate. In L. Carmichael (Ed.), *Manual of child psychology.* Chap. 4. New York: Wiley [116].

PRESTON, M. G. 1940. Concerning the determination of trait variability. *Psychometrika*, 5, 275–281 [301].

PRIBRAM, K. H. 1958a. Comparative neurology and the evolution of behavior. In Anne Roe & G. G. Simpson (Eds.), *Behavior and evolution.* Pp. 140–164.

PRIBRAM, K. H. 1958a. (*Cont.*)
New Haven: Yale Univer. Press [289, 291, 296].

PRIBRAM, K. H. 1958b. Neocortical function in behavior. In H. F. Harlow & C. Woolsey (Eds.), *Biological and biochemical bases of behavior.* Madison: Univer. Wisconsin Press [89–90].

PRIBRAM, K. H. 1960. A review of theory in physiological psychology. *Ann. Rev. Psychol.,* 11, 1–40 [8, 88–91, 98, 105–107, 116, 289–292, 296, 353].

PRIBRAM, K. H. *See* Miller, Galanter, & Pribram, 1960.

PRIBRAM, K. H., & MISHKIN, M. 1956. Analysis of the effects of frontal lesions in monkeys. III. Object alternation. *J. comp. physiol. Psychol.,* 49, 41–45 [89].

PRUETTE, LORINE. 1926. *G. Stanley Hall: a biography of a mind.* New York: Appleton-Century-Crofts [43].

RAVEN, J. C. 1938. Guide to using Progressive Matrices. London: Lewis, 1952 [299].

RAY, W. S. 1955. A framework for problem-solving. Laboratory note SCRL 55–8, AFPRTC. Lackland AFB, Texas [282].

REY, A. 1935. *L'intelligence practique chez l'enfant.* Paris: Alcan.

RIBBLE, MARGARET A. 1944. Infantile experience in relation to personality development. In J. McV. Hunt (Ed.), *Personality and the behavior disorders.* Chap. 20. New York: Ronald [274].

RICHARDSON, S. K. 1936. The correlation of intelligence quotients of siblings of the same chronological age levels. *J. juv. Res.,* 20, 186–198 [18].

RIESEN, A. H. 1947. The development of visual perception in man and chimpanzee. *Science,* 106, 107–108 [62, 85, 93, 108, 119, 260].

RIESEN, A. H. 1951. Post-partum development of behavior. *Chicago med. School Quart.,* 13, 17–24 [94].

RIESEN, A. H. 1958. Plasticity of behavior: psychological aspects. In H. F. Harlow & C. N. Woolsey (Eds.), *Biological and biochemical bases of behavior.* Pp. 425–450. Madison: Univer. Wisconsin Press [8, 62, 94, 108, 119, 260, 293].

RIESEN, A. H., CHOW, K. L., SEMMES, J., & NISSEN, H. W. 1951. Chimpanzee vision after four conditions of light deprivation. *Amer. Psychologist,* 6, 282 (Abstract) [94].

RIESEN, A. H., KURKE, M. I., & MELLINGER, JEANNE C. 1953. Interocular transfer of habits learned monocularly in visually naive and visually experienced cats. *J. comp. physiol. Psychol.,* 46, 166–171 [96].

RIESEN, A. H., & MELLINGER, JEANNE. 1956. Interocular transfer of habits in cats after alternating monocular visual experience. *J. comp. physiol. Psychol.,* 49, 516–520 [96].

RIESS, B. F. 1950. The isolation of factors of learning and native behavior in field and laboratory studies. *Ann. N. Y. Acad. Sci.,* 51 (6), 1093–1103 [59].

RIESS, B. F. 1954. The effect of altered environment and of age on mother-young relationships among animals. *Ann. N. Y. Acad. Sci.,* 57, 606–610 [60, 351].

RIFE, D. C., & SNYDER, L. H. 1931. Studies in human inheritance. *Hum. Biol.,* 3, 547–559 [298].

RIMOLDI, H. J. A. 1951. Personal tempo. *J. abnorm. soc. Psychol.,* 46, 283–303 [301].

RIPIN, ROWENA. 1933. A comparative study of the development of infants in an institution with those in homes of low socio-economic status. *Psychol. Bull.,* 30, 680–681 [27].

ROBBINS, LILLIAN C. *See* Ausubel, Robbins, & Blake, 1957.

ROBERTS, J. A. F. 1941. The negative association between intelligence and fertility. *Hum. Biol.,* 13, 410–412 [337].

ROGERS, C. R. 1951. *Client-centered therapy.* Boston: Houghton Mifflin [188].

ROMANES, G. J. 1883a. *Animal intelligence.* New York: Appleton-Century-Crofts [45].

ROMANES, G. J. 1883b. *Mental evolution in animals.* New York: Appleton-Century-Crofts, 1884 [45].

ROMANES, G. J. [349].

ROSE, J. E., & WOOLSEY, C. N. 1949. The relations of thalamic connections, cellular structure and evocable electrical activity in the auditory region of the cat. *J. comp. Neurol.*, 91, 441–466 [89].

ROSENZWEIG, S. 1933. Preferences in the repetition of successful and unsuccessful activities as a function of age and personality. *J. genet. Psychol.*, 42, 423–441 [261].

ROSVOLD, H. E. 1959. Physiological psychology. *Ann. Rev. Psychol.*, 10, 415–454 [90].

ROUSSEAU, J. [5].

RUSSELL, D. 1956. *Children's thinking.* New York: Ginn [110].

SAUDEK, R. 1934. A British pair of identical twins reared apart. *Char. Pers.*, 3, 17–39 [20].

SCHMIDT, BERNADINE G. 1946. Changes in personal, social, and intellectual behavior of children originally classified as feebleminded. *Psychol. Monogr.*, 60, No. 5, 144.

SCHNEIRLA, T. C. 1956. Interrelationships of the 'innate' and the 'acquired' in instinctive behavior. In *Colloque Internat sur l'Instinct Animale.* Pp. 387–432. Paris: Masson et Cie.

SCHNEIRLA, T. C. 1957. The concept of development in comparative pschology. In D. B. Harris (Ed.), *The concept of development.* Minneapolis: Univer. Minnesota Press.

SCHWESINGER, G. C. 1933. *Heredity and environment: Studies in the genesis of psychological characteristics.* New York: Macmillan [326].

SCOTT, EILEEN M., & NISBET, J. D. 1955. Intelligence and family size in an adult sample. *Eugen. Rev.*, 46, 233–235 [337].

SCOTT, J. P. 1945. Social behavior, organization and leadership in a small flock of domestic sheep. *Comp. Psychol. Monogr.*, 18, No. 4 (Whole No. 96) [268–269].

SCOTT, J. P. 1958. Critical periods in the development of social behavior in puppies. *Psychosom. Med.*, 20, 42–53 [269].

SCOTT, J. P. *See* Fuller & Scott, 1954.

SCOTT, J. P. & CHARLES, MARGARET S. 1954. Genetic differences in the behavior of dogs: A case of magnification by thresholds and by habit formation. *J. genet. Psychol.*, 84, 175–188 [6].

SCOTT, J. P., FREDERICSON, E., & FULLER, J. L. 1951. Experimental exploration of the critical period hypothesis. *Personality*, 1 (2) [268–270].

SCOTT, J. P., & FULLER, J. L. 1951. Research on genetics and social behavior. *J. Hered.*, 42, 191–197 [268].

SCOTT, J. P., & MARSTON, MARY-'VESTA. 1950. Critical periods affecting the development of normal and maladjustive social behavior of puppies. *J. genet. Psychol.*, 77, 26–60 [268–269].

SCOTT, T. H. *See* Melzack & Scott, 1957.

SCOVILLE, W. B. *See* Henry & Scoville, 1952.

SEARS, R. R. 1944. Experimental analysis of psychoanalytic phenomena. In J. McV. Hunt (Ed.), *Personality and the behavior disorders.* Chap. 9. New York: Ronald [133, 253].

SEARS, R. R., & WISE, G. W. 1950. Relation of cup feeding in infancy to thumb-sucking and the oral drive. *Amer. J. Orthopsychiat.*, 20, 123–138 [262].

SEASHORE, H. G. *See* Bennett, Seashore, & Wesman, 1947.

SELZ, O. 1922. *Zur Psychologie des produktiven Denkens und des Irrtums.* Bonn: Cohen [200, 282].

SENN, M. J. E. 1958. How the Russians bring up their children. *McCall's Magazine*, October, 86 (1), pp. 36ff.

SERRA, MARY C. 1953a. How to develop concepts and their verbal representations. *Elem. Sch. J.*, 53, 275–285 [281].

SERRA, MARY C. 1953b. A study of fourth grade children's comprehension of certain verbal abstractions. *J. exp. Educ.*, 22, 103–118 [281].

SETTLAGE, P. H. *See* Harlow, Meyer, & Settlage, 1951.

SEWALL, W. H. 1944. Differential fertility in completed Oklahoma farm families. *Amer. sociol. Rev.*, 9, 427–434 [337].

SHANNON, C. E., & MCCARTHY, J. (Eds.) 1956. *Automata studies.* (Annals of mathematical studies, No. 34.) Princeton, N. J.: Princeton Univer. Press [296].

SHARP, STELLA E. 1898. Individual psychology: A study in psychological method. *Amer. J. Psychol.*, 10, 329–391 [12].

Shaw, J. C. *See* Newell, Shaw, & Simon, 1958.

Shepard, J. F., & Breed, F. S. 1913. Maturation and use in the development of an instinct. *J. anim. Behav.*, 3, 274–285 [53–54].

Sherrington, C. S. 1893. A note on the knee-jerk and the correlation of action of antagonistic muscles. *Proc. Roy. Soc., London*, ser. B. 52, 556–559. (From Brazier, 1959) [48].

Sherrington, C. S. 1906. *The integrative action of the nervous system*. New York: Scribner's [48, 91].

Shirley, Mary M. 1931. A motor sequence favors the maturation theory. *Psychol. Bull.*, 28, 204–205 [51, 61].

Shirley, Mary M. 1933. *The first two years*. Minneapolis: Univer. Minnesota Press. 2 vols. [51, 255, 350].

Sholl, D. A. 1956. The organization of the cerebral cortex. New York: Wiley [91].

Shuttleworth, F. K. 1935a. The nature *versus* nurture problem. I. Definition of the problem. *J. educ. Psychol.*, 26, 561–578 [323].

Shuttleworth, F. K. 1935b. The nature *versus* nurture problem. II. The contributions of nature and nurture to individual differences in intelligence. *J. educ. Psychol.*, 26, 655–681 [323].

Siegel, A. I. 1953. Deprivation of visual form definition in the ring dove: II. Perceptual-motor transfer. *J. comp. physiol. Psychol.*, 46, 249–252 [96].

Simmons, K. *See* Ebert & Simmons, 1943.

Simmons, Virginia C. 1960. Why waste our five-year-olds? *Harper's Magazine*, 220, No. 1319, 71 ff. [278].

Simms, V. M. *See* Brownell & Simms, 1946.

Simon, H. A. *See* Newell, Shaw, & Simon, 1958.

Simon, T. *See* Binet & Simon, 1905, 1908, 1911, 1916.

Simpson, B. R. 1939. The wandering IQ. *J. psychol.*, 7, 351–367 [28].

Sinnott, E. W., Dunn, L. C., & Dobzhansky, T. 1958. *Principles of genetics*. New York: McGraw-Hill [41, 331].

Skeels, H. M. *See* Wellman, Skeels, & Skodak, 1940.

Skeels, H. M., & Dye, H. B. 1939. A study of the effects of differential stimulation on mentally retarded children. *Proc. Amer. Assoc. ment. Def.*, 44, 114–136 [31, 149, 266].

Skeels, H. M., Updegraff, Ruth, Wellman, Beth L., & Williams, H. M. 1938. A study of environmental stimulation: An orphanage preschool project. *Univer. Iowa Stud. Child Welf.*, 15, No. 4 [28, 264].

Skinner, B. F. 1950. Are theories of learning necessary? *Psychol. Rev.*, 57, 211–220 [67].

Skinner, B. F. 1957. *Verbal behavior*. New York: Appleton-Century-Crofts.

Skinner, B. F. 1959. A case history in scientific method. In S. Koch (Ed.), *Psychology: a study of a science*. Vol. 2, 359–379. *General systematic formulations, learning, and special processes*. New York: McGraw-Hill [272].

Skodak, M. *See* Wellman, Skeels, & Skodak, 1940.

Slater, G. W. 1958. *A study of the influence which environment plays in determining the rate at which a child attains Piaget's 'operational' level in his early number concepts*. Unpublished doctor's dissertation, Birmingham Univer. (From Smedslund, 1961) [295].

Smedslund, J. 1959. Apprentissage des notions de la conservation et de la transitivité du poids. *Études d'Épistémol. génét.*, 9, 85–124 [207, 228, 280, 295].

Smedslund, J. 1960. Transitivity of preference patterns as seen by pre-school children. *Scand. J. Psychol.*, 1, 49–54 [213, 295].

Smedslund, J. 1961. The acquisition of conservation of substance and weight in children. *Scand. J. Psychol.*, 2, 1–10 [273, 280–281, 295].

Smith, K. U. *See* Daniel & Smith, 1947.

Smith, S. 1942. Language and non-verbal test performance of racial groups in Honolulu before and after a fourteen year interval. *J. genet. Psychol.*, 26, 51–93 [338].

Snyder, L. H. *See* Rife & Snyder, 1931.

Socrates [255].

Spalding, D. A. 1902. Instinct: with original observations on young animals. *Pop. Sci. Mon.*, 61, 126–142 [53, 65].

SPALLANZANI [39].

SPEARMAN, C. 1904. "General intelligence" objectively determined and measured. *Amer. J. Psychol.*, 15, 201–293 [16, 298, 300].

SPEARMAN, C. 1923. *The nature of intelligence and the principles of cognition.* London: Macmillan [233, 359].

SPEARMAN, C. 1927. *The abilities of man.* New York: Macmillan [17, 257, 299, 301, 311].

SPENCE, K. W. 1942. Theoretical interpretions of learning. In F. A. Moss (Ed.), *Comparative psychology.* Chap. 11. New York: Prentice-Hall [66, 68].

SPENCE, K. W. 1944. The nature of theory construction in contemporary psychology. *Psychol. Rev.*, 51, 47–68.

SPENCE, K. W. 1951. Theoretical interpretations of learning. In S. S. Stevens (Ed.), *Handbook of experimental psychology.* Chap. 18. New York: Wiley [66].

SPIEGEL, H. See Kardiner & Spiegel, 1947.

SPITZ, R. A. 1945. Hospitalism: an inquiry into the genesis of psychiatric conditions in early childhood. *Psychoanal. Stud. Child.*, 1, 53–74 [33, 149, 264, 274].

SPITZ, R. A. 1946a. Hospitalism: a follow-up report. *Psychoanal. Stud. Child*, 2, 113–117 [33–34, 122, 149, 264, 274].

SPITZ, R. A. 1946b. Anaclitic depression. *Psychoanal. Stud. Child*, 2, 313–342 [33–34, 122, 149, 264, 274].

SPITZ, R. A. 1946c. The smiling response: a contribution to the ongogenesis of social relations. *Genet. Psychol. Monogr.*, 34, 57–125 [122].

SRB, A. M., & OWEN, R. D. 1957. *General genetics.* San Francisco: W. H. Freeman [41].

STEPHENS, F. E., & THOMPSON, R. B. 1943. The case of Millan and George, identical twins reared apart. *J. Hered.*, 34, 109–114 [20].

STERN, W. 1912. *The psychological methods of testing intelligence.* Trans. by G. M. Whipple. Baltimore: Warwick & York, 1914 [15].

STERN, W. 1914. *The psychology of early childhood.* Trans. from 3rd ed. by Anna Burwell. New York: Holt, 1924.

STEWART, NAOMI. 1947. A.G.C.T. Scores of army personnel grouped by occupations. *Occupations*, 26, 5–41 [17].

STICE, G. F. See Cattell, Stice, & Kristy, 1957.

STOCKS, P., & KARN, M. N. 1933. A biometric investigation of twins and their brothers and sisters. *Ann. Eugen., Cambridge*, 5, 1–55 [18].

STODDARD, G. D. 1939. The IQ: Its ups and downs. *Educ. Rec.*, 20, 44–57 [28].

STODDARD, G. D. 1943. *The meaning of intelligence.* New York: Macmillan [13, 26].

STODDARD, G. D., & WELLMAN, BETH L. 1940. Environment and the IQ. *Yearb. Nat. Soc. Stud. Educ.*, 39 (I), 405–442 [26].

SUCHMAN, J. R. 1960a. Inquiry training and science education. In H. Ruchlis (Ed.), *Laboratories in the classrooom.* New York: Science Materials Center [282].

SUCHMAN, J. R. 1960b. Inquiry training in the elementary school. *Sci. Teacher*, 27 (No. 27), 42–47 [282–285].

SULLIVAN, ANNE [268].

SUTHERLAND, H. E. G. 1929. The relationship between IQ and size of family. *J. educ. Psychol.*, 30, 81–91 [337].

SUTHERLAND, H. E. G. 1930. The relationship between IQ and size of family in the case of fatherless children. *J. genet. Psychol.*, 38, 161–170 [337].

SUTHERLAND, H. E. G., & THOMSON, G. H. 1926. The correlation between intelligence and size of family. *Brit. J. Psychol.*, 17, 81–92 [337].

SUTTER, J. See Tabah & Sutter, 1954.

SWAMMERDAM, J. 1672. *Miraculum naturae sive uteri muliebris fabrica.* Leiden (From Needham, 1959) [37–38].

SZEMINSKA, ALINA. 1935. Essa d'analyse psychologique du raisonnement mathématique. *Cahiers de Ped. Exp. et de Psychol. de l'Enfant*, 7 [113].

SZEMINSKA, ALINA. See Piaget & Szeminska, 1941.

TABAH, L., & SUTTER, J. 1954. Le niveau intellectuel des enfants d'une meme famille. *Ann. hum. Génét.*, 19 (Pt. 2), 120–150 [342].

TAYLOR, G. A. *See* Gates & Taylor, 1925.

TERMAN, L. M. 1916. *The measurement of intelligence.* Boston: Houghton Mifflin [16–17, 43].

TERMAN, L. M. [43].

TERMAN, L. M., *et al.* 1925. *Genetic studies of genius. The mental and physical traits of a thousand gifted children.* Vol. 1. Stanford, Calif.: Stanford Univer. Press [17].

TERMAN, L. M., & ODEN, MALITA H. 1947. *Genetic studies of genius. The gifted child grows up.* Vol. 4. Stanford, Calif.: Stanford Univer. Press [17].

THOMPSON, HELEN. *See* Gesell & Thompson, 1929.

THOMPSON, W. R. *See* Fuller & Thompson, 1960.

THOMPSON, W. R. *See* Hebb & Thompson, 1954.

THOMPSON, W. R., & HERON, W. 1954. The effects of restricting early experience on the problem-solving capacity of dogs. *Canad. J. Psychol.* [8, 17–31, 103–106, 139, 155, 263–265, 269, 316, 353, 356].

THOMSON, G. H. 1939. *The factorial analysis of human ability.* Boston: Houghton Mifflin [301].

THOMSON, G. H., *et al.* of the Scottish Council for Research in Education. 1933. *The intelligence of Scottish children: a national survey of an age group.* London: Univer. London Press [338, 341].

THOMSON, G. H., *et al.* of the Scottish council for Research in Education. 1949. *The trend of Scottish intelligence.* London: Univer. London Press [337–342].

THOMSON, G. H., *et al.* of the Scottish Council for Research in Education. 1953. *Social implications of the 1947 mental survey.* London: Univer. London Press [337–340].

THORNDIKE, E. L. 1898. Animal intelligence. *Psychol. Rev. Monogr. Suppl.,* 2, No. 8 [46].

THORNDIKE, E. L. 1905. The measurement of twins. *Arch. Phil. Psychol. sci. Meth.,* 1, 1–64 [323].

THORNDIKE, E. L. 1911. *Animal intelligence.* New York: Macmillan [46–48, 151].

THORNDIKE, E. L. 1913a. *Educational psychology. The psychology of learning.* Vol. II. New York: Columbia Univer. Press [323, 333].

THORNDIKE, E. L. 1913b. *The original nature of man.* New York: Columbia Univer. Press [323, 333].

THORNDIKE, E. L., & WOODWORTH, R. S. 1901. The influence of improvement in one mental function upon the efficiency of other functions. *Psychol. Rev.,* 8, 247–261, 384–395, 553–564 [66, 106].

THORNDIKE, R. L. 1933. The effect of the interval between test and retest on the constancy of the IQ. *J. educ. Psychol.,* 24, 543–549 [21].

THORNDIKE, R. L. 1940. "Constancy" of the IQ. *Psychol. Bull.,* 37, 167–186 [21].

THORNDIKE, R. L. 1948. Growth of intelligence during adolescence. *J. genet. Psychol.,* 72, 11–15 [27].

THURSTONE, L. L. 1926. *The nature of intelligence.* New York: Harcourt, Brace & World [311].

THURSTONE, L. L. 1935. *The vectors of the mind.* Chicago: Univer. Chicago Press [300].

THURSTONE, L. L. 1938. *Primary mental abilities.* Chicago: Univer. Chicago Press [17, 257, 299–301, 311].

TINBERGEN, N. 1951. *The study of instinct.* London: Oxford Univer. Press [35, 65].

TITCHENER, E. B. 1909. *Experimental psychology of the thought processes.* New York: Macmillan [200, 282].

TOLMAN, E. C. 1932. *Purposive behavior in animals and men.* New York: Appleton-Century-Crofts [68–69, 107, 351].

TOLMAN, E. C. 1937. The acquisition of string pulling in rats: conditioned response or sign-gestalt? *Psychol. Rev.,* 44, 195–211 [68].

TOLMAN, E. C. 1938. The determiner of behavior at the choice point. *Psychol. Rev.,* 45, 1–41 [69].

TOLMAN, E. C. 1948. Cognitive maps in rats and men. *Psychol. Rev.,* 56, 144–155 [48, 68].

TOLMAN, E. C., & BRUNSWIK, E. 1935. The organism and the causal texture of the environment. *Psychol. Rev.,* 42, 43–77 [68].

TREDGOLD, A. F. 1915. *Mental deficiency.* (2nd Ed.) Baltimore: Wood [298].

TREDGOLD, A. F., & SODDY, K. 1956. *A textbook of mental deficiency.* (9th Ed.) Baltimore: Williams & Wilkins.

TRYON, R. C. 1929. The interpretation of the correlation coefficient. *Psychol. Rev.,* 36, 419–445 [301].

TRYON, R. C. 1935. A theory of psychological components—an alternative to "mathematical factors." *Psychol. Rev.,* 42, 425–454 [301].

TRYON, R. C. 1940. Genetic differences in maze learning in rats. *Yearb. Nat. Soc. Stud. Educ.,* 39 (I), 111–119 [330].

TUDDENHAM, R. D. 1948. Soldier intelligence in World Wars I and II. *Amer. Psychologist,* 3, 149–159 [339].

TYLER, LEONA E. 1953. Changes in children's scores on Primary Mental Abilities Tests over a three-year period. *Amer. Psychologist,* 8, 448–449 [257].

UNITED NATIONS. 1953. *The determinants and consequences of population trends.* ST/SOA Series A. Popul. Stud. No. 17. New York: United Nations [337].

UNITED NATIONS. 1955. *Proceedings of the World Population Conference, Rome, 1954.* New York: United Nations, Dept. Social Affairs [337].

UPDEGRAFF, RUTH. See Skeels, Updegraff, Wellman, & Williams, 1938.

VALENTINE, C. W. 1942. *The psychology of early childhood: A study of mental development in the first years of life.* Cleveland: Sherwood Press [110].

VAN LEEUWENHOEK, A., & HAM, J. 1677. Observationes de natis genetali animalculis. *Phil. Trans. Roy. Soc.,* 12 (No. 142), 1040. (From Needham, 1959.) [38].

VARON, EDITH J. 1936. Alfred Binet's concept of intelligence. *Psychol. Rev.,* 43, 32–49 [13].

VERNON, P. E. 1938. *The assessment of psychological qualities by verbal methods, a survey of attitude tests, rating scales and personality questionnaires.* Report No. 83, Medical Research Council, Industrial Health Research Board. London: His Majesty's Stationery Office [311].

VERNON, P. E. 1948. Changes in abilities from 14 to 20 years. *Adv. Sci.* 5, 138 [26].

VERNON, P. E. 1950. *The structure of human abilities.* London: Methuen [300–301].

VERNON, P. E. 1954. The use of intelligence test scores in population studies. *Eugen. Quart.,* 1, 221–224 [26].

VON HALLER, A. 1767. Ad generationem. In *Opera Anatomica Minora* (Tom. II). Lusanne: Grasset. (From Needham, 1959.) [40].

VON NEUMANN, J. 1956. Probabilistic logics and the synthesis of reliable organisms from unreliable components. In C. E. Shannon & J. McCarthy (Eds.), *Automata studies.* Pp. 43–98. (Annals of mathematical studies, No. 34.) Princeton, N. J.: Princeton Univer. Press [87].

VON NEUMANN, J. 1958. *The computer and the brain.* New Haven: Yale Univer. Press [8, 87, 108, 297, 353].

VON SENDEN, M. 1932. *Raum- und Gestaltauffassung bei operierten Blindgeborenen vor und nach der Operation.* Leipzig: Barth, 1932 [62, 85, 93, 97].

WADE, M. 1952. Behavioral effects of prefrontal lobectomy, lobotomy and circumsection in the monkey (Macaca Mulatta). *J. comp. Neurol.,* 96, 179–207 [89].

WALK, R. D. See Gibson & Walk, 1956.

WATSON, J. B. 1914. *Behavior, an introduction to comparative psychology.* New York: Holt, Rinehart & Winston [47–48, 175, 290].

WATSON, J. B. 1919. *Psychology from the standpoint of a behaviorist.* Philadelphia: Lippincott [106].

WATSON, J. B. 1924. *Behaviorism.* New York: Norton [65].

WATSON, J. B. 1928. *Psychological care of infant and child.* New York: Norton [5].

WATSON, J. B. [351].

WELLMAN, BETH L. 1938. The intelligence of preschool children as measured by the Merrill-Palmer scale of performance tests. *Univer. Iowa Stud. Child Welf.,* 15, No. 3 [31].

WELLMAN, BETH L. 1940. Iowa studies on the effects of schooling. *Yearb. Nat. Soc. Stud. Educ.*, 39, 377–399 [30].

WELLMAN, BETH L. *See* Skeels, Updegraff, Wellman & Williams, 1938.

WELLMAN, BETH L., SKEELS, H. M., & SKODAK, M. 1940. Review of McNemar's critical examination of Iowa studies. *Psychol. Bull.*, 37, 93–111 [26, 29, 31].

WERKMEISTER, W. H. 1940. *A philosophy of science.* New York: Harper [294].

WERTHAM, F. 1934. *The brain as an organ.* New York: Macmillan [49].

WERTHEIMER, M. 1920. *Über Schlussprozesse im produktiven Denken.* Berlin, Leipzig: Vereinig [255].

WERTHEIMER, M. 1945. *Productive thinking.* New York: Harper.

WESMAN, A. G. *See* Bennett, Seashore, & Wesman, 1947.

WHEELER, L. R. 1942. A comparative study of the intelligence of East Tennessee mountain children. *J. educ. Psychol.*, 33, 321–334 [339].

WHEELER, R. H. 1940. *The science of psychology.* (2nd Ed.) New York: Crowell [293].

WHITE, R. W. 1959. Motivation reconsidered: the concept of competence. *Psychol. Rev.* 66, 297–333 [179, 261].

WHITESIDE, F. *See* Ojemann, Levitt, Lyle, & Whiteside, 1955.

WIENER, N. 1948. *Cybernetics.* New York: Wiley [111].

WIGGINS, D. M. *See* Chapman & Wiggins, 1925.

WILKINSON, F. R. *See* Ojemann & Wilkinson, 1939.

WILLIAMS, ELIZABETH, & SCOTT, J. P. 1953. The development of social behavior patterns in the mouse in relation to natural periods. *Behavior*, 6, 35–64 [268].

WILLIAMS, H. M. *See* Skeels, Updegraf, Wellman, & Williams, 1938.

WILLIAMS, K. *See* Hebb & Williams, 1946.

WILLOUGHBY, R. R. 1928. Fertility and parental intelligence. *Amer. J. Psychol.*, 40, 671–672 [337].

WILLOUGHBY, R. R., & COOGAN, MARGUERITE. 1940. The correlation between intelligence and fertility. *Hum. Biol.*, 12, 114–119 [341].

WINGFIELD, A. H. 1928. *Twins and orphans: The inheritance of intelligence.* London: Dent [18].

WISE, G. W. *See* Sears & Wise, 1950.

WISSLER, C. 1901. The correlation of mental and physical traits. *Psychol. Monogr.*, 3, No. 16 [12].

WOHLWILL, J. F. 1959. Un essai d' apprentissage dans le domaine de la conservation du nombre. *Études d'Épistémol. génét.*, 9, 125–135 (From Smedslund, 1961) [210, 281].

WOHLWILL, J. F. 1960. Developmental studies of perception. *Psychol. Bull.*, 57, 249–288 [110].

WOLF, A. 1943. The dynamics of the selective inhibition of specific functions in neuroses. *Psychosom. Med.*, 5, 27–38. Reprinted in S. S. Tomkins (Ed.), *Contemporary psychopathology.* Chap. 31. Cambridge: Harvard Univer. Press, 1943 [97].

WOLF, KATHE. *See* Hetzer & Wolf, 1928.

WOLFE, J. B. 1936. Effectiveness of token-rewards for chimpanzees. *Comp. Psychol. Monogr.*, 12, (5), Ser. No. 60 [175].

WOLFF, C. F. 1759. *Theoria Generationis.* Halle (From Needham, 1959) [40, 111, 349].

WOLFF, C. F. 1768. Deformatione intestinorum praecipue, tum et de aminio spurio, allisque partibus embryonis gallinacei nodum visis. *Novi Comment. Acad. Sci. Imp. Petropol.*, 12. Also 1769, 13 (From Needham, 1959) [40, 111, 349].

WOLFLE, D. 1954. *America's resources of specialized talent.* New York: Harper [17].

WOODROW, H. 1838. The relation between abilities and improvement with practice. *J. educ. Psychol.* 29, 215–230 [301].

WOODROW, H. 1939. Factors in improvement with practice. *J. Psychol.*, 7, 55–70 [301].

WOODWORTH, R. S. 1941. Heredity and environment: a critical survey of recently published material on twins and foster children. *Soc. Sci. Res. Coun. Bull.*, No. 47 [20, 253, 324–328].

WOODWORTH, R. S. *See* Thorndike & Woodworth, 1901.

WOODYARD, ELLA. *See* Harrell, Woodyard, & Gates, 1955.

WOOLEY, H. T. 1925. The validity of standards of mental measurement in young childhood. *School & Soc.*, 21, 476–482 [27].

WOOLSEY, C. N. 1958. Organization of somatic sensory and motor areas of the cerebral cortex. In H. F. Harlow & C. N. Woolsey (Eds.), *Biological and biochemical bases of behavior*. Pp. 63–81. Madison: Univer. Wisconsin Press [93].

WRIGHT, S. 1921a. Systems of mating. I. The biometric relations between parent and offspring. *Genetics*, 6, 111–123 [325].

WRIGHT, S. 1921b. Correlation and Causation. *J. agric. Res.*, 20, 557–585 [325].

WRIGHT, S. 1923. The theory of path coefficients: A reply to Niles' criticism. *Genetics*, 8, 239–255 [325].

WRIGHT, S. 1931. Statistical methods in biology. *J. Amer. statis. Ass. Suppl.*, 26, 155–163 [325].

YATES, N., & BRASH, H. 1941. An investigation of the physical and mental characteristics of a pair of like twins reared apart from infancy. *Ann. Eugen.* 11, 89–101 [20].

YERKES, R. M. *See* Yoakum & Yerkes, 1920.

YOAKUM, C. S., & YERKES, R. M. 1920. *Army mental tests*. New York: Holt [17].

YOUNG, J. Z. *See* Gerard & Young, 1937.

ZEAMAN, D. *See* House & Zeaman, 1959.

ZEIGARNISK, B. 1927. Über das Behalten von erledigten und unerledigten Handlungen. *Psychol. Forsch.*, 9, 1–85 [261].

ZENER, K. 1937. The significance of behavior accompanying conditioned salivary secretion for theories of the conditioned response. *Amer. J. Psychol.*, 50, 384–403 [71].

ZOLL, J. *See* Echlin, Arnett, & Zoll, 1952.

Subject Index